Ultimate Genetic Algorithms with Python

Build Intelligent and Adaptive AI Systems with Genetic Algorithms in Python for Machine Learning, Deep Learning, and Multi-Agent Domains

Indrajit Kar

Zonunfeli Ralte

www.orangeava.com

First Published: September 2025

Published By: Orange Education Pvt Ltd, AVA®

Address: 9, Daryaganj, Delhi, 110002, India

275 New North Road Islington Suite 1314 London,
N1 7AA, United Kingdom

ISBN (PBK): 978-93-49888-33-3
ISBN (E-BOOK): 978-93-49888-78-4

Dedicated To

My Beloved Parents,
My Family

And

All The People Who Have Contributed
To My AI Journey So Far

- Indrajit

My Beloved Parents

And

The People of Mizoram

- Zonunfeli

About the Authors

Indrajit Kar is a distinguished AI thought leader, innovator, and author with over 21 years of experience driving transformative AI-led products and platforms across industries. He has led high-impact teams delivering end-to-end solutions in Artificial Intelligence, Machine Learning, Generative AI, and Data Science–guiding projects from design to deployment and scaling.

As Head of AI, Indrajit spearheads large-scale initiatives that deliver measurable business impact for global clients. His expertise spans Generative AI, LLM architectures, MLOps, NLP, and Computer Vision, with a proven track record of integrating LLMs and autonomous AI agents into real-world applications across e-commerce, healthcare, life sciences, telecommunications, and manufacturing.

A trusted advisor to C-level executives, he helps enterprises unlock business value through AI product and platform transformations, bridging the gap between research and enterprise-scale implementation. He has authored two books, including one on Generative AI, published more than 27 research papers, filed 21 patents, and earned eight Best Paper Awards.

Zonunfeli Ralte is a pioneering AI leader, entrepreneur, and researcher with over 16 years of experience in Analytics and AI. As the founder of Northeast India's first AI company, she has positioned her organization at the forefront of applied AI, earning recognition as one of the most influential voices in both regional and global AI landscapes. She has been honored with the prestigious *Women in AI* award for her contributions.

Her interdisciplinary expertise blends strategic business insight with deep technical acumen, enabling her to lead initiatives that align enterprise goals with advanced AI capabilities. She has helped organizations harness data, machine learning, and deep learning to drive innovation, efficiency, and strategic decision-making.

A committed academic and thought leader, Zonunfeli has published 11 research papers in IEEE forums, six of which won Best Paper Awards. Her research spans LLMs, Deep Learning, and Computer Vision, highlighting her ability to push AI boundaries, while ensuring real-world relevance.

About the Technical Reviewer

Avijit K is a seasoned technology leader with over 20 years of experience in Data Science and Artificial Intelligence. He holds a PhD in computer science from a top-tier university and has led numerous high-impact industry projects across Machine Learning, Deep Learning, Computer Vision, Natural Language Processing, and related technologies.

In his current role as CEO and Investor, Avijit drives the strategic direction of his organization, fostering innovation across technology operations, Artificial Intelligence, data analytics, infrastructure, and software development. Over the course of his career, he has guided close to 150 companies in successfully adopting and scaling AI, ML, and data science initiatives. He has also mentored over 30 developers, helping them grow into accomplished professionals.

Avijit is also the recipient of multiple accolades and awards recognizing his contributions to the field of artificial intelligence and his impact on technology-driven business transformation.

Acknowledgments

I extend my deepest appreciation to my family—parents, wife, in-laws, and children—whose steadfast encouragement and belief in me have been the cornerstone of this journey. Heartfelt thanks to Orange Education Pvt Ltd for their unwavering support, patience, confidence and trust in my vision. I am also grateful to my companies for providing opportunities to develop GenAI applications, which have been instrumental in gathering the insights shared here. I thank everyone who supported me, seen and unseen. Their guidance and encouragement have profoundly shaped this journey.

- Indrajit Kar

To my family—parents, sisters, and cousins—whose unwavering support has been the cornerstone of this journey. I am grateful to the people of Mizoram, especially Aizawl and Ramthar Veng, whose rich culture inspired my perspectives and writing. Heartfelt thanks to Orange Education Pvt Ltd and my co-author Indrajit Kar for their trust and patience in bringing this comprehensive work to fruition, covering the evolving field of AI in a single volume. I also thank the companies I have been associated with for fostering growth and providing opportunities to develop GenAI applications, which have greatly shaped the insights shared in this work.

- Zonunfeli Ralte

Preface

In the age of exponential technological advancement, the demand for intelligent, adaptive, and robust optimization systems has never been greater. From solving classical engineering problems to fueling cutting-edge innovations in artificial intelligence, **Genetic Algorithms (GAs)** and their evolutionary relatives have risen as transformative tools. Inspired by the principles of natural selection and Darwinian evolution, these algorithms offer a biologically inspired pathway to solving some of the most complex and high-dimensional optimization problems across science and industry.

This book is designed to serve as a **comprehensive and accessible guide** to Genetic Algorithms, catering to a diverse audience that includes students, researchers, data scientists, AI engineers, and business practitioners. The chapters progress logically—from foundational concepts and algorithmic building blocks to specialized libraries such as DEAP and PyGAD, before moving on to a variety of applications that illustrate the versatility and effectiveness of GAs in real-world scenarios.

What sets this work apart is its **integrative perspective**. The content not only explains the mechanics of Genetic Algorithms—such as population initialization, selection strategies, crossover, mutation, and convergence—but also dives into their synergy with **emerging fields** such as Deep Learning, Computer Vision, Natural Language Processing (NLP), Reinforcement Learning, and **Generative Agentic AI**. Each application chapter is supported by hands-on coding examples, simulation experiments, and comparative analyses to bridge the gap between theory and practice.

The concluding chapters invite readers to imagine the future of GAs in **self-evolving AI systems, multi-agent collaboration frameworks, and adaptive optimization pipelines.** These ideas position Genetic Algorithms not just as optimization tools, but as foundational building blocks in the evolution of intelligent systems.

So, whether you are just beginning your exploration or seeking to deepen your expertise, this book provides both the **conceptual clarity and practical fluency** needed to harness the power of Genetic Algorithms in reshaping our digital world.

Let us now embark on this evolutionary journey together.

Chapter 1. Introduction to Genetic Algorithms: This chapter lays the groundwork by tracing the origins of Genetic Algorithms and their foundational components–selection, crossover, and mutation. It contrasts GAs with Darwinian evolution and modern AI paradigms such as Deep Learning. Concepts such as extrema and execution flow are introduced to contextualize GA operation.

Chapter 2. Fundamentals of Genetic Algorithms: Building on the basics, this chapter dives into metaheuristics, niching techniques, population sampling strategies, and detailed breakdowns of fitness, selection, and termination mechanisms. It offers a rigorous understanding of how GAs adapt and converge over generations.

Chapter 3. Overview of Genetic Algorithm Libraries: A practical comparison of popular GA libraries–PyGAD and DEAP–is presented with toy examples. Code walkthroughs highlight performance differences, hyperparameter tuning, and GA modeling through mathematical simulation frameworks.

Chapter 4. Genetic Algorithms and Their Applications: This chapter explores two classic application domains–Traveling Salesman Problem (TSP) and Fraud Analytics. Readers are guided through solution structures, dataset references (for example, TSPLib), and neural network integrations using genetic representations.

Chapter 5. Foundation of Evolutionary Algorithms: It expands the scope from GAs to the broader class of Evolutionary Algorithms (EAs), including classical, advanced, and deep evolutionary variants. The chapter also introduces Particle Swarm Optimization (PSO), showcasing its relevance and simulation for price optimization issues.

Chapter 6. Advanced Evolutionary Algorithms: This chapter focuses on the application of advanced EAs to real-world challenges, particularly in supply chain optimization. Through DEAP and PyGAD code samples (including GPU acceleration), it explores Swarm Intelligence, overlapping methods, PSO, and Ant Colony Optimization.

Chapter 7. Metaheuristic Optimization Algorithms: A deep dive into various metaheuristics–ACO, Differential Evolution, and MOEAs. The chapter highlights their theoretical foundations, algorithmic flow, and the broader optimization landscape in which GAs operate.

Chapter 8. Application of Evolutionary Algo (GAs) and Generative Agentic AI: This innovative chapter blends Bee Hive Optimization with Generative AI concepts. It covers PyGMO implementations, multi-agent swarm systems, and the synergy between agentic AI and nature-inspired algorithms such as Artificial Bee Colony and GAs.

Chapter 9. Applying Genetic Algorithm to Machine Learning: Focusing on ML use cases, this chapter explains how GAs can be used for feature selection and hyperparameter tuning. Real-world applications and hands-on implementations demonstrate how GA-guided search can boost ML model performance.

Chapter 10. Applying Deep Learning to Genetic Algorithm: This chapter explores Neural Architecture Search, NEAT, and weight optimization in neural networks. It emphasizes how GAs complement or outperform backpropagation in some deep learning tasks, particularly in neural topology evolution.

Chapter 11. Applying Computer Vision Application to Genetic Algorithms: GAs are applied to optimize visual features, CNN parameters, and classification models. Through tuning learning rates and activation functions, this chapter shows how GAs can enhance vision-based tasks, and their accuracy and generalizability.

Chapter 12. Applying NLP to Genetic Algorithms: It introduces GA use in NLP through RAG systems, prompt engineering, embedding optimization, and sentiment analysis. The chapter combines evolutionary strategies with language models for richer semantic understanding, and better feature engineering.

Chapter 13. Applying Reinforcement Learning to Genetic Algorithms: This chapter showcases how GAs can be used to optimize reward functions, tune exploration-exploitation balances, and evolve intelligent agents in games. It concludes with a comparative analysis of GAs vs traditional RL methods such as Q-learning.

Chapter 14. The Future of Genetic Algorithms: The book concludes by projecting GAs into future landscapes such as adaptive multi-agent systems, Generative Agentic AI, and MCP (Model Context Protocol). It includes implementation of the best practices and pro tips to harness the full potential of GA systems in the emerging AI ecosystems.

Get a Free eBook

We hope you are enjoying your recently purchased book! Your feedback is incredibly valuable to us, and to all other readers looking for great books.

If you found this book helpful or enjoyable, we would truly appreciate it, if you could take a moment to leave a short review with a 5 star rating on Amazon. It helps us grow, and lets other readers discover our books.

As a thank you, we would love to send you a free digital copy of this book, and a **30%** discount code on your next cart value on our official websites:

www.orangeava.com

www.orangeava.in (For Indian Subcontinent)

☑ **Here's how:**

Leave a review for the book on Amazon.

Take a screenshot of your review, and send an email to **info@orangeava.com** (it can be just the confirmation screen).

Once, we receive your screenshot, we will send you the digital file, within 24 hours.

Thank you so much for your support – it means a lot to us!

Downloading the code bundles and colored images

Please follow the links or scan the QR codes to download the ***Code Bundles and Images*** of the book:

https://github.com/ava-orange-education/Ultimate-Genetic-Algorithms-with-Python

The code bundles and images of the book are also hosted on ***https://rebrand.ly/wdb92je***

In case there's an update to the code, it will be updated on the existing GitHub repository.

Errata

We take immense pride in our work at **Orange Education Pvt Ltd,** and follow best practices to ensure the accuracy of our content to provide an indulging reading experience to our subscribers. Our readers are our mirrors, and we use their inputs to reflect and improve upon human errors, if any, that may have occurred during the publishing processes involved. To let us maintain the quality and help us reach out to any readers who might be having difficulties due to any unforeseen errors, please write to us at :

errata@orangeava.com

Your support, suggestions, and feedback are highly appreciated.

DID YOU KNOW

Did you know that Orange Education Pvt Ltd offers eBook versions of every book published, with PDF and ePub files available? You can upgrade to the eBook version at **www.orangeava.com** and as a print book customer, you are entitled to a discount on the eBook copy. Get in touch with us at: **info@orangeava.com** for more details.

At **www.orangeava.com**, you can also read a collection of free technical articles, sign up for a range of free newsletters, and receive exclusive discounts and offers on Print Books and eBooks.

PIRACY

If you come across any illegal copies of our works in any form on the internet, we would be grateful if you would provide us with the location address or website name. Please contact us at **info@orangeava.com** with a link to the material.

ARE YOU INTERESTED IN AUTHORING WITH US?

If there is a topic that you have expertise in, and you are interested in either writing or contributing to a book, please write to us at **business@orangeava.com**. We are on a journey to help developers and tech professionals to gain insights on the present technological advancements and innovations happening across the globe and build a community that believes Knowledge is best acquired by sharing and learning with others. Please reach out to us to learn what our audience demands and how you can be part of this educational reform. We also welcome ideas from tech experts and help them build learning and development content for their domains.

REVIEWS

Please leave a review. Once you have read and used this book, why not leave a review on the site that you purchased it from? Potential readers can then see and use your unbiased opinion to make purchase decisions. We at Orange Education would love to know what you think about our products, and our authors can learn from your feedback. Thank you!

For more information about Orange Education, please visit **www.orangeava.com**.

Table of Contents

Chapter 1
Introduction to Genetic Algorithms

Introduction

"*We used to think our fate was in the stars. Now we know, in large measure, our fate is in our genes.*" - James Watson. The science of genetics began with foundational contributions by Charles Darwin and Gregor Mendel. Darwin's theory of natural selection explained how species adapt over time, while Mendel's discovery of inheritance through genes provided the mechanism of trait transmission. Together, these theories form the backbone of evolutionary biology, demonstrating that traits beneficial for survival are passed down through generations, leading to gradual adaptation. This concept inspired the development of Genetic Algorithms (GAs) in artificial intelligence, which mimic biological evolution to solve complex optimization problems. In GAs, potential solutions evolve over successive generations through processes analogous to selection, crossover, and mutation. Just as nature optimizes organisms to fit their environment, genetic algorithms evolve solutions to optimize outcomes, allowing AI to efficiently explore large problem spaces and identify optimal or near-optimal solutions. This biologically inspired approach has made GAs useful in AI for tasks such as machine learning, optimization problems, and evolving neural networks, helping AI systems adapt and improve by simulating the way organisms evolve in nature.

In this chapter, we will learn about the components of GAs, focusing on the core aspects such as selection, crossover, and mutation. We will compare Darwinian evolution to genetic algorithms, examining the similarities and differences in their principles. We will also explore how genetic algorithms relate to deep learning, highlighting key distinctions and shared concepts. Additionally, we will delve into the concepts of extrema and minima, which are critical to understanding the optimization process, and provide a detailed overview of the execution process of GAs, including the mathematical foundations and practical steps involved.

Structure

In this chapter, we will discuss the following topics:

- History
- Components of Genetic Algorithms
- Core Components of Genetic Algorithms
- Darwinian Evolution Versus Genetic Algorithms: Comparison and Principles
- Genetic Algorithms Versus Deep Learning
- Extrema and Minima
- Execution Process of Genetic Algorithms

History

The development of modern genetics is rooted in the work of two pivotal figures: Charles Darwin and Gregor Mendel. Darwin, known as the father of evolution, initially struggled to find direction in life, spending time outdoors studying nature rather than pursuing a medical or ministerial career as his father had hoped. His passion for nature led him to a pivotal role as a naturalist aboard the HMS Beagle in 1831, where he observed species' adaptations in different environments. These observations inspired his theory of natural selection, which he cautiously published in *Origin of Species* in 1859. Despite initial religious opposition and his incomplete understanding of heredity, Darwin's theory gained scientific acceptance.

Gregor Mendel, a poor farmer's son from Czechoslovakia, later provided the missing piece in Darwin's theory. Joining a monastery to continue his education without financial burdens, Mendel conducted experiments on pea plants, where he discovered how traits were passed down through generations. He introduced the concept of "*elements*," now known as genes, and identified dominant and recessive traits. Mendel's work was initially overlooked, but it later became foundational to understanding heredity when rediscovered in the early 1900s by several biologists.

Mendel's discovery of genetic inheritance, along with Darwin's theory of natural selection, laid the groundwork for modern evolutionary biology. While Darwin's ideas faced controversy but gained fame quickly, Mendel's work went unnoticed during his lifetime, only to be recognized decades later, completing the understanding of how traits evolve and pass through generations.

Survival of the Fittest *refers to the mechanism within Charles Darwin's theory of natural selection, where individuals best adapted to their environment are more likely to survive and reproduce. These "fit" individuals pass on their favorable traits to their offspring, while those less adapted may not survive to reproduce, leading to the gradual* *prevalence of advantageous traits in a population over time. This concept is often simplified as the "survival of the fittest," meaning that fitness in an evolutionary context relates to an organism's ability to survive and leave behind more offspring.*

***Theory of Evolution** is the scientific explanation for how species change over time through processes such as natural selection. Charles Darwin proposed that all species, including humans, evolved from common ancestors, gradually diversifying into the multitude of life forms we see today. Evolution occurs as individuals with advantageous traits survive and reproduce, passing those traits to future generations. Over long periods, these small, incremental changes accumulate, leading to the emergence of new species and adaptations that better fit organisms to their environments.*

The Early Pioneers of Genetic Algorithms

John von Neumann, a future pioneer of computer science, was born in 1903. Von Neumann displayed exceptional talent from a young age, leading him to earn a degree in chemical engineering and a PhD in mathematics by the age of 23. He joined Princeton University in 1929, later becoming a founding member of the Institute of Advanced Studies. Throughout his career, von Neumann contributed significantly to mathematics, physics, and economics, and played a leading role in the atomic bomb project during World War II. He was also a key figure in the invention of the digital computer, developing the "*von Neumann architecture*," which became the foundational model for most computers. In 1953, von Neumann invited Nils Barricelli to explore artificial life using digital computers. This work led to Barricelli creating the first Genetic Algorithm (GA) software, aiming to simulate evolutionary processes within a computer. Others, such as Alexander Fraser, Hans-Joachim Bremermann, George Box, George Friedman, and Lawrence Fogel, also contributed to the development of GAs, applying evolutionary concepts to solve biological and engineering problems. This laid the foundation for a surge in genetic algorithm research in the 1970s and 1980s, driven by increasing computational power and interest in biologically inspired computing methods.

So now you know, GAs are optimization techniques inspired by the principles of natural evolution. By mimicking processes such as selection, crossover, and mutation, GAs are capable of finding optimal or near-optimal solutions to complex problems. The core components of GAs play a critical role in guiding the evolution of solutions, ensuring the population evolves effectively toward the desired outcome. Understanding these fundamental components—such as populations, fitness evaluation, genetic operations, and adaptation—provides insight into how GAs simulate biological evolution to tackle challenging computational tasks. Further, we delve into the core components that make genetic algorithms a powerful tool for problem-solving.

Components of Genetic Algorithms

To fully grasp how genetic algorithms mimic the principles of natural evolution, it is essential to understand the key processes that drive both biological evolution and algorithmic optimization. These processes include populations, selection, crossover, mutation, fitness, generations, and adaptation. Each of these elements plays a crucial role in guiding the evolutionary process, whether in nature or within a computational model. By exploring how these components function and interact, we can better appreciate how GAs draw inspiration from evolutionary theory to solve complex optimization problems, improving solutions over time through mechanisms that parallel natural selection and adaptation.

- **Populations:** In both Darwinian evolution and genetic algorithms, a population represents a collection of individuals. In evolution, the population is a group of organisms belonging to the same species that interact and reproduce. Their traits evolve based on natural selection over many generations. In genetic algorithms, a population consists of potential solutions to an optimization problem. Each individual represents a different candidate solution, and through processes such as selection, crossover, and mutation, the population evolves over multiple generations. Maintaining a diverse population ensures that the search space is well explored, increasing the likelihood of finding an optimal solution.

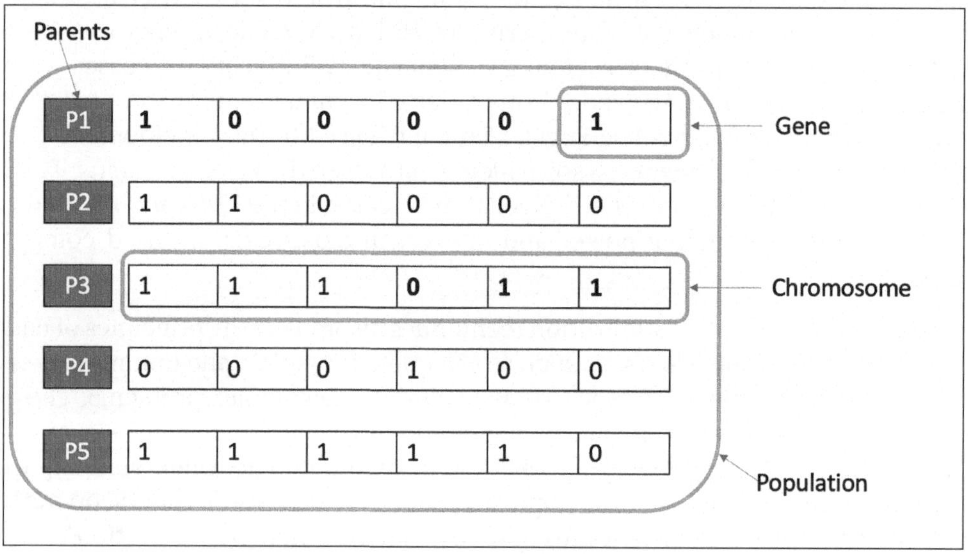

Figure 1.1 (a): *Gene, Chromosome, and Populations with many parents*

- **Selection:** Selection is a mechanism where individuals with higher fitness are chosen to reproduce and pass on their traits. In Darwinian evolution, natural selection ensures that individuals better adapted to their environment are more likely to survive and reproduce, thus passing advantageous traits to the next generation. In GAs, the fitness function determines the quality of each solution, and individuals with higher fitness scores are given a greater chance of being selected to create offspring for the next generation. This process ensures that favorable solutions are preserved and that the algorithm converges towards optimal results.

- **Crossover (Recombination):** Crossover is the process of combining the genetic information of two parent individuals to produce offspring, leading to new variations. In Darwinian evolution, genetic recombination occurs during sexual reproduction, mixing genes from two parents to create genetic diversity in the population. In genetic algorithms, crossover involves taking portions of two parent solutions and merging them to form new offspring solutions. This allows the next generation to inherit successful traits from both parents, enhancing the search for better solutions. Crossover introduces diversity and helps genetic algorithms explore new areas of the solution space effectively.

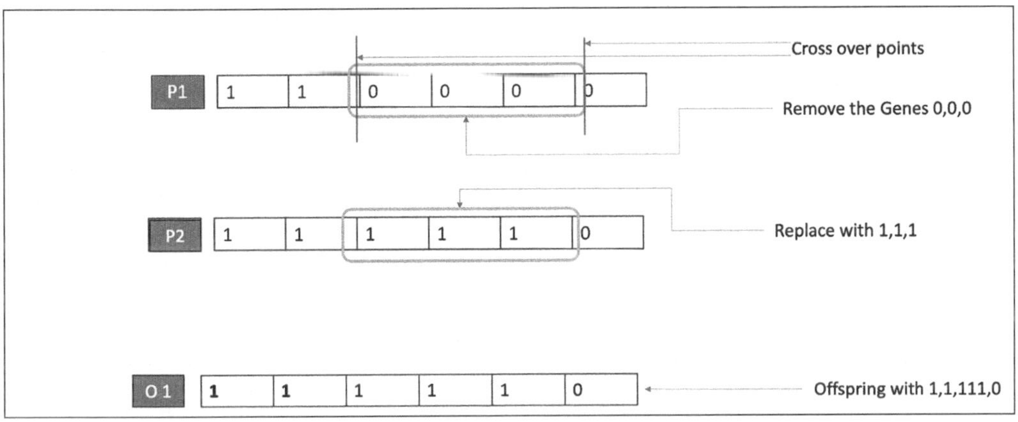

Figure 1.1 (b): *Recombination process and Crossover points*

- **Mutation:** Mutation is a random alteration that introduces new traits or variations into the population. In Darwinian evolution, mutations occur naturally as random changes in an organism's DNA, sometimes resulting in beneficial traits that improve fitness. In genetic algorithms, mutation is a process that randomly modifies parts of an individual solution, ensuring genetic diversity and preventing premature convergence. Mutation enables exploration of the solution space by introducing new characteristics that may lead to better solutions. It is a crucial mechanism to avoid getting stuck in local optima and helps maintain a healthy level of variation in the population.

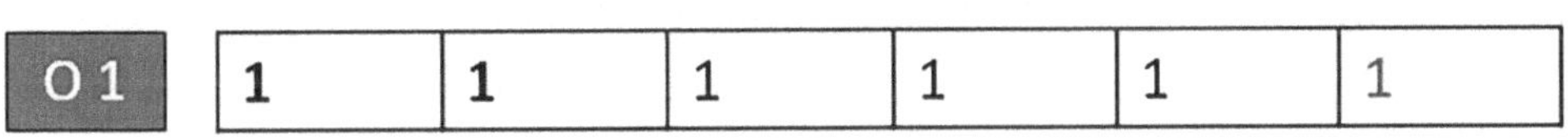

Figure 1.2: Mutation

- **Fitness:** Fitness refers to how well an individual performs in its environment or problem context. In Darwinian evolution, fitness is a measure of an organism's ability to survive and reproduce, determined by its adaptations to the environment. Organisms with higher fitness have a greater chance of passing their genes to the next generation. In genetic algorithms, fitness is determined by an objective function that evaluates the quality of each solution. Solutions with higher fitness scores are more likely to be selected for reproduction, ensuring that favorable traits are carried forward to subsequent generations, moving closer to the optimal solution.
- **Generations:** Generations represent the successive cycles in which a population evolves. In Darwinian evolution, each generation consists of individuals that survive, reproduce, and pass on their traits, allowing species to evolve gradually over thousands to millions of years. In genetic algorithms, each generation represents an iteration of the algorithm, where a new population of solutions is created from the previous one using selection, crossover, and mutation. Over multiple generations, the quality of the population improves as more optimal solutions emerge, leading to the convergence of the algorithm towards the best possible answer to the given problem.
- **Adaptation:** Adaptation is the process of evolving traits that improve an individual's ability to thrive in its environment. In Darwinian evolution, adaptation occurs as individuals with beneficial traits are more likely to survive and reproduce, passing these traits to future generations. This process gradually shapes species to better fit their environment. In genetic algorithms, adaptation refers to the evolution of a population of solutions to solve an optimization problem more effectively. Through selection, crossover, and mutation, the population is refined over generations, with solutions becoming progressively better at achieving the desired outcome, thereby adapting to the problem's requirements.
- **Genotype:** In Darwinian evolution, the genotype is the genetic makeup of an organism—the specific sequence of DNA that determines its hereditary traits. It is the information encoded in the genes that influences traits such as height, eye color, or metabolic processes. The genotype provides the blueprint for building the organism.

  In genetic algorithms, the genotype is the encoded representation of a potential solution. It is often represented as a string of binary values or symbols, containing the information that defines a particular solution. This encoded information undergoes operations such as selection, crossover, and mutation to evolve better solutions over generations.
- **Phenotype:** The phenotype refers to the observable characteristics or traits of an organism, which are the result of the interaction between its genotype and

the environment. Traits such as size, behavior, or flower color are part of an organism's phenotype, influenced by both genetics and environmental factors.

In genetic algorithms, the phenotype is the expressed version of the solution—the actual candidate that can be evaluated for its fitness. It is derived by decoding the genotype and applying it to solve the problem at hand. The fitness function evaluates the phenotype to determine how effective the solution is, guiding the evolutionary process toward better solutions.

- **Termination:** In Darwinian Evolution, termination does not have a fixed endpoint in Darwinian evolution. Natural selection is an ongoing process without a predefined goal or endpoint—species continuously adapt to changing environments. Evolutionary processes might only "*terminate*" when a species becomes extinct, unable to adapt to environmental changes, competition, or catastrophic events.

  In Genetic Algorithms, Termination refers to the condition or criterion that stops the evolutionary process. Genetic algorithms are designed to run until a specific condition is met. Common termination criteria include:

  - Reaching a maximum number of generations.
  - Finding a solution that meets or exceeds a predefined fitness threshold.
  - Observing little to no improvement in the best solution for a set number of generations (convergence).
  - Running out of computational resources, such as time or memory.

Common Confusion: *Genetic programming (GP) and Genetic Algorithms (GA) are both evolutionary algorithms inspired by natural selection, but they differ in focus. Genetic algorithms are used to solve optimization problems by evolving a set of potential solutions (usually represented as fixed-length strings or chromosomes) through selection, crossover, and mutation. In contrast, genetic programming evolves entire computer programs or algorithms. GP generates variable-length trees representing programs and optimizes them to perform a specific task. Essentially, GAs optimize solutions, while GP evolves algorithms or models, making GP more flexible in terms of problem-solving complexity.*

In the next section, we will compare Darwinian evolution with genetic algorithms. Comparing Darwinian evolution with genetic algorithms is essential because it highlights how principles from natural selection can be applied to problem-solving in computational contexts. Darwinian evolution provides a framework for understanding how organisms adapt and survive through generations, while genetic algorithms leverage these principles to evolve solutions to complex optimization problems. This comparison not only enhances our understanding of how genetic algorithms function but also illustrates the interdisciplinary nature of artificial intelligence, where concepts from biology inform computational techniques. By examining these parallels, we gain insights into both the biological and algorithmic processes that drive adaptation and optimization.

Core Components of Genetic Algorithms

The three core components of genetic algorithms–selection, crossover, and mutation–are essential for effectively evolving a population towards an optimal solution. Selection ensures that individuals with higher fitness have a better chance of contributing to the next generation, simulating the natural principle of "*survival of the fittest*." Crossover facilitates the mixing of genetic material from two parents, creating offspring that may inherit the best traits from both, allowing exploration of new areas of the solution space. This recombination is crucial for enhancing the diversity of the population and combining successful features. Mutation introduces random changes to individual genes, preventing premature convergence to suboptimal solutions and maintaining genetic diversity. Together, these components balance exploration (searching different areas of the solution space) and exploitation (focusing on the best solutions), driving the population to evolve towards higher fitness over generations.

Let us understand by a detailed explanation of the different types of selection, mutation, and crossover methods used in genetic algorithms, along with examples involving chromosomes and genes.

Selection Methods

Selection is the process of choosing individuals from the current population to become parents for the next generation. It determines which individuals will contribute their genetic material to the offspring.

1. **Roulette Wheel Selection**
    - **Description**: Each individual is assigned a probability of selection proportional to its fitness value. Think of it as a roulette wheel, where each segment is proportional to the fitness.
    - **Example**: Suppose we have four chromosomes with fitness values [10, 30, 20, 40]. The probabilities for each are [0.1, 0.3, 0.2, 0.4]. The wheel is spun, and individuals are selected based on these probabilities.
    - **Analogy**: If a chromosome represents [1, 0, 1, 1, 0], its likelihood of being selected depends on how fit it is compared to others.
2. **Tournament Selection**
    - **Description**: A subset of the population is randomly chosen, and the fittest individual in this subset is selected as a parent.

- **Example**: From a population of chromosomes [A, B, C, D, E], a tournament selects [B, C, E]. If B has the highest fitness, it is selected.
- **Benefit**: This method ensures that stronger individuals are more likely to be chosen but still allows weaker individuals a chance.

3. **Rank Selection**
   - **Description**: Individuals are ranked based on fitness, and selection probabilities are assigned based on their rank rather than fitness value.
   - **Example**: Chromosomes [A, B, C, D] are ranked such that D is best and A is worst. Selection probabilities are proportional to the ranks [1, 2, 3, 4] rather than their fitness scores.
   - **Benefit**: Prevents domination by a few highly fit individuals and maintains population diversity.
4. **Elitism**
   - **Description**: A few of the best individuals from the current population are carried over to the next generation without modification.
   - **Example**: If chromosome X is the best, it is directly passed to the next generation to ensure high-quality solutions are preserved.

Crossover Methods

Crossover combines two parent chromosomes to create offspring. It simulates genetic recombination and creates diversity in the population.

1. **Single-Point Crossover**
   - **Description**: A single crossover point is selected, and genetic material is exchanged between parents after this point.
   - **Example**: Consider two parents:
     - **Parent 1**: [1, 0, 1, | 0, 1, 0]
     - **Parent 2**: [0, 1, 0, | 1, 0, 1]
     - **Crossover Point**: | represents the crossover point. The offspring would be [1, 0, 1, 1, 0, 1] and [0, 1, 0, 0, 1, 0].
   - **Benefit**: Allows the mixing of genetic information, potentially leading to better solutions.
2. **Two-Point Crossover**
   - **Description**: Two points are selected, and the genetic material between these points is swapped.

- **Example**:
  - **Parent 1**: [1, 0, | 1, 0, 1, | 0]
  - **Parent 2**: [0, 1, | 0, 1, 0, | 1]
  - **Offspring**: [1, 0, 0, 1, 0, 0] and [0, 1, 1, 0, 1, 1].
- **Benefit**: Provides more variety than single-point crossover.

3. **Uniform Crossover**
   - **Description**: Each gene is selected randomly from either parent with a given probability.
   - **Example**:
     - **Parent 1**: [1, 0, 1, 0, 1, 0]
     - **Parent 2**: [0, 1, 0, 1, 0, 1]
     - If the probability of selecting from Parent 1 is 0.5, an offspring could be [1, 1, 0, 0, 0, 1].
   - **Benefit**: Allows more control over genetic diversity and produces a more diverse set of offspring.

Mutation Methods

Mutation introduces small random changes in individuals to maintain genetic diversity and prevent premature convergence.

1. **Bit Flip Mutation**
   - **Description**: Randomly flip one or more bits in the chromosome.
   - **Example**:
     - Chromosome: [1, 0, 1, 0, 1, 1]
     - **Mutation Point**: Flip the third bit to get [1, 0, 0, 0, 1, 1].
   - **Benefit**: Ensures that new genetic material is introduced into the population.
2. **Gaussian Mutation**
   - **Description**: For real-valued genes, add Gaussian noise to a randomly selected gene.
   - **Example**: If the gene value is 2.5 and Gaussian noise with mean 0 and standard deviation 0.1 is added, it might become 2.55.
   - **Benefit**: Useful when optimizing real-valued parameters, allowing small perturbations to explore the solution space.

3. **Swap Mutation**
    - **Description**: Two genes within the chromosome are swapped.
    - **Example**:
        - Chromosome: [1, 0, 1, 0, 1, 1]
        - **Swap Genes**: Swap positions 2 and 5 to get [1, 1, 1, 0, 0, 1].
    - **Benefit**: Helps in problems such as the traveling salesman, where swapping cities might yield better solutions.
4. **Scramble Mutation**
    - **Description**: A subset of genes is chosen, and their positions are shuffled randomly.
    - **Example**:
        - Chromosome: [1, 2, 3, 4, 5, 6]
        - **Scramble Genes** between positions 2 and 5: [1, 5, 4, 3, 2, 6].
    - **Benefit**: Introduces diversity and helps escape local optima.
5. **Inversion Mutation:**
    - **Description**: A segment of the sequence is selected and then inverted (reversed).
    - **Example**: In the sequence [1, 2, 3, 4, 5], if the segment [2, 3, 4] is selected, it will be reversed to [4, 3, 2], resulting in [1, 4, 3, 2, 5].
    - **Purpose**: Inversion mutation is particularly effective in changing the order within subgroups, which can help escape local optima.
6. **Insert Mutation:**
    - **Description**: A random element is selected and inserted into a different position within the permutation.
    - **Example**: Given a sequence [1, 2, 3, 4, 5], if 3 is selected and inserted after 5, the new sequence becomes [1, 2, 4, 5, 3].
    - **Purpose**: Useful for generating new permutations by slightly modifying the order of elements.

Example of a Chromosome Representation

Let us consider a chromosome represented by [1, 0, 1, 1, 0, 1], where:

- Each digit is a **gene**, and the entire sequence is the **chromosome**.
- Different selection, crossover, and mutation methods determine which chromosomes reproduce and how genes are mixed to form new offspring.

- For instance:
  - **Selection** might pick this chromosome because of its high fitness.
  - **Single-point crossover** might exchange part of it with another chromosome.
  - **Mutation** might flip the third gene from 1 to 0.

Darwinian Evolution Versus Genetic Algorithms

So now that we understand, genetic algorithms are an abstraction of Darwinian evolution applied to solve optimization problems. Both follow principles of selection, crossover, and mutation, relying on the "*survival of the fittest*" to improve solutions over generations. However, they differ fundamentally in their context, mechanism of selection, speed, and purpose. Darwinian evolution is a natural, long-term process focused on species' adaptation and survival, whereas genetic algorithms are artificial, fast-paced processes designed to find optimal or near-optimal solutions in a defined problem space. We will understand them in more detail.

Principles and Similarities

Both Darwinian evolution and GAs are based on the concept of adaptation through selection. Darwinian evolution, proposed by Charles Darwin, explains how organisms adapt to their environments over successive generations through natural selection. Individuals with advantageous traits are more likely to survive and reproduce, passing these beneficial traits on to their offspring, thereby gradually shaping the population.

Similarly, GAs are inspired by Darwinian principles. In GAs, potential solutions to a problem are represented as individuals in a population. These solutions undergo processes analogous to natural selection, crossover (recombination), and mutation, which generate new individuals. Over successive generations, "*fitter*" solutions–those closer to the optimization goal–are more likely to be retained, thereby refining the solution space.

Differences	Darwinian Evolution	Genetic Algorithms
Natural vs. Artificial Environment	This occurs in nature without human intervention, where the fitness of individuals is determined by environmental pressures.	GAs are computational simulations that occur within a defined problem space, and fitness is evaluated using an objective function designed by the user.

Selection Mechanism	The selection process is driven by environmental factors, such as predators, climate, and availability of resources, and may involve numerous factors beyond direct fitness.	Selection is algorithmically determined by evaluating how well each individual solution meets the predefined objective, making it a simplified and idealized form of selection.
Timeframe	Evolution in nature occurs over thousands to millions of years, making it a slow and gradual process.	GAs operate much faster within a computational setting, allowing evolution-like processes to converge in minutes or hours.
Mutation and Variation	Mutation is a natural and random change in genes, while genetic recombination introduces variation. The effects are typically small-scale, and only some mutations prove beneficial.	Mutation rates, crossover mechanisms, and variation are adjustable and can be controlled based on the problem requirements, making GAs more deterministic.
Fitness and Goal	The concept of fitness in natural evolution is about survival and reproductive success, which is influenced by complex interactions in the ecosystem.	Fitness is problem-specific and defined by a mathematical function that measures how good a particular solution is. GAs have a clear and specific optimization goal, unlike the open-ended goals of natural evolution.

Table 1.1: *Darwinian Evolution Versus Genetic Algorithms*

Let us understand how these concepts relate to deep learning. In the next section, we will explain the comparison between genetic algorithms and deep learning, highlighting their similarities.

Genetic Algorithms Versus Deep Learning

Genetic Algorithms (GAs) and deep learning are both powerful tools for solving complex problems, but they operate based on different underlying principles. Despite their distinct approaches, many core components of GAs have analogous concepts in deep learning. By comparing elements such as populations, selection, crossover, mutation, and fitness, we can better understand how these two methodologies adapt, optimize, and converge towards solutions. This comparison not only highlights the similarities between evolutionary optimization and neural network learning but also provides insights into how the principles of biological evolution can be reflected in modern artificial intelligence techniques. In *Table 1.2*, we explore how the ten core components of GAs find their counterparts in deep learning.

Components	Genetic Algorithms	Deep Learning
Populations	A set of candidate solutions to a problem, which evolve over successive generations.	The concept of populations is akin to a batch of data. In each training iteration, a batch of data is used to update the neural network, enabling diverse examples to contribute to the learning process.
Selection	The process of choosing the best individuals from a population based on fitness.	Selection is like gradient descent. Parameters are updated based on gradients, effectively selecting weight adjustments that minimize loss, similar to selecting high-fitness individuals to propagate.
Crossover (Recombination)	Combining parts of two parent solutions to produce new offspring with inherited traits.	Crossover is analogous to layer combinations or model ensemble techniques. For instance, combining features or using weights from different models to form a better representation is similar to recombination in GAs.
Mutation	Random alterations to parts of an individual to introduce diversity.	Mutation can be compared to adding noise during training, such as through dropout, which prevents overfitting by altering nodes randomly, helping the model generalize better.
Fitness	A measure of how well a solution performs regarding the optimization goal.	The fitness is equivalent to the loss function in deep learning, which evaluates the performance of the neural network. A lower loss indicates better fitness in representing or solving the problem.
Generations	Successive iterations in which a population evolves and improves.	Generations in deep learning are like training epochs. In each epoch, the model processes the entire training dataset, refining the weights progressively to minimize loss.
Adaptation	The process of evolving traits to better solve a problem.	Adaptation is represented by the model's ability to learn and adjust its weights based on backpropagation, thereby better fitting the data over time and adapting to the learning task.

Genotype	The encoded representation of a solution, such as a binary string or set of parameters.	The genotype can be compared to the model's internal parameters (weights and biases). These parameters encode the learned information from the data, representing the model's internal state.
Phenotype	The expressed version of a solution, which can be evaluated for its effectiveness.	The phenotype in deep learning is the output of the model, which is the prediction or classification based on the current state of the parameters. It is what is directly observed and evaluated against the ground truth.
Termination	The stopping condition for the evolutionary process.	Termination in deep learning is akin to the stopping criteria for training, such as reaching a maximum number of epochs, convergence to a minimum loss, or achieving a specified accuracy. It ensures that training stops when further improvement is unlikely or unnecessary.

***Table 1.2**: Genetic Algorithms Versus Deep Learning*

To understand the similarities and differences between genetic algorithms and deep learning, it is helpful to see how both approaches operate in practice. Genetic algorithms and deep learning are inspired by natural processes but apply these principles in different ways to solve computational problems. Genetic algorithms use a population of solutions, evolving them over generations to find the best outcome, while deep learning adjusts parameters iteratively to minimize loss and improve predictive accuracy.

We will first understand a simple binary genetics algorithm using PyTorch, then a toy code example of both techniques, genetic algorithms and deep learning, implemented in PyTorch, with annotations to highlight their core components and compare their analogous functions in each context.

PyTorch *is an open-source machine learning library primarily developed by Facebook's AI Research lab. It is designed for flexibility and ease of use, enabling researchers and developers to create dynamic neural networks. PyTorch offers a rich ecosystem for building deep learning models, with features such as automatic differentiation, tensor computation, and GPU acceleration. Its intuitive interface and support for various architectures make it a popular choice for both academic research and industry applications.*

PyGAD *is a Python library specifically designed for implementing genetic algorithms. It provides a simple interface for users to create, manage, and evolve populations of potential solutions to optimization problems. PyGAD supports various functionalities,* *such as selection, crossover, mutation, and fitness evaluation, making it easy to integrate genetic algorithms into projects. The library is compatible with frameworks such as NumPy and TensorFlow, allowing for seamless incorporation into machine learning workflows, including those built with PyTorch.*

The following code block shows the evolution of a solution, one using a biologically inspired GA approach and the other using a gradient-based deep learning approach.

Below is a PyTorch implementation of a simple binary Genetic Algorithm (GA) that solves the OneMax problem–maximizing the number of ones in a binary string. The code includes detailed comments and plots the best and average fitness over generations to help you understand how the algorithm evolves over time. OneMax problem we will understand in the upcoming chapters.

Simple binary genetic algorithm (GA)

```
import torch
import matplotlib.pyplot as plt

# Genetic Algorithm parameters
population_size = 100       # Number of individuals in the
                            population
chromosome_length = 20      # Length of each binary string
                            (chromosome)
mutation_rate = 0.01        # Probability of flipping each bit
                            during mutation
crossover_rate = 0.7        # Probability of performing crossover
                            between pairs
num_generations = 50        # Number of generations to evolve

# Initialize the population randomly with 0s and 1s
population = torch.randint(0, 2, (population_size, chromosome_
length))

def fitness_function(population):
    «»»
    Fitness is the sum of bits in the chromosome.
    For the OneMax problem, the goal is to maximize this sum.
    «»»
    fitness = population.sum(dim=1)
    return fitness

def selection(population, fitness):
    «»»
    Roulette Wheel Selection:
    Select individuals probabilistically based on their fitness.
    «»»
```

```
    # Normalize fitness to probabilities
    selection_probs = fitness.float() / fitness.sum()
    # Select indices of individuals to form the mating pool
    selected_indices = torch.multinomial(selection_probs,
population_size, replacement=True)
    # Create the selected population
    selected_population = population[selected_indices]
    return selected_population

def crossover(population, crossover_rate):
    «»»
    Single-point crossover between pairs of individuals.
    «»»
    new_population = population.clone()
    for i in range(0, population_size - 1, 2):
        if torch.rand(1).item() < crossover_rate:
            # Select a crossover point
            crossover_point = torch.randint(1, chromosome_length,
(1,)).item()
            # Perform crossover between pairs
            new_population[i, crossover_point:], new_
population[i+1, crossover_point:] = \
            population[i+1, crossover_point:], population[i,
crossover_point:]
    return new_population

def mutation(population, mutation_rate):
    «»»
    Bit-flip mutation applied to the population.
    «»»
    mutation_mask = torch.rand(population.size()) < mutation_rate
    population[mutation_mask] = 1 - population[mutation_mask]
    return population

# Lists to record fitness over generations
best_fitness_over_time = []
avg_fitness_over_time = []

# Main Genetic Algorithm loop
for generation in range(num_generations):
    # Evaluate fitness
    fitness = fitness_function(population)
    # Record best and average fitness
    best_fitness = fitness.max().item()
    avg_fitness = fitness.float().mean().item()
    best_fitness_over_time.append(best_fitness)
    avg_fitness_over_time.append(avg_fitness)
```

```
    # Selection
    selected_population = selection(population, fitness)
    # Crossover
    crossed_population = crossover(selected_population,
crossover_rate)
    # Mutation
    mutated_population = mutation(crossed_population, mutation_
rate)
    # Update population
    population = mutated_population
    # Print progress
    print(f›Generation {generation+1}: Best Fitness = {best_
fitness}, Avg Fitness = {avg_fitness:.2f}›)

# Plotting the results
plt.figure(figsize=(10, 6))
plt.plot(best_fitness_over_time, label='Best Fitness')
plt.plot(avg_fitness_over_time, label='Average Fitness')
plt.xlabel('Generation')
plt.ylabel('Fitness')
plt.title('Fitness over Generations')
plt.legend()
plt.grid(True)
plt.show()

Generation 1: Best Fitness = 15, Avg Fitness = 10.33
(truncated)......
Generation 50: Best Fitness = 19, Avg Fitness = 15.86
```

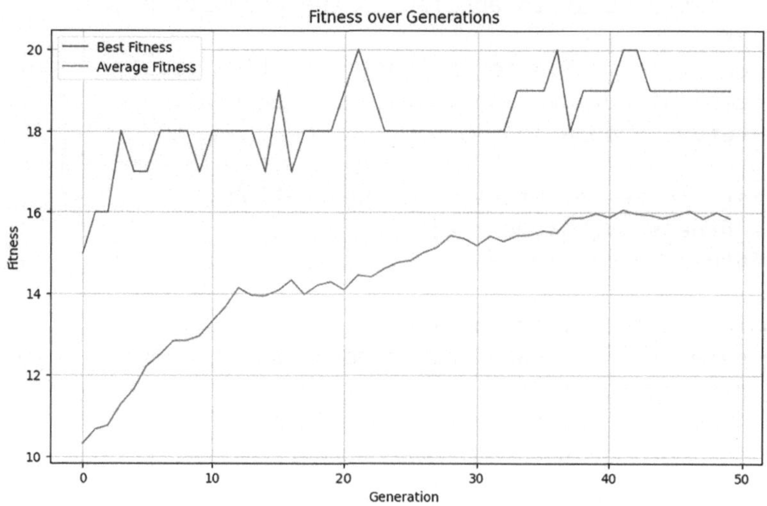

Figure 1.3: *The plot illustrates the fitness performance of a genetic algorithm over multiple generations, showcasing two key metrics:* **Best Fitness** *and* **Average Fitness**

The Best Fitness curve (in blue) indicates the highest fitness score achieved by any individual in the population during each generation, reflecting the optimal solutions found. As seen in the graph, this value fluctuates significantly at the beginning but eventually stabilizes around a higher level, suggesting that the algorithm is successfully exploring the solution space and converging towards better solutions.

Conversely, the Average Fitness curve (in orange) represents the mean fitness score across the entire population for each generation. This line shows a more gradual upward trend, indicating consistent improvement in the population's overall performance. The divergence between the two curves suggests that while individual solutions may vary, the population as a whole is trending towards higher fitness levels, demonstrating the effectiveness of the genetic algorithm in optimizing solutions across generations.

Understanding the Outcomes:

- **Best Fitness:** Represents the highest fitness value found in the population for each generation.
- **Average Fitness:** Represents the mean fitness of the entire population for each generation.
- **Evolution Trend:** Both curves should show an upward trend, indicating improvement in the population's overall fitness.

Feel Free to Experiment:

- **Adjust Parameters:** Try changing the **`mutation_rate`**, **`crossover_rate`**, **`population_size`**, or **`num_generations`** to see how they affect the algorithm's performance.
- **Different Fitness Functions:** Modify the **`fitness_function`** to solve different optimization problems.
- **Observation:** Pay attention to how the algorithm converges and how genetic diversity affects the search for optimal solutions.

The below PyTorch-based GA example demonstrates how to find an optimal solution by minimizing the sum of squares of a genotype. It starts with generating a random population of solutions (each represented as a tensor) and iteratively evolves the population through generations using a fitness function, selection, crossover, and mutation. The fitness function evaluates each solution, with better solutions being selected as parents. Offspring are generated using crossover, combining parent solutions, and then subjected to mutation to introduce diversity. After 20 generations, the final solution is chosen as the one with the best fitness value.

Genetic Algorithm (GA) Example in PyTorch

```
import torch
import random
```

```
# Core Components Definitions:
# Population: A set of random solutions (genotypes).
population_size = 10
genotype_length = 5
population = [torch.randn(genotype_length) for _ in range
(population_size)]  # Populations

# Fitness Function
def fitness(solution):
    return -torch.sum(solution ** 2)  # Minimize the sum of
squares for simplicity

# GA Parameters
num_generations = 20
mutation_rate = 0.1

for generation in range(num_generations):  # Generations
    # Calculate fitness of each solution
    fitness_values = [fitness(ind) for ind in population]

    # Selection: Select parents based on fitness
    sorted_population = [x for _, x in sorted(zip(fitness_values,
population), key=lambda pair: pair[0], reverse=True)]
    parents = sorted_population[:2]  # Select the two best
individuals

    # Crossover: Create new offspring by combining parents
    offspring = []
    for _ in range(population_size // 2):
        parent1, parent2 = random.sample(parents, 2)
        crossover_point = random.randint(1, genotype_length - 1)
        child1 = torch.cat((parent1[:crossover_point],
parent2[crossover_point:]))
        child2 = torch.cat((parent2[:crossover_point],
parent1[crossover_point:]))
        offspring.extend([child1, child2])

    # Mutation: Randomly alter some offspring genes
    for child in offspring:
        if random.random() < mutation_rate:
            mutation_index = random.randint(0, genotype_length - 1)
            child[mutation_index] += torch.randn(1).item()  #
Mutation

    # Create the new population
    population = parents + offspring[:population_size - len
(parents)]
```

```
# Final solution
best_solution = sorted(population, key=lambda x: fitness(x),
reverse=True)[0]
print("Best solution:", best_solution)
Best solution: tensor([-0.1051, -0.3039, 0.0575, -0.1835,
0.4139])
```

The output shows the best solution found as a tensor with five values, representing optimized parameters for the given problem.

Mapping Core Components:

- **Populations:** `population = [torch.randn(genotype_length) for _ in range(population_size)]`
- **Selection:** `parents = sorted_population[:2]`
- **Crossover (Recombination):** Combining genes from two parents using slicing (`torch.cat`).
- **Mutation:** `child[mutation index] += torch.randn(1)`
- **Fitness:** `def fitness(solution):`
- **Generations:** for generation in `range(num_generations):`
- **Adaptation:** Population evolves over generations.
- **Genotype:** Individual solutions, represented by `torch.randn(genotype_length)`.
- **Phenotype:** In this toy example, the phenotype is the same as the genotype, as it is directly evaluated.
- **Termination:** Stopping after `num_generations`.

This example illustrates the use of a simple PyTorch neural network, SimpleModel, which represents a candidate solution (genotype) being trained to approximate a linear function. The network is trained using Mean Squared Error (MSE) as the loss function, with the Stochastic Gradient Descent (SGD) optimizer. The training loop (representing generations) updates the model parameters iteratively over 100 epochs. In each iteration, the loss (fitness value) is computed, and the weights are adjusted to minimize the loss, similar to the selection, crossover, and mutation steps in genetic algorithms. After 100 epochs, the final model is obtained as the best solution.

Deep Learning Example in PyTorch

```
import torch
import torch.nn as nn
import torch.optim as optim

# Core Components Definitions:
```

```
# Model (Genotype): A neural network representing a candidate
solution
class SimpleModel(nn.Module):
    def __init__(self):
        super(SimpleModel, self).__init__()
        self.fc = nn.Linear(1, 1)

    def forward(self, x):
        return self.fc(x)

# Create model (Phenotype: The expression of the solution)
model = SimpleModel()

# Define loss function (Fitness function)
criterion = nn.MSELoss()  # Fitness
optimizer = optim.SGD(model.parameters(), lr=0.01)

# Training data
x_train = torch.tensor([[1.0], [2.0], [3.0], [4.0]])
y_train = torch.tensor([[2.0], [4.0], [6.0], [8.0]])

# Training loop (Generations: Each epoch updates the model)
num_epochs = 100
for epoch in range(num_epochs):  # Generations
    # Forward pass
    outputs = model(x_train)
    loss = criterion(outputs, y_train)  # Calculate fitness (loss)

    # Backward pass and optimization (Selection, Crossover, Mutation)
    optimizer.zero_grad()
    loss.backward()  # Compute gradients for parameter updates (like
mutation)
    optimizer.step()  # Update weights (adaptation)

    # Print loss every 20 epochs (Termination is defined after `num_
epochs`)
    if (epoch+1) % 20 == 0:
        print(f'Epoch [{epoch+1}/{num_epochs}], Loss: {loss.
item():.4f}')

# Final model (best solution)
 Epoch [20/100], Loss: 0.1040
Epoch [40/100], Loss: 0.0337
Epoch [60/100], Loss: 0.0298
Epoch [80/100], Loss: 0.0264
Epoch [100/100], Loss: 0.0235
   Trained Model Weight: tensor([[1.8729]])
```

The above output shows that the model is effectively learning to minimize its error over the epochs, resulting in improved performance by the end of training.

Mapping Core Components with Deep Learning:

- **Populations:** The population is implicitly represented by the weights initialized randomly.
- **Selection:** Selection is analogous to gradient descent, choosing weight adjustments that minimize the loss.
- **Crossover (Recombination):** Not directly applicable, but a layer or model ensemble could be analogous.
- **Mutation:** Weight updates through backpropagation (`loss.backward()`) introduce changes, similar to mutations.
- **Fitness:** Loss function (`nn.MSELoss()`) measures the model's performance.
- **Generations:** Each epoch in training (for epoch in `range(num_epochs)`) acts as a generation.
- **Adaptation:** Model weights adjust during training to minimize the loss, improving fitness.
- **Genotype:** The parameters of the model (`model.parameters()`) represent the internal information.
- **Phenotype:** The model's output (`outputs = model(x_train)`) is the expression of the parameters used to evaluate performance.
- **Termination:** Defined by the `num_epochs (training stops after a fixed number of epochs)`.

One of the key concepts in deep learning, local and global maxima and minima, refer to the points in a loss function where the value of the function is at its highest or lowest relative to nearby points. A **local maximum** is a point where the loss function has a higher value than its immediate neighbors but is not necessarily the highest overall; similarly, a **local minimum** is where the loss is lower than that of nearby points. In contrast, a **global maximum** is the absolute highest point in the entire loss landscape, while a **global minimum** is the lowest point achievable across all possible configurations. Finding the global minimum is desirable in training deep learning models, as it corresponds to the best performance on the training data, but the presence of multiple local minima can complicate optimization, potentially leading to suboptimal solutions.

Extrema and Minima

Understanding local and global maxima and minima is key to ensuring that genetic algorithms effectively search the entire solution space and avoid prematurely converging to suboptimal solutions. It also aids in designing and fine-tuning the GA to improve its robustness and efficiency in finding the global optimum.

Here is a 3D plot representing a solution space with multiple local and global optima. This fitness landscape illustrates the complexity that a genetic algorithm must navigate when searching for the best solution. The peaks represent maxima (which could be local or global), and the valleys represent minima. The challenge for genetic algorithms is to avoid getting trapped in these local optima and instead find the global optimum that yields the best result for the problem being optimized.

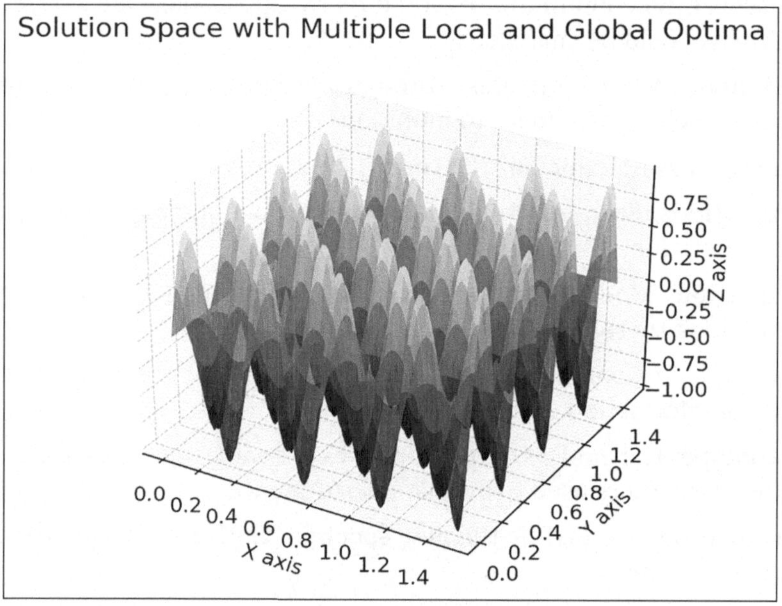

Figure 1.4: *Solution space with multiple global and local minimum*

Now that we understand solution space, let's understand Global and Local Minima/ Maxima.

Here is a 3D plot illustrating the global and local minima and maxima. The peaks and valleys represent points of high and low values in the function, similar to the local and global optima seen in optimization problems. The marked points (red, blue, cyan, and magenta) highlight different types of extrema, such as global and local maxima/ minima.

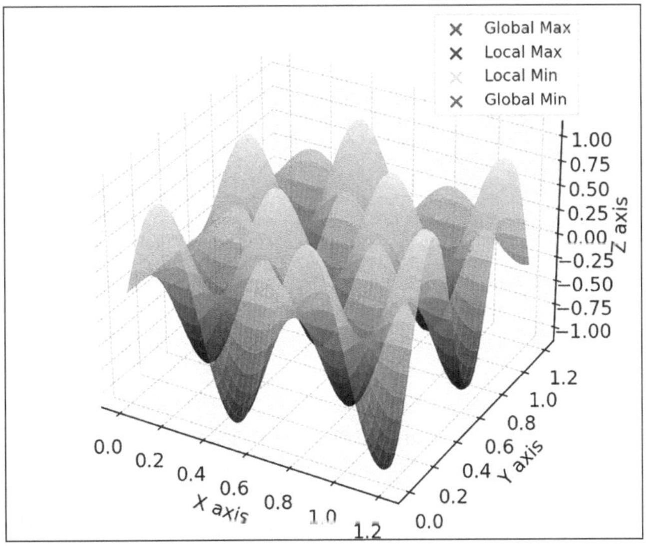

Figure 1.5: *3D Plot showing global and local minima/maxima*

Many conventional search and optimization algorithms, especially those that rely on gradients, often become trapped in a local maximum instead of locating the global one. This occurs because any slight modification near a local maximum typically degrades the performance score. In contrast, genetic algorithms are less susceptible to this issue and are more likely to find the global maximum. This advantage arises from using a population of candidate solutions rather than focusing on a single option. Additionally, crossover and mutation operations frequently produce new candidate solutions that differ significantly from previous ones. This effectiveness persists as long as we maintain diversity within the population and prevent premature convergence, a topic we will discuss in the next section.

Following is an example of how you can implement both Genetic Algorithms (using the PyGAD library) and Deep Learning (using PyTorch) to identify local and global maxima/minima of a solution space. The code will involve training a neural network to fit a function and using a GA to optimize the function. We will use PyGAD to solve the optimization problem for the given solution space.

First, you will need to install the PyGAD library :

```
!pip install pygad # PyGAD API version 3.3.1[ latest while we are
                    writing this book]
```

```
Installing collected packages:
pygad Successfully installed pygad-3.3.1
```

When the message above is displayed, it indicates that the software has been successfully installed with the latest version.

Example: Deep Learning (PyTorch) and Genetic Algorithm (PyGAD) to Identify Maxima/Minima

Deep Learning Approach Using PyTorch

In this example, we will create a simple neural network to approximate the target function and identify its extrema.

```
import torch
import torch.nn as nn
import torch.optim as optim
import numpy as np

# Define the target function (same function used to create the
solution space)
def target_function(x):
    return np.sin(5 * np.pi * x) * np.cos(5 * np.pi * x)

# Create synthetic training data
x_train = torch.tensor(np.linspace(0, 1.5, 100).reshape(-1, 1),
dtype=torch.float32)
y_train = torch.tensor(target_function(x_train).reshape(-1, 1),
dtype=torch.float32)

# Define a simple neural network
class SimpleNet(nn.Module):
    def __init__(self):
        super(SimpleNet, self).__init__()
        self.fc1 = nn.Linear(1, 10)
        self.fc2 = nn.Linear(10, 10)
        self.fc3 = nn.Linear(10, 1)

    def forward(self, x):
        x = torch.relu(self.fc1(x))
        x = torch.relu(self.fc2(x))
        return self.fc3(x)

# Initialize model, loss function, and optimizer
model = SimpleNet()
criterion = nn.MSELoss()
optimizer = optim.Adam(model.parameters(), lr=0.01)

# Train the model
num_epochs = 1000
for epoch in range(num_epochs):
    outputs = model(x_train)
    loss = criterion(outputs, y_train)
```

```
        optimizer.zero_grad()
        loss.backward()
        optimizer.step()

# Predict and find extrema using the trained model
x_test = torch.tensor(np.linspace(0, 1.5, 100).reshape(-1, 1),
dtype=torch.float32)
y_pred = model(x_test).detach().numpy()

# Identify local minima and maxima
local_max = []
local_min = []
for i in range(1, len(y_pred) - 1):
    if y_pred[i] > y_pred[i - 1] and y_pred[i] > y_pred[i + 1]:
        local_max.append((x_test[i].item(), y_pred[i].item()))
    elif y_pred[i] < y_pred[i - 1] and y_pred[i] < y_pred[i + 1]:
        local_min.append((x_test[i].item(), y_pred[i].item()))

print("Local Maxima (Deep Learning):", local_max)
print("Local Minima (Deep Learning):", local_min)
```

```
  y_train = torch.tensor(target_function(x_train).reshape(-1, 1),
dtype=torch.float32)
```

```
Local Maxima (Deep Learning): [(0.43939393758773804,
0.05530213564634323)] Local Minima (Deep Learning):
[(0.3636363744735718, -0.1417413353919983), (1.1515151262283325,
-0.0616307333111763)]
```

Genetic Algorithm Approach Using PyGAD

Using PyGAD, we will define a fitness function that the GA will use to optimize the function and find the extrema.

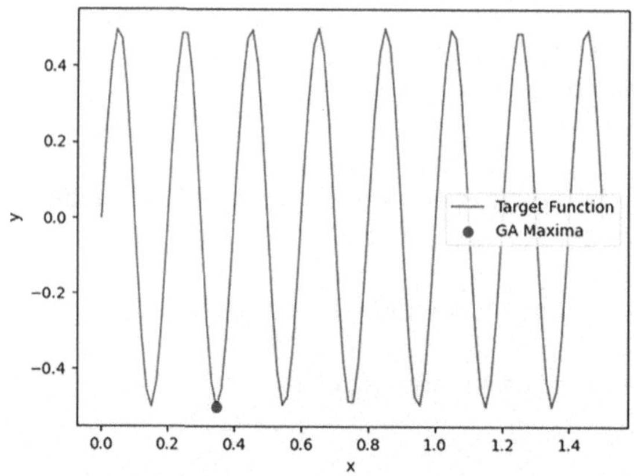


```
Global Maximum (GA): x = 0.3496107067088243, y = -0.49996260718337937
```

Figure 1.6: *Plot showing global and local minima/maxima*

The plot shows the target function used for optimization, which has multiple peaks and valleys, representing local and global extrema. The red dot labeled "GA Maxima" indicates the global maximum identified by the Genetic Algorithm (GA). The GA explored the solution space and found this point to be the highest value within the defined domain. The oscillatory nature of the function highlights the challenges of distinguishing between local and global maxima, which the GA effectively navigates by utilizing crossover, mutation, and selection mechanisms to explore and converge on the optimal solution.

Key Insights:

- **Deep Learning** is useful for approximating functions and can help identify local and global extrema, but it requires proper training and enough data to converge.
- **Genetic Algorithms** provide a robust way of optimizing functions, especially in complex landscapes where there are multiple peaks and valleys. GAs avoid getting trapped in local optima by exploring a diverse solution space.

Execution Process of Genetic Algorithms

Let us go back to section "*Core Components of Genetic Algorithms*," where we explain all the components, for example, Population Selection, Crossover (Recombination), Mutation, Fitness, Generations, Adaptation, and Termination. It is crucial to understand the execution process along with the underlying mathematics. So let us explore it one by one.

The following flowchart illustrates the Genetic Algorithm (GA) process. It begins with an initial population of candidate solutions, followed by iterative steps: creating the population, selecting the fittest individuals, applying crossover to combine parent traits, and performing mutation to introduce variation. Fitness evaluation is performed to determine the quality of each solution. A new population is created from the fittest individuals, and the process repeats until a stopping condition is met. The final output is the solution with the highest fitness value. The process emulates evolution to iteratively improve solutions.

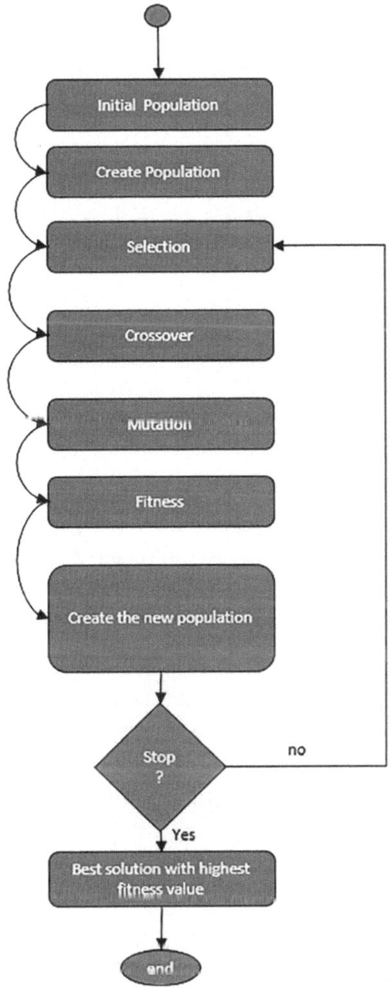

Figure 1.7: *The execution process of GA*

Execution Process of Genetic Algorithms

The following is a theoretical explanation of the execution process of genetic algorithms (GAs), using input data denoted as X. This includes relevant equations to describe each step.

Initialization (Create Population)

Start by generating an initial population of candidate solutions (genotypes), typically represented as vectors of real or binary values. If P represents the population, and N is the population size, each individual solution `X_i` is initialized randomly:

$$P = \{X_1, X_2, \ldots, X_N\}, \qquad X_i \sim \mathit{Random}\ (\mathit{Range})$$

where `X_i` is sampled from a range defined by the problem.

Fitness Evaluation

The fitness of each individual is evaluated using a predefined fitness function $f(X)$. This function quantifies how good each solution is in solving the problem:

$$F_i = f(X_i), \qquad \forall X_i \in P$$

The fitness function can vary depending on the problem; for minimization, it could be the negative of the objective value, and for maximization, it could be the value itself.

Selection

Selection involves choosing individuals from the population to become parents for the next generation, based on their fitness values. One common selection technique is roulette wheel selection, where the probability of selecting an individual `X_i` is proportional to its fitness value:

$$p_i = \frac{F_i}{\sum_{j=1}^{N} F_j}$$

Alternatively, tournament selection or rank selection can also be used.

Crossover (Recombination)

Crossover combines the genetic information of two parents to create offspring. For two parents `X_a` and `X_b`, a new child `X_child` can be produced using a crossover point k:

$$X_{\text{child}} = [X_a[:k], X_b[k:]]$$

This recombination allows for the mixing of features and helps explore new areas of the solution space.

Mutation

Mutation is applied to introduce random variations, ensuring genetic diversity in the population. For a solution **X_i**, each element **X_{i,j}** is mutated with a small probability **p_mut**:

$$X'_{i,j} = X_{i,j} + \epsilon, \quad \textbf{with probability } p_{\text{mut}}$$

where epsilon is random noise, such as Gaussian noise.

Create the New Population (Generations)

A new population is formed by combining selected parents, offspring generated through crossover, and mutated individuals. This iterative process continues for multiple generations, with each generation being an improvement over the previous one:

$$P_{\text{new}} = \{X_{\text{selected}}, X_{\text{crossover}}, X_{\text{mutated}}\}$$

Adaptation

The process of adaptation occurs over generations as the population evolves towards better solutions. The population becomes fitter as weaker individuals are replaced by better offspring, following the principle of "*survival of the fittest.*"

Termination

The algorithm stops when a termination condition is met, such as reaching a maximum number of generations (**G_max**), finding a solution that meets a desired fitness threshold (**F_target**), or when improvements fall below a certain threshold over several iterations:

$$\text{Terminate if } F_{\text{best}} \geq F_{\text{target}} \quad \text{or} \quad \text{generation count} = G_{\text{max}}$$

Conclusion

In conclusion, this chapter has provided an in-depth understanding of genetic algorithms by exploring their key components, such as selection, crossover, and mutation, and examining how these aspects contribute to the evolutionary process. We compared the principles of Darwinian evolution and genetic algorithms, as well as their connections to deep learning, to highlight the shared and distinct characteristics of these optimization approaches. The discussion on extrema and minima was essential to understanding the challenges of optimization, and we further covered the complete execution process of genetic algorithms, including the underlying mathematical concepts.

In the next chapter, we will delve deeper into variations on traditional genetic algorithms and explore the termination criteria–when and how to effectively stop the genetic algorithm process, hyperparameter tuning, and advanced GA.

Chapter 2
Fundamentals of Genetic Algorithms

Introduction

In the previous chapter, we explored the fundamental components of genetic algorithms, focusing on core aspects such as selection, crossover, and mutation. We also compared genetic algorithms to Darwinian evolution, highlighting both their similarities and differences, and examined the connections between genetic algorithms and deep learning, pointing out the key distinctions and shared concepts. Furthermore, we discussed the concepts of extrema and minima, providing insight into their importance in the optimization process, and outlined the execution process of genetic algorithms from both mathematical and practical perspectives.

In this chapter, we will delve into the foundational concepts of genetic algorithms, starting with an **overview of metaheuristic algorithms**, which provide the overarching strategies that genetic algorithms fall under. We will explore how these high-level approaches are used to solve complex optimization problems where traditional methods fall short.

Next, we will discuss **niching in genetic algorithms**, a crucial technique for maintaining diversity in the population, which prevents the algorithm from converging prematurely to suboptimal solutions. We will also go deeper into the importance of creating a strong **initial population and sampling** methods, which set the foundation for successful optimization.

Further, we will examine **fitness evaluation** as the key measure that determines the quality of solutions, and how various **selection methods** guide the evolution process. Finally, we will look into different **termination criteria** to understand when and how to conclude the optimization process efficiently, ensuring that the Genetic Algorithm finds an optimal solution without unnecessary computation.

Structure

In this chapter, we will discuss the following topics:

- Overview of Metaheuristics Algorithms
- Niching in Genetic Algorithms
- More into Initial Population and Sampling
- More into Fitness
- More into Selection
- More into Termination

Overview of Metaheuristics Algorithms

Even though we will cover more about metaheuristics algorithms in *Chapter 7, Metaheuristic Optimization Algorithms*, Genetic Algorithms (GA) belong to the evolutionary computing category and are one of many population-based metaheuristics methods used to evolve a set of potential solutions over time, leveraging principles of natural selection and genetics. Metaheuristic algorithms can be divided into two main types:

- Trajectory-based methods
- Population-based methods

As mentioned earlier, genetic algorithms fall under population-based methods, specifically under evolutionary computing. Following is a brief explanation of each category and algorithm:

- **Trajectory-based methods (S-metaheuristics)**: Explore the search space using a single solution trajectory to find an optimal or near-optimal solution.
    - **Simulated Annealing (SA)**: Inspired by the annealing process in metallurgy, it probabilistically accepts worse solutions to avoid getting stuck in local optima.
    - **Tabu Search (TS)**: Uses memory structures to avoid revisiting recently explored solutions, thus enabling a broader search.
    - **Greedy Randomized Adaptive Search Procedure (GRASP)**: Combines greedy heuristics with randomization to find good solutions iteratively.
    - **Iterated Local Search (ILS)**: Applies local optimization multiple times, restarting from perturbed versions of previously found solutions.
    - **Guided Local Search (GLS)**: Uses penalties to escape local optima, guiding the search towards more promising areas.

  - **Variable Neighborhood Search (VNS)**: Systematically changes neighborhoods during the search to find better solutions.
- **Population-based methods (P-metaheuristics)**: Utilize a population of candidate solutions and evolve them over time.
- **Evolutionary Computing (EC)**: Algorithms inspired by biological evolution to improve populations of solutions.
  - **Genetic Algorithm (GA)**: Uses selection, crossover, and mutation to evolve a population towards better solutions.
  - **Differential Evolution (DE)**: Optimizes by combining existing solutions with weighted differences between others.
  - **Genetic Programming (GP)**: Evolves computer programs instead of numerical solutions.
  - **Evolutionary Programming (EP)**: Focuses on evolving the parameters of candidate solutions.
  - **Evolutionary Strategies (ES)**: Similar to genetic algorithms but emphasizes self-adaptation of mutation rates.
  - **Cultural Algorithms (CA)**: Incorporate shared knowledge to influence the evolution of solutions.
  - **Co-Evolution (CoE)**: Evolves multiple interacting populations to achieve optimal solutions.
- **Swarm Intelligence (SI)**: Algorithms inspired by the collective behavior of social entities.
  - **Particle Swarm Optimization (PSO)**: Models the social behavior of birds or fish to find optimal solutions.
  - **Ant Colony Optimization (ACO)**: Simulates the foraging behavior of ants to find paths in a graph.
  - **Artificial Bee Colony (ABC)**: Mimics the behavior of bees searching for nectar to optimize functions.
  - **Bat Algorithm (BA)**: Inspired by the echolocation behavior of bats to navigate the search space.
  - **Firefly Algorithm (FA)**: Uses the flashing behavior of fireflies to attract and explore new solutions.
  - **Wolf Search Algorithm (WSA)**: Models the hunting behavior of wolves to optimize the solution.

Now that we understand the different types of metaheuristic algorithms, let us explore the different types of genetic algorithms. After that, we will dive deeper into the genetic algorithm execution process, starting with sampling, and explain why sampling is necessary.

Different types of Genetic Algorithms (GA) are suited to various optimization problems. The Simple GA is general-purpose and easy to implement, while Steady-State GA maintains diversity with gradual changes. Generational GA excels in large search spaces, and Elitist GA ensures convergence by preserving top solutions. Parallel GA leverages parallel resources for large-scale problems, and Adaptive GA adjusts parameters dynamically to avoid premature convergence. Hybrid GA combines GA with other techniques, and Multi-objective GA optimizes conflicting objectives. Distributed GA handles decentralized control, Differential GA aids numerical optimization, and Immune GA uses immune principles to sustain diversity. The choice depends on the problem's nature, computational resources, and convergence needs. Let us understand them with description, steps, and applications.

Simple Genetic Algorithm (SGA)

- **Description**: The Simple Genetic Algorithm is the most basic form of GA. It uses selection, crossover, and mutation to evolve the population.
- **Steps**:
  1. Generate an initial population of candidate solutions.
  2. Evaluate the fitness of each solution.
  3. Select parents based on fitness.
  4. Apply crossover and mutation to create offspring.
  5. Replace the old population with the new population and repeat until convergence.
- **Application**: Suitable for solving general optimization problems where computational resources are not a constraint.

Steady-State Genetic Algorithm (SSGA)

- **Description**: Instead of replacing the entire population, only a few individuals are replaced in each generation. It maintains a steady state by keeping most of the population intact.
- **Steps**:
  1. Generate an initial population.
  2. Select a small number of parents.
  3. Apply crossover and mutation to produce a few offspring.

4. Evaluate the offspring and replace the worst individuals in the population.

- **Application**: Useful in maintaining diversity and allowing a more gradual convergence. It is more efficient when fewer changes are needed in each generation.

Generational Genetic Algorithm

- **Description**: The entire population is replaced with a new one in each generation. This method helps maintain a high diversity within the population.
- **Steps**:
  1. Generate an initial population.
  2. Select parents and generate offspring using crossover and mutation.
  3. Replace the entire population with the new offspring.
- **Application**: This approach is effective for avoiding premature convergence but can be computationally expensive.

Elitist Genetic Algorithm

- **Description**: In an elitist GA, the best individuals (elite) are retained across generations to ensure the best solutions are not lost.
- **Steps**:
  1. Generate an initial population.
  2. Evaluate and select the best individuals as elites.
  3. Generate offspring from selected parents.
  4. Replace the population but retain the elite individuals.
- **Application**: Suitable for avoiding loss of good solutions during evolution, helping in faster convergence to the optimal solution.

Parallel Genetic Algorithm (PGA)

- **Description**: PGAs run multiple subpopulations (islands) in parallel. Each subpopulation evolves independently and occasionally shares individuals.
- **Types**: There are two primary types of PGAs:
  - **Coarse-grained PGA**: Subpopulations evolve independently for many generations before exchanging individuals.
  - **Fine-grained PGA**: Individuals are distributed across processors, and evolution occurs through neighborhood-based interactions.

- **Application**: Efficient for large-scale problems and takes advantage of parallel computing resources for faster convergence.

Adaptive Genetic Algorithm (AGA)

- **Description**: An adaptive GA changes its parameters, such as crossover probability or mutation rate, during the evolution process based on the performance of the population.
- **Steps**:
  1. Start with an initial population and fixed parameters.
  2. Monitor the population's diversity and adjust parameters accordingly to maintain diversity and avoid premature convergence.
- **Application**: Suitable for dynamic optimization problems where the landscape is changing, or when adaptation is needed to prevent getting stuck in local optima.

Hybrid Genetic Algorithm (HGA)

- **Description**: HGA combines GA with other optimization techniques like hill climbing, simulated annealing, or local search. The purpose is to combine the exploration capability of GA with the fast convergence of other optimization methods.
- **Steps**:
  1. Run GA to explore the search space.
  2. Apply a local optimization method to refine the solution.
- **Application**: Effective for problems requiring both global exploration and local refinement. Examples include engineering design optimization.

Multi-objective Genetic Algorithm (MOGA)

- **Description**: MOGAs are designed to handle optimization problems with multiple objectives that need to be optimized simultaneously. The goal is to find a set of solutions representing the trade-offs between objectives.
- **Algorithm Examples**:
  - **NSGA-II (Non-dominated Sorting Genetic Algorithm II)**: Uses non-dominated sorting and crowding distance to maintain diversity in the Pareto front.
  - **SPEA2 (Strength Pareto Evolutionary Algorithm 2)**: Keeps an archive of non-dominated solutions to guide the search process.

- **Application**: Suitable for real-world optimization problems involving multiple conflicting objectives, such as cost versus performance.

Distributed Genetic Algorithm

- **Description**: Similar to parallel GAs, but with decentralized control. Multiple populations (called subpopulations or demes) evolve independently and exchange individuals occasionally.
- **Steps**:
  1. Subpopulations evolve separately for several generations.
  2. Migration is performed to exchange individuals among subpopulations.
- **Application**: Suitable for large-scale optimization problems where distributed resources can be used effectively to speed up computation.

Differential Genetic Algorithm (DGA)

- **Description**: Combines principles of Differential Evolution (DE) with GA, using differential mutation to create new individuals based on weighted differences between existing ones.
- **Steps**:
  1. Generate a new individual using the weighted difference of other individuals in the population.
  2. Combine this new individual with traditional crossover and mutation.
- **Application**: Useful for numerical optimization problems where differential approaches can guide the search more efficiently.

Immune Genetic Algorithm (IGA)

- **Description**: Inspired by the immune system, this approach incorporates immune operators such as vaccination and antibody generation. It focuses on maintaining diversity and enhancing the population's adaptability.
- **Steps**:
  1. Incorporate immune mechanisms, such as vaccination of individuals.
  2. Perform selection, crossover, and mutation as in traditional GA.
- **Application**: Useful for avoiding premature convergence and maintaining population diversity in complex search spaces.

Having explored the various types of genetic algorithms and their unique characteristics, it is important to understand how a well-chosen initial population can significantly impact the efficiency and outcome of these algorithms. The initialization phase, often overlooked, plays a crucial role in determining whether the algorithm converges to an optimal solution or gets stuck in suboptimal regions.

In the next section, we will dive deeper into strategies for generating the initial population, including different sampling methods and their influence on performance. We will explore how techniques such as random sampling, Latin Hypercube Sampling, and quasi-random sequences can improve the diversity and quality of the initial candidate solutions, setting the foundation for successful optimization. However, let us understand that an important topic, **Niching** techniques, are applied **after** the initial population is generated and during the evolutionary process. Specifically, niching comes into play when the population is evolving through multiple generations. It works alongside **selection**, **crossover**, and **mutation** to maintain diversity and ensure that the Genetic Algorithm can explore multiple optimal or near-optimal solutions.

Niching in Genetic Algorithms

Niching refers to techniques used in Genetic Algorithms (GAs) to promote and maintain diversity in the population by encouraging the formation of multiple subpopulations, or "*niches*," that can explore different regions of the search space. Niching helps GAs to effectively explore **multimodal** functions, which have multiple local optima. Without niching, a GA may converge prematurely to a single solution, missing out on potentially better solutions.

The preceding plot represents a **multimodal function** with multiple peaks, each representing a potential optimum. The peaks highlighted as **Niche 1**, **Niche 2**, and **Niche 3** correspond to different regions of the search space that the GA can explore and converge to. Niching ensures that the population is distributed across these different peaks, rather than converging to only one of them.

Types of Niching Techniques

- **Fitness Sharing:**
    - **Concept**: The fitness of an individual is reduced based on its proximity to other individuals, effectively reducing the reproductive potential of individuals in crowded regions.
    - **Purpose**: This encourages individuals to spread out and fill different regions of the search space.
    - **Example**: If many individuals occupy a niche, the fitness value for all individuals in that niche will be reduced, thereby promoting the exploration of other niches.

- **Crowding**:
    - **Concept**: In this approach, offspring replace individuals that are most similar to them, rather than replacing random individuals.
    - **Purpose**: This prevents similar individuals from dominating the population and maintains diversity by ensuring that each niche can be preserved.
    - **Types**:
        - **Deterministic Crowding**: Pairs of parents are compared with their offspring, and the more similar one replaces the parent.
        - **Probabilistic Crowding**: Similar to deterministic, but replacement is based on a probabilistic criterion.
- **Clearing**:
    - **Concept**: Individuals in densely populated niches are "*cleared*," and only a limited number of the best individuals in each niche are allowed to survive.
    - **Purpose**: This prevents any niche from overcrowding and encourages a balanced spread across multiple peaks in the search space.
- **Speciation**:
    - **Concept**: The population is divided into subpopulations (species) that evolve independently.
    - **Purpose**: By allowing separate evolution of subpopulations, speciation helps preserve and optimize multiple peaks in a multimodal fitness landscape.
    - **Example**: Species might be formed based on similarity metrics, such as genetic distance, with each species focusing on a different peak.
- **Genetic Drift**:
    - **Concept**: Introducing slight changes in the genetic material to encourage individuals to explore different niches.
    - **Purpose**: This ensures that some individuals can escape a crowded peak and explore other parts of the search space.

Importance of Niching

- **Avoid Premature Convergence**: Niching helps to prevent the entire population from converging to a single local optimum too quickly, especially in multimodal landscapes.
- **Multimodal Optimization**: It is particularly useful when we are interested in finding multiple optima in a problem, such as in **multi-objective optimization** or **robust optimization**.

- **Real-world Applications**: In practical applications, there are often multiple valid solutions to a problem, and niching can help identify a diverse set of solutions to choose from.

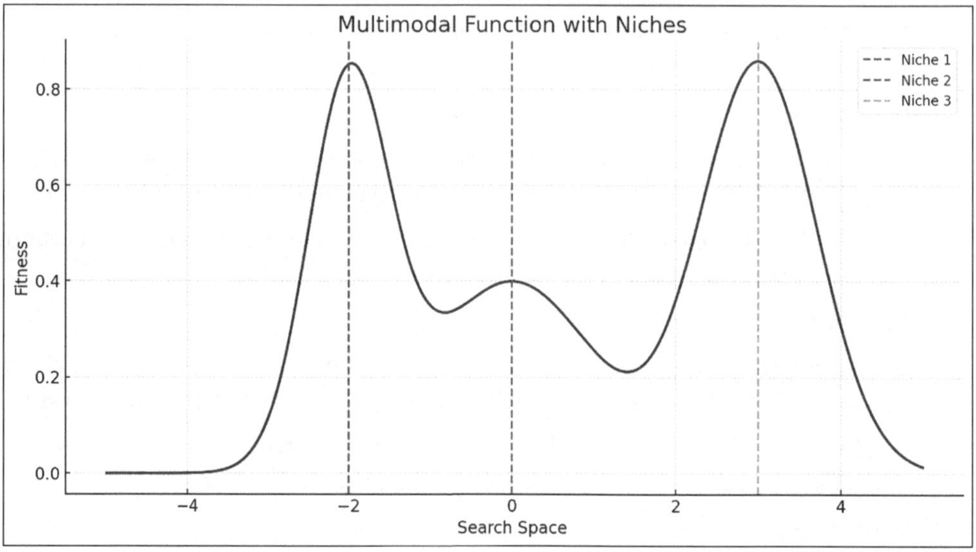

Figure 2.1: *Multimodal function with multiple peaks, each corresponding to a different niche*

Using niching techniques, the GA can distribute its population across the different niches (peaks), allowing the algorithm to explore and optimize multiple regions simultaneously. This increases the likelihood of finding a global optimum and prevents the algorithm from getting stuck in suboptimal solutions.

The following code implements two genetic algorithms (GAs) to solve a multimodal optimization problem, one using a standard fitness function and the other using a fitness-sharing technique (niching) to maintain diversity in the population. The fitness function is defined to create a multimodal landscape with three peaks, and the goal of the GA is to find solutions corresponding to these peaks.

The first GA runs without niching, simply maximizing the fitness function, which leads to convergence around the highest peak. In contrast, the second GA uses a modified fitness function with niching, which applies fitness sharing to promote diversity by penalizing solutions that are too similar to others in the population. This helps the GA explore and preserve solutions around different peaks, not just the global optimum.

Finally, both GAs are run, and the fitness evolution is plotted for each. The best solutions are retrieved and printed to compare how the niching strategy affects the solution's diversity and fitness. The plots visually show how fitness changes across generations, comparing the behavior of the GAs with and without niching.

```
import pygad
import numpy as np
import matplotlib.pyplot as plt

# Define the multimodal fitness function
def fitness_function(ga_instance, solution, solution_idx):
    # Multimodal function with three peaks
    return (
        np.exp(-(solution[0] + 2) ** 2) +  # Peak 1
        1.5 * np.exp(-solution[0] ** 2) +  # Peak 2
        np.exp(-(solution[0] - 3) ** 2)    # Peak 3
    )

# Define a modified fitness function for niching (fitness sharing)
def fitness_function_with_niching(ga_instance, solution, solution_
idx):
    # Calculate base fitness
    base_fitness = fitness_function(ga_instance, solution,
solution_idx)

    # Apply fitness sharing to maintain diversity
    sharing_radius = 1.5  # Radius within which fitness sharing is
applied
    niche_count = 0

    # Loop over the entire population to compute niche count
    for other_solution in ga_instance.population:
        distance = np.linalg.norm(solution - other_solution)
        if distance < sharing_radius:
            niche_count += 1

    # Apply fitness sharing by dividing the base fitness by the
niche count
    if niche_count > 0:
        shared_fitness = base_fitness / niche_count
    else:
        shared_fitness = base_fitness

    return shared_fitness

# Parameters for the genetic algorithm
num_generations = 50
num_parents_mating = 4
sol_per_pop = 20
num_genes = 1
gene_space = {'low': -5, 'high': 5}
```

```
# Run the GA without niching
ga_without_niching = pygad.GA(
    num_generations=num_generations,
    num_parents_mating=num_parents_mating,
    fitness_func=fitness_function,
    sol_per_pop=sol_per_pop,
    num_genes=num_genes,
    gene_space=gene_space,
    parent_selection_type=»sss»,
    keep_parents=2,
    crossover_type=»single_point»,
    mutation_type=»random»,
    mutation_percent_genes=20
)
ga_without_niching.run()

# Run the GA with niching (fitness sharing)
ga_with_niching = pygad.GA(
    num_generations=num_generations,
    num_parents_mating=num_parents_mating,
    fitness_func=fitness_function_with_niching,
    sol_per_pop=sol_per_pop,
    num_genes=num_genes,
    gene_space=gene_space,
    parent_selection_type=»sss»,
    keep_parents=2,
    crossover_type=»single_point»,
    mutation_type=»random»,
    mutation_percent_genes=20
)
ga_with_niching.run()

# Plotting the results
fig, axes = plt.subplots(1, 2, figsize=(15, 6))

# Plot for GA without niching
axes[0].plot(ga_without_niching.best_solutions_fitness, col-
or='blue', label="Without Niching")
axes[0].set_title("GA Without Niching: Generation vs Fitness")
axes[0].set_xlabel("Generation")
axes[0].set_ylabel("Fitness")
axes[0].legend()

# Plot for GA with niching
axes[1].plot(ga_with_niching.best_solutions_fitness, color='red',
label="With Niching")
axes[1].set_title("GA With Niching (Fitness Sharing): Generation
```

```
vs Fitness")
axes[1].set_xlabel("Generation")
axes[1].set_ylabel("Fitness")
axes[1].legend()

plt.show()

# Get the best solutions for each problem
solution_without_niching, fitness_without_niching, _ = ga_without_
niching.best_solution()
solution_with_niching, fitness_with_niching, _ = ga_with_niching.
best_solution()

print("Best Solution Without Niching:", solution_without_niching)
print("Fitness of Best Solution Without Niching:", fitness_with-
out_niching)

print("Best Solution With Niching:", solution_with_niching)
print("Fitness of Best Solution With Niching:",
fitness_with_niching)
```

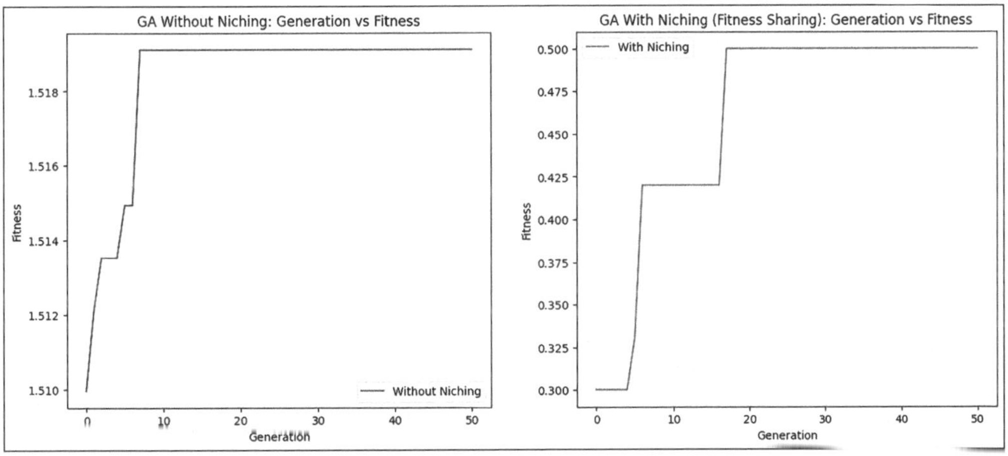

Figure 2.2: *By comparing the two plots, you should be able to observe how niching helps prevent premature convergence and promotes the exploration of multiple regions in the search space, leading to potentially better global optimization*

In the next chapters, we will further improve this plot in our Hyperparameter tuning section.

In *Chapter 1, Introduction to Genetic Algorithms*, we gave an overview of "Initial Population and sampling." In the following, we are going deeper into this topic.

Initial Population and Sampling

In the previous chapter, *Figure* 1.7 illustrates that the first step in a Genetic Algorithm (GA) involves creating an initial population of valid candidate solutions, known as individuals, which are selected randomly. Since genetic algorithms represent each individual using a chromosome, the initial population consists of a set of chromosomes. Let us understand what a chromosome is in the real sense.

The following figure illustrates the relationship between chromosomes, genes, and DNA. The larger structure shown is a chromosome, which contains tightly coiled DNA. Zooming in, we see the DNA double helix, where specific segments are labeled as "*genes*." Each gene represents a distinct section of DNA responsible for coding particular traits. Genes are the fundamental units of heredity, found at specific locations on chromosomes. Chromosomes, in turn, are structures within cells that contain all of an organism's genetic material, helping transmit information from one generation to the next.

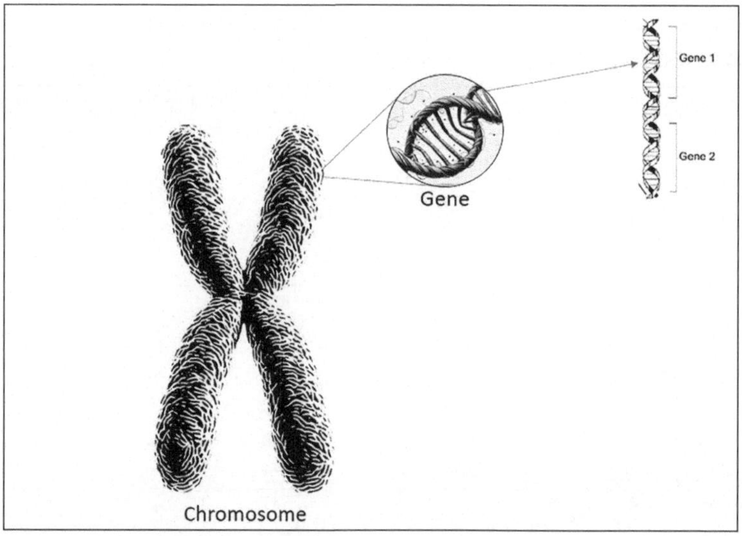

Figure 2.3: *Relationship between chromosomes, genes, and* DNA

Now that you have a complete understanding of genes, chromosomes, and DNA, let us explore genotype and phenotype in more detail.

- **Genotype** refers to the specific combination of alleles (versions of genes) that an organism has. In the table, the alleles for each characteristic, such as Vocalization (V), Scent marking (S), or Body language (BL), represent different possible genetic makeups for that trait. The combination of all these alleles across different genes constitutes the genotype of an individual.
- **Phenotype** refers to the observable characteristics or traits resulting from the genotype and its interaction with the environment. The traits listed, such

as communication style, habitat, body covering, and sensory abilities, are the physical or behavioral manifestations of the underlying genetic makeup. Thus, the phenotype is influenced by the combination of the alleles present in the genotype.

Genotype

Gene	Characteristic	Alleles
Gene 1	Communication Style	Vocalization (V), Scent marking (S), Body language (BL)
Gene 2	Habitat	Forest (F), Desert (D), Water (W), Grassland (G)
Gene 3	Body Covering	Fur (F), Feathers (FTH), Scales (S), Shells (SH)
Gene 4	Sensory Abilities	Night vision (NV), Acute hearing (AH), Electroreception (ER)

Phenotype

Figure 2.4: *This table helps visualize the concept of genotype*

Now, going back to *Figure* 1.7, the initial population in genetic algorithms refers to the starting set of candidate solutions, often generated randomly or using specific sampling methods. It serves as the foundation for evolving solutions towards optimality through processes such as selection, crossover, and mutation. A diverse and well-distributed initial population increases the chances of covering different regions of the search space, avoiding premature convergence on suboptimal solutions. Sampling techniques such as pseudo-random, quasi-random, and Latin Hypercube ensure diversity. The quality and variability of the initial population significantly influence the efficiency and success of the genetic algorithm in finding an optimal or near-optimal solution.

Let us understand each sampling method.

- **Pseudo-random Sampling**: Points are randomly distributed throughout the search space. This method uses a standard random number generator to produce candidate locations, which may lead to uneven coverage with clustering or gaps.
- **Quasi-random Sampling**: Quasi-random points aim for a more uniform distribution compared to pseudo-random sampling. This approach attempts to systematically fill the search space, reducing clustering and providing a more consistent spread of points.
- **Box-Muller Sampling**: The Box-Muller method is used to generate random numbers that follow a normal (Gaussian) distribution. The points are centered around a mean value, with a higher density towards the center, which is useful when the solution is expected to be near the mean.
- **Central Limit Theorem Sampling**: Points generated using the Central Limit Theorem approach are normally distributed, resulting in a higher density near the center. This is suitable for scenarios where candidate solutions are expected to follow a natural distribution with most values clustering around a central point.

- **Sobol Sequence**: Sobol sequences are a type of quasi-random sequence designed to cover the search space uniformly. It is often used in numerical integration and optimization because it provides better uniformity compared to purely random sequences.
- **Latin Hypercube Sampling**: Latin Hypercube Sampling (LHS) ensures that the sample space is divided evenly, with each region sampled only once. This method reduces the likelihood of clustering and ensures that each dimension of the search space is well-represented, improving exploration.

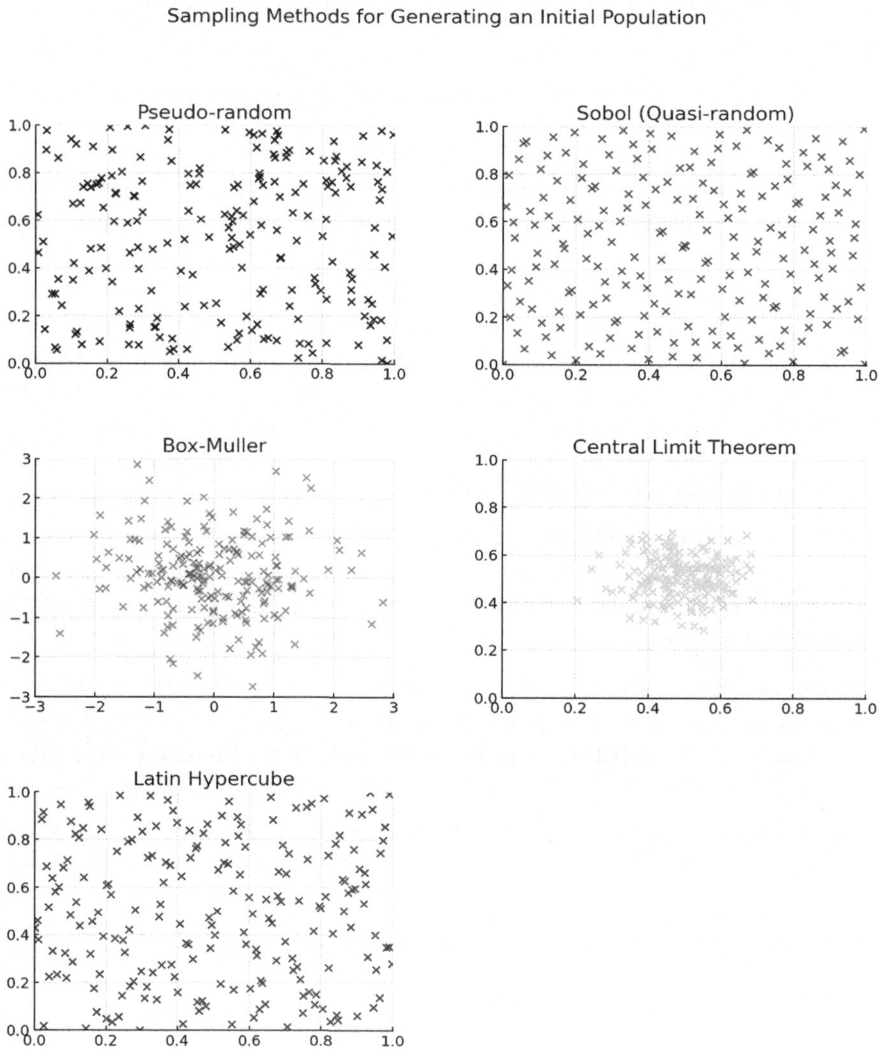

Figure 2.5: *Sampling Methods for Generating an Initial Population*

Sobol and quasi-random sampling are related concepts, and Sobol sequences are a specific type of quasi-random sampling.

The following is a small code snippet that demonstrates how to use PyGAD (v3.3.1) to solve a simple optimization problem using a genetic algorithm. In this example, we will optimize a function to find the values of inputs that minimize the sum of their squares.

You can install the correct version of PyGAD using the following command before running the script: We are using ame: pygad Version: 3.3.1

```
import pygad
import numpy as np

# Define the fitness function
def fitness_function(ga_instance, solution, solution_idx):
    # Objective is to minimize the sum of squares
    return -np.sum(np.square(solution))

# Parameters for the genetic algorithm
num_generations = 50
num_parents_mating = 4
sol_per_pop = 10
num_genes = 5
gene_space = {'low': -10, 'high': 10}

# Create an instance of the PyGAD class
ga_instance = pygad.GA(
    num_generations=num_generations,
    num_parents_mating=num_parents_mating,
    fitness_func=fitness_function,
    sol_per_pop=sol_per_pop,
    num_genes=num_genes,
    gene_space=gene_space,
    parent_selection_type=»sss»,  # Stochastic Universal Sampling
    keep_parents=2,
    crossover_type=»single_point»,
    mutation_type=»random»,
    mutation_percent_genes=20
)

# Run the genetic algorithm
ga_instance.run()

# Plot the result
ga_instance.plot_fitness()

# Get the best solution
solution, solution_fitness, solution_idx = ga_instance.best_solution()
print("Best Solution:", solution)
print("Fitness of the Best Solution:", solution_fitness)
```

The fitness function calculates the negative sum of squares of the input to minimize the value, as the genetic algorithm maximizes the fitness function. Key genetic algorithm parameters include the number of generations, the number of parents for mating, the number of solutions per population, the number of genes per solution, and the gene value range (–10 to 10). A GA instance is initialized with selection, crossover, and mutation settings. It runs using **ga_instance.run()**, with fitness evolution plotted via **ga_instance.plot_fitness()**. The best solution is retrieved with **ga_instance.best_solution()**. The fitness function and parameters can be adjusted for specific optimization tasks.

Best Solution: [0.61035681 -0.35299535 -0.21309226 -0.26779176 -0.12316718]

Fitness of the Best Solution: -0.6294320429237426

Next, we will modify the previous code to include the **Latin Hypercube Sampling** technique to generate the initial population. We will then compare the fitness evolution to see if using this technique changes the fitness values compared to a random initial population. We will also explain how using a more systematic sampling technique such as **Latin Hypercube Sampling** can provide a better foundation for genetic algorithms by generating a more diverse initial population, increasing the likelihood of finding optimal solutions more effectively.

To do this, we will use **scipy.stats.qmc.LatinHypercube** to generate the initial population.

```
import pygad
import numpy as np
from scipy.stats import qmc
import matplotlib.pyplot as plt

# Define the fitness function
def fitness_function(ga_instance, solution, solution_idx):
    # Objective is to minimize the sum of squares
    return -np.sum(np.square(solution))

# Parameters for the genetic algorithm
num_generations = 50
num_parents_mating = 4
sol_per_pop = 10
num_genes = 5
gene_space = {'low': -10, 'high': 10}
```

Latin Hypercube Sampling (LHS) is used via scipy.stats.qmc.LatinHypercube to generate the initial population for the genetic algorithm. The sampled points are scaled to fit within the specified **gene_space** range (–10 to 10). The LHS-generated population is then passed to the GA instance using the **initial_population** parameter. The fitness evolution over generations is visualized using **ga_instance.plot_fitness()**, which helps track the optimization progress.

```
# Use Latin Hypercube Sampling to generate the initial population
lhs_sampler = qmc.LatinHypercube(d=num_genes)
initial_population = lhs_sampler.random(sol_per_pop)
initial_population = qmc.scale(initial_population, gene_
space['low'], gene_space['high'])

# Create an instance of the PyGAD class using the initial
population
ga_instance = pygad.GA(
    num_generations=num_generations,
    num_parents_mating=num_parents_mating,
    fitness_func=fitness_function,
    sol_per_pop=sol_per_pop,
    num_genes=num_genes,
    initial_population=initial_population,  # Use the
LHS-generated initial population
    parent_selection_type="sss",  # Stochastic Universal Sampling
    keep_parents=2,
    crossover_type="single_point",
    mutation_type="random",
    mutation_percent_genes=20
)

# Run the genetic algorithm
ga_instance.run()

# Plot the fitness evolution
ga_instance.plot_fitness()

# Get the best solution
solution, solution_fitness, solution_idx = ga_instance.best_solution()
print("Best Solution with Latin Hypercube Sampling:", solution)
print("Fitness of the Best Solution with Latin Hypercube Sampling:",
solution_fitness)

Best Solution with Latin Hypercube Sampling: [-0.00734819
-0.01104071  0.01835571 -0.03613743  0.06688635]
Fitness of the Best Solution with Latin Hypercube Sampling:
-0.006292522768996095
```

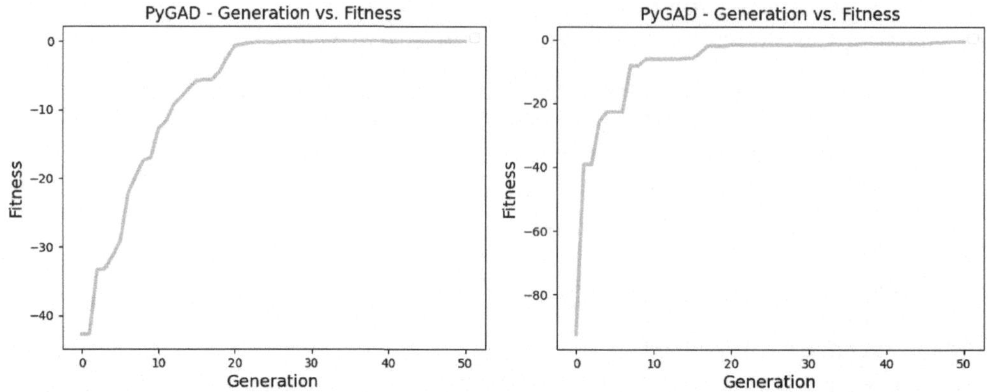

Figure 2.6: *The two fitness plots represent the evolution of fitness over generations for two different initialization strategies used in the genetic algorithm. Uniform Sampling (Latin Hypercube Sampling) in Plot 1 seems to provide a more effective initialization, leading to a better starting point and a more consistent fitness improvement*

Random Sampling in Plot 2 resulted in a population that started further from the optimal solution, showing rapid but inconsistent improvement.

Genetic algorithms (GA) begin with an initial population of candidate solutions, and the population size must be chosen carefully. A large population size does not always enhance performance, and research suggests that the optimal size depends on the length of the encoded chromosomes. For instance, chromosomes with 32 bits may require a larger population size than those with 16 bits for effective optimization.

Before we move into the next section, let us first understand what maximization and minimization problems are. These concepts are fundamental to optimization, helping us define the goals of a genetic algorithm – whether we aim to find the maximum value of a function (maximization) or the minimum value (minimization). Understanding these distinctions is key to effectively formulating and solving real-world optimization problems.

In the previous chapter, we gave an overview of "*Fitness in GA*." In the following, we are going deeper into this topic.

Fitness in GA

We know from *Chapter 1, Introduction to Genetic Algorithms*, that a fitness function is a measure used by genetic algorithms to evaluate how good a particular solution is relative to the problem being solved. It assigns a numerical value, often called the fitness score, to each individual in the population, representing the quality of that solution. The genetic algorithm uses this score to determine which individuals are selected for reproduction, favoring those with higher fitness to pass on their traits to future generations. The fitness function plays a crucial role, as it guides the search process, whether the goal is maximization or minimization, by identifying promising solutions in the search space.

The fitness function in a genetic algorithm is directly related to whether the problem is a maximization or minimization problem:

- **Maximization**: In a maximization problem, the goal is to find the highest possible value of the objective function. In this case, the fitness function is designed to directly represent the objective value, meaning that higher fitness values correspond to better solutions. The genetic algorithm selects individuals based on their fitness, striving to maximize this value over generations.
- **Minimization**: In a minimization problem, the goal is to find the lowest possible value of the objective function. To align this with the genetic algorithm's approach to maximizing fitness, the fitness function is typically transformed. This is done by taking the negative of the objective value or by using a reciprocal transformation so that minimizing the objective function effectively becomes a problem of maximizing the fitness.

So, regardless of whether the underlying problem is one of maximization or minimization, the genetic algorithm framework always works by maximizing the fitness function. The fitness function is therefore adapted accordingly to reflect the specific optimization goal.

In general, converting a maximization problem to a minimization problem allows for consistency in handling the objective, simplifies the implementation, and aligns with the fitness evaluation mechanism of most Genetic Algorithm frameworks. In GAs, it is common to convert a maximization problem to a minimization problem in the following scenarios:

- **Standardization of the GA Framework**: Many GA implementations are designed to solve minimization problems by default. Since the algorithm inherently selects solutions with higher fitness, it is easier to convert a maximization problem into a minimization one by changing the fitness function. For instance, you could take the negative of the objective function, effectively converting the maximization goal into minimizing a negative value.
- **Simplification for Fitness Evaluation**: When the objective function's behavior or range is easier to express or compute in a minimization form, it might be beneficial to convert it. This helps in maintaining a consistent evaluation process, especially when you need to combine different objective functions or perform transformations.
- **Penalty-based Constraints Handling**: If there are constraints, converting the problem to a minimization form allows for penalty terms to be added. This way, infeasible solutions are assigned high penalty values, making them less desirable, which fits naturally with minimization.

- **Compatibility with Penalty Methods**: If you are using penalty methods to handle constraints, representing the problem as a minimization problem allows you to add penalties to the objective value for constraint violations. This ensures that solutions with constraint violations have higher fitness values to minimize, making them less favorable.

Let us understand with code. You will be provided with a code example using PyGAD (v3.3.1) to demonstrate both a **maximization problem** and its corresponding **minimization conversion** using a fitness function. We will solve both versions and visualize the fitness evolution in each case to see the effect of converting a maximization problem to a minimization problem.

For demonstration purposes, we will use a simple objective function: the **sum of the elements**. The objective is to **maximize** the sum, but we will also convert it to a **minimization** problem to illustrate the process.

```
import pygad
import numpy as np
import matplotlib.pyplot as plt

The objective function calculates the sum of elements in a solu-
tion. For fitness, maximization directly uses the sum, while minimi-
zation negates the sum to transform it into a minimization problem.
The genetic algorithm is run twice: once for maximization and once
for minimization. Fitness evolution is plotted for both cases to
compare their convergence.

# Define the objective function (sum of the elements)
def objective_function(solution):
    return np.sum(solution)

# Define the fitness function for the maximization problem
def fitness_function_max(ga_instance, solution, solution_idx):
    return objective_function(solution)

# Define the fitness function for the minimization problem (con-
verted)
def fitness_function_min(ga_instance, solution, solution_idx):
    return -objective_function(solution)

# Parameters for the genetic algorithm
num_generations = 50
num_parents_mating = 4
sol_per_pop = 10
num_genes = 5
gene_space = {'low': 0, 'high': 10}
```

```
# Run the GA for maximization problem
ga_max = pygad.GA(
    num_generations=num_generations,
    num_parents_mating=num_parents_mating,
    fitness_func=fitness_function_max,
    sol_per_pop=sol_per_pop,
    num_genes=num_genes,
    gene_space=gene_space,
    parent_selection_type="sss",
    keep_parents=2,
    crossover_type="single_point",
    mutation_type="random",
    mutation_percent_genes=20
)
ga_max.run()

# Run the GA for minimization problem
ga_min = pygad.GA(
    num_generations=num_generations,
    num_parents_mating=num_parents_mating,
    fitness_func=fitness_function_min,
    sol_per_pop=sol_per_pop,
    num_genes=num_genes,
    gene_space=gene_space,
    parent_selection_type="sss",
    keep_parents=2,
    crossover_type="single_point",
    mutation_type="random",
    mutation_percent_genes=20
)
ga_min.run()

# Plotting the results
fig, axes = plt.subplots(1, 2, figsize=(15, 6))
# Plot for Maximization
axes[0].plot(ga_max.best_solutions_fitness, color='blue',
label="Maximization")
axes[0].set_title("Maximization Problem: Generation vs Fitness")
axes[0].set_xlabel("Generation")
axes[0].set_ylabel("Fitness")
axes[0].legend()

# Plot for Minimization
axes[1].plot([-fitness for fitness in ga_min.best_solutions_fitness],
color='red', label="Minimization (Converted)")
axes[1].set_title("Minimization Problem (Converted): Generation
vs Fitness")
```

```
axes[1].set_xlabel("Generation")
axes[1].set_ylabel("Fitness")
axes[1].legend()

plt.show()

# Get the best solutions for each problem
solution_max, fitness_max, _ = ga_max.best_solution()
solution_min, fitness_min, _ = ga_min.best_solution()

print("Best Solution (Maximization):", solution_max)
print("Fitness of Best Solution (Maximization):", fitness_max)

print("Best Solution (Minimization):", solution_min)
print("Fitness of Best Solution (Minimization, converted to
positive):", -fitness_min)
```

```
Best Solution (Maximization): [9.34030385 9.74208153 9.97411047
9.45732248 9.96655698]
Fitness of Best Solution (Maximization): 48.48037530387502
Best Solution (Minimization): [0.50239853 0.12086237 0.29883104
0.01256197 0.43276639]
Fitness of Best Solution (Minimization, converted to positive):
1.367420306978837
```

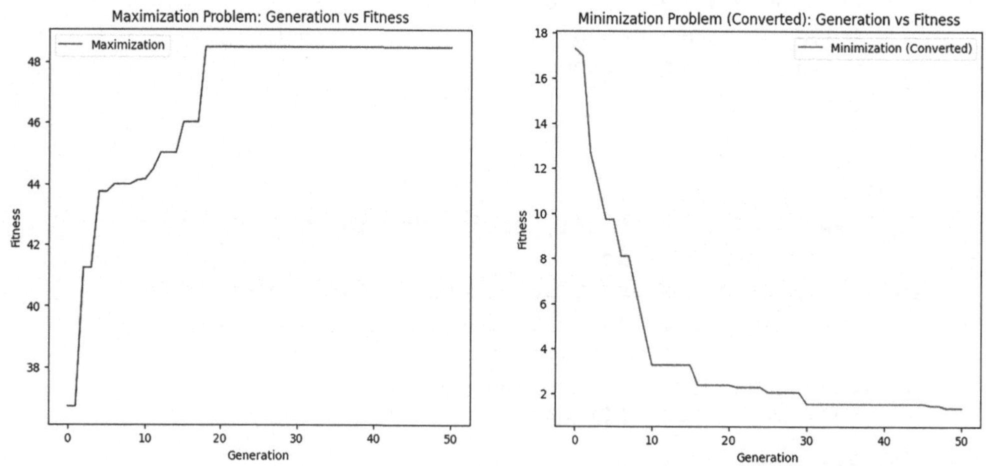

***Figure** 2.7: You can see that the convergence behavior remains similar, but the representation differs because of the fitness transformation. In the maximization problem, the fitness values will increase over generations as the GA tries to maximize the sum*

In the minimization problem, the fitness values will be negative, as we are minimizing by taking the negative of the sum. In the plot, we convert the values back to positive for easy comparison.

Having established the importance of generating an effective initial population and exploring the fitness function, it is now time to delve into the core mechanisms that drive evolution in genetic algorithms–selection. Selection operators determine which individuals get to contribute to the next generation, directly impacting the algorithm's balance between exploration and exploitation. In the following section, we will explore different selection methods and their selective pressures.

Once we have a good understanding of selection, we will move on to discuss termination criteria, which define when the evolutionary process should end, ensuring an efficient balance between computation time and solution quality.

In *Chapter 1, Introduction to Genetic Algorithms*, we gave an overview of "*Selection in* GA," In the following, we are going deeper into this topic.

Selection in GA

Selection in GA is the process of choosing individuals from the current population to create offspring for the next generation. This process mimics natural selection, where individuals with higher fitness have a better chance of reproducing, thus passing their genes to the next generation. Selection ensures that better solutions contribute more to the future population, gradually improving the quality of solutions. Various selection methods, such as roulette wheel selection, tournament selection, rank-based selection, and elitism, are used to choose which individuals reproduce, each with its unique way of balancing between preserving high-quality solutions and maintaining genetic diversity.

Selective pressure refers to the degree to which better-performing individuals are favored during selection. High selective pressure means that only the fittest individuals are selected, leading to faster convergence towards an optimal solution. However, too much pressure can reduce population diversity and cause premature convergence to a local optimum. On the other hand, low selective pressure allows a wider range of individuals, including those with lower fitness, to reproduce, promoting diversity but slowing down the optimization process. The balance of selective pressure is crucial to ensure that the algorithm converges efficiently without losing the potential to explore other promising regions of the solution space.

Exploration and exploitation are two opposing aspects of the search process in genetic algorithms. Exploration is the ability to investigate a wide area of the solution space, ensuring the algorithm does not miss out on potentially better solutions by focusing only on the known good regions. It prevents the GA from getting stuck in local optima by introducing new genetic variations. Exploitation, on the other hand, is the refinement of the currently known good solutions to optimize them further. A successful GA must balance these two aspects effectively: exploration to discover new potential solutions and exploitation to improve the quality of these solutions. Selection methods and selective pressure play an essential role in determining the balance between exploration and exploitation to achieve the best possible outcome.

Selection Methods in Genetic Algorithms

- **Elitism:**
  - **Description**: The best individuals in the population are always preserved for the next generation without alteration.
  - **Selective Pressure**: **Highest**. This ensures that the best solutions are never lost, which accelerates convergence.
  - **Exploration vs. Exploitation**: Elitism focuses heavily on **exploitation**—preserving top-performing solutions, leading to rapid convergence but potentially reduced diversity.
- **Fitness-Proportionate Selection (FPS):**
  - **Description**: Also known as **Roulette Wheel Selection**, where the probability of selecting an individual is proportional to its fitness relative to the total fitness of the population.
  - **Selective Pressure**: Moderate to high. Individuals with higher fitness have a higher chance of being selected, which drives towards better solutions.
  - **Exploration vs. Exploitation**: FPS provides a balance between exploration and exploitation, but it can lead to premature convergence if fitness differences are high.
- **Rank-Based Selection**:
  - **Description**: Individuals are ranked based on their fitness, and selection is based on rank rather than absolute fitness value.
  - **Selective Pressure**: **Moderate**. This method avoids problems related to large differences in fitness, ensuring individuals with lower fitness also have a chance of being selected.
  - **Exploration vs. Exploitation**: This method encourages **exploration** more than FPS since it ensures that even less fit individuals contribute to the next generation, preventing premature convergence.
- **Stochastic Universal Sampling (SUS)**:
  - **Description**: A variant of fitness-proportionate selection, where a single spin of the wheel is used with multiple evenly spaced pointers to select individuals, ensuring that all individuals have a chance of being selected.

- **Selective Pressure**: **Moderate**. This method reduces variance in the selection process, ensuring more even distribution and diversity.
- **Exploration vs. Exploitation**: **Balanced** between exploration and exploitation, as SUS selects individuals more uniformly, providing a better chance for less-fit individuals to be chosen.

- **Tournament Selection**:
  - **Description**: A set number of individuals is randomly chosen, and the fittest among them is selected for reproduction. The tournament size can control selective pressure.
  - **Selective Pressure**: This can vary from **low to high** depending on tournament size. Larger tournament sizes result in higher selective pressure.
  - **Exploration vs. Exploitation**: Smaller tournament sizes encourage **exploration** by allowing weaker individuals to be selected, while larger tournaments focus more on **exploitation**.
- **Random Selection**:
  - **Description**: Individuals are selected randomly, without considering their fitness.
  - **Selective Pressure**: **Lowest**. There is no bias towards fit individuals, which means any individual can be selected.
  - **Exploration vs. Exploitation**: This method maximizes **exploration**, ensuring the search space is explored broadly but at the expense of slower convergence towards optimal solutions.

Selective Pressure and Search Dilemma

- **Selective Pressure**: Refers to how strongly the selection process favors the fittest individuals.
  - **High Selective Pressure**: Ensures that only the best individuals reproduce, which can lead to rapid convergence but may risk getting stuck in local optima.
  - **Low Selective Pressure**: Increases diversity by allowing weaker individuals to contribute, thereby promoting exploration but slowing convergence.
- **Search Dilemma (Exploration versus Exploitation)**:
  - **Exploration**: Refers to the ability to search new and diverse areas of the solution space, preventing premature convergence.
  - **Exploitation**: Focuses on refining and optimizing current best solutions to achieve convergence faster.

The different selection methods provide a balance between **selective pressure** and **exploration vs. exploitation** to achieve an optimal evolutionary search strategy, depending on the problem at hand.

After understanding the various selection methods and their impact on guiding the evolutionary process, it is important to consider when and how to conclude this iterative search. This brings us to the concept of **termination**, which determines the appropriate stopping point for the algorithm, ensuring that computational resources are efficiently utilized while still achieving a high-quality solution.

In *Chapter 1, Introduction to Genetic Algorithms*, we gave an overview of "*Termination in* GA." In the following, we are going deeper into this topic so that our fundamentals are strong before we proceed to the next advanced chapters

Termination in GA

Termination in GA refers to the criteria or conditions used to stop the algorithm from running further generations. It plays a critical role in ensuring the GA runs for an appropriate amount of time to find a suitable solution without unnecessary computation. The termination condition can vary depending on the problem and the specific goals of the optimization process. The selection of a proper termination condition is vital to strike a balance between computational efficiency and solution quality.

There are several common **termination criteria** used in GAs:

- **Maximum Generations**: The algorithm stops after running a pre-defined number of generations. This is a straightforward and commonly used approach to ensure the GA does not run indefinitely. It provides a predictable endpoint, but it might stop before finding an optimal solution if the number is too low or run longer than necessary if the number is too high.
- **Fitness Convergence**: The GA terminates when there is no significant improvement in the best fitness value over a specified number of generations. This implies that the algorithm has potentially converged to an optimal or near-optimal solution. However, this criterion can lead to premature termination if the GA gets stuck in a local optimum without exploring other parts of the solution space.
- **Fitness Threshold**: The algorithm stops once a specific fitness value is reached. This criterion is used when there is a known acceptable fitness level that defines a good solution. Once the GA achieves this fitness value, there is no need to continue the evolution process, thereby saving computational resources.
- **Stall Generations**: The algorithm terminates if the population's fitness does not change significantly over a set number of consecutive generations. This

indicates that the GA has exhausted its ability to find better solutions and has likely reached a point of stagnation.

- **Computation Time Limit**: The GA can be set to stop after a fixed amount of time, which is especially useful when the time available for computation is constrained.

Termination is important in GAs because it helps ensure that computational resources are used effectively and efficiently. Without proper termination criteria, a GA might run for an unnecessarily long time, consuming significant time and computational power without any meaningful improvement in the solution. Conversely, terminating too early may result in a suboptimal solution, as the algorithm might not have had sufficient time to explore the solution space adequately or refine promising candidates. Choosing the right termination condition depends on the specific optimization problem, available computational resources, and the desired balance between solution quality and computational cost. Proper termination helps ensure that the GA can produce high-quality solutions within a reasonable time frame, effectively achieving the goal of optimization.

Conclusion

In this chapter, we have explored key components of genetic algorithms, including initial population strategies, selection methods, niching techniques, and termination criteria. These concepts are fundamental to ensuring that genetic algorithms effectively balance exploration and exploitation, allowing them to converge towards an optimal solution while avoiding premature convergence.

In the next chapter, we will delve into popular genetic algorithms libraries such as **DEAP**, **PyTorchGA**, and **PyGAD**. We will discuss the advantages and disadvantages of each library, implement both DEAP and PyGAD on the same problem, and provide a hands-on toy example to compare their performance and code structure. Topics such as the parameters and hyperparameters of GA, and modeling genetic algorithms through mathematical models and simulations, will also be covered.

CHAPTER 3
Overview of Genetic Algorithm Libraries

Introduction

Coding is crucial in the field of deep learning because it enables researchers and developers to translate complex mathematical models into functional algorithms, allowing experimentation and implementation of new ideas. By coding, one can customize neural network architectures, optimize training processes, and efficiently handle data, which are all essential for achieving state-of-the-art performance. Moreover, coding skills allow practitioners to explore open-source frameworks, modify pre-existing models, and contribute innovations that push the boundaries of what deep learning can accomplish. In short, coding bridges the gap between theoretical knowledge and practical application, making breakthroughs in deep learning possible.

This chapter introduces popular genetic algorithm libraries such as DEAP, PytorchGA, and PyGAD, discussing the advantages and disadvantages of each. Additionally, these libraries will be implemented on the same problem, providing a toy example, and an analysis of the differences in the resulting code will be conducted.

Structure

In this chapter, we will discuss the following topics:

- Introduction to PyGAD with PyTorch
- Introduction to DEAP: Features and Strengths
- Comparing DEAP and PyGAD: Code Differences and Performance
- Implementing a Toy Example: Hands-On Problem-Solving
- Analyzing the Code: Differences in Performance and Structure
- Parameters and hyperparameters of GA from the Previous Chapter
- Modeling Genetic Algorithms: Mathematical Model of GA, Simulation in GA

Introduction to PyGAD

PyGAD is a Python library designed to implement genetic algorithms for optimizing machine learning models, with a focus on neural networks. PyGAD provides an easy-to-use interface to create custom genetic algorithm workflows, allowing developers to tailor the evolutionary process according to their requirements. In previous chapters, this library was used; however, it was not discussed in depth. The latest version is 3.3.1 and can be found here: https://pygad.readthedocs.io/en/latest/releases.html.

PyGAD's flexibility lies in its ability to work seamlessly with other deep learning frameworks such as TensorFlow or PyTorch, which means it can optimize neural network weights directly. Its main features include customizable fitness functions, multi-objective optimization, built-in mutation and crossover functions, and support for parallel processing, making it an efficient choice for training models where conventional optimizers may fail to converge to optimal solutions.

Additionally, PyGAD offers several utilities that simplify the setup of genetic algorithm components. Defining parameters such as population size, crossover type, mutation rate, and gene space is straightforward, allowing for rapid prototyping. Its ability to visualize evolution results, such as tracking the best solution across generations, aids in understanding how well the genetic algorithm is performing. PyGAD can handle multiple types of crossover techniques, including single-point and uniform crossovers, which provide versatility in mixing genetic information. It also includes adaptive mutation strategies that help maintain diversity within the population, which is crucial in avoiding local optima during the search process.

PyGAD is particularly beneficial for problems with non-differentiable objective functions or where derivative-based optimization is impractical. Unlike gradient-based methods, genetic algorithms do not require the calculation of gradients, making them suitable for a wider variety of optimization tasks, including those with noisy or discontinuous search spaces. Overall, PyGAD brings a powerful yet user-friendly genetic algorithm toolkit to the deep learning community, enabling the application of evolutionary strategies to complex problems. Next, let us understand PyGAd modules.

PyGAD Modules

As a deep learning practitioner, learning about the attributes, methods, and classes in PyGAD is essential for understanding how genetic algorithms can be used to solve optimization problems, which are common in deep learning tasks such as hyperparameter tuning, feature selection, and neural network optimization. Understanding these attributes allows you to control the behavior of the genetic algorithm, making it adaptable to various tasks. Mastering the genetic operators and parent selection methods can help you create a diverse and optimized population, which is critical for achieving better model performance.

`pygad.GA`

This is the core class for implementing genetic algorithms. It includes methods for initialization, running generations, applying genetic operators such as crossover and mutation, and finding the best solution.

- **Initialization**: Setting up parameters such as population size, number of generations, and gene space.
- **Genetic Operators**: Methods for crossover, mutation, and parent selection.
- **Fitness Function**: Custom user-defined function to evaluate solutions.

Genetic Operators:

- **Crossover**: Types include single-point, two-point, uniform, and so on.
- **Mutation**: Mutation probabilities and gene space handling.

Parent Selection Methods: Techniques such as roulette wheel, tournament, and rank selection to choose parents for crossover.

Let us understand the methods and attributes under the `pygad.GA` class:

- **`run()`**: Executes the genetic algorithm, iterating through the specified number of generations.
- **`crossover()`**: Performs crossover between selected parents, with options such as single-point, two-point, and uniform crossover.
- **`mutation()`**: Applies mutations to offspring based on the specified mutation type and probability.
- **`select_parents()`**: Implements parent selection using methods such as roulette wheel, tournament selection, and so on.
- **`plot_fitness()`**: Plots the fitness values over generations to visualize optimization progress.
- **`best_solution()`**: Returns the best solution found, including its fitness and generation.

Attributes in `pygad.GA`:

- **`population_size`**: Specifies the number of individuals in each generation.
- **`num_generations`**: Defines how many generations will be evolved.
- **`fitness_func`**: A custom user-defined function that evaluates the quality of each solution.
- **`gene_space`**: Specifies the possible values for each gene, providing bounds or discrete options.
- **`mutation_percent_genes`**: Defines the percentage of genes to be mutated in each offspring.

Let us understand the methods and attributes under the Genetic Operators: These components allow users to control the genetic algorithm's evolution process and introduce variability into the population.

Methods:

1. **`crossover()`**: Defines how to combine genes from parents to produce offspring. Different types include single-point, two-point, and uniform crossover.

2. **`mutation()`**: Introduces small random changes to offspring's genes to maintain genetic diversity. Types of mutations, including random, adaptive, and so on, are covered.

3. **`select_parents()`**: Selects parents based on different selection strategies such as roulette wheel, rank selection, or tournament selection.

Attributes:

1. **`crossover_type`**: Determines the type of crossover to use.

2. **`mutation_type`**: Defines the mutation strategy.

3. **`mutation_probability`**: Sets the probability that a gene will undergo mutation.

Let us understand the methods and attributes under the `pygad.GA` class. These methods and attributes allow users to control how individuals are chosen for producing the next generation, thereby influencing the convergence and diversity of the population.

Methods:

1. **`select_parents()`**: Implements the strategy for choosing parents for crossover. This method allows for selecting the best individuals for the next generation.

Attributes:

- **`parent_selection_type`**: Defines the strategy to be used for selecting parents. Some common strategies include:
  - **Roulette Wheel Selection**: Assigns a probability of selection to each individual based on its fitness.
  - **Tournament Selection**: Randomly selects a few individuals and chooses the one with the highest fitness.
  - **Rank Selection**: Ranks individuals based on fitness and assigns selection probabilities accordingly.

Aside from the preceding, other notable classes in PyGAD include: These classes enable extending PyGAD's functionality for more complex optimization problems, especially involving neural networks. For more information, refer to the PyGAD Documentation, https://pygad.readthedocs.io/en/latest/pygad.html .

1. **pygad.nn**: Contains functions for implementing neural networks.
2. **pygad.gann**: Genetic Algorithm for Neural Networks, helps optimize neural network parameters using genetic algorithms.

If you recall from *Chapter 1, Introduction to Genetic Algorithms*, where we introduced PyGAD code, in this section, we will optimize the code with the new attributes and modules provided by PyGAD. Here are the detailed changes:

1. **Parent Selection Type**: We changed the **parent_selection_type** to "**tournament**" to improve the selection of high-quality parents, which helps maintain diversity while ensuring better genetic material for the next generation.
2. **Mutation Type**: We opted for **mutation_type="adaptive"** to dynamically adjust the mutation probability. This helps balance the exploration of new solutions and the exploitation of the best solutions found so far, allowing for more robust optimization as the algorithm progresses.
3. **Crossover Type**: We replaced **crossover_type** with "**uniform**" crossover, which allows each gene in an offspring to be chosen randomly from either parent. This approach increases genetic diversity in the population, which can improve the chances of finding a global optimum.
4. **Keep Parents**: The **keep_parents** attribute is reduced to 1 (previously 2), retaining fewer parents between generations. This encourages more diversity and avoids premature convergence by allowing more new individuals in the population, rather than preserving too many old individuals.
5. **Mutation Percentage**: The **mutation_percent_genes** is increased to 30% (previously 20%). This increased mutation rate ensures that a greater portion of the genes in the offspring undergo mutations, enhancing diversity and reducing the likelihood of getting stuck in local optima.

These changes collectively enhance the performance of the genetic algorithm by improving parent quality, encouraging population diversity, and dynamically balancing the exploration and exploitation phases throughout the optimization process. Let us understand with a code; the explanations are given before every section.

```
import pygad
import numpy as np

# Define the fitness function
def fitness_function(ga_instance, solution, solution_idx):
    # Objective is to minimize the sum of squares
```

```
    return -np.sum(np.square(solution))

# Parameters for the genetic algorithm
num_generations = 50
num_parents_mating = 4
sol_per_pop = 10
num_genes = 5
gene_space = {'low': -10, 'high': 10}

# Create an instance of the PyGAD class
ga_instance = pygad.GA(
    num_generations=num_generations,
    num_parents_mating=num_parents_mating,
    fitness_func=fitness_function,
    sol_per_pop=sol_per_pop,
    num_genes=num_genes,
    gene_space=gene_space,
    parent_selection_type=»tournament»,  # Using tournament
selection for better diversity
    keep_parents=1,  # Retain fewer parents to promote diversity
    crossover_type=»uniform»,  # Use uniform crossover for better
genetic diversity
    mutation_type=»adaptive»,  # Adaptive mutation to balance
exploration and exploitation
    mutation_percent_genes=[20, 40]  # Provide a list with 2 values
for adaptive mutation
)

# Run the genetic algorithm
ga_instance.run()

# Plot the result
ga_instance.plot_fitness()

# Get the best solution
solution, solution_fitness, solution_idx = ga_instance.best_solu-
tion()
print("Best Solution:", solution)
print("Fitness of the Best Solution:", solution_fitness)
```

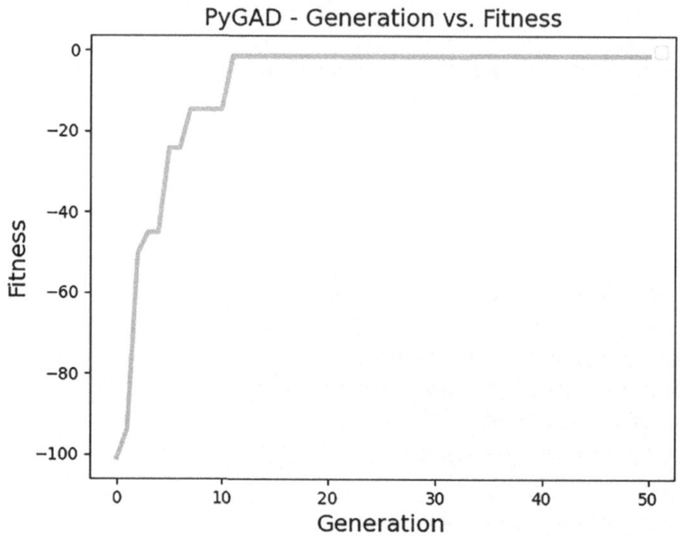

Figure 3.1: *The plot above shows Fitness Curve*

```
Best Solution: [ 0.36216862 -0.1925282   1.02223633 -0.41528862
-0.03886852]
Fitness of the Best Solution: -1.3871757321149936
```

It seems that despite the changes, the fitness value has worsened, indicating that the current approach may be overexploring or introducing too much randomness. Let us make some further adjustments:

1. **Reduce Mutation Percent**: Lower the mutation percent to reduce the chance of disrupting good solutions.
2. **Change Parent Selection Type**: Switching to tournament selection could provide a balance between exploration and exploitation.
3. **Fine-tune Gene Space**: Narrow down the gene space to focus more closely on optimal regions.

We have to update the code to incorporate these refinements to see if we can achieve better optimization.

```
# Define the fitness function
def fitness_function(ga_instance, solution, solution_idx):
    # Objective is to minimize the sum of squares
    return -np.sum(np.square(solution))

# Parameters for the genetic algorithm
num_generations = 150  # Increase number of generations for more
optimization
```

```
num_parents_mating = 6  # Increase number of parents for better
exploration
sol_per_pop = 20  # Increase population size for greater diversity
num_genes = 5
gene_space = {'low': -5, 'high': 5}  # Narrow down gene space to
focus more on optimal regions

# Create an instance of the PyGAD class
ga_instance = pygad.GA(
    num_generations=num_generations,
    num_parents_mating=num_parents_mating,
    fitness_func=fitness_function,
    sol_per_pop=sol_per_pop,
    num_genes=num_genes,
    gene_space=gene_space,
    parent_selection_type=»tournament»,  # Use tournament selection
to balance exploration and exploitation
    keep_parents=1,  # Retain fewer parents to promote diversity
    crossover_type=»two_points»,  # Use two-point crossover for
better diversity
    mutation_type=»adaptive»,  # Adaptive mutation to balance
exploration and exploitation
    mutation_percent_genes=[5, 15]  # Reduce mutation percentage to
focus search
)

# Run the genetic algorithm
ga_instance.run()

# Plot the result
ga_instance.plot_fitness()

# Get the best solution
solution, solution_fitness, solution_idx = ga_instance.best_solu-
tion()
print("Best Solution:", solution)
print("Fitness of the Best Solution:", solution_fitness)
```

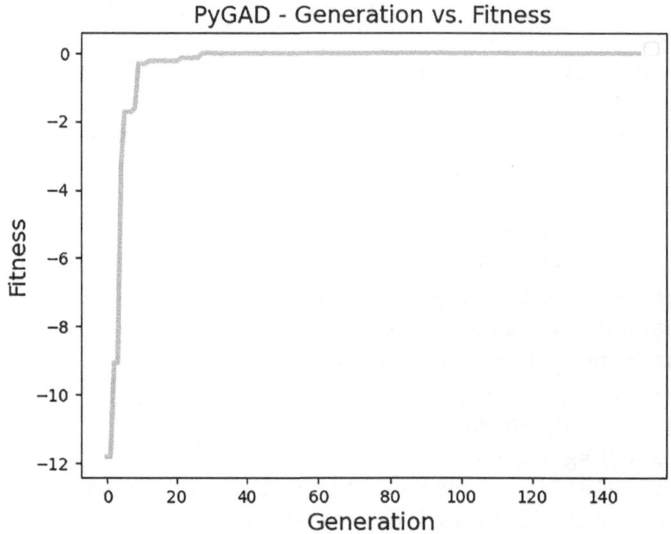

Figure 3.2: *The plot above shows Fitness Curve*

```
Best Solution: [-0.00598024 -0.0090543  -0.03459727 -0.03292129
-0.03057321]
Fitness of the Best Solution: -0.00333324706201267
```

In the preceding section, we have adjusted the genetic algorithm by narrowing down the gene space, reducing the mutation rate, and switching back to tournament selection to balance exploration and exploitation. These changes should help improve the results. However, this single-objective optimization. **Single-objective optimization** involves finding the best solution for a problem with only one objective or goal, typically minimizing or maximizing a single function. The solution is often represented by the optimal value of this function.

Multi-objective optimization, on the other hand, involves optimizing two or more conflicting objectives simultaneously. Instead of a single optimal solution, multi-objective algorithms aim to find a set of solutions called the Pareto front, which represent different trade-offs between the objectives, none of which can be improved without sacrificing another. Examples of multi-objective algorithms include NSGA-II and MOEA/D. Py GAD 3.2.0 supports multi-objective optimization.

The Non-Dominated Sorting Genetic Algorithm II (NSGA-II).

The Non-dominated Sorting Genetic Algorithm II (NSGA-II) is a popular multi-objective optimization algorithm based on genetic algorithms. It aims to find a set of optimal solutions, called the Pareto front, for problems with two or more conflicting objectives. NSGA-II is widely used in evolutionary computation due to its effectiveness in handling complex optimization problems.

Key features of NSGA-II include:

- **Non-Dominated Sorting**: Solutions are ranked based on the concept of dominance. A solution is said to dominate another if it is at least as good in all objectives and better in at least one. The algorithm uses a ranking system to sort the population into different layers of dominance.
- **Crowding Distance Calculation**: To maintain diversity among the solutions, NSGA-II uses a crowding distance measure. This measure determines how close each solution is to its neighbors, ensuring that the solutions are well-spread across the Pareto front.
- **Elitism**: NSGA-II uses an elitist approach, meaning the best solutions from both the current and previous generations are preserved, ensuring that the quality of the solution does not degrade over time.
- **Fast Sorting Mechanism**: NSGA-II introduces an efficient sorting mechanism that helps reduce the computational complexity compared to the earlier NSGA, making it suitable for larger populations and more complex problems.

Single-Objective and Multi-Objective Optimization

Let us explore single-objective and multi-objective optimization using real-world examples:

- **Single-objective optimization** focuses on optimizing one criterion, such as minimizing fuel cost.
- **Multi-objective optimization** balances multiple criteria, such as minimizing fuel cost, delivery time, and maximizing customer satisfaction simultaneously, where solutions are evaluated based on how well they trade-off among the objectives.

Let us explore single-objective and multi-objective optimization using real-world examples:

Single-Objective Optimization Example: Consider a **delivery company** trying to minimize its fuel cost for deliveries. The company's goal is to find the optimal route that results in the lowest fuel consumption. In this case, the objective is singular: **minimize fuel cost**. This type of problem is a typical single-objective optimization problem, where there is only one clear metric that needs optimization. The company can use algorithms such as the genetic algorithm, traveling salesman approach, or other routing techniques to minimize the distance and thus the fuel used.

Multi-Objective Optimization Example: Now let us consider the same delivery company, but with additional goals. Suppose the company wants to optimize **delivery time**, **fuel cost**, and **customer satisfaction** simultaneously. Here, the company has to consider:

1. **Minimize Fuel Cost:** Reducing the fuel consumption to save costs.
2. **Minimize Delivery Time:** Deliver packages as fast as possible.
3. **Maximize Customer Satisfaction:** Ensure deliveries are timely, without any delays or damages.

These objectives often conflict with each other; for instance, minimizing delivery time might increase fuel consumption, and the routes that save fuel might not always be the fastest. This type of optimization is called **multi-objective optimization**. The company would need to find an optimal trade-off solution where all three objectives are considered, typically leading to a set of "*Pareto optimal*" solutions where no objective can be improved without degrading another. Such solutions balance the different goals to achieve an acceptable compromise across all objectives.

Let us understand with a code where we combine two objectives (minimizing the sum of squares and maximizing the sum of values) using a weighted sum. We build upon the previous code. We will cover this in more detail in *Chapter 7, Metaheuristic Optimization Algorithms.*

```
# Define the fitness function for multi-objective optimization
def fitness_function(ga_instance, solution, solution_idx):
    # Objectives: Minimize the sum of squares and maximize the sum
of the solution values
    objective1 = -np.sum(np.square(solution))  # Minimize sum of
squares
    objective2 = np.sum(solution)  # Maximize sum of values

    # Combine objectives (Pareto-based approach could also be used
for true multi-objective optimization)
    # For simplicity, we will just return a weighted sum
    weight1 = 0.5
    weight2 = 0.5
    return weight1 * objective1 + weight2 * objective2

# Parameters for the genetic algorithm
num_generations = 150  # Increase number of generations for more
optimization
num_parents_mating = 6  # Increase number of parents for better
exploration
sol_per_pop = 20  # Increase population size for greater diversity
num_genes = 5
```

```
gene_space = {'low': -5, 'high': 5}  # Narrow down gene space to
focus more on optimal regions

# Create lists to store objectives across generations
objective1_history = []
objective2_history = []

# Create an instance of the PyGAD class
ga_instance = pygad.GA(
    num_generations=num_generations,
    num_parents_mating=num_parents_mating,
    fitness_func=fitness_function,
    sol_per_pop=sol_per_pop,
    num_genes=num_genes,
    gene_space=gene_space,
    parent_selection_type=»tournament»,  # Use tournament selection
to balance exploration and exploitation
    keep_parents=1,  # Retain fewer parents to promote diversity
    crossover_type=»two_points»,  # Use two-point crossover for
better diversity
    mutation_type=»adaptive»,  # Adaptive mutation to balance
exploration and exploitation
    mutation_percent_genes=[5, 15]  # Reduce mutation percentage to
focus search
)

# Run the genetic algorithm and collect objective values across
generations
for generation in range(num_generations):
    ga_instance.run()
    best_solution, _, _ = ga_instance.best_solution()
    objective1 = -np.sum(np.square(best_solution))
    objective2 = np.sum(best_solution)
    objective1_history.append(objective1)
    objective2_history.append(objective2)

# Plot the result
fitness_history = ga_instance.best_solutions_fitness
generations = range(len(objective1_history))

plt.figure(figsize=(12, 6))

# Plot objective 1 (minimize sum of squares)
plt.plot(generations, objective1_history, label='Objective 1:
Minimize Sum of Squares', color='r')

# Plot objective 2 (maximize sum of values)
```

```
plt.plot(generations, objective2_history, label='Objective 2:
Maximize Sum of Values', color='b')

plt.xlabel('Generation')
plt.ylabel('Objective Value')
plt.title('Objectives Over Generations')
plt.legend()
plt.grid()
plt.show()

# Run the final generation to get the final solution
# The final run is not necessary as it has already run in the loop.

# Get the best solution
solution, solution_fitness, solution_idx = ga_instance.best_solution()
print("Best Solution:", solution)
print("Fitness of the Best Solution:", solution_fitness)
```

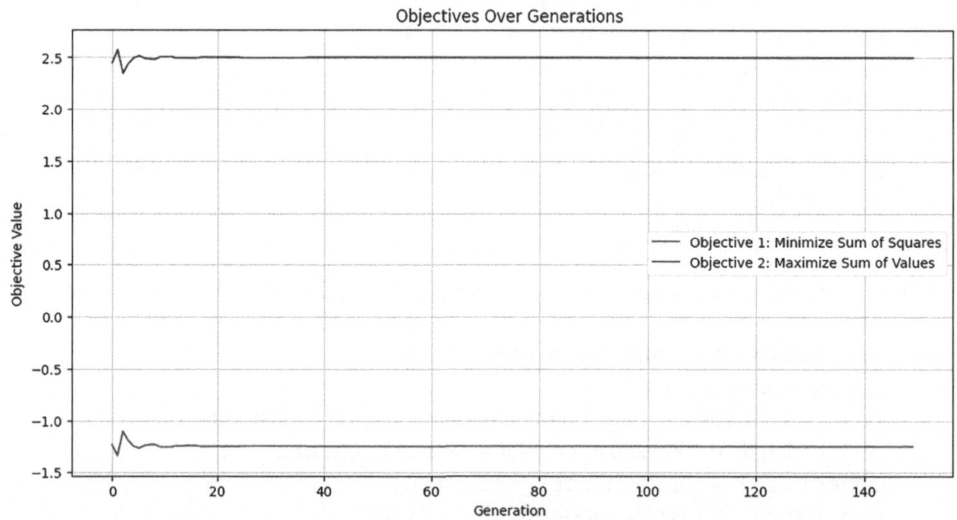

Figure 3.3: *The plot above shows mathematical modeling with GA minimizing the sum of squares and maximizing the sum of values*

```
Best Solution: [0.49965527 0.49987381 0.49982668 0.49992517
0.50013799]
Fitness of the Best Solution: 0.6249999052793438
```

The output indicates the best solution found by the genetic algorithm:

- **`Best Solution: [0.49965527, 0.49987381, 0.49982668, 0.49992517, 0.50013799]`**: This array represents the optimal set of values for the five genes, each approximately around 0.5.

- **`Fitness of the Best Solution: 0.6249999052793438`**: This value is the fitness score of the best solution. Since the fitness function combines two objectives (minimizing the sum of squares and maximizing the sum of values) using a weighted sum, a positive fitness score means the genetic algorithm has managed to find a good balance between the objectives. The values are close to 0.5, which seems to achieve an equilibrium between minimizing and maximizing the given objectives.

The positive fitness value indicates that the solution has a high sum of the elements while also minimizing their squares, as per the combined weighted fitness function. Could we have done this with Deep learning instead?

Deep learning might struggle to handle the complexity and trade-offs in multi-objective optimization without additional modifications and techniques, whereas Genetic Algorithms are well-suited to naturally deal with such scenarios. For problems where objectives are conflicting and a range of possible trade-off solutions is needed, Genetic Algorithms provide a more straightforward and efficient approach. Therefore, GA is preferred for multi-objective optimization problems like the one given. Let us understand why:

- **Single-Objective Optimization**: Deep learning can handle single-objective optimization problems, such as finding optimal routes, by training a model using reinforcement learning or other optimization techniques. However, these approaches generally require large amounts of data to create a model that learns the patterns effectively. For tasks such as finding the best route, deep learning can use historical data but might struggle to generalize well without extensive, high-quality datasets.
- **Multi-Objective Optimization**: The real challenge is in the multi-objective optimization scenario, where there are multiple conflicting goals (such as minimizing delivery time while minimizing fuel cost). Deep learning models typically optimize one objective function (such as minimizing a loss function) and are not naturally suited to balancing multiple conflicting objectives without complex and specialized architectures.
- **Genetic Algorithms**: Genetic Algorithms are inherently more flexible for multi-objective optimization because they simulate evolution, allowing multiple candidate solutions to evolve simultaneously. They can efficiently explore a broad solution space, maintaining diversity, which makes them well-suited to handle complex trade-offs between multiple objectives.
- **Handling Multiple Trade-offs**: In multi-objective optimization problems, the solutions must often balance conflicting goals. Genetic Algorithms can maintain a **Pareto front**, which represents a set of solutions where improving one objective cannot be done without compromising another. Deep learning does not naturally maintain a Pareto front, requiring additional mechanisms

(such as multi-head networks or reinforcement learning with tailored reward functions) to achieve a balance.

PyGAD Integrations

PyGAD Keras: PyGAD provides integration with Keras, allowing users to optimize deep learning models by applying genetic algorithms. With PyGAD Keras, weights of a neural network are evolved using GA to enhance model performance, making it suitable for cases where traditional backpropagation might not be effective. It offers an alternative way of training models, focusing on population-based search and global optimization capabilities.

PyGAD PyTorch: Similar to its Keras integration, PyGAD also supports PyTorch, allowing the use of genetic algorithms to train PyTorch models. Instead of using gradient-based methods such as Stochastic Gradient Descent (SGD), PyGAD applies genetic algorithms to evolve model parameters, which can be useful for tasks where gradient information is unavailable or unreliable. This approach offers flexibility for training complex models with non-standard objective functions or loss surfaces.

The PyTorch below implements a genetic algorithm entirely from scratch to optimize; it is a multi-object optimization code, a solution by minimizing the sum of squares while maximizing the sum of values. It begins by generating a random population of solutions and iteratively evolves the population through crossover and mutation over a set number of generations. The custom **`crossover()`** and **`mutate()`** functions are used to create offspring and introduce genetic variation. At each generation, the best individuals are selected as parents for the next generation. The optimization progress is tracked by recording the values of the objectives across generations, and the results are visualized using plots to illustrate the progress toward finding the optimal solution.

```
import torch
import torch.nn as nn
import torch.optim as optim
import numpy as np
import matplotlib.pyplot as plt

# Define the fitness function for multi-objective optimization
def fitness_function(solution):
    # Objectives: Minimize the sum of squares and maximize the sum
of the solution values
    objective1 = -torch.sum(solution ** 2)  # Minimize sum of
squares
    objective2 = torch.sum(solution)  # Maximize sum of values

    # Combine objectives (Pareto-based approach could also be used
for true multi-objective optimization)
```

```
    # For simplicity, we will just return a weighted sum
    weight1 = 0.5
    weight2 = 0.5
    return weight1 * objective1 + weight2 * objective2

# Parameters for the genetic algorithm
num_generations = 150  # Increase number of generations for more
optimization
population_size = 20  # Increase population size for greater
diversity
num_genes = 5
gene_space = {'low': -5, 'high': 5}  # Narrow down gene space to
focus more on optimal regions
mutation_rate = 0.1

# Create the initial population
population = torch.empty((population_size, num_genes)).uniform_
(gene_space['low'], gene_space['high'])

# Create lists to store objectives across generations
objective1_history = []
objective2_history = []

# Define crossover function
def crossover(parent1, parent2):
    crossover_point = torch.randint(1, num_genes - 1, (1,)).item()
    child1 = torch.cat((parent1[:crossover_point],
parent2[crossover_point:]))
    child2 = torch.cat((parent2[:crossover_point],
parent1[crossover_point:]))
    return child1, child2

# Define mutation function
def mutate(solution):
    if torch.rand(1).item() < mutation_rate:
        mutation_index = torch.randint(0, num_genes, (1,)).item()
        solution[mutation_index] += torch.randn(1).item()
    return solution

# Run the genetic algorithm and collect objective values across
generations
for generation in range(num_generations):
    # Calculate fitness of each solution
    fitness_values = torch.tensor([fitness_function(ind) for ind in
population])

    # Select the top individuals as parents
```

```
    sorted_indices = torch.argsort(fitness_values, descending=True)
    parents = population[sorted_indices[:population_size // 2]]

    # Crossover to create offspring
    offspring = []
    for i in range(0, len(parents), 2):
        parent1, parent2 = parents[i], parents[i + 1]
        child1, child2 = crossover(parent1, parent2)
        offspring.extend([child1, child2])

    # Mutate offspring
    offspring = [mutate(child) for child in offspring]

    # Create the new population
    population = torch.vstack((parents, torch.stack(offspring)
[:population_size - len(parents)]))

    # Record objectives for the best solution
    best_solution = population[0]
    objective1 = -torch.sum(best_solution ** 2).item()
    objective2 = torch.sum(best_solution).item()
    objective1_history.append(objective1)
    objective2_history.append(objective2)

# Plot the result
generations = range(len(objective1_history))

plt.figure(figsize=(12, 6))

# Plot objective 1 (minimize sum of squares)
plt.plot(generations, objective1_history, label='Objective 1:
Minimize Sum of Squares', color='r')

# Plot objective 2 (maximize sum of values)
plt.plot(generations, objective2_history, label='Objective 2:
Maximize Sum of Values', color='b')

plt.xlabel('Generation')
plt.ylabel('Objective Value')
plt.title('Objectives Over Generations')
plt.legend()
plt.grid()
plt.show()

# Get the best solution
best_solution = population[0]
fitness_of_best_solution = fitness_function(best_solution).item()
```

```
print("Best Solution:", best_solution.numpy())
print("Fitness of the Best Solution:", fitness_of_best_solution)
```

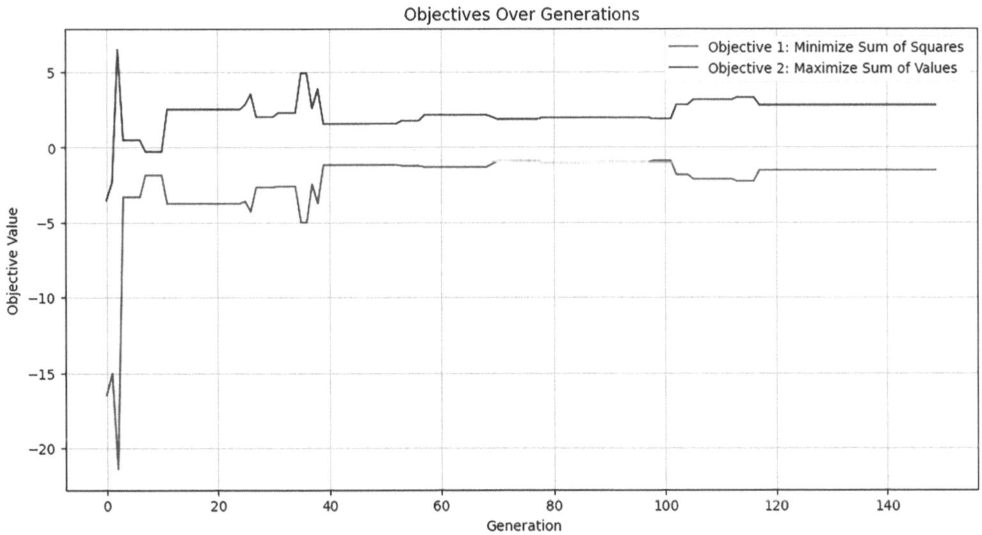

Figure 3.4: *The plot above shows mathematical modeling with PyTorch with GA minimizing the sum of squares and maximizing the sum of values*

```
Best Solution: [0.626692   0.6003643  0.55396163 0.5420197
0.45500118]
Fitness of the Best Solution: 0.6085869073867798
```

The PyTorch code implements a genetic algorithm to optimize a solution represented by a simple neural network model using pygad and TorchGA. The SimpleModel class represents candidate solutions, and the GA iteratively evolves a population to find optimal values that minimize the sum of squares while maximizing the sum of values. The code uses TorchGA to create an initial population and **pygad** to manage the evolutionary process, including selection, crossover, and mutation. The objectives are recorded across generations, and the results are plotted to illustrate the optimization progress, ultimately yielding the best solution found by the GA.

To use the **pygad.torchga** module and import the TorchGA class in Google Colab, you first need to install pygad. Use the following steps:

Import the **TorchGA** class from `pygad.torchga`: **from pygad.torchga import TorchGA**, this will allow you to use the **TorchGA** class for integrating genetic algorithms with PyTorch models.

```
import torch
import torch.nn as nn
import torch.optim as optim
import numpy as np
```

```
import matplotlib.pyplot as plt
from pygad.torchga import TorchGA
import pygad

# Define the neural network model representing the solution
class SimpleModel(nn.Module):
    def __init__(self, num_genes):
        super(SimpleModel, self).__init__()
        self.fc = nn.Linear(num_genes, 1)

    def forward(self, x):
        return self.fc(x)

# Parameters for the genetic algorithm
num_generations = 150  # Number of generations
population_size = 20  # Population size
num_genes = 5
mutation_rate = 0.1

gene_space = {'low': -5, 'high': 5}  # Gene range for initialization

# Create an instance of the PyTorch model
model = SimpleModel(num_genes)

# Create the initial population using torchga
ga_instance = TorchGA(model=model, num_solutions=population_size)

# Create lists to store objectives across generations
objective1_history = []
objective2_history = []

# Define the fitness function for multi-objective optimization
def fitness_function(ga_instance, solution, solution_idx):
    # Convert solution to a torch tensor
    solution_tensor = torch.tensor(solution, dtype=torch.float32)

    # Objectives: Minimize the sum of squares and maximize the sum
of the solution values
    objective1 = -torch.sum(solution_tensor ** 2)  # Minimize sum of
squares
    objective2 = torch.sum(solution_tensor)  # Maximize sum of
values

    # Combine objectives (Pareto-based approach could also be used
for true multi-objective optimization)
    # For simplicity, we will just return a weighted sum
    weight1 = 0.5
```

```
        weight2 = 0.5
        return (weight1 * objective1 + weight2 * objective2).item()

    # Initialize the genetic algorithm using PyGAD
    initial_population = ga_instance.population_weights

    ga = pygad.GA(
        num_generations=num_generations,
        num_parents_mating=5,
        initial_population=initial_population,
        fitness_func=fitness_function,
        mutation_percent_genes=10,
        mutation_type=›random›,
        crossover_type=›single_point›
    )

    # Run the genetic algorithm and collect objective values across
    generations
    ga.run()

    # Extract the fitness history
    best_solutions = ga.best_solutions_fitness
    for solution in ga.best_solutions:
        best_solution_tensor = torch.tensor(solution, dtype=torch.
    float32)
        objective1 = -torch.sum(best_solution_tensor ** 2).item()
        objective2 = torch.sum(best_solution_tensor).item()
        objective1_history.append(objective1)
        objective2_history.append(objective2)


    # Get the best solution
    best_solution, best_solution_fitness, _ = ga.best_solution()
    fitness_of_best_solution = fitness_function(ga, best_solution, 0)
    print("Best Solution:", best_solution)
    print("Fitness of the Best Solution:", fitness_of_best_solution)
```

```
Best Solution: [0.49662609 0.50732505 0.50423829 0.50754301
0.51474639 0.50092976]
Fitness of the Best Solution: 0.7498208284378052
```

Here are the main differences between the PyTorch native GA code and the **pygad.torchga (TorchGA)** code:

Feature	PyTorch Native GA	TorchGA (pygad.torchga)
Library Usage	Implements Genetic Algorithm (GA) operations manually using PyTorch tensors, coding each GA step from scratch (fitness evaluation, selection, crossover, mutation).	Uses TorchGA with PyGAD, which abstracts most GA operations like evolution, crossover, mutation, and fitness evaluation, simplifying implementation.
Population Handling	Initial population is manually created using `torch.empty()` and evolves through custom logic per generation.	Uses TorchGA for population initialization and relies on PyGAD for population evolution, encapsulating population handling.
Crossover and Mutation Implementation	Custom crossover and mutation functions are implemented using PyTorch operations, allowing full control over crossover points and mutation conditions.	PyGAD handles crossover and mutation with predefined types (e.g., single_point, two_point, uniform) and mutation strategies, easing usage but limiting customization.
Fitness Function Evaluation	Fitness function is manually evaluated on each solution, with results used for selection and evolution.	Fitness function is provided to the `pygad.GA` class, which handles solution evaluation automatically each generation.
Selection of Parents	Custom logic selects parents based on sorted fitness values, typically by selecting top individuals.	Uses PyGAD's predefined selection methods (e.g., tournament, roulette, rank), making selection easier.
Level of Control vs. Abstraction	Offers full control over the GA workflow, ideal for highly customized implementations.	Provides abstraction via PyGAD, enabling quick setup but less granular control.
Code Complexity	More verbose and complex, with every GA step manually implemented, including population management, crossover, mutation, and selection.	Code is concise, as TorchGA and PyGAD handle most operations internally, resulting in fewer lines and improved readability.

Figure 3.5: *Comparison of Genetic Algorithm implementation between PyTorch Native GA and TorchGA*

So the **PyTorch Native GA** approach requires more code and gives complete flexibility to modify any aspect of the Genetic Algorithm, while the **TorchGA (`pygad.torchga`)** approach simplifies the process by leveraging PyGAD's abstractions, making it faster to implement but less customizable.

In the next section, we will discuss another library: DEAP. DEAP is the older library, first released in 2010, while PyGAD was introduced later, around 2020. DEAP's longer presence in the community means it has a more established user base and a wide range of use cases.

DEAP provides a low-level API that allows for greater flexibility, whereas PyGAD offers a simpler, high-level interface. DEAP is designed with modularity, enabling advanced customization, while PyGAD focuses on ease of use for common optimization problems.

DEAP Single-Objective Optimization

Distributed Evolutionary Algorithms in Python or DEAP is an open-source library for evolutionary computation. It is designed for rapid prototyping and testing of evolutionary algorithms. DEAP offers a flexible framework for creating custom optimization algorithms, including genetic algorithms, genetic programming, and multi-objective optimization.

Modules in DEAP:

- **creator**: Used to create custom classes for individuals, fitness functions, and other evolutionary components.
- **base**: Provides the fundamental algorithms for evolutionary operations.
- **tools**: Contains commonly used tools for selection, mutation, and crossover.
- **algorithms**: Implements standard evolutionary algorithms such as eaSimple and eaMuPlusLambda.

Differences from PyGAD:

Algorithms	Execution	Structure
DEAP	Provides a low-level API, requiring more manual setup and greater customization, which makes it highly flexible for creating diverse evolutionary algorithms.	Designed with modularity, enabling users to create individuals and their evolutionary operators in a highly customizable manner.
PyGAD	Provides a high-level API that is easier to use and more focused on traditional genetic algorithms. PyGAD is more user-friendly for straightforward optimization tasks.	Offers a simpler, more integrated structure, with features such as defining fitness functions, mutation, and crossover directly through easy-to-configure parameters.

Table 3.1: DEAP vs. PyGAD

In this section, we will reuse the niching code under the section *Chapter 2, Fundamentals of Genetic Algorithms*, "*Niching in Genetic Algorithms*" and convert it to DEAP code. The DEAP library provides a more modular approach to setting up evolutionary algorithms compared to PyGAD, allowing greater control over the individual components of the genetic algorithm.

PyGAD to DEAP Code Conversation

We started by defining the fitness function for a multimodal problem, aiming to optimize three different peaks. To implement niching (fitness sharing), we adjusted the fitness calculation based on the proximity of individuals in the population, thereby promoting diverse solutions by reducing the fitness of closely clustered individuals. This helps maintain multiple optimal solutions across different niches in the fitness landscape.

```
from deap import base, creator, tools, algorithms
import numpy as np
import matplotlib.pyplot as plt
import random

# Define the multimodal fitness function
def fitness_function(individual):
    x = individual[0]
    return (
        np.exp(-(x + 2) ** 2) +  # Peak 1
        1.5 * np.exp(-x ** 2) +  # Peak 2
        np.exp(-(x - 3) ** 2),   # Peak 3
    )

# Define a modified fitness function for niching (fitness sharing)
def fitness_function_with_niching(individual, population,
sharing_radius=1.5):
    base_fitness = fitness_function(individual)[0]
    niche_count = 0

    for other_individual in population:
        distance = np.linalg.norm(np.array(individual)
- np.array(other_individual))
        if distance < sharing_radius:
            niche_count += 1

    shared_fitness = base_fitness / niche_count if niche_count > 0
else base_fitness
    return shared_fitness,

# Register necessary components for DEAP
creator.create("FitnessMax", base.Fitness, weights=(1.0,))
creator.create("Individual", list, fitness=creator.FitnessMax)

toolbox = base.Toolbox()
toolbox.register("attr_float", random.uniform, -5, 5)
toolbox.register("individual", tools.initRepeat,
```

```
creator.Individual, toolbox.attr_float, n=1)
toolbox.register("population", tools.initRepeat, list, toolbox.
individual)

toolbox.register("mate", tools.cxUniform, indpb=0.5)
toolbox.register("mutate", tools.mutGaussian, mu=0, sigma=1,
indpb=0.1)
toolbox.register("select", tools.selStochasticUniversalSampling)

def run_ga(fitness_func, num_generations=200, pop_size=50,
cxpb=0.7, mutpb=0.2):
    toolbox.register("evaluate", fitness_func)
    population = toolbox.population(n=pop_size)

    stats = tools.Statistics(lambda ind: ind.fitness.values)
    stats.register("avg", np.mean)
    stats.register("min", np.min)
    stats.register("max", np.max)

    population, logbook = algorithms.eaSimple(
        population, toolbox, cxpb=cxpb, mutpb=mutpb, ngen=num_
generations,
        stats=stats, verbose=False
    )

    return population, logbook

# Run the GA without niching
population_without_niching, logbook_without_niching = run_ga
(fitness_function)

# Run the GA with niching
# Create an initial population for niching
population_with_niching = toolbox.population(n=50)
# Using lambda to pass population as argument to the fitness
function
toolbox.register("evaluate", lambda ind: fitness_function_with_
niching(ind, population_with_niching))
population_with_niching, logbook_with_niching = run_ga(lambda
ind: fitness_function_with_niching(ind, population_with_niching))

# Plotting the results
fig, axes = plt.subplots(1, 2, figsize=(15, 6))

# Plot for GA without niching
axes[0].plot(logbook_without_niching.select("max"), color='blue',
label="Without Niching")
```

```
axes[0].set_title("GA Without Niching: Generation vs Fitness")
axes[0].set_xlabel("Generation")
axes[0].set_ylabel("Fitness")
axes[0].legend()

# Plot for GA with niching
axes[1].plot(logbook_with_niching.select("max"), color='red',
label="With Niching")
axes[1].set_title("GA With Niching (Fitness Sharing): Generation
vs Fitness")
axes[1].set_xlabel("Generation")
axes[1].set_ylabel("Fitness")
axes[1].legend()

plt.show()

# Get the best solutions for each problem
best_without_niching = tools.selBest(population_without_niching,
k=1)[0]
best_with_niching = tools.selBest(population_with_niching, k=1)
[0]

print("Best Solution Without Niching:", best_without_niching)
print("Fitness of Best Solution Without Niching:", fitness_func-
tion(best_without_niching))

print("Best Solution With Niching:", best_with_niching)
print("Fitness of Best Solution With Niching:", fitness_func-
tion(best_with_niching))
est Solution Without Niching: [-0.0614603862925156]
Fitness of Best Solution Without Niching: (1.5177614980484635,)
Best Solution With Niching: [0.17221471254824317]
Fitness of Best Solution With Niching: (1.4654314535540411,)
```

The major changes when converting the PyGAD code to DEAP are:

- **Library Change**: Switched from PyGAD to DEAP, which is more modular and requires more setup for individuals and operators.
- **Fitness Function**: In DEAP, fitness functions are registered via toolbox and directly used for evaluation.
- **Population and Individuals**: Created individuals and populations explicitly using creator and toolbox in DEAP, unlike PyGAD, where parameters are defined within the GA class.
- **Evolutionary Process**: DEAP requires the manual combination of operators, population initialization, and statistics gathering, whereas PyGAD abstracts much of this process.

- **Fitness Sharing**: Implemented fitness sharing manually within the niching function, while PyGAD uses a straightforward fitness evaluation across the population.

PyTorch to DEAP Code Conversation

In this section, the code demonstrates how to use genetic algorithms to train a simple neural network for regression using PyTorch. The data is created using make_regression and is standardized before being converted into PyTorch tensors. The genetic algorithm is used to evolve the weights of the neural network without relying on traditional gradient-based training methods. Crossover and mutation operators are implemented to introduce new individuals into each generation, allowing the network to gradually optimize its performance.

Two variants of the GA are run: one with niching and one without. Niching penalizes individuals that are too similar to others, thereby maintaining diversity in the population and avoiding premature convergence. Both runs are evaluated for their performance, and the results are visualized by plotting the best fitness scores over generations. The comparison aims to show the effectiveness of niching in maintaining diverse and high-quality solutions in the GA.

```
import torch
import torch.nn as nn
import numpy as np
import matplotlib.pyplot as plt
from sklearn.datasets import make_regression
from sklearn.model_selection import train_test_split
from sklearn.preprocessing import StandardScaler

# Create a synthetic dataset for regression
X, y = make_regression(n_samples=200, n_features=1, noise=15)
X_train, X_test, y_train, y_test = train_test_split(X, y, test_
size=0.2, random_state=42)

# Scale the data
scaler_X = StandardScaler()
scaler_y = StandardScaler()
X_train = scaler_X.fit_transform(X_train)
X_test = scaler_X.transform(X_test)
y_train = scaler_y.fit_transform(y_train.reshape(-1, 1)).ravel()
y_test = scaler_y.transform(y_test.reshape(-1, 1)).ravel()

# Convert data to PyTorch tensors
X_train_tensor = torch.FloatTensor(X_train)
y_train_tensor = torch.FloatTensor(y_train)
```

```
# Define a simple neural network model
class SimpleNN(nn.Module):
    def __init__(self):
        super(SimpleNN, self).__init__()
        self.fc1 = nn.Linear(1, 1)

    def forward(self, x):
        return self.fc1(x)

# Genetic Algorithm Parameters
population_size = 20
num_generations = 100
mutation_rate = 0.1

# Initialize population
population = [SimpleNN() for _ in range(population_size)]

# Fitness function: Mean Squared Error on training data
def evaluate_fitness(model, X, y):
    model.eval()
    with torch.no_grad():
        predictions = model(X).squeeze()
        loss = torch.mean((predictions - y) ** 2)
    return -loss.item()  # Negative because we want to maximize
fitness

# Function for crossover between two parents
def crossover(parent1, parent2):
    child = SimpleNN()
    with torch.no_grad():
        for param_child, param_p1, param_p2 in zip(child.
parameters(), parent1.parameters(), parent2.parameters()):
            param_child.data = (param_p1.data + param_p2.data) /
2
    return child

# Function for mutation
def mutate(model, mutation_rate):
    with torch.no_grad():
        for param in model.parameters():
            if np.random.rand() < mutation_rate:
                param.data += torch.randn_like(param) * 0.1

# Run the Genetic Algorithm with and without niching
best_fitnesses_without_niching = []
best_fitnesses_with_niching = []
```

```
for use_niching in [False, True]:
    # Initialize population
    population = [SimpleNN() for _ in range(population_size)]
    best_fitnesses = []

    for generation in range(num_generations):
        # Evaluate fitness for each individual in the population
        fitnesses = [evaluate_fitness(individual, X_train_tensor,
y_train_tensor) for individual in population]

        # Apply niching: Penalize individuals that are too
similar to others
        if use_niching:
            sharing_radius = 0.1
            for i in range(len(population)):
                for j in range(len(population)):
                    if i != j:
                        distance = torch.norm(torch.cat([p.view
(-1) for p in population[i].parameters()]) -
                                              torch.cat([p.view
(-1) for p in population[j].parameters()]))
                        if distance < sharing_radius:
                            fitnesses[i] -= 0.1  # Penalize fitness
if individuals are too similar

        # Select the top 50% individuals
        sorted_indices = np.argsort(fitnesses)[::-1]
        top_individuals = [population[i] for i in sorted_
indices[:population_size // 2]]

        # Generate new offspring through crossover
        offspring = []
        for _ in range(population_size - len(top_individuals)):
            parent1, parent2 = np.random.choice(top_individuals,
2, replace=False)
            child = crossover(parent1, parent2)
            mutate(child, mutation_rate)
            offspring.append(child)

        # Form the new population
        population = top_individuals + offspring

        # Record the best fitness
        best_fitnesses.append(max(fitnesses))

    # Store results for plotting
    if use_niching:
```

```
            best_fitnesses_with_niching = best_fitnesses
        else:
            best_fitnesses_without_niching = best_fitnesses

    # Plotting the best fitness over generations
    plt.figure(figsize=(15, 6))

    # Plot for training without niching
    plt.plot(range(num_generations), best_fitnesses_without_niching,
    color='blue', label="Without Niching")
    # Plot for training with niching
    plt.plot(range(num_generations), best_fitnesses_with_niching,
    color='red', label="With Niching")

    plt.xlabel("Generation")
    plt.ylabel("Fitness (Negative MSE)")
    plt.title("GA Training Neural Network: Generation vs Best Fitness
    (With and Without Niching)")
    plt.legend()
    plt.show()
```

In the plot, we can observe the performance of the Genetic Algorithm with and without niching over 100 generations. The **straight line (blue)** represents the GA without niching, while the **zig-zag line (red)** represents the GA with niching.

The GA without niching consistently achieves a higher fitness, demonstrating stable convergence. On the other hand, the GA with niching shows more fluctuation, indicating that the fitness-sharing technique maintains diversity in the population, but often at the expense of slower convergence. Niching helps prevent the algorithm from getting stuck in a single peak, hence maintaining multiple solutions, but this comes at a cost of reduced overall fitness.

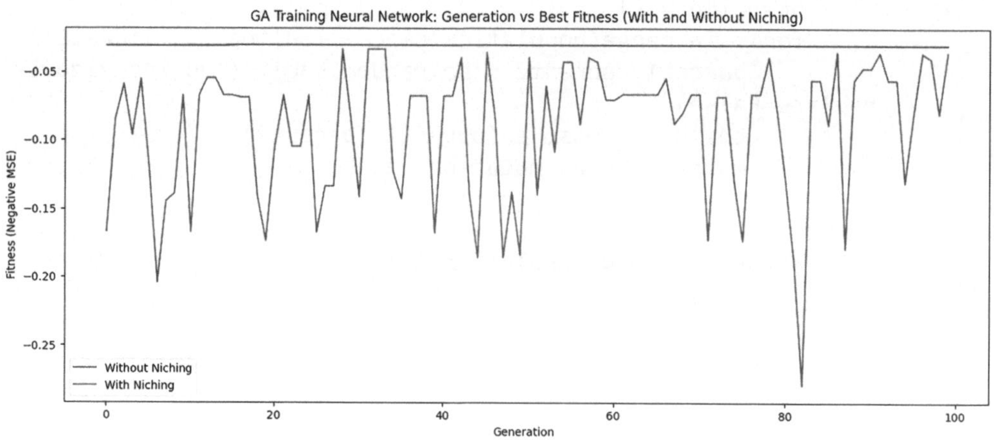

Figure 3.6: *The plot above shows the fitness plot of the model*

```
from deap import base, creator, tools, algorithms
import numpy as np
import matplotlib.pyplot as plt
import torch
import torch.nn as nn
from sklearn.datasets import make_regression
from sklearn.model_selection import train_test_split
from sklearn.preprocessing import StandardScaler
import random

# Create a synthetic dataset for regression
X, y = make_regression(n_samples=200, n_features=1, noise=15)
X_train, X_test, y_train, y_test = train_test_split(X, y, test_
size=0.2, random_state=42)

# Scale the data
scaler_X = StandardScaler()
scaler_y = StandardScaler()
X_train = scaler_X.fit_transform(X_train)
X_test = scaler_X.transform(X_test)
y_train = scaler_y.fit_transform(y_train.reshape(-1, 1)).ravel()
y_test = scaler_y.transform(y_test.reshape(-1, 1)).ravel()

# Define a simple neural network model
class SimpleNN(nn.Module):
    def __init__(self):
        super(SimpleNN, self).__init__()
        self.fc1 = nn.Linear(1, 1)

    def forward(self, x):
        return self.fc1(x)

# Register necessary components for DEAP
creator.create("FitnessMax", base.Fitness, weights=(1.0,))
creator.create("Individual", list, fitness=creator.FitnessMax)

toolbox = base.Toolbox()
toolbox.register("attr_float", random.uniform, -5, 5)
toolbox.register("individual", tools.initRepeat, creator.Individual,
toolbox.attr_float, n=1)
toolbox.register("population", tools.initRepeat, list,
toolbox.individual)

def evaluate_fitness(individual):
    model = SimpleNN()
    model.fc1.weight.data.fill_(individual[0])
    model.fc1.bias.data.fill_(0)
```

```
    X_train_tensor = torch.FloatTensor(X_train)
    y_train_tensor = torch.FloatTensor(y_train)
    model.eval()
    with torch.no_grad():
        predictions = model(X_train_tensor).squeeze()
        loss = torch.mean((predictions - y_train_tensor) ** 2)
    return -loss.item(),

toolbox.register("mate", tools.cxBlend, alpha=0.5)
toolbox.register("mutate", tools.mutGaussian, mu=0, sigma=1,
indpb=0.1)
toolbox.register("select", tools.selTournament, tournsize=3)
toolbox.register("evaluate", evaluate_fitness)

def run_ga(num_generations=100, pop_size=20, cxpb=0.7, mutpb=0.2,
use_niching=False):
    population = toolbox.population(n=pop_size)

    stats = tools.Statistics(lambda ind: ind.fitness.values)
    stats.register(«avg», np.mean)
    stats.register("min", np.min)
    stats.register("max", np.max)

    best_fitnesses = []

    for generation in range(num_generations):
        fitnesses = list(map(toolbox.evaluate, population))
        if use_niching:
            sharing_radius = 0.1
            for i in range(len(population)):
                for j in range(len(population)):
                    if i != j:
                        distance = abs(population[i][0] -
population[j][0])
                        if distance < sharing_radius:
                            fitnesses[i] = (fitnesses[i][0] - 0.1,)

        for ind, fit in zip(population, fitnesses):
            ind.fitness.values = fit

        offspring = toolbox.select(population, len(population))
        offspring = list(map(toolbox.clone, offspring))

        for child1, child2 in zip(offspring[::2], offspring[1::2]):
            if random.random() < cxpb:
                toolbox.mate(child1, child2)
                del child1.fitness.values
```

```
                del child2.fitness.values

        for mutant in offspring:
            if random.random() < mutpb:
                toolbox.mutate(mutant)
                del mutant.fitness.values

        population[:] = offspring
        invalid_ind = [ind for ind in population if not ind.fitness.
valid]
        fitnesses = map(toolbox.evaluate, invalid_ind)
        for ind, fit in zip(invalid_ind, fitnesses):
            ind.fitness.values = fit

        record = stats.compile(population)
        best_fitnesses.append(record[‹max›])
        print(f»Gen {generation}: {record}»)

    return best_fitnesses

# Run the GA without niching
best_fitnesses_without_niching = run_ga(use_niching=False)

# Run the GA with niching
best_fitnesses_with_niching = run_ga(use_niching=True)

# Plotting the results
plt.figure(figsize=(15, 6))
plt.plot(range(len(best_fitnesses_without_niching)), best_fitnesses_
without_niching, color='blue', label="Without Niching")
plt.plot(range(len(best_fitnesses_with_niching)), best_fitnesses_with_
niching, color='red', label="With Niching")
plt.xlabel("Generation")
plt.ylabel("Fitness (Negative MSE)")
plt.title("GA Training Neural Network: Generation vs Best Fitness
(With and Without Niching)")
plt.legend()
plt.show()
```

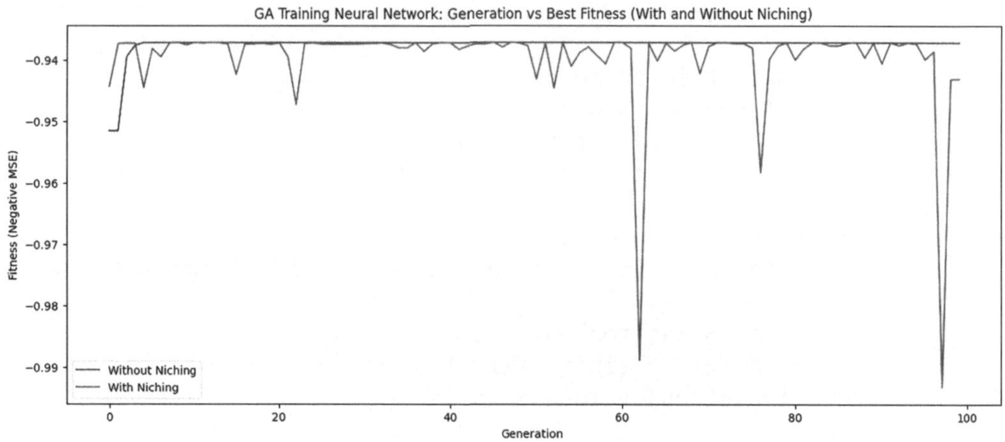

Figure 3.7: *The plot above shows the fitness plot of the model*

```
Gen 0: {'avg': -4.725197812914848, 'min': -15.542619705200195,
'max': -0.9515320658683777}
Gen 99: {'avg': -1.1147283697128296, 'min': -1.7287766933441162,
'max': -0.9430373907089233}
```

The results for generation 99, shown as **`{'avg': -1.1147283697128296, 'min': -1.7287766933441162, 'max': -0.9430373907089233}`**, summarize the population's fitness statistics:

1. **avg (−1.11)**: The average fitness of the population is approximately −1.11. This gives an idea of how well the average individual is performing in terms of minimizing the Mean Squared Error (MSE).
2. **`min` (−1.73)**: The worst-performing individual has a fitness of −1.73.
3. **`max` (−0.94)**: The best-performing individual has a fitness of −0.94, indicating the lowest error in the population.

The negative values represent MSE (since we negate it to maximize fitness). Lower values indicate better performance.

As you can see that the line flattens out, somewhere between Gen10 and Gen20, we can do multiple steps to ensure achieving smoother growth in fitness over generations. Changes include:

- Increased mutation probability (**`mutpb`**) and mutation strength for better exploration.
- Higher crossover probability (**`cxpb`**) to allow more gene recombination.
- Increased population size and number of generations to improve convergence.
- Increased selection pressure through larger tournament size (**`tournsize`**).

- Reduced the niching sharing radius to maintain diversity without heavily penalizing individuals.

This leads to our next topic Hyperparameter tuning

Hyperparameter

Hyperparameter tuning plays a crucial role in optimizing the performance of machine learning models. By carefully adjusting parameters such as learning rate, regularization strength, and model complexity, we can significantly improve model accuracy, convergence speed, and robustness. Tuning these hyperparameters ensures that our models can generalize well to new data, avoiding issues such as overfitting or underfitting. Without effective tuning, even a well-designed model might fail to reach its potential, leading to suboptimal outcomes and missed opportunities for insights.

In evolutionary algorithms, achieving a consistent improvement in the fitness curve is crucial for finding optimal solutions. Various optimization strategies can help guide the population toward better fitness values while maintaining genetic diversity and avoiding premature convergence. This section outlines several key strategies for enhancing the fitness curve, including adjustments to mutation rates, selection pressure, crossover methods, and population dynamics. By employing these techniques, we can create a more effective evolutionary process that yields higher quality solutions over time, Examples of some of these techniques are listed as follows:

- **Adjust Mutation Rate**: Increase the mutation probability or apply an adaptive mutation rate that changes with each generation. Use higher mutation rates in early generations for better exploration, gradually decreasing as the population converges.
- **Increase Selection Pressure**: Use a larger tournament size or employ elitism to ensure the fittest individuals are consistently selected for reproduction. While stronger selection pressure can promote faster convergence, it is essential to balance it with genetic diversity.
- **Experiment with Crossover Methods**: Try different crossover operators such as two-point crossover or a blend crossover with a higher alpha value. Increasing crossover probability facilitates the rapid spread of beneficial traits.
- **Increase Population Size**: A larger population size enhances genetic diversity and allows for a more thorough exploration of the solution space. This can help prevent premature convergence and support a more gradual improvement in fitness.
- **Use Adaptive Parameters**: Implement adaptive mechanisms for crossover and mutation rates. High crossover rates can diversify the gene pool in the early stages, and gradually reducing these rates can help the population converge.

- **Adjust Fitness Sharing Radius**: If niching is used, reducing the sharing radius helps maintain diversity without overly penalizing individuals, allowing multiple good solutions to coexist and improve simultaneously.
- **Increase Number of Generations**: Allow more generations to provide the population with sufficient time to evolve. This can give the algorithm the opportunity for a steady improvement in solutions.
- **Incorporate Elitism**: Use elitism to ensure the best individuals always survive to the next generation. This helps retain good solutions throughout the evolutionary process and contributes to smoother fitness progression.

The complete program containing the code snippets shown in this section can be found in *Chapter* 3 notebook: https://github.com/ava-orange-education/Ultimate-Genetic-Algorithm-with-Python .

```
Gen 199: {'avg': -0.14349979844689367, 'min': -0.8860036730766296,
'max': -0.05527617409825325} "
```

In generation 199, the average fitness is -0.143, indicating an overall improvement. The worst fitness is -0.886, while the best fitness achieved is -0.055, showing that the population has evolved to produce individuals with lower errors. Lower fitness values represent better solutions, as this metric is based on minimizing the mean squared error.

The multiple instances of starting from "`Gen 0`" indicate that the code runs the genetic algorithm multiple times, with different parameter configurations (for example, with and without niching). Each new instance of the genetic algorithm starts from an initial generation (`Gen 0`) because it creates a new population and begins evolving it from scratch.

This repetition allows for comparison between different approaches (such as using niching or not), helping evaluate which one yields better results for the given problem.

Conclusion

In this chapter, we explored PyGAD and DEAP, comparing their strengths and discussing their use in both single and multi-objective optimization problems. PyGAD's advantages lie in its simplicity, whereas DEAP offers a more customizable approach. We delved into converting PyGAD to DEAP code and even extended it to PyTorch for practical problem-solving. A toy example demonstrated genetic algorithm implementation, and we analyzed code differences in terms of performance. Finally, we reviewed the mathematical modeling, hyperparameters, and parameters of genetic algorithms.

In the next chapter, we will explore combinatorial optimization using genetic algorithms for problems such as the Traveling Salesman Problem. We will also cover constraint satisfaction and scheduling, focusing on solving resource allocation challenges. Additionally, we will dive into multi-objective optimization, balancing multiple conflicting objectives, and explore applications in game strategy development for AI and game theory. Finally, we will discuss real-world financial applications, such as portfolio optimization.

CHAPTER 4
Genetic Algorithms and Their Applications

Introduction

In the previous chapters, you have learned how to structure a genetic algorithm, explored different types of optimizations, and understood the use of fitness functions. You have also gained experience working with libraries such as PyGAD and DEAP for implementing genetic deep learning algorithms.

Optimization plays a pivotal role in addressing complex challenges across various domains, including logistics, finance, and data analytics. Finding the most efficient solution among countless possibilities often requires sophisticated methods capable of navigating large and intricate solution spaces. This chapter focuses on two significant optimization problems: the Traveling Salesman Problem (TSP) and fraud analytics. It explores how genetic algorithms, inspired by the principles of natural selection and genetics, offer powerful tools for solving these problems effectively.

The TSP exemplifies a classic optimization challenge where the goal is to determine the shortest possible route that visits a set of cities exactly once and returns to the starting point. Traditional computational methods become impractical as the number of cities increases, making genetic algorithms a valuable alternative for finding near-optimal solutions efficiently. In the domain of fraud analytics, detecting fraudulent activities within vast amounts of data presents a significant hurdle. Genetic algorithms enhance fraud detection by optimizing neural network parameters, improving the system's ability to identify complex fraudulent patterns. By examining these two problem types, we demonstrate the versatility and effectiveness of genetic algorithms in solving complex optimization issues.

Structure

This chapter is structured as follows:

Optimization Problem Types

- **Traveling Salesman Problem (TSP):**
  - Detailed Steps on Solving TSP Using Genetic Algorithms
  - Reference to **TSPLib** for Experiments
- **Fraud Analytics:**
  - Application of Genetic Algorithms in Fraud Detection
  - Chromosome Representation and Neural Network Implementation for Fraud Detection Using Genetic Algorithms

Optimization Problem Types

This section introduces various types of optimization problems to which genetic algorithms can be applied effectively. Optimization is a fundamental concept in problem-solving, involving the identification of the best solution from a set of possibilities. Depending on the nature of the problem—whether it involves discrete choices, satisfying constraints, optimizing continuous functions, or dealing with multiple objectives—different approaches are necessary. Genetic algorithms are versatile tools that can handle a wide range of optimization tasks, including combinatorial optimization, constraint satisfaction, continuous function optimization, multi-objective trade-offs, dynamic changes, and uncertainty. Understanding these different types of optimization problems provides a foundation for utilizing genetic algorithms in diverse real-world applications.

Combinatorial Optimization

In combinatorial optimization, the goal is to find the best solution from a discrete set of possible solutions. Problems such as the Traveling Salesman Problem (TSP), scheduling, or knapsack problems fall under this category. Genetic algorithms are effective for combinatorial optimization because they can search a large solution space using selection, crossover, and mutation to evolve optimal or near-optimal solutions.

Example: Supply Chain Route Planning

Finding the optimal routes for delivering goods to minimize transportation costs and maximize efficiency is a combinatorial optimization problem, similar to the TSP.

Constraint Satisfaction

Constraint satisfaction involves finding a solution that meets a set of constraints or conditions. Examples include the n-queens problem or Sudoku. Genetic algorithms can be applied here by encoding possible solutions as chromosomes and then using penalty functions to enforce the satisfaction of constraints during the fitness evaluation. GAs help evolve solutions that meet all or most of the problem's constraints.

Example: University Timetabling

Scheduling lectures for different courses such that no students or teachers have conflicts and room capacities are not exceeded involves satisfying multiple constraints, such as room availability and conflict-free time slots.

Continuous Function Optimization

Continuous function optimization deals with finding the maximum or minimum of a continuous mathematical function, often involving real-valued parameters. Genetic algorithms are suitable for these problems since they can handle complex, multi-modal, or non-linear functions by evolving populations of real-valued solutions. Operators such as real-coded crossover and mutation allow GAs to explore the continuous search space efficiently.

Example: Aerospace Design

Optimizing the shape of an aircraft wing to minimize drag while maintaining lift and stability involves optimizing a continuous function, requiring adjustments to aerodynamic parameters.

Function approximation involves finding the optimal parameters for a model (for example, coefficients in a polynomial) to minimize the difference between predicted and actual values. Genetic algorithms are used here to evolve sets of parameters that optimize this function, making it a continuous optimization problem.

Symbolic regression aims to discover the best mathematical expression that fits a given dataset. GAs are used to evolve expressions, combining various mathematical operators and constants. This task falls under continuous optimization because it requires evaluating and improving a continuous function, searching for an optimal solution within the space of possible expressions.

Multi-Objective Optimization

In multi-objective optimization, we have touched upon this in *Chapter* 3; the goal is to optimize more than one objective simultaneously. This often results in trade-offs between conflicting objectives (for example, minimizing cost while maximizing quality). Genetic algorithms are commonly used here, as they can maintain a diverse set of solutions that approximate the Pareto front, allowing decision-makers to choose the most preferred trade-off.

Example: Balancing

A company wants to optimize delivery time, fuel cost, and customer satisfaction simultaneously; there are conflicting objectives that need to be balanced. Minimizing delivery time might require faster routes, which can increase fuel costs, while minimizing costs might lead to longer delivery times, potentially reducing customer satisfaction. Genetic algorithms can be employed to evolve a set of possible solutions that consider trade-offs between these objectives, resulting in a Pareto front from which the company can choose the most suitable balance, such as a solution that offers reasonable delivery times while maintaining customer satisfaction and minimizing operational costs.

Product Design: In automobile manufacturing, optimizing both vehicle safety and fuel efficiency simultaneously involves balancing multiple conflicting objectives, where a genetic algorithm can help find the best trade-offs.

Dynamic Optimization

In dynamic optimization, the objective function or constraints change over time. Genetic algorithms can be adapted to solve these problems by maintaining population diversity and using techniques such as memory-based approaches to adapt to the changing landscape.

Examples include time-varying scheduling or adapting to real-time changes in resource allocation. To be specific, **Power Grid Management**: Allocating power in a grid where supply, demand, and network conditions change over time requires a dynamic optimization approach to keep the system stable and cost-effective.

Stochastic Optimization

Stochastic optimization deals with uncertainty and randomness in the objective function or constraints. For instance, some of the parameters may have probabilistic distributions. Genetic algorithms can incorporate stochastic elements by evaluating solutions using Monte Carlo simulations or probabilistic fitness functions.

Example: Financial Portfolio Optimization

Optimizing a portfolio considering uncertain market returns involves stochastic optimization. Genetic algorithms can be used to find the best asset allocation strategy based on probabilistic returns.

Discrete Optimization

Discrete optimization involves finding the best solution from a finite set of possibilities, where the variables are typically discrete or categorical (for example, binary or integer values). Though similar to combinatorial optimization, this category also includes problems that do not necessarily involve combinatorial complexity, such as choosing the best set of features for a model.

Example: Feature Selection in Machine Learning

Selecting the optimal subset of features from a given dataset to maximize model accuracy while minimizing complexity is a discrete optimization problem involving binary decisions (select or not select).

Global versus Local Optimization

Global Optimization aims to find the overall best solution in the entire search space, often involving challenging landscapes with multiple local optima. Genetic algorithms excel at global optimization due to their population-based approach and ability to escape local optima.

Example: Pharmaceutical Drug Design

Finding the optimal molecular structure for a drug that minimizes side effects and maximizes efficacy involves exploring a large, multi-modal search space, which is a global optimization problem.

Local Optimization, on the other hand, focuses on finding the optimal solution within a neighborhood or region of the search space. Genetic algorithms are generally used for global optimization, but local search techniques can be hybridized with them to refine solutions.

Example: Tuning Industrial Processes

Optimizing a specific process parameter, such as temperature in a chemical reaction to maximize yield, is often solved with local optimization if it is assumed the process is near the optimum.

Integer Programming

Integer programming involves optimization problems where some or all of the decision variables must be integers. Genetic algorithms are used for solving such problems when traditional methods such as branch-and-bound are computationally infeasible due to the problem's complexity.

Example: Production Planning

Determining the number of each product type to manufacture, subject to resource constraints such as materials and labor, while maximizing profit is an integer programming problem since the production numbers must be integers.

Heuristic Search and Metaheuristics

While this is not a specific category of optimization, heuristic search and metaheuristics, such as genetic algorithms, simulated annealing, particle swarm optimization, and ant colony optimization, are techniques used to solve various types of optimization problems. These methods are particularly useful when the problem space is vast and traditional methods are ineffective.

Example: Urban Traffic Signal Optimization

Metaheuristic approaches such as genetic algorithms can be used to optimize traffic light timings to minimize congestion and improve traffic flow.

Compositional Optimization

This category refers to optimization tasks where the objective function is composed of multiple sub-objectives, possibly with different forms or types. Genetic algorithms can be effective for such problems by evolving composite solutions that consider different components simultaneously.

Example: Optimizing Composite Manufacturing

Manufacturing composite materials requires considering multiple sub-objectives such as weight, strength, and cost. A genetic algorithm can evolve solutions to optimize all these sub-objectives simultaneously.

Machine Learning Optimization

Genetic algorithms are also used to optimize hyperparameters, neural network architectures, and model weights in machine learning. This is a broad area, and the optimization problem can be classified based on the specific nature of what is being optimized–typically involving continuous and discrete variables or a combination of both.

Example: Neural Network Hyperparameter Tuning

Genetic algorithms can be used to find the optimal set of hyperparameters (for example, learning rate, number of layers) for training a deep learning model for image classification.

Robust Optimization

Robust optimization aims to find solutions that perform well under uncertainty or variability in problem parameters. Genetic algorithms can be used to search for solutions that are less sensitive to changes in parameters, making them robust against unexpected scenarios.

Example: Mechanical Design under Vibration

Designing a mechanical structure to withstand vibrations, where there are uncertainties in load conditions, requires robust optimization to ensure the design performs well across all possible conditions.

Mixed-Integer Nonlinear Programming (MINLP)

This type of problem involves optimizing both integer and real-valued (continuous) decision variables, with potentially non-linear objective functions and constraints. Genetic algorithms can be applied to search for optimal or near-optimal solutions in these complex problem spaces.

Example: Hybrid Power System Design

Optimizing the design of a renewable energy system (for example, solar and wind) involves both integer decisions (for example, number of turbines) and continuous decisions (for example, size of panels), with non-linear efficiency constraints.

Constrained Optimization with Penalty Functions

When dealing with hard constraints that must be satisfied, GAs often transform the problem into an unconstrained form using penalty functions. The challenge here is to balance between exploring feasible solutions and handling penalties appropriately to converge on a valid solution.

Example: Structural Engineering Design

Optimizing the design of a bridge, where hard constraints such as stress limits must be satisfied, can be approached using genetic algorithms with penalty functions to handle infeasible designs until an optimal and feasible design is found.

There can be numerous other examples beyond those mentioned, each demonstrating the versatility of genetic algorithms in solving a wide range of optimization problems across different domains. In the next section, let us dive into some of these areas with code examples, starting with the very famous Traveling Salesman Problem (TSP).

Traveling Salesman Problem (TSP)

The **Traveling Salesman Problem (TSP)** was first formulated in the 1930s and 1940s. The problem was originally studied by mathematicians and researchers interested in optimization and operations research.

- In the **1930s**, the problem was described by mathematicians such as Karl Menger in relation to problems in graph theory.
- The term "*Traveling Salesman Problem*" and the formalization of the problem as we know it today were popularized in the **1940s**, largely due to the work of researchers such as **Hassler Whitney** and **Merrill Flood**. Flood, who worked for the RAND Corporation, is particularly noted for bringing the TSP to a broader audience as a formal optimization challenge.

The TSP gained significant attention during the **mid-20th century** when it became a benchmark problem for developing optimization algorithms and continues to be a fundamental problem in computer science and mathematics. Genetic algorithms were first applied to the **TSP** in the **1980s**. One of the earliest notable works was by **John Holland**, the pioneer of genetic algorithms, and his students. They demonstrated how GAs could be used to tackle complex combinatorial optimization problems such as TSP. In the mid-1980s, **David Goldberg** and **Robert Lingle** applied genetic algorithms specifically to solve TSP, highlighting their ability to find good approximate solutions for the problem's large solution space.

Regarding companies that face TSP-like challenges:

- **Amazon:**
  - **Delivery Route Optimization**: Amazon needs to find optimal delivery routes for its logistics network, especially for its "*last-mile*" delivery. The problem involves determining the most efficient way to deliver packages to multiple locations while minimizing time and fuel costs.
  - **Warehouse Picking**: In Amazon's fulfillment centers, robots or workers need to pick items from multiple locations, which also involves optimizing the sequence of locations to minimize travel.
- **Flipkart (or other e-commerce companies):**
  - **Logistics and Distribution**: Like Amazon, Flipkart must manage efficient routing for its delivery trucks and last-mile delivery operations. Optimizing the delivery path is crucial for ensuring fast delivery while reducing operational costs.
- **FedEx, UPS, and DHL:**
  - **Courier and Delivery Services**: These logistics companies face similar routing problems every day, as they need to determine the best routes

for delivering packages to customers, which involves solving large-scale TSP-like problems.

- **Food Delivery Services (for example, DoorDash, Uber Eats, Zomato):**
    - **Driver Routing**: Food delivery companies need to optimize the routes their drivers take to pick up food from restaurants and deliver it to customers, minimizing delivery times while considering constraints such as traffic and customer preferences.
- **Ride-sharing Companies (for example, Uber, Lyft):**
    - **Ride Assignment and Route Planning**: Ride-sharing platforms need to solve variations of the TSP when assigning drivers to passengers and determining the optimal routes, especially for carpool or multi-passenger services.
- **Manufacturing Companies:**
    - **Material Handling and Production**: Companies such as **Siemens**, **Toyota**, or **BMW** need to optimize the movement of materials between different stages of production. The goal is to minimize the total distance travelled by parts or robots within a factory, which is similar to TSP.
- **Retail Chains (for example, Walmart, Target):**
    - **Inventory Replenishment**: These companies need to optimize delivery routes for replenishing products across their retail stores from distribution centers, minimizing fuel costs and delivery times.

All these companies use TSP or TSP-like optimization problems to improve efficiency, reduce operational costs, and enhance customer satisfaction. Genetic algorithms are a useful tool in these contexts because they can effectively explore large, complex solution spaces and provide good approximate solutions to the TSP.

The TSP can be both a **closed path** or an **open path**, depending on how the problem is defined:

- **Closed Path (Tour)**: In the traditional version of TSP, the path is **closed**, meaning that the salesman must return to the starting city after visiting all other cities exactly once. This forms a **tour** where the last city is directly connected to the first city, completing a loop. This version is often called the **"circuit TSP"** or **"Hamiltonian cycle"** problem, as it involves finding a cycle that visits all nodes with minimal cost.
- **Open Path**: In some variations of TSP, the path is **open**, meaning that the salesman is not required to return to the starting point. This type of problem is often referred to as an **"Open TSP"** or a **"Hamiltonian path"** problem. The goal is still to visit all cities exactly once, but the path does not necessarily end at the starting point. This variation can be used in scenarios where returning to the start is not needed or is not cost-effective.

Examples of Application:

- **Closed Path (Tour): Delivery of Goods**: A delivery truck starting from a depot and needing to return after delivering goods to multiple locations represents a closed-path TSP.
- **Open Path: School Bus Routing**: A school bus picking up students from multiple locations and then reaching the school without returning to the starting point can be modelled as an open-path TSP.

Solving the TSP Using a Genetic Algorithm

In the context of solving the **Traveling Salesman Problem (TSP)** using a **genetic algorithm (GA)**, we can describe the key concepts, learned in *Chapter 1, Introduction to Genetic Algorithms*, and *Chapter 2, Fundamentals of Genetic Algorithms* – **chromosome**, **genes**, **genotype**, **phenotype**, **initialization**, **selection**, **crossover**, **mutation**, **fitness**, and **generation**—as follows:

- **Chromosome**
    - A **chromosome** represents a **candidate solution** to the TSP.
    - In TSP, the chromosome is often represented as a sequence of cities that the salesman will visit. For example, if there are 5 cities labeled A, B, C, D, E, a possible chromosome could be [A, C, D, B, E], representing the order in which the cities will be visited.
- **Genes**
    - A **gene** represents a **single component** of the solution.
    - In the context of TSP, each gene represents a city in the list of cities to be visited. For instance, in the chromosome [A, C, D, B, E], each letter (A, C, D, B, E) is a gene that represents one city.
- **Genotype**
    - The **genotype** is the internal representation of the solution.
    - For TSP, the genotype is the sequence of cities in the order they are visited. In this case, it could be represented as an ordered list or array, such as [A, C, D, B, E].
- **Phenotype**
    - The **phenotype** is the **expressed version** of the genotype, that is, what the solution looks like in the real world.
    - For TSP, the phenotype could be visualized as a **route on a map**, showing the path connecting the cities in the order specified by the genotype.

- **Initialization**
  - **Initialization** refers to creating an initial population of chromosomes to start the genetic algorithm.
  - For TSP, this is done by generating random permutations of the cities to create a **diverse initial population**. For instance, different chromosomes such as [A, C, B, D, E] and [D, A, B, E, C] could be used as starting points.
- **Selection**
  - **Selection** is the process of choosing parent chromosomes from the current population to generate offspring.
  - For TSP, the selection is based on the **fitness** of each chromosome, where fitter solutions (shorter total travel distances) are more likely to be selected for reproduction. Common selection methods include **roulette wheel** and **tournament selection.**
- **Crossover**
  - **Crossover** is the process of combining two parent chromosomes to produce offspring.
  - For TSP, special types of crossover, such as **ordered crossover (OX)** or **partially mapped crossover (PMX)**, are used to create offspring while preserving valid sequences of cities. The goal is to inherit parts of the route from both parents to potentially create a better solution.
- **Mutation**
  - **Mutation** introduces small random changes in the chromosome to maintain genetic diversity and explore new parts of the solution space.
  - In TSP, a common mutation operation is **swap mutation**, where two cities in the chromosome are randomly swapped (for example, swapping cities C and E in [A, C, D, B, E] to get [A, E, D, B, C]). Mutation helps prevent the algorithm from getting stuck in local optima.
- **Fitness**
  - **Fitness** is a measure of how good a solution (chromosome) is.
  - For TSP, the fitness is usually the **inverse of the total travel distance** (since the goal is to minimize the distance). A shorter route will have a higher fitness value, making it more desirable.
- **Generation**
  - **Generation** refers to one complete iteration of the genetic algorithm, where a new set of potential solutions (routes) is created from the existing population through genetic operators such as selection, crossover, and mutation.

The following shows what a **generation** entails in the context of TSP:

- **Fitness Evaluation**: In each generation, all the **chromosomes** (routes) in the population are evaluated based on their **fitness**. For TSP, the fitness of each chromosome is often determined by the **total travel distance**, with shorter distances having higher fitness.
- **Selection**: Based on their fitness, a set of **parent chromosomes** is selected from the current population. Chromosomes with higher fitness are more likely to be selected, representing better solutions for creating the next generation of routes.
- **Crossover**: Selected parents undergo **crossover** to produce new **offspring**. For TSP, this could mean combining two parents to create a new route that hopefully inherits good characteristics from both. This ensures diversity in the search space, potentially leading to better solutions.
- **Mutation**: After crossover, **mutation** is applied to some offspring to introduce variability. Mutation helps in exploring new parts of the solution space that may not be reached by crossover alone, preventing premature convergence to suboptimal solutions.
- **Replacement**: A new **population** is formed by replacing some or all of the previous generation's chromosomes with newly created offspring. Depending on the GA strategy, the best solutions from the previous generation might also be retained (known as **elitism**).
- **Repeat**: The new population then undergoes the same process: fitness evaluation, selection, crossover, and mutation, forming the next generation.

Each **generation** represents an incremental improvement in finding the optimal route to solve TSP. As the genetic algorithm evolves through multiple generations, the solutions are expected to converge toward a shorter and more optimal route for visiting all cities.

- **Early Generations**: These may consist of poorly optimized, random routes since the population is just beginning to evolve.
- **Middle Generations**: The routes start to improve as better chromosomes are selected, and crossover and mutation help refine the solution.
- **Later Generations**: Ideally, the population begins to converge towards an optimal or near-optimal solution, representing an efficient route with minimal travel distance.

The goal is that with each new **generation**, the overall fitness of the population improves, and the genetic algorithm gets closer to solving the TSP optimally or achieving a good approximation. The process continues until a specified number of generations is reached, or a satisfactory solution is found.

Next, we will download the dataset from TSPLib, a well-known library, and apply GA-based machine learning and deep learning.

TSPlib

TSPlib is a well-known library of sample instances for the **Traveling Salesman Problem (TSP)** and related combinatorial optimization problems. It serves as a benchmark dataset for researchers to test, compare, and validate algorithms developed for TSP and other related problems. It was introduced in the early 1990s by **Gerhard Reinelt** as a standard repository to facilitate consistent experimentation in the field of optimization. TSPlib has played a vital role in advancing research in combinatorial optimization and is particularly influential in TSP studies. It offers a standardized set of problem instances that facilitate the development and benchmarking of new algorithms. TSPlib enables researchers to test their algorithms under consistent conditions, leading to better methods for solving real-world optimization problems, particularly in routing and logistics.

Key Features of TSPlib

- **Collection of Problem Instances:**
    - TSPlib contains a diverse collection of TSP instances with varying levels of complexity, including both symmetric and asymmetric TSPs. It also includes instances for related problems such as the **Vehicle Routing Problem (VRP)** and the **Hamiltonian Cycle Problem (HCP)**.
    - The TSP instances are often based on real-world data, such as city coordinates, road distances, or synthetic data that simulate different optimization challenges. Some popular instances are **berlin52**, **eil51**, and **att532**, where the number denotes the number of cities.
- **Symmetric vs. Asymmetric TSP:**
    - **Symmetric TSP (STSP)**: The distance between any two cities is the same in both directions. Most of the instances in TSPlib are symmetric, meaning the distance matrix is mirrored.
    - **Asymmetric TSP (ATSP)**: The distance from city A to city B may not be equal to the distance from city B to city A. ATSP instances are also included in the library, representing scenarios such as one-way streets or different costs in each direction.
- **Data Representation:**
    - TSPlib problem instances are provided in a standardized text format that defines the number of nodes (cities), distances between them, and sometimes additional information such as edge weights.

- The format includes metadata such as `NAME`, `TYPE`, `COMMENT`, `DIMENSION`, `EDGE_WEIGHT_TYPE`, and so on, making it easy for researchers to parse the data and apply their optimization algorithms.

- **Standard Benchmark for Comparison**:
  - TSPlib has become a de facto standard for comparing TSP algorithms, such as genetic algorithms, ant colony optimization, simulated annealing, and branch-and-bound techniques. The availability of well-known instances allows researchers to compare the performance of different methods on the same problems.
- **Problem Sizes**:
  - The instances in TSPlib range from small problems with **10-20 cities** to large, challenging problems with **thousands of cities**, such as **pr2392**, which contains 2,392 cities.
  - This range makes TSPlib suitable for both evaluating new algorithms in their early stages on smaller instances and testing their scalability on large, complex instances.
- **Optimal Solutions**:
  - For many of the instances, the **optimal solutions** are known, which makes it possible to compare an algorithm's solution quality against the best-known solution.
  - This helps in evaluating the efficiency of heuristics and approximate algorithms when solving NP-hard problems such as TSP.
- **Widely Used in Research:**
  - TSPlib has been instrumental in the development of optimization heuristics and exact algorithms for TSP. The library's problem instances are used extensively in academic papers, theses, and optimization challenges.

Example of Using TSPlib:

- **Accessing an Instance**: Researchers typically access an instance from TSPlib, which provides the coordinates or distances between cities. For example, the **berlin52** instance defines 52 cities in Berlin with their respective coordinates.
- **Algorithm Application**: An algorithm (for example, genetic algorithm) can be implemented to solve the TSP using berlin52. The coordinates are used to calculate the distance matrix, and the algorithm seeks to minimize the total distance.
- **Comparative Analysis**: The results (that is, the route found and its total distance) are compared against the known optimal solution for berlin52 to evaluate the algorithm's performance.

Related Problems in TSPlib:

Apart from TSP, TSPlib also contains instances for related problems, such as:

- **Vehicle Routing Problem (VRP)**: Where multiple vehicles are used to visit the nodes, and the goal is to minimize the total route cost while respecting vehicle capacities.
- **Hamiltonian Cycle Problem (HCP)**: Finding a cycle that visits each vertex exactly once and returns to the starting point.

Real-World Applications of TSPlib Instances:

- TSPlib's instances are often derived from **geographical** or **logistical data**, which can be directly related to real-world routing problems faced by delivery companies, city planners, and logistics firms.
- For example, instances based on **European cities** or **network design** provide a practical foundation for testing algorithms in scenarios that resemble actual logistical challenges.

TSP Experimentation

We will conduct 5 experiments, and finally, by integrating these elements, we will efficiently search for high-quality solutions to the TSP, leveraging both exploitation and exploration to avoid local optima and aim for the global optimum.

Experiment 1

The first code in the book *Chapter* 4, uses a **genetic algorithm** to solve the **Traveling Salesman Problem (TSP)** for the **Berlin52** dataset. It first loads the dataset, calculates the distance matrix, and initializes a population of random routes. The fitness function evaluates each route by calculating the total distance, and selection is based on probability proportional to fitness scores.

The **genetic operations** include:

1. **Selection**: Choose parents based on their fitness.
2. **Crossover**: Create offspring by combining segments from two parents.
3. **Mutation**: Introduce variability by swapping cities within a route with a certain mutation rate.

The algorithm evolves the population over a set number of generations, applying elitism (keeping the best routes), crossover, and mutation to create new generations. After running for 500 generations, the **best route** found is plotted to visualize the solution.

Final Best Distance: 8758.27633749122

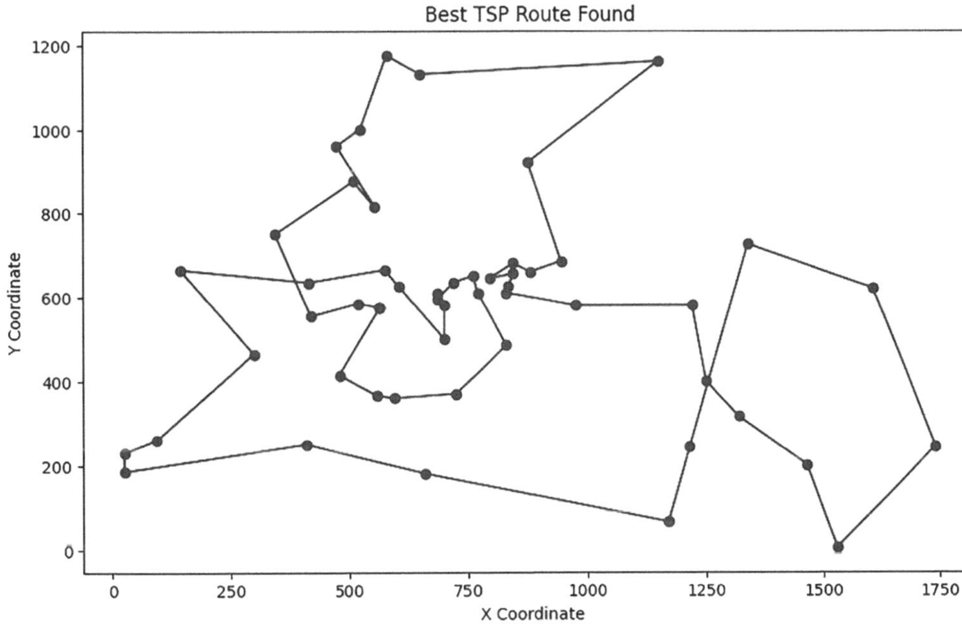

Figure 4.1: *The image illustrates the path of a travelling salesman*

Experiment 2

The second code in the *Chapter* 4 notebook applies a genetic algorithm to solve the Traveling Salesman Problem (TSP) using the PyGAD library, specifically for the Berlin52 dataset. The dataset is loaded, and a distance matrix is calculated for all city pairs. The GA starts with a population of random routes, where each route is represented as a chromosome (list of cities in a certain order).

The fitness function calculates the total distance of a route, with fitness being the negative of the distance since the goal is to minimize it. A tournament selection is used to choose parents, and two-point crossover and random mutation operators are used to evolve the population over 50 generations. The best route found and its distance is displayed, and Matplotlib and Seaborn are used to visualize the best route and the evolution of the fitness over generations as follows.

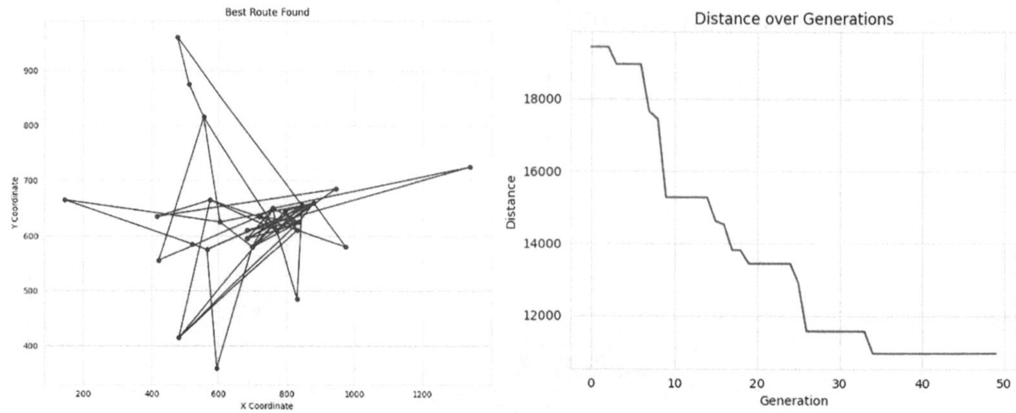

Figure 4.2: *The image illustrates the path of a travelling salesman, and on the right, distance over time, 50 generations*

Best Ever Distance = 10955.501285078455

Experiment 3

The third code in the *Chapter* 4 notebook uses a genetic algorithm to solve the Traveling Salesman Problem (TSP) using the Berlin52 dataset, a classic benchmark problem in combinatorial optimization. The dataset is loaded by reading a compressed file containing city coordinates, and the Euclidean distance between each pair of cities is calculated to form the distance matrix. The fitness function is defined to calculate the total distance of a given route, which the genetic algorithm seeks to minimize. The GA is implemented using the pygad library, with parameters such as population size, crossover probability, mutation rate, and the number of generations configured. Genetic operators such as tournament selection, two-point crossover, and swap mutation are used to evolve the population over generations, aiming to find the shortest possible route that visits all cities exactly once.

After running the GA, the best solution found is printed, showing the optimal route and its distance. The code also includes visualizations: one to display the route found by the GA, and another to show the evolution of the fitness (that is, the total distance) across generations, indicating how the algorithm converges towards an optimal solution. These visualizations help demonstrate the progress of the genetic algorithm in solving the TSP and provide insight into how well the solution improves over time as follows.

Best Ever Distance = 12317.52667708653

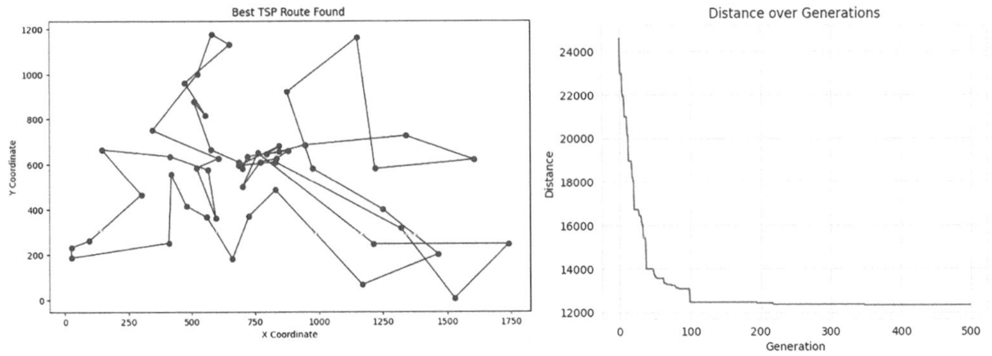

Figure 4.3: *The image illustrates the improved path of a travelling salesman, and on the right, distance over time for 500 generations*

Experiment 4

In this code, a GA is implemented to solve the TSP using the Berlin52 dataset, and the exploration-exploitation trade-off is tracked throughout the GA run. The TSP data is loaded from a compressed file, and the distance matrix is calculated between nodes (cities) using Euclidean distance. The goal of the GA is to minimize the total distance, which is represented as a fitness function that returns the negative of the total travel distance for a given solution (route). The algorithm runs for a maximum of 500 generations, with each generation involving crossover, mutation, and selection to create a new population of potential solutions.

The key aspect of this code is the tracking of exploration and exploitation. Exploration refers to searching new areas of the solution space to find better solutions, while exploitation focuses on improving current solutions. A threshold is used to determine whether the GA should continue exploring or switch to exploiting promising solutions. The **`on_generation`** callback tracks whether the fitness improves from one generation to the next. If there is an improvement, the algorithm shifts to exploitation; if not, it switches back to exploration. This behavior is tracked using **`exploration_count`** and **`exploitation_count`** to visualize the exploration vs. exploitation ratio over generations, helping to assess how the algorithm balances discovering new solutions and refining existing ones. Finally, the best route found and the fitness evolution are visualized to show the progress of the algorithm over time.

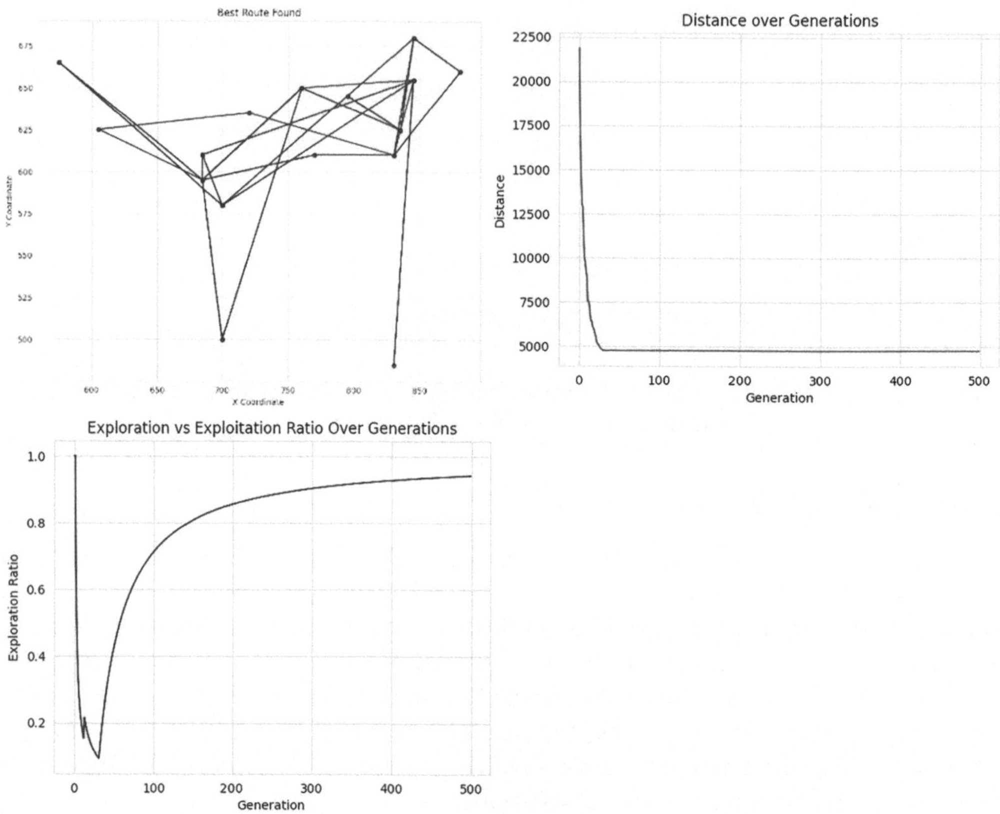

Figure 4.4: *The last plot indicates that the genetic algorithm is not transitioning effectively from exploration to exploitation, leading to a lack of convergence*

Experiment 5

The second code uses a **genetic algorithm** with **PyGAD** to solve the **Traveling Salesman Problem (TSP)** for the **Berlin52** dataset. The dataset is loaded and parsed to obtain the city coordinates, and a **distance matrix** is calculated using **Euclidean distance**.

The genetic algorithm is configured with a custom **fitness function** to evaluate each route based on the total travel distance, which the GA attempts to minimize. Custom **crossover** (Order Crossover) and **mutation** functions are implemented to generate new offspring and introduce diversity, respectively.

The GA is run for **500 generations**, and the **best route** found is plotted using **Matplotlib** to visualize the optimal path connecting all cities. The code also prints the **best fitness** (inverse of the total distance) and the **best total distance** after running the GA.

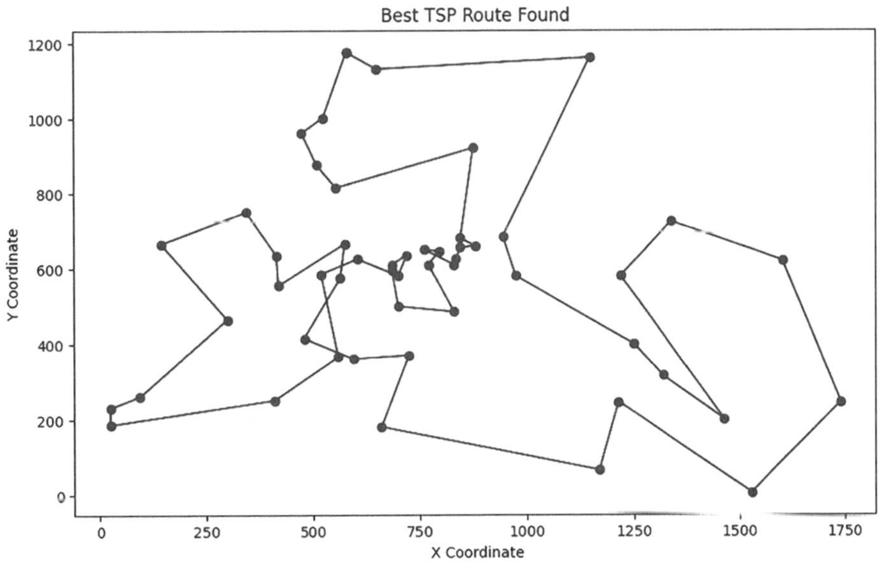

Figure 4.5: The image illustrates the path of an improved travelling salesman

Best Distance: 9357.894621107172

1. **Initial Population (Exploration)**
    - **Diverse Starting Points**: The initial population is generated by creating random permutations of city indices:

```
def create_initial_population(sol_per_pop, num_genes):
    initial_population = []
    for _ in range(sol_per_pop):
        individual = list(range(num_genes))
        random.shuffle(individual)
        initial_population.append(individual)
    return np.array(initial_population)
```

    - **Effect**: This randomization ensures that the GA starts with a diverse set of solutions, promoting the exploration of different regions in the solution space.

2. **Fitness Function (Guiding Exploitation)**
    - **Objective Evaluation**: The fitness function evaluates the total distance of each route and inversely relates it to fitness:

```
def fitness_func(ga_instance, solution, solution_idx):
    # Calculates total_distance and returns fitness = 1 / total_
distance
```

    - **Effect**: By assigning higher fitness scores to shorter routes, the GA is guided to exploit areas of the solution space that lead to better (shorter) tours.

3. **Selection Process (Exploitation)**

   - **Parent Selection Type**: The GA uses **steady-state selection** (**parent_selection_type="sss"**), favoring the selection of fitter individuals for reproduction.
   - **Elitism**: The parameter **keep_elitism=2** ensures that the top 2 individuals are carried over to the next generation unchanged.
   - **Effect**: This process exploits the best solutions found so far, ensuring that high-quality genetic material is preserved and propagated.

4. **Crossover Operation (Both Exploitation and Exploration)**

   - **Custom Crossover Function**: Implements **Order Crossover (OX)** suitable for TSP:

   ```
   def crossover_func(parents, offspring_size, ga_instance):
       # Combines genetic material from two parents to create 
   offspring
   ```

   - **Exploitation Aspect**: By combining segments from the best parents, the GA exploits existing good solutions to create potentially better offspring.
   - **Exploration Aspect**: Crossover introduces new gene combinations, allowing the GA to explore new solutions that were not present in the parent population.

5. **Mutation Operation (Exploration)**

   - **Custom Mutation Function**: Performs swap mutations on the offspring:

Python

   ```
   def mutation_func(offspring, ga_instance):
       # Swaps two cities in the route with a certain probability
   ```

   - **Effect**: Mutation introduces random alterations, enabling the exploration of new areas in the solution space and maintaining genetic diversity.

6. **Genetic Algorithm Parameters (Balancing Exploitation and Exploration)**

   - **Mutation Probability**: Set to 0.01, balancing the introduction of new genetic variations without disrupting the convergence process.
   - **Number of Generations**: Running for 500 generations allows sufficient time for the GA to exploit good solutions and explore new ones.
   - **Population Size**: A size of 100 ensures a diverse pool of individuals for both exploitation and exploration.

7. **Overall Balance**

   - **Exploitation**: Achieved through selection pressure favoring fitter individuals, elitism preserving the best solutions, and crossover combining good traits.

- **Exploration**: Maintained via mutation introducing variability, diverse initial population, and crossover generating new gene sequences.

The code effectively applies both exploitation and exploration through:

- **Selection and Elitism**: Favoring and preserving the best solutions to exploit known good areas.
- **Crossover and Mutation**: Introducing new genetic combinations and random variations to explore the solution space.
- **Parameter Tuning**: Balancing mutation rates, population size, and the number of generations to ensure neither exploitation nor exploration dominates excessively.

By integrating these elements, the GA searches efficiently for high-quality solutions to the TSP, leveraging the strengths of both exploitation and exploration to avoid local optima and strive towards the global optimum.

In the next section, we will solve an insurance fraud problem using the Connected graph and GA.

Fraud Analytics

Fraud analytics is an area that leverages advanced techniques to detect fraudulent activities by analyzing complex relationships between entities. Graph analytics plays a significant role in this domain, where data is represented as a graph with nodes and edges. In the context of fraud detection, nodes typically represent entities such as individuals, accounts, or transactions, while edges represent relationships between these entities, such as money transfers or shared addresses. By analyzing the structure of these connections, patterns of fraudulent behavior can be identified effectively, helping to uncover hidden relationships that might indicate fraud.

The dataset "**`advanced synthetic accident data`**" contains information on accidents, with columns such as **`AccidentID`**, **`CarID`**, **`Driver`**, **`Passengers`**, **`Witness`**, **`DateOfAccident`**, and **`Location`**.

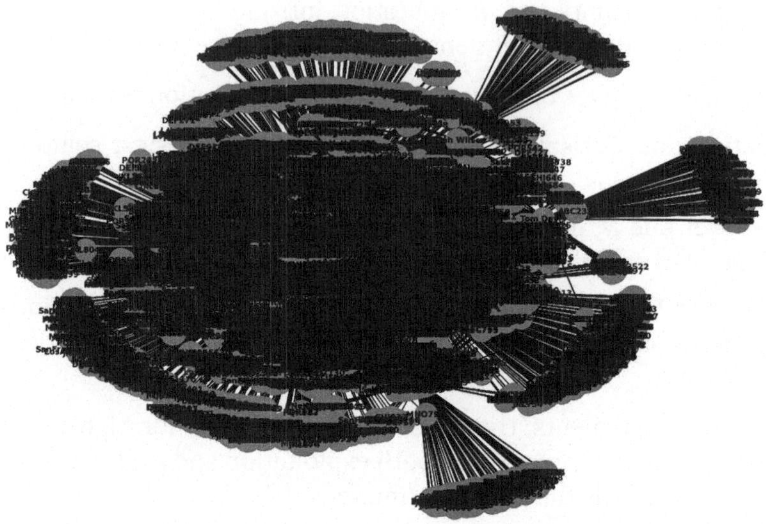

Figure 4.6: *The image illustrates a dense network graph from the fraud dataset, showing clusters of patterns; refer to the code for a better view*

You can use this code to generate a network graph, the code can be found in **Chapter_4_fraud.ipynb**

```
import pandas as pd
import networkx as nx
import matplotlib.pyplot as plt

# Load the dataset
file_path = '/content/sample_data/advanced_synthetic_accident_data.
xlsx'
df = pd.read_excel(file_path, sheet_name='Sheet1')

# Construct the graph
G = nx.Graph()

# Add nodes for unique entities in the dataset
for _, row in df.iterrows():
    G.add_node(row['AccidentID'], type='accident')
    G.add_node(row['CarID'], type='car')
    G.add_node(row['Driver'], type='driver')
    G.add_node(row['Passenger1'], type='passenger')
    G.add_node(row['Passenger2'], type='passenger')
    G.add_node(row['Witness'], type='witness')

    # Add edges between nodes to represent relationships
    G.add_edge(row['Driver'], row['CarID'], relationship='driver_
of')
```

```
    G.add_edge(row['Driver'], row['AccidentID'], relationship='
involved_in')
    G.add_edge(row['Passenger1'], row['AccidentID'], relationship
='involved_in')
    G.add_edge(row['Passenger2'], row['AccidentID'], relationship
='involved_in')
    G.add_edge(row['Witness'], row['AccidentID'], relationship
='witness_of')

# Draw the graph to visualize it
plt.figure(figsize=(12, 8))
nx.draw(G, with_labels=True, node_size=500, font_size=8, font_
weight='bold')
plt.show()
```

Application of Genetics Algorithm to Fraud Detection

To apply a Genetic Algorithm (GA) for fraud detection using a graph representation, you can proceed as follows:

Steps to Implement Genetic Algorithm for Fraud Detection

1. **Graph Representation:**
   - **Nodes:** Represent entities such as Driver, Passenger1, Passenger2, CarID, and Witness. Each entity can be a node in the graph.
   - **Edges:** Represent relationships between these entities. For instance, an edge between Driver and `CarID` represents the association of the driver with a vehicle, and edges between Passenger and `AccidentID` represent their involvement in an accident.
2. **Constructing the Graph:**
   - Use a graph-based library such as NetworkX to create a graph where each entity in the dataset is a node and the relationships are edges.
   - Label edges with information such as accident date, type of relationship (for example, driver-of, witness-of), and so on.
3. **Feature Engineering:**
   - Extract graph features such as the degree centrality of nodes, clustering coefficients, and betweenness centrality, which may indicate potentially fraudulent activity if nodes are highly connected or form unusual patterns.
   - Compute similarity between different nodes or detect subgraphs that frequently occur in fraudulent claims.

4. **Genetic Algorithm for Fraud Detection:**
    - **Chromosome Representation:** Each chromosome can represent a subset of relationships or a set of rules to identify suspicious patterns (for example, high connectivity of a witness to multiple accidents).
    - **Population Initialization:** Generate an initial population of potential fraud detection rules. These could be patterns such as "*a driver involved in multiple accidents within a short timeframe with different passengers.*"
    - **Fitness Function:** Define a fitness function to evaluate the chromosomes. A good fitness function could be one that maximizes the detection of known fraudulent cases while minimizing false positives.
    - Selection, Crossover, Mutation:
        - Use selection to pick the best-performing chromosomes based on the fitness function.
        - Apply crossover to combine parts of two chromosomes, potentially finding better patterns.
        - Use mutation to introduce random changes, helping to explore a wider solution space.
5. **Evaluation and Iteration:**
    - Evaluate the evolved rules on a validation set to determine their effectiveness in identifying fraud.
    - Iterate the process to refine the rules, ultimately aiming to develop a set of rules that can generalize well to new, unseen data.

In the context of using Genetic Algorithms (GAs) for fraud detection, a **chromosome representation** is a way of encoding potential solutions to the problem you are trying to solve, which is identifying fraud in this case.

A **chromosome** in GAs is a data structure that represents a candidate solution to the problem. It is typically represented as an array (or vector) of parameters, values, or rules that describe a potential solution.

In this case, the fraud detection problem using a graph involves identifying suspicious patterns or relationships between entities (for example, drivers, cars, passengers, witnesses). Each chromosome can be used to represent these patterns or subsets of relationships.

Chromosome Representation for Fraud Detection

- **Relationships as Genes:**
    - Each **gene** in a chromosome represents a particular type of relationship or pattern in the graph.

- For example, genes might represent relationships such as "*Driver is linked to more than one AccidentID within a short period*" or "A *Witness is linked to multiple accidents involving the same CarID*."
- A chromosome, therefore, is a combination of multiple genes, each specifying a particular aspect of these relationships.

- **Example of a Chromosome:**
  - Let us say you have a graph where each node represents an entity (Driver, Witness, Car, Accident, and so on), and edges represent their relationships.
  - A chromosome could be represented as:
    - **Gene 1**: A rule that finds Drivers involved in more than 3 accidents within a year.
    - **Gene 2**: A rule that identifies Witnesses linked to more than 5 accidents (high connectivity).
    - **Gene 3**: A rule that flags Passengers who were involved in accidents with more than one different driver.

The entire chromosome represents a potential detection strategy that combines these rules, and the effectiveness of this chromosome can be evaluated based on how well it identifies known fraud cases.

- **High Connectivity Example:**
  - In the graph, a **witness with high connectivity** means that a particular witness node is linked to multiple accident nodes.
  - High connectivity might indicate that this person is suspicious if they frequently appear as a witness in different accidents, especially if the accidents involve different vehicles and drivers.
  - A chromosome can capture this type of pattern by having a gene that represents a threshold for the number of connections (witnesses involved in more than X accidents).

Genetic Algorithm Uses Chromosomes for Fraud Detection:

- **Population:** The GA starts with a population of chromosomes, where each chromosome represents a different set of potential rules or relationships to detect fraud.
- **Fitness Evaluation:** Each chromosome is evaluated based on its **fitness**, which in this case could be how accurately the set of rules identifies fraudulent behavior. The fitness function might consider factors like:
  - Number of fraudulent cases correctly identified (true positives).
  - Number of legitimate cases incorrectly flagged as fraud (false positives).

- **Selection, Crossover, and Mutation:**
  - **Selection:** Chromosomes with better fitness are more likely to be selected to pass their "genes" to the next generation.
  - **Crossover:** Combines parts of two chromosomes to create new offspring. For example, part of a rule for identifying drivers could be combined with part of a rule for witnesses, potentially discovering new patterns.
  - **Mutation:** Introduces random changes to some genes, allowing the algorithm to explore new solutions and avoid being stuck in local optima.

By representing relationships and patterns within the graph as chromosomes, the GA evolves over time to find effective combinations of rules that can help identify fraudulent activities.

Neural Network Implementation of Fraud

The code in the notebook, Chapter 4_fraud,ipynb uses several major Python libraries to implement a genetic algorithm for optimizing a neural network aimed at detecting fraud based on synthetic accident data. The code primarily relies on pandas for data manipulation, NumPy for numerical operations, PyGAD for the genetic algorithm, and PyTorch for handling neural network calculations and GPU acceleration. The dataset is preprocessed by removing non-numeric columns, converting categorical variables into dummy variables, and scaling numerical features with StandardScaler. The data is then split into training and testing sets and further converted into tensors suitable for GPU computation using PyTorch.

The genetic algorithm is implemented using PyGAD to optimize the weights of a simple feedforward neural network. The genetic algorithm evolves a population of candidate solutions (representing weights) over a specified number of generations, attempting to maximize the accuracy of predictions on training data. The fitness function evaluates each solution by computing the forward pass of the neural network and assessing the accuracy of the predictions. The model architecture involves two hidden layers, each with a ReLU activation function, and a final output layer. Throughout the process, the code also uses callbacks to track the accuracy of the best solution in each generation, and plots the evolution of accuracy over time to visualize the progress of the genetic optimization with Test Accuracy: 0.48625180897250364 and Fitness after 200 generations is Fitness = 0.6157742402315485

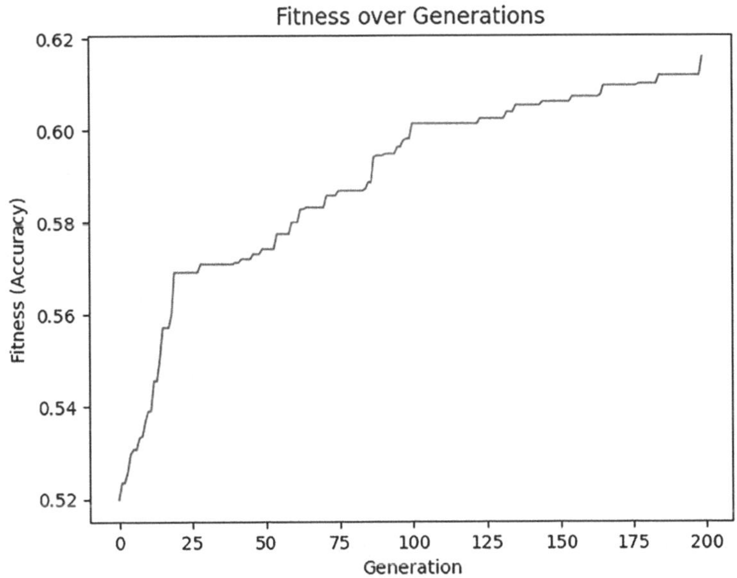

Figure 4.7: *The image illustrates fitness scores over time for 200 generations*

Conclusion

Genetic algorithms provide versatile and powerful methods for solving complex optimization problems such as the Traveling Salesman Problem and enhancing fraud detection systems. By mimicking evolutionary processes, they efficiently search through vast solution spaces to find optimal or near-optimal solutions. This approach is especially valuable in fields that require sophisticated optimization techniques, such as machine learning, logistics, and financial modeling. Genetic algorithms adaptively refine solutions over generations, balancing exploration and exploitation to avoid local optima. Their ability to handle large-scale, nonlinear, and multi-dimensional problems makes them a crucial tool for advancing research and practical applications in various domains.

Next, we will explore the foundations of evolutionary algorithms to further understand their principles and applications.

Chapter 5
Foundation of Evolutionary Algorithms

Introduction

Evolutionary computation is a branch of artificial intelligence inspired by natural evolution, utilizing principles such as selection, mutation, and reproduction to solve complex computational problems. This field can be broadly categorized into two main branches: life simulation and genetic simulation. Life simulation techniques, such as Particle Swarm Optimization and Swarm Intelligence, mimic the collective behavior of biological entities such as birds or insects to explore and optimize search spaces effectively. The Dual-Phase Evolution concept further enhances the optimization process by integrating multiple evolutionary stages to improve convergence and solution quality. These life-inspired methods are valuable for solving optimization problems that require adaptive exploration of large solution spaces.

In this chapter, we will explore the **basic concepts of Evolutionary Algorithms (EAs)**, starting with an overview of what EAs are and the different types that fall under this category. **Evolutionary Algorithms** are optimization techniques inspired by the principles of natural evolution, and we will look into various forms such as **Genetic Algorithms (GAs)**, **Ant Colony Optimization (ACO)**, **Particle Swarm Optimization (PSO)**, and **Differential Evolution (DE)**.

We will also compare **Genetic Algorithms** with other types of EAs to understand their key differences in methods and performance. By using toy examples, we will gain a deeper understanding of each type of EA–how they work and how they can be applied to solve optimization problems. Finally, we will highlight the differences between GAs and other EAs to better understand which methods are most effective in specific situations. This comparison will help us identify the strengths and weaknesses of different evolutionary approaches and determine their suitability for various optimization challenges.

Structure

This chapter is structured as follows:

- Evolutionary Computation
- Basic Concepts of Evolutionary Algorithms
    - Evolutionary Algorithm and Types
    - Classical Evolutionary Algorithms
    - Advanced Evolutionary Algorithms
    - Deep Evolutionary Algorithms
- Genetic Algorithms vs. Evolutionary Algorithms
- Particle Swarm Optimization (PSO)
    - Theory
    - Library
    - Applying Particle Swarm Optimization (PSO) to Price Optimization
    - Simulation
    - Toy Story
    - Results

Evolutionary Computation

This field employs a diverse range of algorithms and methodologies based on evolutionary principles, making it a versatile tool for optimization, problem-solving, and modeling complex systems. The diagram presents the various branches of evolutionary computation, categorizing them broadly into life simulation and genetic simulation, each encompassing a unique approach to mimicking biological processes in a computational setting.

The first branch of evolutionary computation, **life simulation**, includes algorithms that aim to simulate natural behavior and decision-making observed in living organisms. Key examples include **Particle Swarm Optimization (PSO)** and **Swarm Intelligence**. These approaches are inspired by the collective behavior of animals, such as bird flocking and fish schooling, and are useful in addressing optimization problems by exploring the search space collectively. This category also includes concepts such as **Dual-Phase Evolution**, which combines different stages of evolutionary processes to improve the overall optimization and learning process.

On the other hand, **genetic simulation** forms the second significant branch of evolutionary computation, focusing on reproducing biological evolution through mechanisms akin to genetic variation and selection. This branch includes **Genetic**

Programming (GP) and **Genetic Algorithms (GA)**, which are some of the earliest and most widely recognized methods of evolutionary computation. Genetic programming deals with evolving computer programs to solve tasks, while genetic algorithms use a more generic representation for optimization. An extension of this branch is **Gene Expression Programming (GEP)**, which aims to improve the ability to discover efficient solutions by evolving more flexible structures.

Further subdivisions, such as **Genetic and Evolutionary Programming**, emphasize blending various evolutionary techniques to combine the strengths of each method, resulting in a hybrid that is particularly effective for specific problem domains. The integration of **Genetic Algorithms/Evolutionary Algorithms** provides a broader framework, which often encompasses multiple evolutionary strategies to enhance adaptability and problem-solving abilities.

As we explore these branches and subfields, we find that evolutionary computation provides a wide toolkit for addressing problems that are otherwise challenging for conventional techniques. This chapter will delve deeper into each of these areas, highlighting the unique contributions and applications of **Particle Swarm Optimization**, **Swarm Intelligence**, **Genetic Programming**, and more, to illustrate how evolutionary principles have shaped computational intelligence.

Basic Concepts of Evolutionary Algorithms

If you recall from *Chapter 1, Introduction to Genetic Algorithms*, the following process described also looks like the execution of a **genetic algorithm**, which is a type of **evolutionary algorithm**.

Figure 5.1: *The evolution of mankind*

Evolutionary algorithms, in general, are optimization techniques inspired by biological evolution, and **genetic algorithms** are one of the most common forms. We will look into more details in the upcoming sections.

Evolutionary algorithms typically share the following components, which are reflected in the diagram in *Chapter 1, Introduction to Genetic Algorithms, Figure 1.7, The Execution process of* GA.

- **Population of individuals (solutions)**
- **Fitness evaluation** based on an objective function
- **Selection** of the fittest individuals
- **Crossover (recombination)** of selected individuals to produce new offspring
- **Mutation** to introduce diversity
- **Iteration over generations** to improve the solutions

Let us do a quick recap.

1. **Initialize First Population**
   - **Population**: A collection of potential solutions to the problem. Each solution is represented as a **vector** (or individual). These vectors are denoted as $p^1, p^2, \ldots, p^n$. Each vector contains a set of **parameters** (for example, $p^1_{1.}$ $p^1_{2.}$ $p^1_{3.}$ .... $p^1_{n.}$) that define the candidate's solution.
   - These parameters could represent different variables in the problem (such as dimensions in a search space).
   - The population size N refers to the number of solutions, and each vector (solution) is initialized randomly.
2. **Evaluate the Population with the Objective Function**
   - Each individual (vector) in the population is evaluated using a fitness function (objective function) that measures how "*good*" or "*fit*" the individual is in solving the problem.
   - The result of this evaluation assigns a fitness score to each individual based on how well they perform the given task.
3. **Rank the Population and Keep the Best Individuals**
   - After evaluation, the population is ranked based on their fitness scores. The best-performing individuals are kept for the next phase, ensuring that strong candidates have a higher chance of passing on their "*genes*" (parameter values) to the next generation.

4. **Crossover and Recombination**
    - **Crossover** (or recombination) simulates the biological process of reproduction. Two selected individuals (parents) are combined to produce new offspring.
    - In the diagram, parts of vectors (genes from parents) are mixed together. For instance, elements from one parent ($p^1_{1,}$ $p^1_{2,}$) are combined with elements from another parent ($p^2_{1,}$ $p^2_{2,}$), resulting in a new offspring.
    - This process introduces **genetic diversity** by exchanging information between individuals.
5. **Mutation**
    - To maintain diversity and prevent premature convergence to suboptimal solutions, **mutation** is applied. This process randomly perturbs some parameters of the offspring (for example, p^2_2).
    - Mutation introduces slight variations by randomly changing the values of certain genes. In the diagram, this is shown by perturbing certain parameters, which ensures the algorithm continues to explore new areas of the search space.
6. **Form New Offspring/Population**
    - After crossover and mutation, a new generation of individuals (offspring) is formed. These offspring will replace the current population in the next iteration.
    - This new population will go through the same cycle (evaluation, ranking, crossover, mutation).
7. **Repeat for n Generations**
    - The process of evaluation, ranking, crossover, and mutation is repeated for a number of generations (iterations). Over successive generations, the algorithm refines the population, hopefully leading to better and better solutions.
    - After several generations, the best individuals in the population will likely be close to an optimal solution.
8. **Best Individuals**
    - At the end of the process (after several generations), the best individuals are selected. These individuals represent the best solutions found by the algorithm. They will have the highest fitness scores and are the most "**fit**" to solve the optimization problem.

Next, we discuss, classifying the evolutionary algorithms into three "**Classical**", "**Advanced**" and "**Deep**" categories.

Evolutionary Algorithm and Types

Evolutionary computation is an exciting and multidisciplinary area of study that draws inspiration from the process of natural evolution to solve complex computational problems. We can categorize evolutionary algorithms into **Classical Evolutionary Algorithms**, **Advanced Evolutionary Algorithms**, and **Deep Evolutionary Algorithms**. This structured approach highlights the evolutionary timeline and complexity of each algorithm.

- **Classical Evolutionary Algorithms:** Classical evolutionary algorithms form the foundation of evolutionary computation, inspired by biological processes such as natural selection and survival of the fittest. These methods, such as **Genetic Algorithms (GA)**, simulate evolution to solve optimization problems by creating a population of candidate solutions that evolve over time. The mathematical backbone of GAs, as covered in **Mathematical Models of Genetic Algorithms**, helps us understand the underlying dynamics of selection, crossover, and mutation. Similarly, **Evolutionary Programming (EP)** and **Evolution Strategies (ES)** emphasize adaptation and survival through mutation, without focusing on crossover. **Genetic Programming (GP)** extends these ideas to evolve entire programs and symbolic expressions, further demonstrating the wide applicability of classical methods. These algorithms set the stage for further developments in evolutionary computation, offering simple yet powerful techniques for solving a variety of optimization problems.
- **Advanced Evolutionary Algorithms:** As we move beyond the foundational approaches, we explore **Advanced Evolutionary Algorithms**, which build on classical techniques but incorporate newer, often bio-inspired, concepts to tackle more complex problems. For instance, **Ant Colony Optimization (ACO)** models the foraging behavior of ants to solve complex pathfinding and optimization tasks. **Particle Swarm Optimization (PSO)** simulates social behaviors such as bird flocking, where individuals in a population adjust their positions based on personal and group experiences. **Differential Evolution (DE)** focuses on evolving solutions for continuous optimization problems by introducing a unique mutation mechanism. Other advanced algorithms such as **Biogeography-Based Optimization (BBO)** and **Cultural Algorithms** leverage concepts from biogeography and sociology, respectively, to guide the search for optimal solutions. These advanced methods reflect the broadening scope of evolutionary algorithms, demonstrating their ability to adapt and evolve as new biological and social phenomena are discovered.
- **Deep Evolutionary Algorithms:** In the modern era, **Deep Evolutionary Algorithms** represent the convergence of evolutionary computation with deep learning and other complex, data-driven methodologies. These algorithms often operate in high-dimensional, non-convex problem spaces, making them suitable for challenges in machine learning, especially in neural

network optimization. One key example is the **Neuroevolution of Augmenting Topologies (NEAT)** algorithm, which evolves neural networks, optimizing both their weights and structures. In addition, techniques such as **Deep Neuroevolution** apply evolutionary strategies to train deep neural networks more efficiently than gradient-based methods in certain scenarios. The integration of deep learning and evolutionary strategies allows us to explore new frontiers in artificial intelligence, where evolutionary algorithms are adapted to optimize deep models for complex tasks such as image recognition and game-playing. By combining the strengths of both deep learning and evolutionary approaches, these algorithms offer new avenues for tackling increasingly sophisticated and high-dimensional problems in AI research.

Classical Evolutionary Algorithms

These are some of the original methods from evolutionary computation, focusing on using biologically inspired concepts such as selection, crossover, and mutation:

- **Genetic Algorithms (GA)**: One of the most well-known and earliest evolutionary algorithms, based on the process of natural selection and genetics.
- **Mathematical Models of Genetic Algorithms**: These models focus on the theoretical understanding and mathematical formalization of the mechanisms behind genetic algorithms.
- **Evolutionary Programming**: A method used for evolving programs or predicting systems without crossover, mainly emphasizing mutation and selection.
- **Evolution Strategies (ES)**: Focuses on optimization by simulating evolutionary processes, especially useful for continuous parameter optimization.
- **Genetic Programming (GP)**: A branch of genetic algorithms focused on evolving programs or symbolic structures to solve tasks automatically.
- **Evolutionary Algorithm Variations**: Includes various versions and modifications of the basic evolutionary algorithms to enhance performance or adapt to specific problem domains.

Advanced Evolutionary Algorithms

These methods extend, refine, or hybridize the classical techniques and incorporate newer mechanisms, often inspired by different biological or social phenomena.

- **Ant Colony Optimization (ACO)**: Inspired by the foraging behavior of ants, it is used for solving combinatorial optimization problems such as routing and scheduling.

- **Particle Swarm Optimization (PSO)**: Simulates social behavior, such as bird flocking, for optimization tasks by having a swarm of particles adjust their positions based on individual and group experiences.
- **Differential Evolution (DE)**: A method used primarily for continuous optimization problems, it works by evolving populations through mutation, crossover, and selection strategies.
- **Estimation of Distribution Algorithms (EDA)**: Rather than using crossover and mutation, EDA builds probabilistic models to sample new candidate solutions based on learned distribution patterns from the current population.
- **Biogeography-Based Optimization (BBO):** Inspired by the migration patterns and distribution of species across different geographical locations, it applies the principles of biogeography to optimization problems.
- **Cultural Algorithms:** These include a population and a belief space, where information is shared culturally to accelerate the search for an optimal solution.
- **Opposition-Based Learning**: Enhances traditional algorithms by considering opposite solutions during the search process, improving the exploration of the search space.

Other Evolutionary Algorithms

- **Tabu Search**: A metaheuristic that uses memory-based mechanisms to avoid cycling back to previous solutions.
- **Artificial Fish Swarm Algorithm**: Simulates fish swarm behavior to explore global and local optima.
- **Group Search Optimizer**: A technique inspired by group behavior of animals such as pack hunting.
- **Shuffled Frog Leaping Algorithm**: Inspired by the communication between frogs in search of food, combining memetic and genetic algorithms.
- **Firefly Algorithm**: Uses the flashing behavior of fireflies, where more attractive fireflies attract others, simulating optimization.
- **Bacterial Foraging Optimization**: Mimics the foraging behavior of bacteria, where movements in response to stimuli are applied to optimization.
- **Artificial Bee Colony Algorithm**: Inspired by the food-foraging behavior of honeybee swarms.
- **Gravitational Search Algorithm**: Simulates the law of gravity, where agents are attracted to each other based on their masses.
- **Harmony Search**: Mimics the musical improvisation process where musicians attempt to find harmony by adjusting tones.

- **Teaching-Learning-Based Optimization**: Inspired by the teaching-learning process in a classroom setting, improving individual learners' solutions based on the teacher's performance.

Deep Evolutionary Algorithms

This category includes approaches that combine evolutionary strategies with deep learning, focusing on optimizing neural networks and enhancing their structure:

- **Neuroevolution Optimization:** This approach evolves neural networks, adjusting weights and topologies to optimize performance across tasks, often used in reinforcement learning environments.
- **Evolutionary Convolutional Neural Networks**: Evolutionary algorithms are applied to Convolutional Neural Networks (CNNs) to optimize hyperparameters, architectures, and training parameters for deep learning applications such as image recognition.
- **Evolving Autoencoders**: Evolutionary algorithms optimize the structure and learning parameters of autoencoders, which are neural networks that learn unsupervised representations, often used in dimensionality reduction or generative models.
- **Generative Deep Learning and Evolution**: Evolutionary techniques are integrated with generative deep learning models to evolve architectures such as Generative Adversarial Networks (GANs) or Variational Autoencoders (VAEs) to improve the quality and diversity of generated outputs.
- **NeuroEvolution of Augmenting Topologies (NEAT)**: A specific algorithm that evolves both the weights and the topologies of neural networks, NEAT starts with simple networks and gradually evolves more complex structures, which have been successfully applied in control tasks and games.

Genetic Algorithms Versus Evolutionary Algorithms

Genetic Algorithms (GAs) and **Evolutionary Algorithms (EAs)** are both branches of evolutionary computation inspired by the mechanisms of natural selection and genetic processes. While the terms are often used interchangeably, they represent different scopes within the broader field of optimization techniques. Let us dive into the differences, similarities, and specific features that distinguish Genetic Algorithms from other types of Evolutionary Algorithms.

Definition and Scope

- **Evolutionary Algorithms (EAs)**: Evolutionary algorithms refer to a class of optimization techniques that utilize concepts derived from biological evolution, such as selection, mutation, recombination (crossover), and fitness evaluation. They form a broader family of algorithms that includes various specialized methods such as Genetic Algorithms, Evolutionary Strategies, Genetic Programming, and more.
- **Genetic Algorithms (GAs)**: Genetic Algorithms are a specific subset of EAs. They mimic the process of natural evolution more closely by focusing on the genetic representation of solutions, typically in the form of binary strings (though other representations such as real numbers are also possible). GAs use operators such as crossover and mutation to create new generations of potential solutions.

Representation of Solutions

- **Genetic Algorithms**: In GAs, candidate solutions are encoded as "*chromosomes*," which are most commonly represented using binary strings (0s and 1s). Each chromosome represents a potential solution to the problem, and its fitness is evaluated to determine how well it solves the problem at hand. The chromosomes can be thought of as an analogy to DNA, encoding the traits that determine solution quality.
- **Evolutionary Algorithms**: EAs, on the other hand, allow for more flexible representations. The solutions can be encoded as real-valued vectors, permutations, or other structures that suit the specific problem. This flexibility enables EAs to adapt their representations based on the characteristics of the optimization task, providing a more general framework.

Evolutionary Operators

- **Selection**: In both GAs and EAs, selection refers to the process of choosing individuals from the current population based on their fitness. The fitter individuals are more likely to be chosen for reproduction, akin to the "*survival of the fittest*" principle. Common methods include roulette wheel selection, tournament selection, and rank-based selection.
- **Crossover (Recombination)**:
    - In **GAs**, crossover is a central operator, where two parents combine their genetic information to produce offspring. Crossover aims to preserve and mix the good traits of parents, thereby improving the chances of generating better solutions. Types of crossover include one-point, two-point, and uniform crossover.

- In **EAs**, the use of crossover depends on the specific type of algorithm. In some evolutionary strategies, the focus is less on recombination and more on mutation. This means that while crossover may be used in GAs as a primary mechanism for exploration, its use in EAs can vary.

- **Mutation**: Mutation is a process used in both GAs and EAs to introduce small random changes in individuals, which helps maintain diversity in the population and prevents premature convergence. In GAs, mutation typically involves flipping bits in a binary representation. In EAs, mutation can take various forms, such as adding small perturbations to real-valued parameters.

Problem Domain and Applications

- **Genetic Algorithms**: GAs are well-suited to problems that can be easily encoded into binary strings or similar representations. They have been widely applied to optimization problems such as the **Traveling Salesman Problem (TSP)**, knapsack problems, scheduling, and more. GAs excel in problems where solutions can be evaluated relatively easily, but the search space is too large for brute-force methods.

- **Evolutionary Algorithms**: EAs have a broader application scope since they can be tailored to different problem domains by using customized representations and operators. Evolutionary Strategies (a type of EA) are particularly effective for continuous optimization problems, where the solution space is composed of real numbers. Evolutionary algorithms are often used in fields such as engineering design optimization, machine learning (hyperparameter tuning), and game development.

Algorithms	**Strengths**	**Weaknesses**
Genetic Algorithms	GAs are highly effective at exploring large, complex search spaces and avoiding local optima.	GAs rely heavily on crossover and can sometimes struggle with fine-tuning solutions. They may require higher computational resources due to the need to evaluate many generations of solutions.
	The use of crossover allows for the recombination of good traits, which can accelerate convergence toward high-quality solutions.	Representation constraints, such as binary encoding, can be inefficient for some problem domains.

Evolutionary Algorithms	EAs provide flexibility in representation and operators, making them adaptable to a wider range of optimization tasks.	The flexibility of EAs can lead to increased complexity in designing the algorithm for specific problems. Deciding on the representation and the appropriate operators may require domain expertise.
	They can use self-adaptive strategies, where mutation rates and other parameters evolve along with the solutions, allowing for more dynamic control.	EAs may suffer from slower convergence if they lack sufficient selection pressure or diversity.

***Table* 5.1**: GAs *versus* EAs

Diversity Maintenance and Convergence

- **Genetic Algorithms**: GAs often require explicit mechanisms to maintain diversity within the population to prevent premature convergence (that is, getting stuck in local optima). Methods such as maintaining mutation rates, using diversity-preserving selection techniques, or applying elitism (preserving the best individuals across generations) are commonly used.
- **Evolutionary Algorithms**: EAs generally focus on maintaining a balance between exploration (searching for new solutions) and exploitation (refining current solutions). Self-adaptive mutation rates or strategies such as fitness sharing can help EAs maintain diversity and avoid premature convergence. Additionally, some EAs implement a multi-objective optimization approach, balancing multiple goals, which inherently helps maintain diversity.

Both Genetic Algorithms and Evolutionary Algorithms are powerful tools for optimization, but they cater to different needs and problem types. GAs are best for problems where solutions can be represented in discrete forms, and combining good traits can significantly improve the outcome. EAs provide a more general framework, suitable for a wide variety of problems, from combinatorial to continuous optimization. Understanding the differences and strengths of each can help in selecting the appropriate algorithm based on the problem at hand. By leveraging evolutionary principles, both GAs and EAs enable effective exploration of complex search spaces, finding optimal or near-optimal solutions where traditional methods fail.

In addition to **Genetic Algorithms (GAs)**, **Evolutionary Strategies (ES)**, and **Genetic Programming (GP)**, there are several other types of evolutionary and nature-inspired algorithms, as discussed earlier, that fall under the umbrella of **evolutionary computation**. These include:

- **Differential Evolution (DE)**: A population-based optimization algorithm is particularly suited for continuous optimization problems. It involves the combination of different individuals from the population through vector arithmetic, which helps explore the solution space effectively.

- **Particle Swarm Optimization (PSO)**: Inspired by the social behavior of birds or fish, PSO uses a swarm of particles (solutions) to explore the search space. Each particle adjusts its position based on its own experience and that of neighboring particles, allowing for both individual and collective learning.
- **Ant Colony Optimization (ACO)**: Based on the behavior of real ants seeking the shortest path between their nest and a food source, ACO is used mainly for combinatorial optimization problems. The algorithm uses artificial ants to traverse the solution space and deposit pheromones, which help guide other ants towards promising solutions.
- **Estimation of Distribution Algorithms (EDAs)**: Instead of using traditional crossover and mutation operators, EDAs build probabilistic models of promising solutions and sample from these models to generate new candidates, enabling efficient exploration of the search space.
- **Memetic Algorithms (MAs)**: A hybrid approach that combines global evolutionary techniques with local search strategies. Often referred to as "*evolutionary algorithms with individual learning*," MAs leverage the strengths of both global exploration and fine-tuned optimization.
- **Artificial Immune System (AIS)**: Modeled after the human immune system, AIS applies principles such as clonal selection and immune network theory for solving optimization, classification, and anomaly detection problems. AIS algorithms maintain a diverse population of solutions, which makes them suitable for adaptive problem-solving.
- **Cultural Algorithms (CAs)**: CAs extend evolutionary algorithms by incorporating a "*belief space*" that maintains shared knowledge among individuals in the population. This additional component helps guide the search and allows for more efficient exploration.
- **Genetic and Evolutionary Programming (GEP)**: Combines elements of both Genetic Algorithms and Genetic Programming, evolving computer programs or symbolic expressions to solve specific problems. It is useful for problems where an analytical solution needs to be represented in a functional form.
- **Evolutionary Multi-Objective Optimization (EMO)**: Algorithms specifically designed to handle problems with multiple conflicting objectives. Examples include **NSGA-II** (Non-dominated Sorting Genetic Algorithm II) and **SPEA2** (Strength Pareto Evolutionary Algorithm 2), which maintain a set of optimal trade-offs (Pareto front) rather than a single solution.
- **Differential Evolutionary Programming (DEP)**: A variant that uses the principles of differential evolution within the context of genetic programming.

It aims to evolve better computer programs by applying mutations similar to differential evolution's approach.

- **Bee Algorithm**: Inspired by the foraging behavior of honeybees, Bee Algorithms mimic the process by which bees search for and exploit food sources. It involves "scout bees" exploring the search space and "*worker bees*" exploiting promising regions. This type of algorithm is effective for optimization tasks that require both exploration and exploitation to find high-quality solutions.
- **Firefly Algorithm**: The Firefly Algorithm is inspired by the flashing behavior of fireflies. It uses the idea that fireflies are attracted to one another based on the brightness of their flashes. In the optimization context, "*brightness*" is associated with the fitness of the solution, and the algorithm guides the swarm towards the best solution. This method is used for complex optimization tasks involving multi-modal functions.
- **Harmony Search (HS)**: Harmony Search is a music-inspired optimization algorithm where the process of seeking the best harmony among a set of musical instruments is likened to finding the optimal solution in a search space. It uses concepts such as memory consideration, pitch adjustment, and randomization to balance exploration and exploitation.
- **Bat Algorithm (BA)**: The Bat Algorithm is based on the echolocation behavior of bats, which they use to detect prey and navigate. It uses frequency tuning and varying loudness parameters to balance exploration and exploitation, making it effective for global optimization problems.
- **Cuckoo Search (CS)**: Inspired by the brood parasitism of cuckoo birds, this algorithm uses a population of candidate solutions (represented as cuckoo eggs) that compete to replace the solutions in a host population. It uses Lévy flights to explore the search space, which allows it to efficiently avoid local optima.
- **Flower Pollination Algorithm (FPA)**: The Flower Pollination Algorithm is inspired by the pollination process of flowering plants. It combines global and local pollination strategies to solve optimization problems. The algorithm uses the pollinator's behavior to explore the solution space effectively, which is useful in both continuous and discrete optimization.
- **Artificial Bee Colony (ABC)**: The Artificial Bee Colony algorithm is inspired by the foraging behavior of honeybees and focuses on finding the optimal solution by simulating the behaviors of employed bees, onlookers, and scouts. ABC is often used for optimizing numerical problems and can handle non-linear, multi-dimensional optimization.

These various evolutionary and nature-inspired algorithms are used to tackle different kinds of optimization problems based on their specific strengths and adaptability to problem domains. Each method incorporates distinct mechanisms for exploring and exploiting the search space, making them powerful alternatives for solving highly complex, non-linear, and multi-modal problems that traditional optimization techniques find challenging.

Evolutionary algorithms are a specialized form of metaheuristic that uses a population of solutions to evolve and improve over time, making them highly effective for certain complex optimization challenges. Metaheuristics, on the other hand, represent a broader toolkit that encompasses a wide range of optimization strategies for diverse problem domains.

The upcoming section will provide a better understanding of ACO, PSO, and DE by illustrating them through toy examples.

Particle Swarm Optimization (PSO)

In **Particle Swarm Optimization (PSO)**, the term **"particles"** refers to candidate solutions to the optimization problem. Each particle represents a potential solution in the search space, and the goal is to adjust these particles over time to find the optimal or near-optimal solution.

Theory

Here is a breakdown of what particles are and how they work in PSO:

- **Particle as a Candidate Solution**
    - In PSO, each particle is a **vector** in the search space, where each element (dimension) of the vector represents a parameter or variable in the problem you are trying to solve.
    - For example, if you are trying to minimize a function with two variables, each particle could be a 2D vector. x_1, x_2, where x_1 and x_2 are the variables (or parameters) you want to optimize.
- **Position of a Particle**
    - The position of a particle corresponds to a particular solution in the problem space. This position changes as the particle moves through the search space, exploring different regions.
    - The position of a particle is updated over iterations based on the particle's own experience and the experience of neighboring particles.
- **Velocity of a Particle**
    - Each particle also has a **velocity**, which dictates how it moves through the search space. The velocity controls the direction and magnitude of the movement, determining how far and in which direction the particle moves.

- The velocity is influenced by two factors:
  - **Cognitive component**: This is the particle's own memory of the best solution (position) it has found so far, called the **personal best**.
  - **Social component**: This is the particle's awareness of the best solution found by any particle in its neighborhood, called the **global best** (or neighborhood best, depending on the variant of PSO).

- **Swarm of Particles**
  - In PSO, there is not just one particle, but a **swarm** of particles that interact with each other. The particles share information by communicating their best solutions, helping the entire swarm converge toward an optimal solution.
  - The swarm collectively explores the search space, balancing between exploitation (refining known good solutions) and exploration (looking for new potential solutions).

- **Particle Update Rules**
  - At each iteration, the position and velocity of each particle are updated as follows:
    - **Velocity Update**: The particle's velocity is adjusted based on the difference between the particle's current position, its personal best position, and the global best position.
    - **Position Update**: The particle's new position is calculated by adding the updated velocity to its current position.

PSO simulates the motion of particles through the search space, where each particle's movement is influenced by its **personal best position** and the **global best position** found by the entire swarm. The key equations governing the movement of particles are:

- **Velocity Update Equation:**

$$v_i(t+1) = w \cdot v_i(t) + c_1 \cdot r_1 \cdot (p_i - x_i(t)) + c_2 \cdot r_2 \cdot (g - x_i(t))$$

  - $v_i(t)$: Velocity of particle iii at iteration t (how fast it moves).
  - w: **Inertia weight** that controls the influence of the particle's previous velocity, balancing exploration and exploitation.
  - c_1, c_2: **Cognitive** and **social acceleration constants**, respectively, which control the influence of personal best and global best.
  - r_1 and r_2: Random values between 0 and 1, introducing stochastic behavior to the velocity.

- p_i: **Personal best** position of particle iii (the best position found by this particle so far).
- g: **Global best** position found by any particle in the swarm.
- $x_i(t)$: Current **position** of particle i at iteration t.

The velocity update equation calculates the new velocity based on:

- The particle's previous velocity (inertia term).
- The difference between the particle's current position and its personal best (cognitive term).
- The difference between the particle's current position and the global best (social term).

- **Position Update Equation**:

$$x_i(t + 1) = x_i(t) + v_i(t + 1)$$

  - $x_i(t)$: Position of particle iii at iteration t.
  - $v_i(t + 1)$: Updated velocity of particle iii at iteration $t+1$

The position update equation updates the particle's position by adding its current position to its updated velocity. This results in the particle moving to a new location in the search space.

Explanation of the Motion Components

- **Inertia Weight (w)**: The inertia weight helps balance **exploration** and **exploitation**:
  - If www is large, the particle tends to keep moving in its current direction (exploring more).
  - If w is small, the particle slows down and focuses more on exploitation (refining known good areas).
- **Cognitive Component** $c_i \cdot r_i(p_i - x(t))$:
  - This term drives the particle toward its personal best position. The particle "*remembers*" the best solution it has found and tends to return toward it.
- **Social Component** $c_2 \cdot r_2(g - x_i(t))$:
  - This term pulls the particle toward the global best position found by the swarm. Particles share information about the best solution found so far and collectively head toward this solution.

Visualizing the Particle's Motion:

- At each iteration, the particle moves by adjusting its velocity according to both its personal and social experiences.
    - Over time, the swarm of particles explores the search space, with particles adjusting their trajectories based on both individual successes and shared knowledge of the best solutions.

Putting it All Together:

1. **Initialize** the particles with random positions and velocities.
2. **Evaluate** each particle's fitness (how good the current solution is).
3. **Update** the personal best position pi and global best position g based on the current fitness evaluations.
4. **Calculate** the new velocity for each particle using the velocity update equation.
5. **Update** the position of each particle using the position update equation.
6. **Repeat** the process for a set number of iterations or until a stopping criterion is met (for example, no significant improvement in the global best solution).

Example of the Motion:

Let us say a particle represents a solution to an optimization problem, and it is currently at position $x_i(t)$ = [3,4]. Its velocity is $v_i(t)$ = [0.5,−0.2] and the personal and global best positions are p_i=[2,5] and g=[1,6], respectively.

Using the velocity update equation, we compute the new velocity based on these positions and random coefficients. After that, the position update equation moves the particle to a new location based on this updated velocity.

PSO Process Flow Recap:

- Particles "*fly*" through the solution space by adjusting their velocities and positions.
- They are drawn toward their own best positions and the swarm's best-known position.
- Over time, particles converge toward the best solution by balancing exploration and exploitation.

In **Particle Swarm Optimization (PSO)**, the concept of a **neighborhood** refers to a group of particles that share information about their best solutions with each other. This approach draws inspiration from social behavior, such as birds flying in a flock or fish swimming in a school.

Neighborhood in PSO Explained

- **Local vs. Global Best**:
  - In PSO, particles move through the solution space guided by their **personal best** (the best solution a particle has found) and the **neighborhood best** (the best solution found by a defined group of nearby particles).
  - Depending on the type of neighborhood, the **neighborhood best** can either be the best found by all particles (global) or just the best found by a subset of particles (local).
- **Neighborhood Topologies:**
  - **Global Best (gBest)**: In this configuration, the entire swarm is considered as one neighborhood. Each particle is influenced by the best solution found by the entire swarm. This can lead to fast convergence but might risk getting stuck in local optima.
  - **Local Best (lBest)**: In this topology, each particle is influenced only by the best solution found within its local neighborhood. This helps balance exploration and exploitation, potentially avoiding premature convergence by encouraging more diverse movements.
- **Types of Neighborhoods:**
  - **Ring Neighborhood**: Particles are organized in a ring, and each particle shares information with its immediate neighbors. This topology allows for more gradual convergence.
  - **Random Neighborhood**: Particles may randomly select a few other particles to share information with, promoting more exploration.
- **Balancing Exploration and Exploitation:**
  - **Local neighborhoods** enhance **exploration**, as different groups of particles might explore different parts of the solution space. This helps the swarm avoid getting stuck in suboptimal areas.
  - **Global neighborhoods** promote **exploitation**, allowing particles to converge quickly toward the best-known solution.

Purpose of Neighborhoods:

- **Diversity Maintenance**: By dividing the swarm into neighborhoods, PSO maintains diversity in the swarm, which helps in exploring various parts of the solution space and avoiding local optima.
- **Controlled Convergence**: Neighborhoods provide a balance between **global search** (exploring different solutions) and **local search** (refining known good solutions), leading to a more robust optimization process.

Overall, the neighborhood concept in PSO helps ensure that particles are not solely influenced by the global best solution, which reduces the chance of premature convergence and encourages the swarm to thoroughly explore the search space.

Library

There are several Python libraries that implement **Particle Swarm Optimization (PSO)** algorithms, providing ready-made functions to handle the calculations (such as velocity and position updates) under the hood. These libraries make it easy to apply PSO without having to manually code the algorithm from scratch. The following is one such popular library that you can use: **PySwarms**

- **PySwarms** is a popular Python library designed specifically for implementing Particle Swarm Optimization. It is easy to use and provides high-level APIs for PSO, including features such as constraints and parameter tuning.
- It supports both **single-objective** and **multi-objective** optimization

Installation:

```
pip install pyswarms
```

Basic Example:

```
import pyswarms as ps
# Define the objective function (to be minimized)
def objective_function(x):
    return (x ** 2).sum(axis=1)  # Example: Sphere function
# Set up the optimizer
optimizer = ps.single.GlobalBestPSO(n_particles=30, dimensions=2,
options={'c1': 0.5, 'c2': 0.3, 'w': 0.9})
# Perform optimization
best_cost, best_pos = optimizer.optimize(objective_function,
iters=100)
print(f"Best Position: {best_pos}")
print(f"Best Cost: {best_cost}")
```

Key Features:

- Global and local PSO variants
- Constraints handling
- Visualization of swarm movements

Applying Particle Swarm Optimization (PSO) to Price Optimization

Price optimization involves determining the optimal price of a product or service that maximizes a specific objective, such as **profit**, **revenue**, or **sales volume** while considering customer behavior, competitor pricing, and market constraints.

Let us explore how **Particle Swarm Optimization (PSO)** can be applied to this problem step-by-step:

1. **Define the Objective Function:** The objective function in a price optimization problem could be to **maximize profit** or **maximize revenue**, depending on the business goals. For simplicity, let us assume the goal is to maximize profit.

Profit is typically a function of price PPP, sales volume V(P), and cost C, where:

$$\text{Profit}(P) = (P - C) \cdot V(P)$$

- P: The price of the product or service.
- C: The cost of producing the product.
- V(P): The sales volume as a function of price, which often decreases as the price increases (demand elasticity).

The **objective** is to maximize profit by finding the optimal price P, which can be expressed as:

$$\text{Maximize: Profit}(P)$$

2. **Set Up Particles as Price Candidates:** In PSO, each **particle** represents a candidate solution, which in this case is the potential **price** of the product. Each particle's **position** corresponds to a specific price P_1 and its **fitness** is evaluated based on how profitable that price is using the objective function.

For example, if the price range is between $10 and $100, each particle could start at a random price within that range, and PSO will guide the particles to explore different price points in this range.

3. **Initialize the Population (Swarm):** A swarm of particles (price candidates) is initialized, where each particle has

- **Position**: A random price value P_1.
- **Velocity**: A random velocity that controls how the particle moves to a new price value in the next iteration.

Each particle will represent a potential price for the product, such as $25, $50, or $75.

4. **Evaluate the Fitness of Each Particle:** The fitness of each particle is evaluated based on the **profit** it generates at its current price P_1. For each particle (price candidate):

- Calculate the **profit** using the profit function Profit(P)
- The higher the profit, the better the fitness of that particle.

$$\text{Fitness} = \text{Profit}(P_i) = (P_i - C) \cdot V(P_i)$$

5. **Update Personal Best and Global Best**

- **Personal Best**: Each particle keeps track of the best price it has found so far (the price that yielded the highest profit).
- **Global Best**: The entire swarm keeps track of the best price found by any particle (the price with the highest profit across the swarm).

6. **Update Velocity and Position:** The velocity and position of each particle are updated using the following equations:

Velocity Update:

$$v_i(t+1) = w \cdot v_i(t) + c_1 \cdot r_1 \cdot (p_i - P_i(t)) + c_2 \cdot r_2 \cdot (g - P_i(t))$$

Where:

- $v_i(t+1)$: Updated velocity of particle iii at iteration t+1t+1t+1.
- www: Inertia weight (controls the influence of the previous velocity).
- c_1 and c_2: Cognitive and social constants.
- r_1 and r_2: Random factors.
- P_1: Personal best price for particle iii.
- g: Global best price found by any particle.
- $P_i(t)$: Current price for particle iii at iteration ttt.

Position Update:

$$P_i(t+1) = P_i(t) + v_i(t+1)$$

The updated velocity is added to the current price, giving the particle a new price to explore in the next iteration.

7. **Convergence:** Over successive iterations, particles will move through the price space, adjusting their prices based on their own experience (personal best) and the swarm's experience (global best).

- As particles explore the price range, they are guided toward prices that offer higher profits.
- The swarm gradually converges to the price that maximizes profit.

8. **Stopping Criteria:** The process continues until

- A maximum number of iterations is reached.
- The improvement in profit is minimal over successive iterations (indicating convergence to the optimal price).

9. **Best Price Solution:** At the end of the process, the **global best** price found by the swarm is considered the optimal price. This price maximizes the profit based on the demand and cost conditions in the objective function.

Example: Let us say we have a product that costs $20 to manufacture, and we want to find the optimal price between $30 and $100 that maximizes profit.

- Each particle starts with a random price, say $35, $55, $75, and so on.
- At each iteration, the fitness (profit) is calculated for each price based on expected sales volume V(P) (for example, sales drop as prices increase).
- Particles adjust their prices based on both their personal best and the global best prices found so far.
- After several iterations, the swarm converges toward the optimal price, which could be, for example, $58, as it maximizes profit.

Advantages of PSO in Price Optimization:

- **Exploration and Exploitation**: PSO balances exploration (trying new price points) and exploitation (refining good prices) by using both individual and swarm knowledge.
- **Adaptability**: PSO can handle non-linear, complex relationships between price, demand, and profit.
- **Simplicity**: PSO is easy to implement and does not require gradient information (as in other optimization methods such as gradient descent).

Simulation

The simulation using Particle Swarm Optimization (PSO) found the optimal price to be approximately $60. At this price, the maximum profit is $16,000. This result was based on the simplified profit model, where sales volume decreases linearly with increasing price. The PSO algorithm adjusted the price to maximize profit while considering both exploration (trying different prices) and exploitation (refining the best-known prices).

This Python code visualizes the relationship between **price** and **profit** for a product. First, it defines a profit function where profit depends on price, cost, and sales volume (which decreases as price increases). The prices array is created with 100 values between $30 and $100, and for each price, the profit is calculated. The matplotlib library is used to plot the profit against the price.

```
import matplotlib.pyplot as plt
import numpy as np

# Define the profit function again for plotting
def profit(price):
```

```
    cost = 20
    sales_volume = 1000 - 10 * price
    if sales_volume < 0:
        sales_volume = 0
    profit_value = (price - cost) * sales_volume
    return profit_value

# Generate a range of prices to visualize the profit function
prices = np.linspace(30, 100, 100)
profits = [profit(p) for p in prices]

# Plot the profit function and show the optimal price
plt.figure(figsize=(10, 6))
plt.plot(prices, profits, label='Profit vs Price', color='b')
plt.axvline(x=60, color='r', linestyle='--', label=f'Optimal Price =
${60}')
plt.scatter([60], [16000], color='r')  # Optimal point

# Adding labels and title
plt.title('Profit vs Price Before and After Optimization')
plt.xlabel('Price')
plt.ylabel('Profit')
plt.legend()
plt.grid(True)

# Show the plot
plt.show()
```

Figure 5.2: *The evolution of Profit vs Price*

A red vertical dashed line highlights the optimal price ($60), and the dot (red) shows the corresponding maximum profit ($16,000). Labels, a title, and a legend are added for clarity, and the plot is displayed.

Toy Story

Let us say we want to run a **Particle Swarm Optimization (PSO)** algorithm to optimize "*Product Price*" using the dataset, we can break the process into steps. Given that the dataset contains variables such as **`Order_Demand`**, **`Sales_per_Customer`**, **`Order_Profit_Per_Order`**, **`Customer_Segment`**, and **`Product_Category`**, we can build a model that learns the relationship between these factors and product price.

Here is the step-by-step approach to implementing PSO for **Product Price Optimization**:

Step 1: Understand the Dataset

The dataset has the following variables:

- **Product Price** (target variable for optimization).
- **Order Demand** (predictor variable).
- **Sales per Customer** (predictor variable).
- **Order Profit Per Order** (predictor variable).
- **Customer Segment** (categorical predictor).
- **Product Category** (categorical predictor).

We aim to **optimize the price** based on these other variables. The **objective function** for PSO will use this historical data to estimate the profit and demand based on price.

Step 2: Define the Objective Function

The goal is to **maximize the overall profit** based on price. You can model the profit for each order as:

$$\text{Profit} = (\text{Price} - \text{Cost}) \times \text{Order Demand}$$

Where:

- **`Order Demand`** will change based on the price (we can learn this from the dataset).
- **`Cost`** is the fixed or variable cost of producing the product.

Our PSO will explore different price points and use this profit equation as the **objective function** to optimize the price.

Step 3: Prepare the Dataset for Modeling

- Preprocess the data: Normalize or scale numerical features such as **`Order_Demand`**, **`Sales_per_Customer`**, and **`Order_Profit_Per_Order`**.
- One-hot encode or label encodes categorical features such as **`Customer_Segment`** and **`Product_Category`** to convert them into numerical form.

Step 4: Fit a Model to Estimate Demand and Profit Based on Price

You can fit a machine learning model (for example, linear regression, decision tree, or random forest) to predict **Order Demand** and **Order Profit Per Order** based on the price and other factors.

Steps to Train the Model:

- Features: **`Order_Demand`**, **`Sales_per_Customer`**, **`Customer_Segment`**, **`Product_Category`**, and **`Order_Profit_Per_Order`**.
- Target: **Product Price** (dependent variable).

Once the model is trained, we can use it to estimate the demand or profit at different price points during the PSO process.

Step 5: Define the PSO Algorithm

a. **Objective Function for PSO**

To set up the objective function for PSO, you will:

i. Use the model to predict **Order Demand** and **Profit** based on the **Product Price**.

ii. Estimate **Total Profit** based on the model's predictions at each price point.

iii. The goal is to **maximize profit**, so we will minimize the negative of the total profit in PSO.

```
# Objective function for PSO
def profit_function(price, model, other_variables):
    # Predict demand using the model
    demand = model.predict([[price] + other_variables])

    # Define cost (assume fixed cost for now)
    cost = 20

    # Calculate profit
```

```
        profit = (price - cost) * demand

        # Return negative profit to maximize it in PSO
        return -profit
```

b. **Bounds for Price**

You will set the bounds for product price based on historical price data or business constraints. For example, if historical prices ranged between $30 and $100, you could set these bounds for the PSO search space.

```
lower_bound = [30]
upper_bound = [100]
```

Step 6: Implement PSO Algorithm

Using **pyswarm** or any other PSO library, set up the PSO algorithm.

```
from pyswarm import pso
# Define the other variables that are constant for the
optimization
other_variables = [order_demand, sales_per_customer, customer_
segment, product_category]  # Example variables
# Run PSO to find the optimal price
optimal_price, optimal_profit = pso(profit_function, lower_bound,
upper_bound, args=(model, other_variables))

# Output optimal price and corresponding profit
print(f"Optimal Price: {optimal_price}")
print(f"Maximum Profit: {-optimal_profit}")  # Since we minimized
negative profit, return it to positive
```

Step 7: Evaluate Results

Once PSO provides the optimal price, evaluate the results:

- The optimal price should balance demand and profit, considering how changes in price impact **Order Demand** and **Sales per Customer**.
- You can visualize the impact of this new price on profit by plotting the profit function against different prices (as shown in previous visualizations).

Step 8: Segment-Specific Optimization (Optional)

If you want to optimize pricing strategies for different **Customer Segments** or **Product Categories**, you can:

a. Segment the dataset by **`Customer_Segment`** or **`Product_Category`**.

b. Run separate PSO optimizations for each segment to find the optimal price for each customer group or product category.

Results:

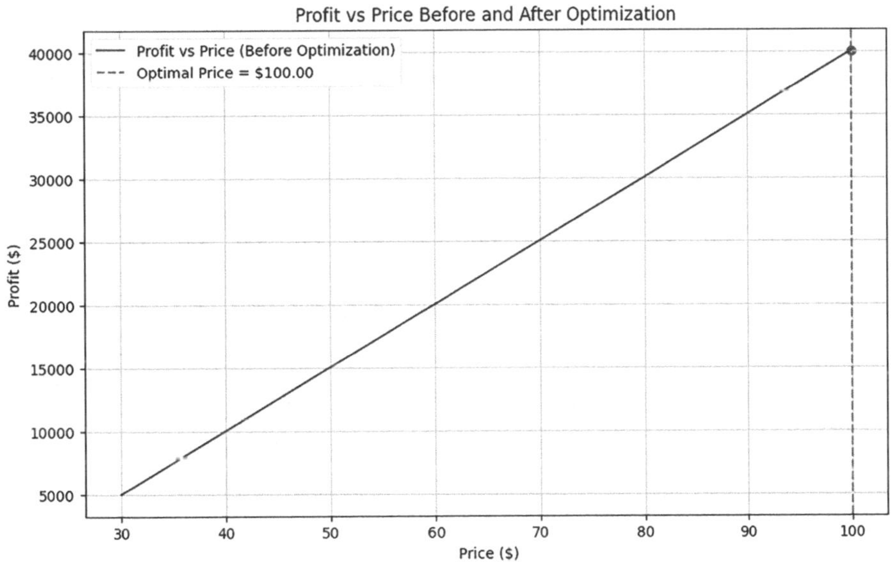

***Figure 5.3:** The result in the plot shows a linear increase in profit as the price increases, and the **optimal price** found by* PSO *is **$100**—the upper limit of the defined bounds*

Analysis:

- **Profit Increases Linearly**: This implies that the higher the price, the greater the profit, assuming a fixed demand. This behavior indicates that there may be no penalty for increasing the price, which could suggest unrealistic conditions in the model.
- **Optimal Price at Upper Bound**: Since the PSO chose the maximum price ($100), it means that, according to the current model, profit keeps increasing without considering any decrease in demand as the price rises.

So, this result is **not ideal** because it implies that setting the highest possible price always leads to the maximum profit, which is unrealistic. In practice, demand usually decreases with increased prices, affecting the total profit. To improve the model, we need to incorporate the **price elasticity of demand**, which would allow the demand to vary realistically as the price changes. This would give a more accurate depiction of how profit changes with price and help find a more reasonable optimal price.

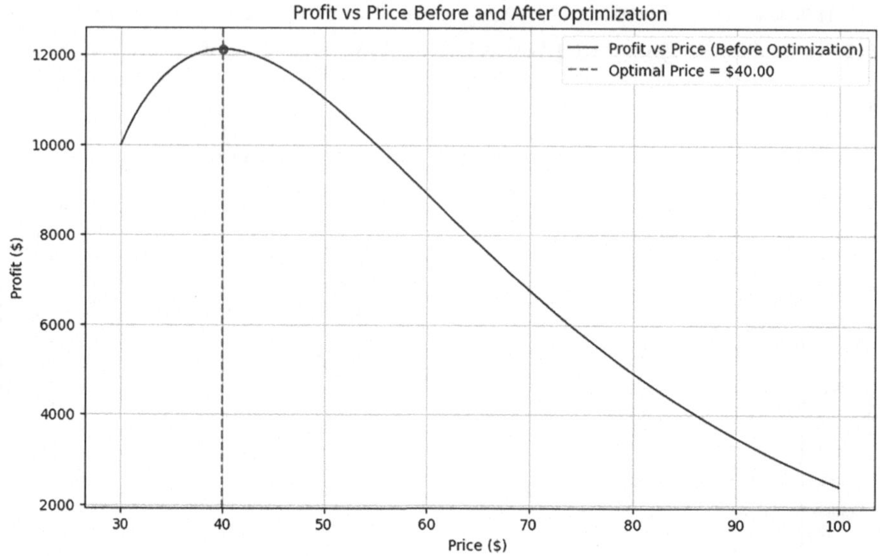

***Figure 5.4**: The plot now shows a more realistic profit behavior as a function of price, based on a **price elasticity of demand** model*

Key Insights from the Plot

- **Profit Curve Shape:**
    - The **profit vs price** curve shows a rise and then a fall, indicating that profit initially increases with price but starts to decline beyond a certain point.
    - This behavior reflects a typical **price elasticity relationship** where increasing the price too much eventually reduces demand significantly, leading to lower profits.
- **Optimal Price:**
    - The **optimal price** found by the PSO algorithm is **$40.00**. This is marked by the red dashed line in the plot.
    - At this price, the **maximum profit** is approximately **$12,000**.
- **Demand-Price Relationship**:
    - The **exponential decrease in demand** as price increases creates a profit peak. Beyond the peak, the reduction in demand outweighs the benefit of a higher price, resulting in lower overall profit.
    - The curve's shape and the optimal point indicate that there is a balance between setting a price high enough for good margins but not so high that demand drops too much.

So, the result is **more realistic** compared to the previous plot, where profit kept increasing indefinitely with higher prices. Here, the model shows an optimal balance between price and demand, capturing a more practical scenario. This type of modeling is essential for real-world pricing strategies, where the goal is to find a sweet spot that maximizes profit by considering both the price and customer demand sensitivity.

To create a **better model** for pricing optimization, we adjusted the **demand-price relationship** to be more realistic by simulating **price elasticity**. Here is what we did:

1. **Introduced a Realistic Demand-Price Relationship**
    - In the original model, the demand was fixed regardless of price, which meant that increasing the price always led to increasing profits–an unrealistic scenario.
    - To reflect real-world behavior, we introduced a **demand-price relationship** where demand decreases **exponentially** as the price increases. This relationship is captured by the formula:

    $$\text{demand} = \text{base\_demand} \times e^{(\text{elasticity} \times (\text{price} - 30))}$$

        - **Base demand** is the starting level of demand when the price is low.
        - **Elasticity** is a negative factor that determines how sensitive demand is to price changes. A negative value means that as the price goes up, demand goes down.

2. **Impact on Optimization**
    - **Profit is now calculated** as the product of (price - cost) and the **demand**, where demand changes with price.
    - This new model allows the PSO to search for a **balance** between setting a high price and maintaining sufficient demand to maximize profit.
    - As a result, the **optimal price** found was **$40.00**, which is lower than the upper bound. This indicates the presence of an equilibrium where profit is maximized without losing too much demand.

So, the previous model unrealistically suggested that higher prices always yield higher profits. The updated model accounts for demand decreasing as prices increase, creating a more practical scenario where profits peak at a reasonable price. This better simulates real-world market conditions, helping find an optimal price that balances revenue and demand.

In the next chapter, we will continue with the practical implementation of PSO, we will also dive into Variants of PACO and do implementation of ACO (Ant colony optimization).

Conclusion

Based on the discussions throughout this content, we explored various types of evolutionary algorithms, from classical to advanced and deep evolutionary approaches, highlighting their theoretical foundations and practical benefits. The comparison between genetic algorithms and evolutionary algorithms provided insight into their respective strengths. In particular, we looked into **Particle Swarm Optimization (PSO)**, covering its theory, library usage, and a practical application to price optimization.

The upcoming chapters will focus on practical applications of **PSO** and **Ant Colony Optimization (ACO)** on real-world datasets, demonstrating their effectiveness in optimizing product pricing and maximizing profit in a business context. These chapters will showcase the full process, from simulation to results, offering hands-on examples for effective optimization.

Chapter 6
Advanced Evolutionary Algorithms

Introduction

This chapter provides a comprehensive exploration of advanced evolutionary algorithms and their practical applications in solving supply chain and price optimization challenges. We begin with an introduction to evolutionary algorithms and metaheuristics, laying the foundation for understanding their differences and similarities in the section Genetic Algorithms vs. Metaheuristics. The chapter is structured to give you an overview of how Evolutionary Algorithms (EA) fit into real-world supply chain management, explaining their role and relevance in optimizing various processes. Next, we move to the practical implementation of evolutionary algorithms, where we discuss the specifics of the supply chain data used in our analyses and how we can apply these algorithms for effective optimization.

In the implementation of the price optimization section, we start by using DEAP as the tool of choice, followed by a step-by-step explanation of the code, which is detailed further into DEAP code and PyGAD code sections. We also introduce advanced implementations such as the PyGAD GPU Code with PyTorch and an improved PyGAD GPU code version, focusing on improving performance through GPU utilization.

Furthermore, the chapter delves into swarm intelligence techniques and the overlapping algorithms that can be applied to supply chain problems. We explore specific algorithms such as Particle Swarm Optimization (PSO) and Ant Colony Optimization (ACO), highlighting their practical application in the context of price optimization and supply chain management. By the end of this chapter, you will gain a deep understanding of both evolutionary and swarm intelligence algorithms, and how they can be effectively applied to optimize complex supply chain and pricing challenges.

Structure

This chapter is structured as follows:

- Genetic Algorithms versus Metaheuristics
- Supply Chain
- Practical Implementation of Evolutionary Algorithms
- Implementation of Price Optimization
- Swarm Intelligence

Genetic Algorithms Versus Metaheuristics

Metaheuristics and **Evolutionary Algorithms (EAs)** are both approaches used for optimization problems, particularly when exact methods are infeasible due to the complexity of the problem. While evolutionary algorithms are a specific type of metaheuristic, the two concepts have important distinctions in terms of scope, methods, and their general characteristics. Let us dive deeper to understand these differences.

Definition and Scope

- **Metaheuristics:**
  - Metaheuristics are high-level frameworks or strategies that guide the search process to find near-optimal solutions for complex optimization problems. They are designed to efficiently explore large search spaces and do not guarantee finding the global optimum, but rather provide good-enough solutions within a reasonable time.
  - Metaheuristics encompass a wide variety of optimization techniques, including **Simulated Annealing (SA)**, **Tabu Search (TS)**, **Genetic Algorithms (GAs)**, **Particle Swarm Optimization (PSO)**, **Ant Colony Optimization (ACO)**, and many more.
  - Metaheuristics can be classified as population-based (for example, GAs, PSO) or single-solution-based (for example, Simulated Annealing, Tabu Search).
- **Evolutionary Algorithms (EAs):**
  - Evolutionary Algorithms are a subset of metaheuristics inspired by the principles of natural evolution. They use mechanisms such as selection, mutation, recombination (crossover), and fitness evaluation to iteratively improve candidate solutions.

- Examples of evolutionary algorithms include **Genetic Algorithms (GAs)**, **Evolutionary Strategies (ES)**, **Genetic Programming (GP)**, and **Differential Evolution (DE)**.
- EAs are population-based approaches, meaning they operate on a group of candidate solutions at each iteration and evolve these solutions over generations.

Inspiration and Mechanisms

- **Metaheuristics:**
  - Metaheuristics are not necessarily inspired by nature or biological systems. They may use general problem-solving concepts, heuristics, or abstract principles to guide the optimization process.
  - Examples include **Simulated Annealing**, which is inspired by the process of annealing in metallurgy, and **Tabu Search**, which uses a memory structure (tabu list) to avoid revisiting previously explored regions of the search space.
- **Evolutionary Algorithms:**
  - EAs are specifically inspired by biological evolution. They mimic the processes of natural selection and genetics, such as **selection, crossover, mutation**, and **survival of the fittest**.
  - The inspiration behind EAs is closely tied to Darwinian evolution, where individuals in a population compete for survival, and the best individuals pass their characteristics to future generations.

Population-Based vs. Single-Solution-Based

- **Metaheuristics**: Metaheuristics can be either **population-based** or **single-solution-based**:
  - **Population-based** metaheuristics, such as **Genetic Algorithms** and **Particle Swarm Optimization**, maintain a set of candidate solutions that evolve over time.
  - **Single-solution-based** metaheuristics, such as **Simulated Annealing** or **Tabu Search**, work with one candidate solution at a time, moving through the search space to find improvements.
- **Evolutionary Algorithms:**
  - EAs are inherently **population-based**, meaning they maintain and evolve a population of solutions through multiple generations. This helps in maintaining diversity within the search and reducing the risk of getting stuck in local optima.

Exploration vs. Exploitation

- **Metaheuristics**: Metaheuristics focus on balancing **exploration** (searching new areas of the solution space) and **exploitation** (refining existing good solutions). Different metaheuristics use different strategies to achieve this balance. For example:
    - **Simulated Annealing** has a "`temperature`" parameter that controls the likelihood of accepting worse solutions, thus enabling exploration early in the process and focusing on exploitation later.
    - **Tabu Search** keeps a list of recently visited solutions to avoid cycling and encourages exploration.
- **Evolutionary Algorithms:**
    - EAs also balance **exploration** and **exploitation**, but they do this by leveraging the diversity within the population of solutions. The **mutation** operator introduces random variations, promoting exploration, while **crossover** recombines good traits from parents to focus on exploitation.
    - The combination of selection pressure and genetic operators helps EAs effectively navigate complex search spaces.

Application Domains and Flexibility

- **Metaheuristics:**
    - Metaheuristics provide a general framework that can be adapted to a wide range of optimization problems, including combinatorial, continuous, and multi-objective problems.
    - Due to their flexibility, metaheuristics can be tailored to specific problem domains by incorporating problem-specific heuristics or constraints.
- **Evolutionary Algorithms:**
    - EAs are particularly well-suited for problems that involve highly complex, nonlinear, or multi-modal search spaces. They are popular for both combinatorial optimization (for example, TSP, knapsack problem) and continuous optimization (for example, parameter tuning).
    - EAs are also used for evolving symbolic expressions or programs in **Genetic Programming**, which is useful in fields such as symbolic regression and automated machine learning.

Convergence Behavior and Solution Quality

- **Metaheuristics:**
    - Metaheuristics are designed to provide "good-enough" solutions rather

than guaranteeing global optimality. They typically focus on finding a balance between solution quality and computation time.

- Different metaheuristics have different convergence characteristics. For instance, **Simulated Annealing** gradually decreases the probability of accepting worse solutions, converging slowly to refine solutions.

- **Evolutionary Algorithms**:
  - The convergence behavior of EAs depends on factors such as population size, mutation rate, and selection pressure. EAs generally aim to improve solution quality over multiple generations, and the presence of a diverse population helps avoid getting trapped in local optima.
  - However, EAs do not guarantee finding the global optimum, especially if the search space is vast and complex.

Next, we will explore supply chain domain, by leveraging evolutionary algorithms in these areas, companies can address the complex challenges of supply chain management more effectively, leading to improved decision-making, cost reductions, and overall supply chain efficiency.

Supply chain

Supply chain management is a highly complex and dynamic process involving numerous interconnected activities such as procurement, production, inventory management, logistics, and demand forecasting. Each of these components has its own set of challenges, making supply chain optimization a difficult task. Some of the key complexities in supply chain management include:

- **Demand Uncertainty**: Accurately predicting demand is challenging due to the fluctuating needs of customers, seasonal variations, and market trends. Inaccurate forecasts can lead to overstocking or stockouts, both of which are costly for companies.
- **Inventory Management**: Balancing the right level of inventory is critical. Holding too much inventory increases costs, while insufficient inventory may result in missed sales opportunities. The optimization of inventory levels becomes difficult when supply and demand are uncertain.
- **Supplier and Vendor Management**: Managing multiple suppliers across different regions involves handling varying lead times, quality issues, and changing costs. Coordinating between vendors to ensure smooth and efficient operations adds another layer of complexity.
- **Logistics and Transportation**: Optimizing routes for transportation and minimizing costs while meeting customer delivery deadlines are major challenges. Variations in fuel prices, traffic, and availability of transport modes complicate logistics planning.

- **Price Optimization**: Setting the right price is crucial to remain competitive while maximizing profitability. This involves accounting for factors such as production costs, competitor pricing, market demand, and customer behaviour, which can all vary widely.
- **Network Design**: The configuration of warehouses, distribution centers, and production facilities must be optimized for cost efficiency, meeting demand, and reducing delivery times. Changes in geopolitical factors, regulations, and supply chain disruptions (for example, natural disasters, pandemics) further complicate network planning.

Evolutionary Algorithms (EA) Fit in Supply Chain

Evolutionary algorithms are well-suited to handle the complexities of supply chain management, as they can solve optimization problems that are difficult for traditional methods. Here are a few areas where EAs can be effectively applied:

- **Demand Forecasting and Inventory Management**: EAs can be used to optimize inventory policies by finding a balance between holding and ordering costs, especially under uncertain demand conditions. They can also help in optimizing replenishment schedules to reduce stockouts and minimize excess inventory.
- **Supplier and Vendor Selection**: EAs can be applied to optimize supplier selection by considering factors such as lead time, cost, and quality. By simulating different scenarios, EAs help in identifying the best suppliers that align with strategic goals.
- **Logistics and Route Optimization**: In logistics, problems such as the **Traveling Salesman Problem (TSP)** or vehicle routing are common, and EAs such as Genetic Algorithms can be used to determine the most efficient routes for delivery. This helps reduce transportation costs, improve delivery times, and enhance overall efficiency.
- **Price Optimization**: EAs can be used to determine the optimal pricing strategy that maximizes profit while considering factors such as competitor pricing, customer behavior, and demand elasticity. By evaluating multiple pricing scenarios, EAs can help in finding the most profitable pricing policy.
- **Network Design**: Evolutionary algorithms can also be used to optimize the configuration of supply chain networks. By simulating different network structures and configurations, EAs can help in finding the most cost-effective network that meets demand requirements, minimizes costs, and remains adaptable to disruptions.
- **Production Scheduling**: EAs can optimize production schedules to reduce production costs and lead times while meeting demand. They are capable of

finding near-optimal schedules when faced with constraints such as machine availability, labor, and raw material supply.

Next, we will begin by downloading the open-source data and working on price optimization problems. The dataset used for analysis comes from DataCo Global and focuses on supply chain activities, which can be analyzed using Python.

Practical Implementation of Evolutionary Algorithms

Practical implementation of evolutionary algorithms involves applying Evolutionary algorithm such as genetic algorithms–to solve complex real-world problems by evolving optimal solutions over successive generations. Let us look into a Supply chain dataset in the next section.

About the Supply Chain Data

The **DataCo SMART Supply Chain** for Big Data Analysis is a dataset designed for analyzing various components of a supply chain. It provides detailed information about supply chain activities, allowing for the application of data analytics, machine learning, and other data-driven approaches to derive insights. Here's what the dataset is generally about:

1. **Supply Chain Activities**:
    - The dataset includes data related to core supply chain activities such as **Provisioning**, **Production**, **Sales**, and **Commercial Distribution**. This provides a complete view of the end-to-end supply chain, from procurement of raw materials to the distribution of finished goods to customers.
2. **Structured and Unstructured Data**:
    - **Structured Data**: The dataset includes tabular data (`DataCoSupplyChainDataset.csv`), which typically contains numerical and categorical data such as product details, order quantities, customer information, inventory levels, sales data, and production details.
    - **Unstructured Data**: The dataset also includes clickstream data (**`tokenized_access_logs.csv`**), representing user interactions, such as web access logs. This data is often used to gain insights into customer behavior, marketing impact, and user engagement.
3. **Product Types**:
    - The dataset involves different types of products such as **Clothing**,

Sports, and **Electronic Supplies**, which helps analyze the supply chain performance across different product categories.

4. **Analysis Capabilities**:
   - The dataset is designed for **Big Data analysis**, allowing the application of **Machine Learning Algorithms** to solve various supply chain-related problems such as price optimization, demand forecasting, inventory management, and so on.
   - It provides opportunities to correlate **structured** and **unstructured data** to derive actionable insights, enabling a more comprehensive analysis of supply chain dynamics, customer preferences, and operational efficiencies.
5. **Variable Descriptions**:
   - A separate file (`DescriptionDataCoSupplyChain.csv`) provides descriptions of each variable in the dataset, helping analysts understand the meaning and significance of different fields and how they can be used for modeling and analysis.

The dataset serves as a foundation for applying **big data analytics** techniques to improve the efficiency and effectiveness of supply chain operations, exploring areas such as **predictive modeling**, **price optimization**, and **demand analysis** to optimize decision-making and enhance business outcomes.

So, next we define a process of using a Genetic Algorithm (GA) to determine an optimal pricing strategy based on a dataset, focusing on maximizing profit or revenue. The steps include defining an objective function, preparing the data, specifically removing Null values, setting up the GA, running the algorithm, and evaluating the results.

Implementation of Price Optimization

To generate an optimal pricing strategy using a Genetic Algorithm (GA) with the cleaned dataset, you would follow these general steps:

Step 1: Define Objective Function

The objective function for the GA should be designed to maximize either profit or revenue. Using the data available, you can calculate these metrics based on pricing strategies, such as:

- **Revenue** = `Product Price * Order Quantity`
- Profit = Benefit per order

The GA will attempt to optimize the **Product Price** variable to maximize the selected objective (for example, revenue or profit).

Step 2: Prepare Data and Define Variables

You would use the following relevant columns from the dataset to inform your model:

- **Product Price**: This is the decision variable that the GA will optimize.
- **Sales per customer**: Represents the sales data, which can be used to assess demand elasticity with respect to price changes.
- **Benefit per order**: Helps to evaluate how changes in price influence overall profit.
- **Order Quantity**: This can be used to measure how different prices affect demand.
- **Customer Segment, Product Category, Geographic Information** (for example, **Customer Country**, **Customer City**): These can be used as features to create customer-specific pricing strategies, allowing the GA to explore variations in pricing across different segments.

Step 3: Set Up the Genetic Algorithm

- **Chromosome Representation**: A chromosome in this context will represent a set of possible prices for products. If there are multiple products or categories, each chromosome could represent a unique pricing strategy for each product.
- **Fitness Function**: The fitness function will evaluate each chromosome (pricing strategy) based on the profit or revenue it generates. For example:

  `Fitness=Total Profit=∑(Benefit per order×Order Quantity)`

  or

  `Fitness=Total Revenue=∑(Product Price×Order Quantity)`

  The GA will maximize this fitness value over generations.
- **Crossover and Mutation**: Implement crossover and mutation to explore different pricing strategies. Crossover will combine successful pricing strategies, while mutation will introduce slight variations to avoid local optima.

Step 4: Run the Genetic Algorithm

a. **Initialization**: Create an initial population of potential pricing strategies.

b. **Selection**: Select the fittest individuals (pricing strategies) based on their revenue or profit performance.

c. **Crossover and Mutation**: Generate new pricing strategies by combining the features of selected individuals and applying mutations.

d. **Iterate**: Repeat the process for a set number of generations or until convergence criteria are met (for example, no significant improvement in fitness value).

Step 5: Evaluate Results

The output of the GA model would include:

- **Optimal Pricing Strategy**: The optimal prices for the products or product categories that maximize profit or revenue.
- **Expected Revenue or Profit**: The maximum revenue or profit that can be obtained using the optimal pricing.
- **Insights for Different Customer Segments**: Depending on how the GA is set up, it may also provide insights into how prices should be adjusted for different customer segments, product categories, or regions.

Example Output:

1. **Optimal Product Prices**: The set of optimized prices for each product or category (for example, Product A: $299, Product B: $399, and so on).
2. **Expected Profit/Revenue**: A value representing the maximum profit or revenue achievable with the given strategy (for example, "`Expected Revenue: $1,500,000`").
3. **Segment-Specific Pricing** (Optional): A matrix or list of prices for different customer segments or regions if you decide to segment your market.

Data Preparation and Feature Selection

Even though there are 51 variables to optimize "`Product Price`," we will consider the following columns from the dataset as influencing variables, These columns provide relevant features to calculate and optimize profit and revenue while considering customer preferences and demand change.

1. `Order_Demand`: This will help in understanding how demand changes with changes in price.
2. `Sales_per_Customer`: Provides insight into the behavior of sales per customer, which can be used to determine price elasticity.
3. `Order_Profit_Per_Order`: Measures how changes in price influence overall profit.
4. `Customer_Segment`: Helps in segmenting customers to potentially identify different pricing strategies for each segment.

5. `Product_Category`: You can optimize pricing based on product categories for a more targeted strategy.

   Let us revisit the diagram from *Chapter 1, Introduction to Genetic Algorithms, Figure 1.7*, to ensure we have a clear understanding of our approach.

Understanding Multiple Product

In a **Genetic Algorithm (GA)**, the **chromosome** represents a **potential solution** in the form of a sequence of genes, where each gene is a **parameter to be optimized**. In the context of the price optimization problem:

- Each **chromosome** would be a **vector of 10 values** if there are **10 products**.
- Each **gene** in the chromosome corresponds to the **price of a specific product**.

  For instance, consider a chromosome represented as:

  [12.5, 15.0, 11.2, 9.8, 14.5, 10.7, 13.9, 16.0, 12.1, 17.4]

- **12.5** is the price for **Product 1**.
- **15.0** is the price for **Product 2**.
- **11.2** is the price for **Product 3**, and so on, up to **Product 10**.

In a GA, multiple chromosomes form a **population**, and each chromosome is evaluated based on a **fitness function**–in this case, the **profit** derived from all product prices. The GA operations, such as:

1. **Selection**: Chooses the best chromosomes for mating based on their fitness.
2. **Crossover**: Combines genes from two parent chromosomes to create offspring.
3. **Mutation**: Randomly alters some genes in a chromosome to maintain diversity.

These operations are used to evolve the population towards better solutions. The goal is to optimize the entire chromosome, meaning finding the best set of prices for all products that maximizes the overall profit.

Using DEAP to get started:

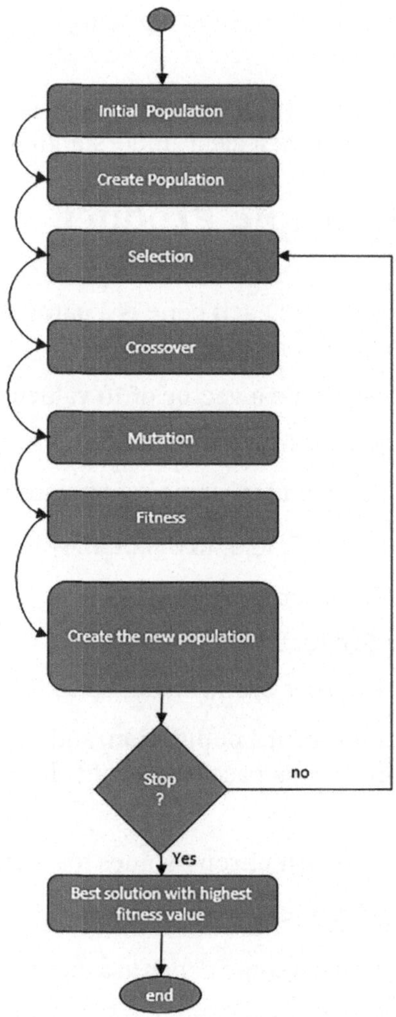

Figure 6.1: *The Execution process of GA (Genetics Algorithm)*

Step-by-Step Explanation

1. **Import Required Libraries**: You need pandas to load your dataset, and DEAP for the genetic algorithm.
2. **Prepare Your Dataset**: Extract only the relevant features that influence the pricing decision.
3. **Define Genetic Algorithm Elements**:
   - **Chromosome Representation**: Each chromosome is a list of potential prices for each product.
   - **Fitness Function**: The fitness function calculates the profit or revenue.

- **Genetic Operators**:
  - **Crossover (mate)**: Blends two chromosomes (pricing strategies) to create offspring.
  - **Mutation (mutate)**: Introduces randomness in the chromosome to explore different strategies.
  - **Selection (select)**: Uses tournament selection to select the fittest individuals for crossover.

4. **Run the Genetic Algorithm**: The GA iterates through multiple generations, and for each generation:
   - **Selection**: The fittest individuals are selected.
   - **Crossover and Mutation**: New offspring are generated through crossover and mutation.
   - The process repeats for a specified number of generations (`NGEN`).
5. **Evaluate Results**: After running for a fixed number of generations, the algorithm outputs the best pricing strategy that maximizes profit or revenue.

Things to Consider:

- **Objective Function**: Here, the objective function is set to maximize profit (`calc_profit`). You could modify it for revenue.
- **Hyperparameters**: Tuning GA parameters (`NGEN`, `CXPB`, `MUTPB`) is crucial to finding good solutions.
- **Data Normalization**: Depending on the range of values, you might need to normalize the data to improve GA performance.

This implementation will help you find an optimal pricing strategy for your products based on historical data.

The DEAP Code

The code in note book "`Price_optimzation_chapter 6`" uses Python's DEAP library to implement a Genetic Algorithm (GA) for optimizing product pricing in a supply chain dataset. It starts by importing necessary libraries such as pandas, NumPy, and DEAP, and then loads and preprocesses the supply chain data. Relevant features such as '`Product Price`,' '`Order Demand`,' and '`Order Profit Per Order`' are extracted, and an objective function is defined to calculate profit and revenue based on the product prices and order quantities. The GA setup involves defining individuals, fitness functions, and using DEAP's genetic operators, such as crossover, mutation, and selection, to evolve the population of potential solutions.

The main genetic algorithm function (`run_ga()`) creates an initial population and evolves it over 50 generations, using a combination of selection, crossover, and mutation to optimize product pricing for maximum profit. During each generation, the fitness of individuals (representing different sets of product prices) is evaluated, and the best fitness value is recorded. The algorithm then prints the best individual solution found, along with its associated fitness (total profit), and plots the progress of the best fitness value across generations, providing a visual representation of the optimization process.

Note: *The current code does not utilize a GPU. The DEAP library, which is used for the genetic algorithm, operates on the CPU.*

So next we will transition to pyGAD:

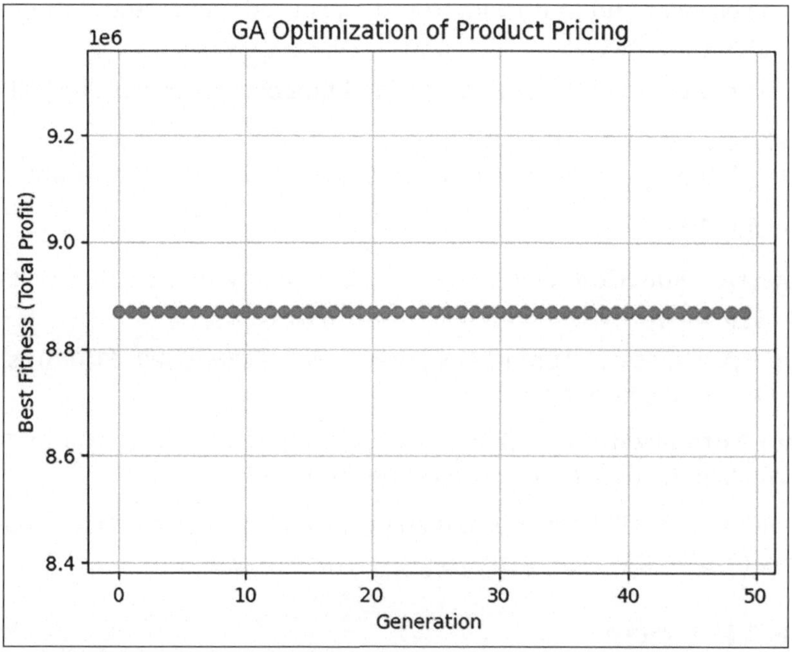

Figure 6.2: *The plot shows the best fitness (total profit) value over 50 generations during the optimization process of product pricing*

The fact that the best fitness value remains constant throughout all generations suggests that the Genetic Algorithm (GA) has not been able to effectively improve the solution beyond the initial population.

This result could indicate several potential issues:

- **Lack of Diversity**: The initial population may lack sufficient diversity, causing the algorithm to converge prematurely to a local optimum without exploring better solutions.

- **Low Mutation or Crossover Probability**: If the mutation rate or crossover rate is too low, the algorithm might not introduce enough variation to explore new solutions effectively, leading to stagnation.
- **Fitness Function Limitations**: The fitness function or the attributes used may not sufficiently differentiate between individuals to drive improvements in the population.
- **Suboptimal Parameter Tuning**: The parameters of the GA, such as the number of generations, population size, or the selection mechanism, might not be well-tuned for this problem, leading to ineffective optimization.

To address this, consider increasing mutation rates, adjusting crossover probabilities, ensuring a diverse initial population, or re-evaluating the fitness function for better differentiation.

Let us try to first convert the code to use the pygad library for the genetic algorithm, to see if we can bring in some improvements, and changing the library differs.

The PyGAD Code

The Second Code Snippet in "**`Price_optimzation_chapter 6`**" uses Python's pygad library to implement a Genetic Algorithm (GA) to optimize product pricing for maximizing profit based on a supply chain dataset. The dataset is loaded and preprocessed to extract relevant features such as '**`Product Price`**,' '**`Order Demand`**,' and '**`Order Profit Per Order`**'. The objective function calculates the total profit based on product prices, order quantity, and profit per order, which is then used as the fitness function to evaluate the performance of different sets of product prices.

The Genetic Algorithm is defined with parameters including 50 generations, 100 solutions per population, and product price bounds between 10 and 500. The GA uses tournament selection, single-point crossover, and random mutation to evolve the population and maximize profit. After running the GA, the best solution (optimized product prices) and its corresponding fitness value (total profit) are printed. The code also visualizes the best fitness values over the generations to show the optimization progress.

The plot remains exactly the same , with no improvement and the time taken is as slow as DEAP.

The current code using pygad does not explicitly utilize GPU acceleration. The pygad library primarily runs computations on the CPU, and it does not directly support GPU usage out of the box. To run a genetic algorithm on a GPU, you would need to use a GPU-accelerated library such as PyTorch or TensorFlow, and integrate the genetic algorithm logic manually.

The PyGAD GPU Code with PyTorch

This code uses Python's pygad library to implement a Genetic Algorithm (GA) for optimizing product pricing in a supply chain dataset. The dataset is loaded and preprocessed using pandas, extracting relevant features such as '**`Product Price`**,' '**`Order Demand`**,' and '**`Order Profit Per Order`**'. The code uses PyTorch to utilize GPU capabilities if available, for efficient computation of profit during the optimization process. The fitness function calculates the total profit based on product prices, order quantity, and profit per order.

The Genetic Algorithm is defined using **`pygad.GA`** with parameters such as 50 generations, 100 solutions per population, and a gene space defining the product price range between 10 and 500. The GA evolves over multiple generations to find the optimal set of product prices that maximize profit. After running the GA, the optimized prices are compared against the original product prices, and the results are visualized through two plots: one showing the actual vs optimized prices and another showing the best fitness value (total profit) over the generations.

The code is faster; however, the output remains the same.

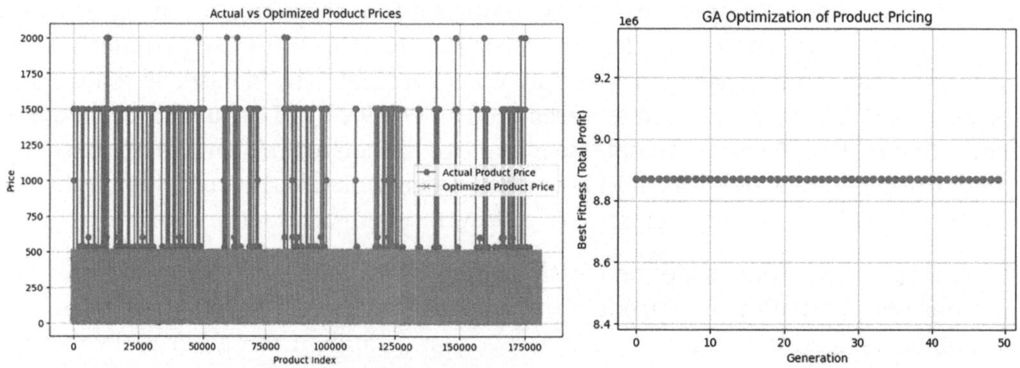

Figure 6.3: *(a) Actual vs. Optimized Product Prices (b) Best Fitness (Total Profit) vs. Iteration*

```
Best Individual: [125.84208884 293.97307803 293.16942188 ...
365.22689189 413.20873036  187.0455644 ]
Best Fitness (Total Profit): 8870218.0
     Product Price   Optimized Price
0          327.75        125.842089
1          327.75        293.973078
2          327.75        293.169422
3          327.75        244.352876
4          327.75        405.287760
```

The **PyGAD GPU Code** shows a constant best fitness value across all generations, indicating that the optimization process is not improving. Here are some improvements to the code that can help the Genetic Algorithm evolve better:

- **Increase Mutation Probability**: To introduce more diversity into the population and prevent premature convergence, the mutation probability can be increased.
- **Improve Fitness Function**: The current fitness function may be too simple or improperly scaled. Scaling the objective function to ensure a wide range of fitness values can make it more effective. It may also be beneficial to normalize the input values before using them.
- **Use Adaptive Parameters**: Use adaptive mutation or crossover rates. This means that as generations proceed, the mutation rate could increase if the population stagnates.
- **Increase Generations and Population Size**: Allowing the algorithm to run for more generations and increasing the population size can provide more opportunity for individuals to evolve better solutions.
- **Add Elitism**: Adding elitism helps retain the best individuals in each generation, ensuring that the highest fitness is not lost during crossover and mutation.

The Improved PyGAD GPU Code

These modifications should help the Genetic Algorithm overcome stagnation and produce more varied and improved results. The `Price_optimzation_chapter 6`, contains the code:

1. **Increased Number of Generations**: The number of generations is increased from 50 to 200 to provide more opportunity for optimization.
2. **Increased Population Size**: The population size is increased from 100 to 200 to allow more diverse solutions.
3. **Increased Number of Parents for Mating**: The number of parents for mating is increased to 40 to improve genetic diversity in each generation.
4. **Modified Fitness Calculation**: Modified calc_profit() to include product prices for better representation of total profit.
5. **Higher Mutation and Crossover Probability**: Increased mutation and crossover probability to introduce more variability.
6. **Elitism**: Added elitism by keeping the top 10 parents to ensure good solutions are not lost.

Let us understand the changed code

1. **Reduced Dataset Size**: The dataset is limited to **20 samples** using **`df.sample()`**, which makes the GA run faster by reducing the number of genes and computational requirements.
2. **Reduced GA Complexity**:
   - **Number of Generations**: Reduced to **10** to limit iterations and shorten runtime.
   - **Population Size**: The number of solutions per population (**`sol_per_pop`**) is set to **20**, and the number of parents mating (**`num_parents_mating`**) is set to **5** to speed up the convergence.
   - **Mutation Percentage**: Reduced to **10%** to limit changes during each generation and maintain stability.
3. **Objective Function and Profit Calculation**: The fitness function calculates total profit based on product prices and demand, simulated using **PyTorch** to allow GPU acceleration when available.

```
Best Fitness (Total Profit): 3452.21630859375
        Product Price  Optimized Price
80120      199.990005        73.632487
19670       50.000000        88.212339
114887      49.980000        90.947041
120110     299.980011        95.229649
56658       39.990002        87.986487
```

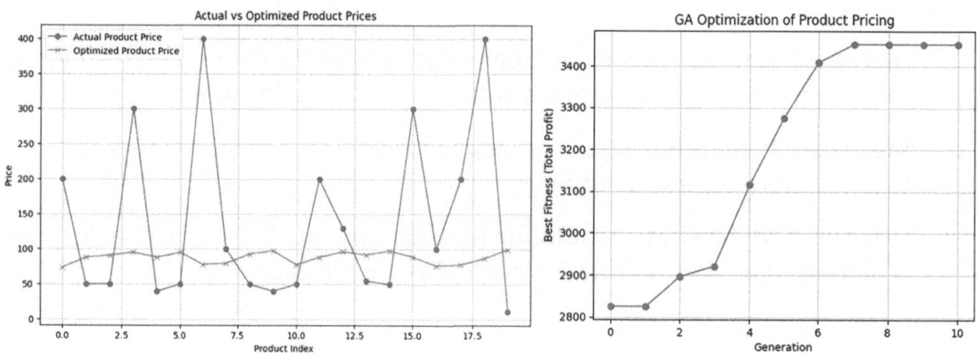

Figure 6.4: *(a) Actual vs. Optimized Product Prices (b) Best Fitness (Total Profit) vs. Iteration*

The code extracts the **optimized product prices** and compares them with the actual prices through visualizations, demonstrating how the GA converges to maximize profit in a shorter time frame.

In the next section, we will focus on Swarm intelligence and its application to price optimization.

Swarm Intelligence

Swarm intelligence algorithms and evolutionary algorithms are both inspired by natural processes and fall under the umbrella of nature-inspired optimization techniques. Swarm intelligence algorithms mimic the collective behaviours of social organisms, such as ants, bees, and birds, to explore and exploit solution spaces. Evolutionary algorithms, on the other hand, simulate the process of natural evolution, using mechanisms such as selection, mutation, and crossover to evolve solutions over generations. Both approaches emphasize adaptation, distributed search, and diversity maintenance, making them effective for solving complex optimization problems where traditional methods may fail to find optimal or near-optimal solutions. The overlap between **swarm intelligence algorithms** and **evolutionary algorithms** exists because both are inspired by nature and involve population-based search techniques. The most common algorithms that share principles between these two fields include.

Overlapping Algorithms

These overlapping algorithms illustrate how swarm intelligence and evolutionary computation share foundational principles, such as population-based search, collaboration, adaptation, and solution evolution.

Running these algorithms is extremely time-consuming and can sometimes take days without the right GPU.

- **Particle Swarm Optimization (PSO)**: While primarily considered a swarm intelligence algorithm inspired by bird flocking and fish schooling, PSO also shares similarities with EAs as it involves a population of solutions (particles) that evolve over time through collaboration and adaptation.
- **Differential Evolution (DE)**: DE is classified as an evolutionary algorithm but also shares swarm-like characteristics as it maintains and evolves a population of potential solutions using differential variations, similar to swarm dynamics.
- **Ant Colony Optimization (ACO) and Artificial Bee Colony (ABC)**: These swarm intelligence algorithms use population-based approaches similar to EAs, where each "*individual*" (ant or bee) represents a potential solution that collectively adapts to optimize the search process.
- **Genetic Swarm Optimization (GSO)**: GSO combines elements of both genetic algorithms (from EA) and swarm intelligence, using swarm-based social interactions along with genetic operations such as mutation and crossover.

Next, we will apply **Particle Swarm Optimization (PSO)** and **Ant Colony Optimization (ACO)** to the price optimization problem.

Particle Swarm Optimization (PSO)

Particle Swarm Optimization (PSO) is a nature-inspired algorithm that simulates the social behavior of birds flocking or fish schooling to find optimal solutions. PSO works by maintaining a population of candidate solutions, called **particles**, which move through the solution space to search for the best possible value for a given target. In our case, the target variable is **Product Price**, and the relevant features are **Order Demand**, **Sales per Customer**, **Order Profit per Order**, **Customer Segment**, and **Product Category**.

We pick it up from the section Particle Swarm Optimization (PSO) in *Chapter* 5, *Foundation of Evolutionary Algorithms*, where describe a toy story on similar lines. However, this time we will apply on the supply chain dataset.

Before that, let us understand how multiple products are presented in the particles.

Understanding Multiple Product

In a **Particle Swarm Optimization (PSO) algorithm**, each solution is represented as a **particle**, and the particle represents a set of parameter values to be optimized, similar to how a chromosome represents a set of genes in a Genetic Algorithm (GA).

If you have **10 products**, each **particle** in PSO will be a **vector of 10 values**, where each value corresponds to the **price of a different product**. For example, consider a particle represented as:

[20.5, 18.0, 22.1, 25.4, 19.5, 21.0, 23.3, 17.8, 26.2, 24.5]

- **20.5** represents the price for **Product 1**,
- **18.0** is the price for **Product 2**,
- **22.1** is the price for **Product 3**, and so on, up to **Product 10**.

Key Differences in PSO:

- **Particle Representation:**
  - Each **particle** is a **candidate solution** to the problem, and in this case, it is a set of **prices for 10 products**.
  - Each particle's position in the solution space represents a potential set of product prices.
- **Swarm and Movement:**
  - In PSO, multiple particles form a **swarm**.

  - Each particle has a **velocity** that determines its movement in the search space. The particle's position (that is, the set of prices) is updated iteratively based on its own experience (**personal best position**) and the experience of the swarm (**global best position**).
  - The **personal best** of each particle is the set of product prices that yielded the highest profit during previous iterations.
  - The **global best** is the set of product prices that yielded the best profit among all particles in the swarm.

- **Optimization Process**: In each iteration, particles adjust their positions based on the **velocity**, which takes into account:
  - **Personal best** (the best solution found by the particle so far).
  - **Global best** (the best solution found by the entire swarm).
  - **Random components** to ensure exploration of the solution space.

  The movement of particles continues until a termination condition is met (for example, a certain number of iterations or the convergence of fitness values).

- **Fitness Evaluation:**
  - Each particle is evaluated based on a **fitness function**–in this case, the **total profit** generated from the set of prices for all 10 products.
  - Particles converge towards an optimal or near-optimal set of prices, with the swarm collectively moving towards the **global best** solution.

Let us now dive into the application.

Step-by-Step Application of PSO for Price Optimization

1. **Data Preparation**:
   - The data is first preprocessed, and the relevant features are extracted: **Order Demand**, **Sales per Customer**, **Order Profit per Order**, **Customer Segment**, and **Product Category**.
   - The dataset is normalized to ensure that all features are on the same scale, which is important for the PSO algorithm to efficiently explore the solution space.

2. **Initialization**:
   - A population of particles is initialized, with each particle representing a possible solution for **Product Price**.
   - The initial positions of the particles are randomly assigned within a defined range, and their initial velocities are also randomized.

   - Each particle has a position that represents a potential set of price values and an associated velocity that defines how they move through the solution space.

3. **Fitness Evaluation**:

   - The **fitness function** is used to evaluate how good each particle's position is in terms of the target variable, **Product Price**.
   - The fitness function is designed to maximize the profit while considering factors such as **Order Profit per Order** and **Sales per Customer**. For example:

     `Fitness` = Order Profit per Order — Penalty for High Price
   - This ensures that the selected price optimizes revenue while balancing customer demand and sales.

4. **Updating Velocity and Position**: Each particle's velocity is updated based on three components:

   - **Inertia**: The previous velocity, which maintains some momentum.
   - **Cognitive Component**: The particle's personal best experience (how well it has done in the past).
   - **Social Component**: The best-known position found by the entire swarm, encouraging particles to move toward better-performing areas.

   The velocity update formula is:

$$v_i^{t+1} = w \cdot v_i^t + c_1 \cdot r_1 \cdot (p_i^{\text{best}} - x_i^t) + c_2 \cdot r_2 \cdot (g^{\text{best}} - x_i^t)$$

5. **Updating Positions**:

   - The new positions of the particles are calculated using their updated velocities:

$$x_i^{t+1} = x_i^t + v_i^{t+1}$$

   - These new positions represent new potential pricing strategies.

6. **Iteration and Convergence**:

   - Steps 3–5 are repeated for a fixed number of iterations or until a stopping criterion is met (for example, minimal change in fitness over several iterations).
   - The swarm gradually converges toward an optimal pricing strategy that balances profit, demand, and other features.

7. **Final Optimization Results**:
   - The **global best position** found by the swarm represents the optimal price for the product.
   - This optimal price takes into account all relevant features, balancing `profit`, `demand`, and `customer segment` preferences.

The pyswarm library provides a simple and user-friendly way to apply Particle Swarm *Optimization to optimization problems. It is best suited for beginners or for use in projects that require straightforward, continuous optimization with relatively small problem sizes. For more advanced applications, users may need to look into more feature-rich and actively maintained optimization libraries.*

The application of this code can be found in **`Price_optimzation_chapter 6`**, This code uses Particle Swarm Optimization (PSO) with the pyswarm library to optimize product pricing in a supply chain dataset. The dataset is loaded and preprocessed, with relevant features such as '**`Product Price`**,' '**`Order Demand`**,' and '**`Order Profit Per Order`**' extracted. The fitness function, which calculates the total profit using PyTorch, is defined to return the negative of the total profit because PSO inherently minimizes the objective function. The PSO algorithm is then set up with bounds for the product prices between 10 and 500, and is run with a swarm size of 100 and 50 iterations. During the optimization process, the best solution (optimized product prices) and corresponding fitness value (total profit) are recorded.

To track the convergence of PSO, a custom fitness function (**`fitness_function_with_logging`**) logs the best fitness value at each iteration. The final optimized product prices are compared against the actual prices, and the results are visualized with two plots: one showing the actual versus optimized product prices, and another showing the PSO convergence over the iterations, demonstrating the progress of the optimization. This approach uses PSO to effectively search the solution space and maximize profit by optimizing the pricing strategy.

```
Stopping search: maximum iterations reached --> 50
Stopping search: maximum iterations reached --> 100
Stopping search: maximum iterations reached --> 50
Stopping search: maximum iterations reached --> 100
Stopping search: maximum iterations reached --> 50
Stopping search: maximum iterations reached --> 100
Best Parameters: {'swarmsize': 50, 'maxiter': 50}
Best Individual: [406.43702678 266.38281898 215.04774499 ...
328.96681219 257.34357029
 198.01694215]
Best Fitness (Total Profit): 8870218.0
   Product Price  Optimized Price
0         327.75       406.437027
1         327.75       266.382819
```

```
2          327.75        215.047745
3          327.75        371.637203
4          327.75        315.629723
```

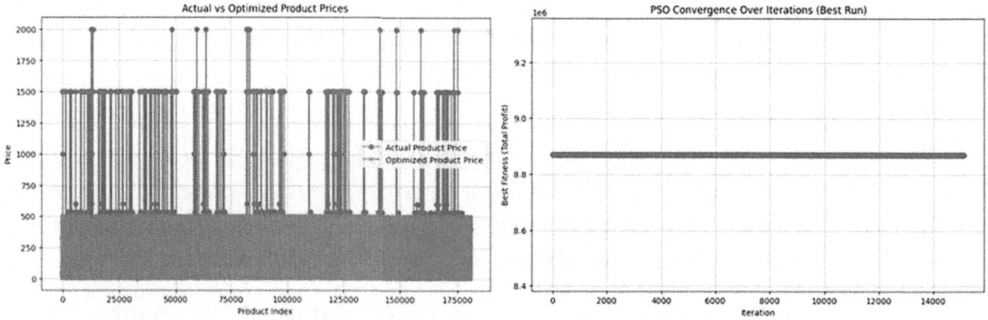

***Figure 6.5**: (a) Actual vs. Optimized Product Prices (b) Best Fitness (Total Profit) vs. Iteration*

Additional implementation of Artificial Bee Colony (ABC), has been implemented in **`Price_optimzation_chapter 6_extended`** using PyGMO: A Python wrapper for the Pagmo library, which provides a collection of optimization algorithms, including multi-objective PSO. We will discuss more about **Artificial Bee Colony (ABC)** in *Chapter* 8, *Application of Evolutionary Algo* (GAs) *and Generative Agentic AI.*

Improving the Current Code

Here are the key changes we made to improve the code:

1. **Realistic Demand-Price Relationship**
    a. Introduced a **demand-price relationship** where **demand decreases exponentially** as the price increases. This simulates **price elasticity**, making the model more realistic compared to a static demand value.
    b. Added a function called **`demand_price_relationship()`** to adjust demand dynamically based on the price, reflecting real-world consumer behavior.
2. **Modified Profit Calculation**
    a. Updated the profit calculation in the **`calc_profit()`** function to incorporate the new demand model.
    b. Used **PyTorch** tensors for the profit calculation, which is useful for leveraging GPU acceleration if available.
    c. The profit is now calculated as: Profit = (Price − Cost) × Order Quantity
    d. The cost is set to $20, and the profit calculation is negative to facilitate maximization through PSO.

3. **PSO Hyperparameter Tuning with Grid Search**
   a. Added **Grid Search** to tune the PSO parameters: **`swarm_sizes`** (different numbers of particles) and **`max_iters`** (different iteration counts).
   b. Used **`itertools.product()`** to iterate through combinations of these parameters to find the best PSO setup, storing the **best solution**, **best fitness**, and **best parameters** for further analysis.
4. **Tracking and Visualization**
   a. Added tracking of **fitness per iteration** by logging the fitness value at each iteration using a custom PSO function (**`fitness_function_with_logging()`**).
   b. Improved the visualizations:
      i. Compared **actual vs optimized product prices** using a line plot.
      ii. Plotted the **PSO convergence** to show the improvement of the solution over iterations.
   c. This makes it easier to see how PSO finds the optimal price and how the profit evolves during the optimization process.

These changes make the optimization more practical and insightful by including dynamic demand adjustment and better parameter tuning, which results in a more realistic optimization outcome.

```
Stopping search: maximum iterations reached --> 50
Stopping search: maximum iterations reached --> 100
Stopping search: maximum iterations reached --> 50
Stopping search: maximum iterations reached --> 100
Stopping search: maximum iterations reached --> 50
Stopping search: maximum iterations reached --> 100
Best Parameters: {'swarmsize': 150, 'maxiter': 100}
Best Individual: [83.59063392 30.         30.72918051 ... 93.06315458
97.54234591
 98.49364503]
Best Fitness (Total Profit): 17508588.0
   Product Price  Optimized Price
0         327.75        83.590634
1         327.75        30.000000
2         327.75        30.729181
3         327.75        79.670020
4         327.75        30.000530
```

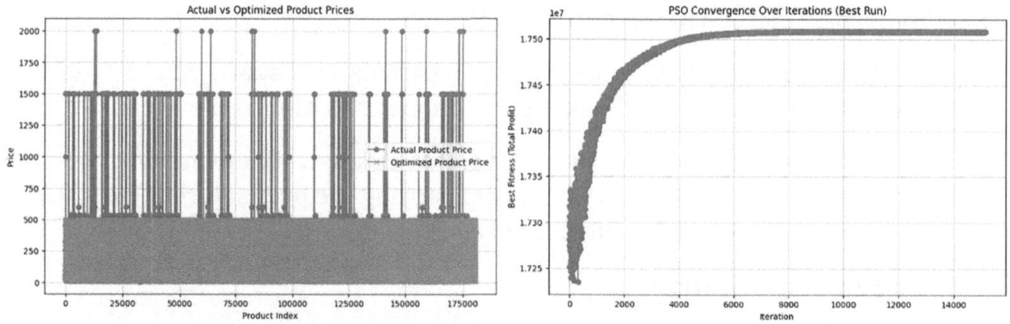

Figure 6.6: *(a) Actual vs. Optimized Product Prices* *(b) Best Fitness (Total Profit) vs. Iteration*

Ant Colony Optimization (ACO)

Ant Colony Optimization (ACO) is an algorithm inspired by the foraging behavior of ants, where artificial ants are used to find optimal paths through a graph. In the context of price optimization, ACO can be adapted to explore different pricing strategies by simulating the behavior of ants searching for the best possible solution.

Next we will explore ACO in detail for now, let's apply ACO to the same Price optimization dataset.

Step-by-Step Application of ACO for Price Optimization:

- **Load the Dataset:**
  - Load the historical product price data.
  - Extract relevant features such as **`Product Price`**, **`Order_Demand`**, **`Sales per Customer`**, and so on, and limit the dataset size to make the proof of concept run quickly.
- **Define the Objective Function**:
  - The objective function, **`calc_profit()`**, calculates total profit for a set of product prices.
  - Profit is computed as **`(product price - cost) * order quantity`** for each product. The negative value is used because ACO tries to **minimize** cost, so converting the objective to a minimization problem is necessary.
- **Custom ACO Implementation:**
  - A custom **`CustomAntColony`** class is used for optimization.
  - **Pheromone Trails** are initialized, representing information from previous solutions.

- The **number of ants** (`num_ants`) and **iterations** (`num_iterations`) determine the number of solutions generated in each cycle.

- **Ants Build Solutions:**
  - Each ant generates a candidate solution by randomly selecting a price for each product within the specified range (30–100).
  - The **`fitness_function()`** evaluates the profit for each solution.
- **Update Pheromones:**
  - After each iteration, the pheromone levels are updated.
  - Pheromones evaporate over time, and are reinforced based on solution quality (**`evaporation_rate`** controls this).
- **Run Optimization:**
  - The run() method repeats the process for a specified number of iterations, maintaining a record of the best solution found and its profit value.
  - After optimization, the best solution (set of product prices) and corresponding profit are returned.
- **Results Visualization:**
  - The optimized product prices are compared with the original prices using line plots.
  - A **convergence plot** shows the change in the best fitness (profit) over iterations to demonstrate how the algorithm progresses towards an optimal solution.

The application of this code can be found in **`Price_optimzation_chapter 6`**, This uses the Ant Colony Optimization (ACO) algorithm from the pants library to optimize product prices based on a supply chain dataset.

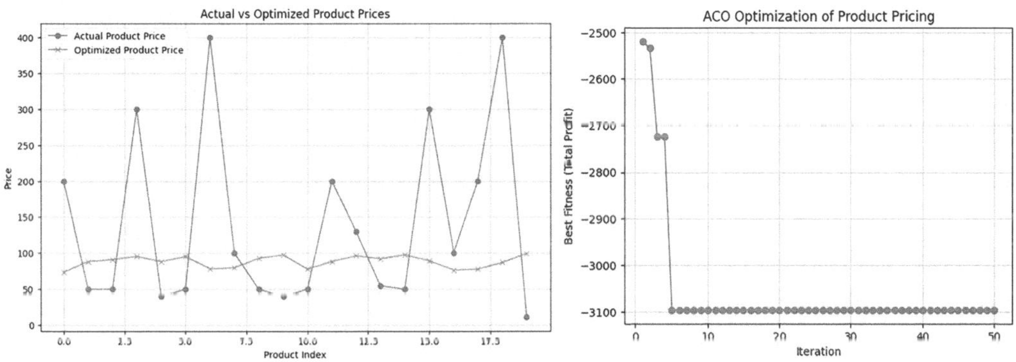

Figure 6.7: *(a) Actual vs. Optimized Product Price (b) Best Fitness (Total Profit) vs. Iteration*

The convergence plot shows that the Ant Colony Optimization (ACO) algorithm quickly finds a solution that minimizes the total cost. The rapid drop in fitness value within the first few iterations indicates that the algorithm quickly identified a better solution. After this point, the fitness value stabilizes, meaning the algorithm likely reached a **local optimum** and did not improve further. This behavior suggests that the early solutions were significantly suboptimal, but the convergence was effective, leading to a stable, if potentially non-global, optimum. The fitness level remaining flat implies that the algorithm did not find further improvements.

Here we have used , scikit-opt, however aco-pants library is a Python package that provides an implementation of Ant Colony Optimization (ACO), a nature-inspired metaheuristic used to solve optimization problems, particularly those involving complex paths or networks. It allows users to model a problem as a "world" of coordinates and solve it with ants simulating possible solutions. The library is versatile, supporting custom distance functions to represent various objective functions. It is especially useful for solving combinatorial optimization problems such as the Traveling Salesman Problem (TSP) and other similar tasks where paths and sequences need to be optimized for efficiency or profit maximization.

The dataset is loaded and preprocessed to extract relevant features such as '**`Product Price`**', '**`Order_Demand`**', and '**`Order Profit Per Order`**'. A fitness function is defined using PyTorch, which calculates the negative of the total profit to facilitate minimization by Ant Colony Optimization (ACO), which inherently minimizes an objective function. The ACO problem is represented by creating a "*world*" with product price points as coordinates, and a custom distance function is defined to determine the "*distance*" between two solutions, effectively guiding the ants to maximize profit.

The ACO solver is configured with a reduced number of ants and steps to allow for faster execution. It then solves the optimization problem to find the best solution (optimized product prices), which is printed and compared against the original prices. The results are also visualized using a plot that shows the actual versus optimized product prices, allowing the user to evaluate the improvements made by the ACO algorithm in optimizing pricing strategy for maximum profit

In **PSO**, a population of particles searches the solution space, with each particle representing a potential price. The optimal solution is found through iterative updates of particle velocities and positions based on individual and collective experiences.

In **ACO**, artificial ants explore different pricing paths, and pheromone trails guide them towards optimal pricing strategies. The best pricing solution is found through probabilistic exploration and pheromone reinforcement.

Both algorithms use relevant features to navigate the search space, ensuring that the final optimized **Product Price** maximizes **profit**, considers **customer demand**, and caters to different **customer segments** and **product categories**.

In the next chapter, we will deep dive into Metaheuristics algorithm and we will explain more about Ant Colony Optimization.

Conclusion

Evolutionary algorithms, including Genetic Algorithms (GA), Particle Swarm Optimization (PSO), and Ant Colony Optimization (ACO), have proven effective for price optimization in supply chain management. By exploring different algorithm types and implementations using DEAP, PyGAD, and GPU acceleration, this Chapter demonstrated the practical advantages of evolutionary algorithms for solving complex, dynamic pricing problems. Swarm intelligence techniques such as PSO and ACO, as well as overlapping approaches, showed the potential to enhance optimization outcomes. Overall, evolutionary algorithms provide a powerful, adaptable toolset for optimizing supply chain operations, helping companies achieve better profitability and operational efficiency.

In the next chapter, we will discuss Optimization, Metaheuristic Algorithms, Ant Colony Optimization (ACO), Differential Evolution (DE), and Multi-Objective Evolutionary Algorithm (MOEA)

CHAPTER 7
Metaheuristic Optimization Algorithms

Introduction

Optimization refers to the process of finding the best possible solution to a problem within a defined set of constraints. It involves maximizing or minimizing an objective function by adjusting variables in a way that meets certain requirements. In computational contexts, optimization plays a key role in improving efficiency, performance, and outcomes across diverse fields, from engineering to artificial intelligence.

Metaheuristic Optimization is a broad category of optimization techniques that mimic natural processes and behaviors to find solutions to complex problems. These methods do not guarantee the optimal solution but aim to find a good enough or near-optimal solution within a reasonable time frame. Inspired by the behaviors of animals and insects, metaheuristic algorithms often model the way swarms of birds, ants, or bees search for food, or how animals evolve over generations. Examples include Ant Colony Optimization (ACO), which simulates how ants find the shortest path to food, and Artificial Bee Colony (ABC) is a popular metaheuristic optimization algorithm inspired by the foraging behavior of honeybees. This nature-inspired approach allows metaheuristic algorithms to explore and exploit the search space efficiently in diverse, dynamic environments.

In this chapter, we will deep dive into **Metaheuristic Optimization**. Before that, we will explore the different types of optimizations and discuss in depth **ACO** and **ABC**, which we touched upon in the previous chapter. These nature-inspired algorithms will provide a deeper understanding of how animal behaviors can be modeled to solve complex optimization problems.

Structure

In this chapter, we discuss the following topics:

- Optimization
- Metaheuristic Algorithms
- Ant Colony Optimization (ACO)
- Differential Evolution (DE)
- Multi-Objective Evolutionary Algorithm (MOEA)

Optimization

The study Metaheuristics: From Design to Implementation by Elias G. Talbi outlines various **Optimization methods**, dividing them into two main categories: **Exact methods** and **Approximate methods**, with further subcategories for each. Here is an explanation of the techniques presented:

Exact Methods

These methods guarantee finding the optimal solution, meaning they will provide the best possible outcome for a given problem. They are often computationally intensive, especially for large problem sizes, but they ensure accuracy.

- **Branch and X:** Refers to techniques based on the "*branch and bound*" principle.
    - **Branch and bound:** A general algorithm for solving combinatorial optimization problems. It systematically explores all possible solutions but prunes branches of the search tree that cannot contain an optimal solution.
    - **Branch and cut:** Combines branch and bound with cutting plane methods to solve integer programming problems more efficiently.
    - **Branch and price:** Uses branch and bound along with column generation (a technique from linear programming) to handle large-scale problems.
- **Constraint Programming:** A technique where relationships between variables are expressed in the form of constraints, and the goal is to find values for the variables that satisfy all the constraints. It is widely used in scheduling, planning, and resource allocation problems.
- **Dynamic Programming:** A method for solving complex problems by breaking them down into simpler subproblems. It is particularly useful for problems exhibiting overlapping subproblems and optimal substructure, such as shortest paths, knapsack problems, and more.

- *A, IDA***: These are graph search algorithms.
    - **A***: A well-known algorithm used to find the shortest path in a graph by exploring the most promising nodes first, guided by heuristics.
    - **IDA***: Iterative Deepening A*, a memory-efficient version of A*, combining depth-first search's space efficiency and A*'s optimality.

Approximate Methods

These methods do not guarantee an optimal solution but aim to find a solution that is "*good enough*" in a reasonable amount of time, which is often more practical for large or complex problems.

- **Heuristic Algorithms:** These are problem-solving methods that use practical techniques to find solutions that are close to optimal. Heuristics are rule-based and can be problem-specific, relying on experience or experimentation rather than a formal guarantee of optimality.
- **Approximation Algorithms:** These provide provable bounds on the quality of the solution and the time required to find it. They are often obtained by relaxing the problem's constraints and finding a close approximation of the optimal solution. For example, they might guarantee a solution within a certain percentage of the optimal.
- **Metaheuristics:** A subset of heuristics, metaheuristics are higher-level frameworks that guide heuristic search methods to find near-optimal solutions. They are flexible, adaptable, and often inspired by natural phenomena.
    - **Single-solution based:** These algorithms work with a single candidate solution and iteratively improve it. Examples include simulated annealing and tabu search.
    - **Population-based:** These algorithms work with a group of candidate solutions and evolve them over time. Examples include genetic algorithms and particle swarm optimization.
- **Problem-Specific Heuristics:** These are tailored and designed to solve a particular problem or class of problems. Unlike metaheuristics, which are generally applicable, problem-specific heuristics exploit the unique characteristics of a given problem to find efficient solutions.

While metaheuristic algorithms have proven highly effective in tackling complex optimization problems by mimicking natural processes, recent advances in optimization have introduced new approaches that leverage deeper mathematical foundations and machine learning techniques. Among these, **Dynamic Programming Optimization (DPO)** and **Proximal Policy Optimization (PPO)** stand out, particularly in fields such as reinforcement learning. These techniques shift the focus from nature-inspired heuristics to more structured, policy-driven optimizations, designed to handle multi-step decision processes and continuous learning environments. In the next sections, we will explore how DPO and PPO build on traditional optimization frameworks while addressing challenges in modern, data-driven contexts.

Newer Optimization

While metaheuristic algorithms have proven highly effective in tackling complex optimization problems by mimicking natural processes, recent advances in optimization have introduced new approaches that leverage deeper mathematical foundations and machine learning techniques. Among these, **Dynamic Programming Optimization (DPO)** and **Proximal Policy Optimization (PPO)** stand out, particularly in fields such as reinforcement learning and training Large Language Models (LLMs). These techniques shift the focus from nature-inspired heuristics to more structured, policy-driven optimizations, designed to handle multi-step decision processes and continuous learning environments. In the next sections, we will explore how DPO and PPO build on traditional optimization frameworks while addressing challenges in modern, data-driven contexts.

Dynamic Programming Optimization (DPO) and **Proximal Policy Optimization (PPO)** are more recent optimization techniques commonly used in fields such as reinforcement learning and control problems. Here is an overview of both.

Dynamic Programming Optimization (DPO)

Dynamic Programming Optimization (DPO) is rooted in **Dynamic Programming (DP)**, a method for solving complex optimization problems by breaking them down into simpler overlapping subproblems. However, **DPO** can refer to advancements in applying DP principles to modern optimization challenges, especially in reinforcement learning.

Key Principles of DP in Optimization:

- **Bellman's Principle of Optimality**: This is the foundation of DP. It states that the solution to an optimization problem can be decomposed into subproblems, and the optimal solution to the entire problem depends on the optimal solution to these subproblems.
- **Recursive Decomposition**: Problems are broken down into stages, where each stage represents a subproblem.
- **Memoization**: Previously computed solutions to subproblems are stored to avoid redundant computations.

In **modern contexts**, DPO might refer to applying DP to large-scale systems, dynamic systems, or optimization problems in fields such as **supply chain management**, **robotics**, and **machine learning**. By leveraging more advanced algorithms, DPO aims to solve **multi-step optimization problems** where decisions at each step affect future outcomes, such as the optimization of policies in **Markov Decision Processes (MDPs)**.

Proximal Policy Optimization (PPO)

Proximal Policy Optimization (PPO) is a type of **policy optimization algorithm** used in **reinforcement learning**. It is a modern variant of policy gradient methods and is widely used because of its simplicity and efficiency.

How PPO Works:

- **Policy Gradient Methods**: In reinforcement learning, policy gradient methods aim to directly optimize the policy (a function that maps states to actions) by improving it through gradient ascent on the expected reward.
- **Clipped Objective Function**: PPO improves on traditional policy gradient methods by introducing a **clipping mechanism** that ensures updates to the policy do not go too far from the current policy. This stabilizes learning and prevents drastic changes that can destabilize training.
- **Trust Region**: By constraining how much the policy can change in each update, PPO keeps the optimization process within a "*safe*" region (the trust region), which ensures better convergence behavior.

Key Features of PPO:

- **Sample Efficiency**: PPO is more sample-efficient than earlier algorithms such as **Trust Region Policy Optimization (TRPO)** because it allows multiple updates from the same batch of data, speeding up learning.
- **Robustness**: PPO is known for its stability, as it carefully controls the extent of policy updates, which avoids catastrophic performance degradation seen in some other algorithms.
- **Wide Use**: PPO has been widely adopted due to its success in challenging environments such as **OpenAI's reinforcement learning environments** and game-playing AIs.

Relation to Metaheuristic Optimization: Although **DPO** and **PPO** are not direct metaheuristic algorithms, they share similarities in how they **explore the solution space** and **optimize** by improving solutions iteratively. In reinforcement learning, PPO especially acts as a bridge between dynamic programming-based methods (such as value iteration) and gradient-based optimization, showing that new techniques often combine elements from both traditional optimization and modern machine learning algorithms.

Extension of Traditional Frameworks

Both **DPO** and **PPO** take core ideas from traditional optimization frameworks and extend them to modern data-driven contexts:

- **DPO** builds on dynamic programming by **approximating solutions** for high-dimensional problems and utilizing **reinforcement learning** to optimize multi-step decision processes in dynamic, real-time environments. It also integrates **function approximators** such as neural networks to handle large-scale problems that traditional DP cannot solve due to computational constraints.
- **PPO** evolves from **gradient-based optimization methods** by adding mechanisms that ensure stability and scalability, addressing the challenges of learning policies in reinforcement learning environments with constantly changing data. It ensures that policies are updated efficiently while maintaining a **safe region of optimization** to avoid performance degradation.

DPO and Its Extension of Traditional Frameworks

Dynamic Programming (DP) is a classical optimization technique that works well for problems that can be broken into overlapping subproblems, particularly in scenarios such as shortest path problems, knapsack problems, or certain control problems. However, traditional DP frameworks encounter **scalability** and **complexity issues** when dealing with large, real-world, data-driven problems that involve more uncertain or dynamic environments.

Challenges in Modern Contexts:

- **Scalability**: DP techniques can suffer from the "*curse of dimensionality*" because they require storing and solving all possible subproblems, which becomes computationally prohibitive for large-scale systems.
- **Real-Time Data**: Traditional DP assumes a static, well-defined problem, but in modern applications (for example, robotics, dynamic systems), decisions often have to be made in real time with new data constantly arriving.
- **Multi-Step Decision Making**: Complex problems often have a sequential nature where decisions at one stage impact future stages, requiring adaptive solutions that handle changing environments.

How DPO Extends Traditional DP:

- **Approximate Dynamic Programming (ADP)** or **Reinforcement Learning (RL)** techniques, such as **Q-learning** and **Temporal Difference (TD)** learning, build on DP by **approximating value functions** for large state-action spaces. These approaches reduce the need to compute or store exact solutions for every possible state, which makes DPO more scalable.

- **Model-Free Approaches**: DPO, in the form of **model-free reinforcement learning**, does not require a complete model of the environment. Instead, it learns directly from interactions with the environment, making it better suited for **uncertain, real-world problems** where models are incomplete or unknown.
- **Policy Optimization**: Instead of computing value functions explicitly, DPO-inspired methods, particularly in reinforcement learning, optimize the policy directly (such as **actor-critic** methods). This direct optimization allows for more efficient learning from large datasets where defining an exact model may be impossible.

Thus, DPO extends the **DP framework** to modern data-driven contexts by handling **high-dimensionality**, using **function approximators** (such as neural networks), and applying **online learning** techniques that adapt to changing environments.

PPO and Building on Traditional Gradient-Based Methods

PPO is primarily used in reinforcement learning and builds on **policy gradient methods**, which directly optimize policies based on gradient ascent. Traditional optimization methods such as **gradient descent** are central to many machine learning techniques, but these methods face specific challenges in modern contexts, especially in reinforcement learning tasks where the environment is non-stationary and decisions evolve over time.

Challenges in Modern, Data-Driven Contexts:

- **Exploration vs. Exploitation**: Policy gradient methods often suffer from instability and require balancing between exploring new strategies and exploiting the current best-known policy. Sudden large updates can lead to instability, especially in environments where actions impact future rewards.
- **High Variance in Policy Gradients**: Policy gradient methods typically have high variance, which can slow down convergence and require careful tuning.
- **Scalability and Efficiency**: Traditional policy optimization methods such as **Trust Region Policy Optimization (TRPO)** attempt to improve stability but are computationally expensive and hard to scale to real-time, large-scale learning problems.

How PPO Addresses These Challenges:

- **Clipped Objective Function**: PPO builds on **gradient-based optimization** but introduces a novel technique where it clips policy updates. By ensuring the updates do not deviate too far from the current policy, PPO avoids the problem of overly large, destabilizing updates that can make training unstable. This improves the **stability** of learning.

- **Trade-Off Between Efficiency and Stability**: PPO strikes a balance between the efficiency of standard policy gradient methods (such as **REINFORCE**) and the stability of more constrained methods such as **TRPO**. It does this without the computational overhead of solving complex optimization constraints that TRPO imposes, making it more scalable and practical in large-scale, data-driven contexts.
- **Multiple Updates per Data Batch**: While many policy gradient methods rely on a single update per batch of data (due to variance and instability), PPO enables **multiple updates** using the same data. This makes PPO highly **sample-efficient**, which is crucial in data-driven environments where obtaining real-world data is expensive or time-consuming.

In essence, both techniques adapt foundational optimization concepts to fit the demands of modern problems, such as **uncertainty**, **high-dimensionality**, and **dynamic, real-time learning**, making them suitable for applications in fields such as **robotics**, **game AI**, **autonomous systems**, **LLMs** and other data-driven domains. Next we focus on Metaheuristic algorithms.

Metaheuristic Algorithms

In this section, we explore **Metaheuristic algorithms**, a diverse class of optimization techniques inspired by natural processes, biological evolution, and the behavior of animals, insects, and social systems. These algorithms are designed to tackle complex, large-scale optimization problems that traditional methods struggle with due to non-linearity, vast search spaces, and uncertainty. By mimicking natural phenomena such as the way ants find food or how birds flock together, metaheuristic algorithms offer a flexible and robust approach to finding near-optimal solutions in a variety of fields, from engineering to artificial intelligence. Below, we present some of the most prominent metaheuristic algorithms that have proven effective across a wide range of applications.

Nature-Inspired Metaheuristic Algorithms

- **Genetic Algorithm (GA):** Inspired by the process of natural selection and genetics.
- **Particle Swarm Optimization (PSO):** Mimics the social behavior of bird flocking or fish schooling.
- **Ant Colony Optimization (ACO):** Simulates the behavior of ants finding the shortest path to food.

- **Artificial Bee Colony (ABC):** Based on the foraging behavior of honey bees.
- **Simulated Annealing (SA):** Mimics the physical annealing process of metals.
- **Firefly Algorithm:** Based on the flashing behavior of fireflies for attracting mates.
- **Bat Algorithm:** Simulates the echolocation behavior of bats in hunting.
- **Grey Wolf Optimizer (GWO):** Mimics the leadership hierarchy and hunting behavior of grey wolves.
- **Cuckoo Search (CS):** Inspired by the brood parasitism of cuckoo birds.
- **Whale Optimization Algorithm (WOA):** Imitates the bubble-net hunting strategy of humpback whales.

Evolutionary and Swarm-Based Metaheuristics

- **Differential Evolution (DE):** Uses vector differences for problem-solving, inspired by GA but focuses on mutation.
- **Harmony Search (HS):** Based on the improvisation process of musicians.
- **Memetic Algorithm (MA):** A combination of genetic algorithms and local search strategies.
- **Bacterial Foraging Optimization (BFO):** Simulates the foraging strategy of E. coli bacteria.
- **Cat Swarm Optimization (CSO):** Inspired by the natural behavior of cats.
- **Cultural Algorithm (CA):** Extends genetic algorithms by including knowledge-sharing mechanisms (cultural evolution).
- **Fish School Search (FSS):** Models the social behavior of fish schools.

Hybrid and Recent Metaheuristics

- **Hybrid Genetic Algorithm (HGA):** Combines genetic algorithms with other techniques such as local search.
- **Hybrid Particle Swarm Optimization (HPSO):** Integrates PSO with additional mechanisms such as mutation or crossover.
- **Multi-Objective Evolutionary Algorithm (MOEA):** Targets multiple optimization objectives simultaneously.
- **Flower Pollination Algorithm (FPA):** Inspired by the pollination process in flowering plants.
- **Elephant Herding Optimization (EHO):** Simulates the behavior of elephant herds.

- **Lion Optimization Algorithm (LOA):** Models the social behavior of lions in hunting and living in prides.
- **Dragonfly Algorithm (DA):** Mimics the dynamic swarming behaviors of dragonflies.
- **Krill Herd (KH):** Simulates the herding behavior of krill in the ocean.

These algorithms are typically used when solving highly complex, multi-modal optimization problems where traditional optimization techniques (such as gradient-based methods) struggle due to large search spaces, non-linearity, or lack of differentiability. They are versatile and can be applied in diverse fields such as engineering, AI, robotics, finance, and logistics.

Ant Colony Optimization (ACO)

In the last chapter, we developed an algorithm to optimize product prices using **Ant Colony Optimization (ACO)** techniques. Now, let us take a closer look at how ants inspire this optimization approach and the mechanisms behind their efficiency. Ants, in their natural environment, exhibit a remarkable ability to find the shortest paths to food sources, despite the complexity of their surroundings. They achieve this by laying down a chemical trail, known as **pheromones**, which guides other ants toward promising paths. Over time, paths with higher pheromone concentrations attract more ants, reinforcing the shortest or most efficient route.

This behavior is the foundation of **heuristics** in ACO, where a problem is solved not by systematically exploring every possibility but by guiding the search process through positive reinforcement (pheromones) and local exploration. The concept of **heuristics** relates to **pheromones** in that heuristics offer a strategy to explore the search space efficiently, just as pheromone trails guide ants toward optimal paths. Through this process, ACO balances **exploration** (searching new paths) and **exploitation** (reinforcing successful ones), mimicking nature's elegant solution to complex problems.

Theory

In ACO, ants traverse through a **graph**, where the nodes represent possible states or locations (such as product prices in your case), and edges between nodes represent the transition between these states (possible moves or decisions). Each ant seeks the optimal solution by moving along the edges, influenced by **pheromone levels** and local **heuristic information**.

- **Pheromone Trails:** The key idea behind ACO is that ants leave **pheromone trails** on the edges as they move from one node to another. The strength of the pheromone on a path τ_{ij} (for the path between node iii and node j) influences the likelihood that subsequent ants will follow the same path.

Each ant probabilistically chooses its next step based on a **transition probability** that considers both pheromone levels and heuristic information. The probability P_{ij}^k that an ant k moves from node iii to node j is given by:

$$P_{ij}^k = \frac{[\tau_{ij}]^\alpha \cdot [\eta_{ij}]^\beta}{\sum_{l \in \text{allowed}} [\tau_{il}]^\alpha \cdot [\eta_{il}]^\beta}$$

- τ_{ij} is the pheromone level on edge (i,j).
- η_{ij} is the heuristic information (for example, inverse of the distance between iii and j, or in the case of pricing, the profitability of choosing a certain price).
- α controls the influence of pheromones.
- β controls the influence of heuristic information.
- The denominator sums over all possible moves from node iii.

This equation ensures that ants are more likely to choose paths with stronger pheromone concentrations and paths that are shorter or more profitable (based on the heuristic η).

- **Pheromone Update:** Once all ants have completed their journeys (from start to destination), the pheromone levels on each path are updated. The **pheromone update** rule is:

$$\tau_{ij} \leftarrow (1 - \rho) \cdot \tau_{ij} + \sum_k \Delta\tau_{ij}^k$$

- P is the **evaporation rate**, which controls the rate at which pheromone evaporates over time. This prevents older solutions from being overemphasized.
- $\Delta\tau_{ij}$ is the pheromone deposited by ant k on edge (i,j).

Each ant deposits pheromone in proportion to the quality of its solution. If ant kkk finds a better solution (shorter path, higher profit), it deposits more pheromone. The pheromone deposit is often modeled as:

$$\Delta\tau_{ij}^k = \begin{cases} Q/L^k & \text{if ant } k \text{ uses edge } (i,j) \\ 0 & \text{otherwise} \end{cases}$$

Where:

- Q is a constant.
- L^k is the length (or cost) of the solution found by ant k.

- **Evaporation Rate** ρ: The **evaporation rate** ρ ensures that pheromone levels do not grow indefinitely and allows the algorithm to "forget" less optimal solutions. It balances exploration and exploitation by preventing older paths from dominating the search space, thus encouraging ants to continue exploring new possibilities. Higher evaporation rates encourage exploration, while lower rates lead to stronger exploitation of existing paths.

Key Elements of ACO

The following are the core components that influence the behavior of the algorithm:

- **Pheromone Trails** τ: These represent accumulated knowledge from past iterations and guide future ants toward promising solutions. The pheromone concentration is updated after each cycle.
- **Heuristic Information** η: This provides problem-specific guidance to the ants, such as favouring shorter distances, lower costs, or higher profits. In your price optimization example, this could be based on expected revenue or market demand.
- **Exploration vs. Exploitation**: ACO must balance exploring new solutions (paths) and exploiting known, successful paths. This is controlled by:
  - **Pheromone Influence** α
  - **Heuristic Influence** β
  - **Evaporation Rate** ρ
- **Solution Construction**: Each ant incrementally builds a solution by selecting one edge at a time, influenced by the transition probabilities, until a complete solution is constructed (for example, all products have optimized prices).
- **Pheromone Update Mechanism**: After all ants complete their solutions, the pheromone levels are updated to reinforce good solutions and weaken less optimal ones. This encourages the ants in future iterations to follow better paths.

Workflow of ACO Algorithm

1. **Initialization**: The pheromone levels on all edges are initialized to the same small value.
2. **Solution Construction**: Each ant constructs a solution by iteratively choosing the next step based on transition probabilities that depend on the pheromone trail and heuristic information.
3. **Pheromone Update**: Once all ants have completed their solutions, the pheromone trails are updated. Paths that were part of better solutions receive more pheromone, and some pheromone evaporates to encourage exploration.

4. **Repeat**: The process is repeated over several iterations until a termination condition is met (for example, a fixed number of iterations or convergence to a satisfactory solution).

So, Ant Colony Optimization uses pheromone trails, heuristic information, and probabilistic decision-making to iteratively build better solutions to complex optimization problems. The algorithm's key parameters, such as **pheromone influence**, **heuristic influence**, and **evaporation rate**, allow for a dynamic balance between exploring new solutions and reinforcing existing ones. Through **pheromone updates** and controlled **evaporation**, ACO converges towards near-optimal solutions over time, making it suitable for real-world applications such as pricing optimization, where solutions need to adapt based on continuously changing market conditions.

Library

There are several Python libraries implement **Ant Colony Optimization (ACO)**

In algorithms, providing ready-made functions to handle the calculations.

1. **PyACO (Python Ant Colony Optimization):**
   - **PyACO** is a Python implementation of the Ant Colony Optimization algorithm. It is simple to use and can be integrated into any optimization workflow, including machine learning model tuning.
   - **Usage**: It is great for problems such as the **traveling salesman problem (TSP)** or optimizing parameter combinations, and it can be adapted for continuous or discrete optimization tasks.

Install:

```
pip install pyaco
```

Example:

```
from pyaco import ACO, Graph

def distance_function(n1, n2):
    # Define a distance function or use heuristic information
    return abs(n1 - n2)

aco = ACO(10, 100, 1.0, 5.0, 0.5, 10, distance_function)
graph = Graph(10, distance_function)
best_solution = aco.solve(graph)
```

2. **ACOTSP (Ant Colony Optimization for TSP):**
   - This is a specific library for solving the **Traveling Salesman Problem (TSP)** using ACO, which can be adapted for similar optimization tasks.

- While it is specific to TSP, you can customize its components for other combinatorial problems, such as **feature selection** or **hyperparameter tuning**.

Install:

```
pip install acotsp
```

3. **ACO-Py: ACO-Py** is a more customizable and flexible Python library that provides a general framework for ACO. You can apply it to different kinds of problems, including parameter tuning, scheduling, and optimization tasks often required in machine learning.

Install:

```
pip install aco-py
```

Example:

```
from aco import ACO
from aco.problem import Problem

class MyProblem(Problem):
    def __init__(self):
        super(MyProblem, self).__init__()
        self.best_solution = None

    def cost(self, solution):
        # Define the cost function for your problem
        return sum(solution)

aco = ACO(ant_count=10, generations=50)
problem = MyProblem()
best_solution = aco.solve(problem)
```

4. **sko.ACA:** The library **sko.ACA** refers to the **Ant Colony Algorithm (ACA)** implemented in the **Scikit-Opt (sko)** package. **Scikit-Opt** is a Python library designed for various swarm intelligence algorithms, including **Genetic Algorithm (GA)**, **Particle Swarm Optimization (PSO)**, **Simulated Annealing (SA)**, and **Ant Colony Algorithm (ACA)**, among others. This package allows users to solve optimization problems, with a focus on combinatorial optimization such as the **Traveling Salesman Problem (TSP)**.

   With **sko.ACA**, you can use the Ant Colony Algorithm to solve problems such as TSP by defining a cost function (for example, calculating the total distance in a TSP). The algorithm will simulate the way ants deposit pheromones and reinforce the shortest paths based on iterations, allowing you to optimize complex solutions.

Install Scikit-Opt:

```
pip install scikit-opt
```

This library is open-source and is actively used for various optimization tasks such as **feature selection**, **hyperparameter tuning**, and classical optimization problems.

Example:

Here's a simple example of using **sko.ACA** for TSP:

```
from sko.ACA import ACA_TSP

# Define the total distance function
def cal_total_distance(routine):
    num_points, = routine.shape
    return sum([distance_matrix[routine[i % num_points],
routine[(i + 1) % num_points]] for i in range(num_points)])

# Initialize ACA with TSP settings
aca = ACA_TSP(func=cal_total_distance, n_dim=num_points, size_
pop=50, max_iter=200, distance_matrix=distance_matrix)

# Run ACA to find the best solution
best_x, best_y = aca.run()
```

Scikit-Opt makes it easy to extend these algorithms to other types of optimization problems, integrating well with other Python tools such as **NumPy** and **Matplotlib** for further analysis and visualization(Scikit-Opt)(PyPI). This library is open-source and is actively used for various optimization tasks such as feature selection, hyperparameter tuning, and classical optimization problems.

Applications of ACO

Ant Colony Optimization (ACO) has been applied in various real-world scenarios where complex, combinatorial optimization problems need to be solved efficiently. Here are three notable applications:

- **Logistics and Supply Chain Management: ACO** is frequently used to optimize routing problems in logistics, such as the **Traveling Salesman Problem (TSP)** and **Vehicle Routing Problem (VRP)**. In logistics, minimizing travel distances, reducing delivery times, and optimizing the path of multiple delivery vehicles is crucial. ACO-based algorithms help in determining the most efficient routes for fleets, minimizing costs related to fuel, time, and vehicle wear.

  Example: Large-scale courier services such as **UPS** or **FedEx** use similar optimization techniques to minimize delivery costs and time while managing thousands of vehicles across complex networks.

- **Telecommunications Networks:** ACO has been applied in **network routing** to find optimal paths for data packets across complex networks, ensuring efficient bandwidth use and minimizing latency. The dynamic nature of network traffic, which is influenced by real-time factors such as congestion, makes ACO ideal for adapting routes to changing conditions.

  Example: **Wireless sensor networks** and **Ad-Hoc networks** use ACO to route data in a decentralized manner, improving data transmission rates and network efficiency.

- **Scheduling and Resource Allocation: ACO** is used in various scheduling applications where limited resources need to be allocated efficiently, such as job-shop scheduling or university timetable scheduling. ACO optimizes the scheduling process by assigning jobs, tasks, or resources in a way that minimizes delays, conflicts, and idle times.

  Example: Manufacturing companies use ACO to optimize the scheduling of machinery, workers, and materials, ensuring maximum productivity while minimizing delays.

- **Price Optimization: ACO** is increasingly applied in **price optimization** to help businesses maximize revenue by determining the best pricing strategy. ACO can simulate customer demand and competitor pricing behavior to find the optimal prices that balance supply, demand, and profitability.

  Example: In **e-commerce** platforms or retail chains, ACO algorithms can be used to dynamically adjust product prices in real-time, taking into account factors such as competitor pricing, customer behavior, and inventory levels.

These applications highlight the power and flexibility of **ACO** in tackling complex optimization problems across a range of industries.

In the last chapter, we discussed one such example, and the code can be found in `Price_optimzation_chapter 6`.

Differential Evolution (DE)

Now that you understand **Nature-Inspired Metaheuristic Algorithms**, let us focus on **Evolutionary and Swarm-Based Metaheuristics**. One of the powerful techniques in this domain is **Differential Evolution (DE)**. Like Genetic Algorithms (GA), DE is part of the family of **evolutionary algorithms** and is inspired by the process of natural evolution. DE excels at solving complex optimization problems by maintaining a population of candidate solutions and improving them iteratively using mutation, crossover, and selection.

Theory

How Differential Evolution Works:

1. **Initialization**: DE begins by initializing a population of candidate solutions, often represented as vectors. These vectors are spread throughout the solution space randomly, ensuring a diverse exploration of potential solutions at the start.

2. **Mutation**: The core of DE lies in its **mutation operation**, where a new candidate solution (often called a "*mutant vector*") is generated by adding the weighted difference between two population vectors to a third one. This process is expressed as:

$$v_i = x_{r1} + F \cdot (x_{r2} - x_{r3})$$

   - v_i is the mutant vector.
   - x_{r1}, x_{r2}, x_{r3} are randomly selected vectors from the population.
   - F is a scaling factor (typically between 0 and 1) that controls the amplification of the difference between two vectors.

   This mutation step is critical as it introduces variability and drives exploration of the solution space.

3. **Crossover**: After mutation, **crossover** is applied to combine the mutant vector with the current candidate solution (known as the "*target vector*") to create a new trial vector. This step helps maintain useful traits from the current solution while incorporating novel information from the mutant vector. The trial vector is formed based on a **crossover probability** CR, which controls the likelihood that the elements from the mutant vector replace those in the target vector.

4. **Selection**: Finally, DE uses a **selection** mechanism to choose the better solution between the trial vector and the target vector. If the trial vector yields a lower value of the objective function (for minimization problems), it replaces the target vector in the population. This step ensures that the population evolves towards better solutions over time.

Key Parameters

- **Population Size**: A larger population increases exploration but adds computational cost.
- **Scaling Factor (F)**: Controls the strength of the mutation and the extent of exploration. Values close to 0.5 are common.

- **Crossover Probability (CR)**: Determines the balance between exploration and exploitation, with typical values ranging from 0.1 to 0.9.

Advantages of Differential Evolution

- **Simple and Efficient**: DE is easy to implement and often requires fewer parameters than other evolutionary algorithms such as Genetic Algorithms.
- **Global Optimization**: DE is well-suited for solving continuous, non-linear, and multi-modal optimization problems, making it a robust method for global optimization.
- **Good Convergence**: It can achieve fast convergence to optimal or near-optimal solutions, especially for problems with a smooth search space.

Applications

Differential Evolution is used in various real-world applications, including:

- **Engineering Design**: Optimizing complex designs such as aircraft wings or automotive components, where many parameters need to be adjusted.
- **Machine Learning**: Hyperparameter tuning of machine learning models, where DE is used to find the best configuration of parameters such as learning rate or the number of neurons in a neural network.
- **Signal Processing**: DE has been applied to optimize filters and algorithms in fields such as audio and image processing.

So, **Differential Evolution (DE)** is a powerful, evolutionary algorithm that effectively balances exploration and exploitation. It's simple mechanics, combined with strong performance on complex problems, make it a popular choice in optimization tasks across industries.

Computer Vision Application

An example of how you can build a toy neural network using **PyTorch** and **PyGAD** for hyperparameter tuning with **Differential Evolution (DE)**. The DE will be used to tune the hyperparameters of the neural network, such as the learning rate and the number of neurons in the hidden layer.

We will use **PyGAD** (a Python library for Genetic Algorithms) to implement the DE optimization strategy, and **PyTorch** to create the neural network. The code can be found in the jupyter notebook **"Chapter 7"**.

Step 1: Install Required Libraries

First, install the necessary libraries: as shown in jupyter notebook

Step 2: Define the Neural Network and Dataset

We will define a simple feedforward neural network in **PyTorch** and use the **MNIST** dataset as an example.

Step 3: Define the Fitness Function for PyGAD

The fitness function will evaluate how well the neural network performs with the given hyperparameters. We will optimize the learning rate and the number of neurons in the hidden layer.

Step 4: Configure and Run Differential Evolution Using PyGAD

Now, we set up **PyGAD** for the **Differential Evolution** process, where the population contains different configurations of hyperparameters, and it evolves towards the best solution over several generations.

We initialize and configure the **PyGAD GA** instance to simulate the **Differential Evolution** process, which will be used to find the optimal hyperparameters for the neural network model. Here is what we are configuring step-by-step:

a. **Number of Generations (`num_generations`)**: We specify that the GA will evolve over **10 generations**. Each generation aims to improve the solutions by selecting the best parents, applying crossover, and mutating offspring.

b. **Number of Parents Mating (`num_parents_mating`)**: We set **5 parents** to mate in each generation. These parents will be selected from the population based on their fitness scores.

c. **Fitness Function (`fitness_func`)**: The **fitness function** is defined to evaluate how well a solution performs. In our case, it trains the neural network for a few iterations and uses the negative of the loss value as the fitness score. Lower loss values correspond to better solutions.

d. **Population Size (`sol_per_pop`)**: The population size is set to **10**. This means there will be 10 possible solutions (sets of hyperparameters) in each generation.

e. **Number of Genes (`num_genes`)**: We have **2 genes** in each solution: the **learning rate** and the **number of neurons in the hidden layer**. These genes will be evolved to optimize the performance of the neural network.

f. **Initial Range for Genes (`init_range_low` and `init_range_high`)**: The initial range for the genes (hyperparameters) is specified. The learning rate will start between **0.0001** and **0.01**, and the number of neurons in the hidden layer will start between **50** and **200**. This ensures a good spread across possible values.

g. **Mutation Parameters (`mutation_percent_genes`, `mutation_type`)**: We specify that **10%** of the genes will be mutated during each generation, and the mutation type is set to **random**. This helps maintain genetic diversity in the population.

h. **Crossover Type (`crossover_type`)**: The crossover type is set to **single point**, meaning that two parents are combined by swapping their genes at a randomly chosen crossover point.

By configuring these parameters, we create an instance of a **Genetic Algorithm** that mimics the behavior of **Differential Evolution**–iteratively improving solutions (that is, hyperparameters) over multiple generations. The idea is to converge towards the set of hyperparameters that result in the best neural network performance by continually evolving and refining candidate solutions.

Once configured, we call **`ga_instance.run()`** to start the optimization process. After all generations are completed, the **`ga_instance.best_solution()`** function provides us with the optimal hyperparameters found during the evolution process.

Step 5: Evaluate the Best Solution

Finally, evaluate the best hyperparameters found by **Differential Evolution** on the full dataset.

Step 6: Add Visualization of Gradients and Loss

We will collect the gradients of the model parameters during training and plot their magnitudes before and after using DE to tune the hyperparameters.

Step 7: Explanation

a. **Loss Plot**: We visualize the **loss** before and after applying DE. The plot shows how the loss decreases during training, both before and after the hyperparameters are tuned using Differential Evolution. The **before DE plot** will likely show a slower or less optimal decrease in loss compared to the **after DE plot**, which should reflect improved performance due to better hyperparameters.

b. **Gradient Magnitude Plot**: We also plot the **gradient norms** to observe how the gradients change during training. Before tuning with DE, gradients might fluctuate more, whereas after tuning, the gradients should stabilize and potentially converge faster, reflecting a more optimized training process.

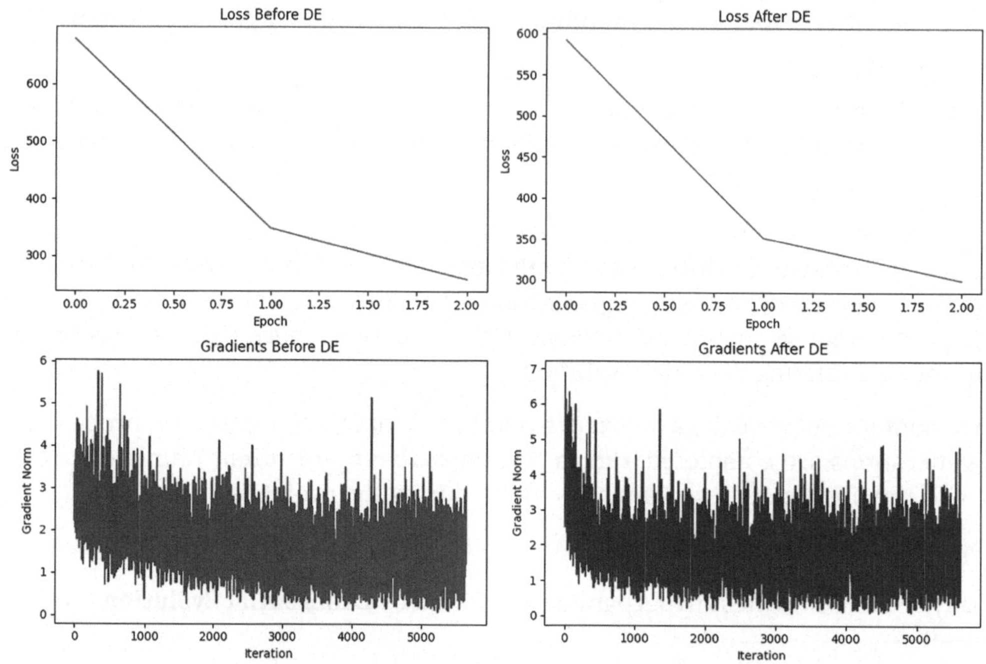

Figure 7.1: *Best solution found: Learning rate: 0.0030205213296474053, Hidden size: 157, Fitness: -32.18541920185089*

Visualization

- **Before DE**: You will likely see a slower decrease in loss and larger fluctuations in gradient magnitudes, indicating that the initial hyperparameters (random values) were not ideal.
- **After DE**: With optimized hyperparameters, the loss should decrease faster, and the gradients should behave more smoothly, indicating improved convergence behavior.

This visualization gives you a clear understanding of how **Differential Evolution** improves both the **training process** and **gradient dynamics**, ultimately leading to better optimization of the neural network.

This simple example showcases how **Differential Evolution (DE)** can be applied to tune neural network hyperparameters such as **learning rate** and **hidden layer size** for better performance on a machine learning task.

In *Chapter 3, Overview of Genetic Algorithm Libraries*, we spoke about multi-object optimization and introduced NSGA-II, under the section **Single-objective and multi-objective optimization**, where we combine two objectives (minimizing the sum of squares and maximizing the sum of values) using a weighted sum. We build upon the previous code. Let us take a deep dive into it.

Multi-Objective Evolutionary Algorithm (MOEA)

A **Multi-Objective Evolutionary Algorithm (MOEA)** is a type of evolutionary algorithm that aims to solve **multi-objective optimization problems**, where there arc two or more conflicting objectives that need to be optimized simultaneously. Unlike traditional optimization problems that focus on a single objective, **MOEAs** are used when you need to optimize multiple objectives, which often cannot be easily combined into a single objective function.

Key Concepts in MOEA

- **Multiple Objectives**: In many real-world problems, there are conflicting objectives. For instance, when designing an electric vehicle, one may need to minimize both **cost** and **weight** while maximizing **battery range**. These objectives are often in conflict—minimizing weight might require expensive lightweight materials, whereas minimizing cost might result in increased weight. MOEAs help to balance such competing objectives.
- **Pareto Front**: **MOEAs** do not produce a single solution but rather a set of **Pareto optimal solutions**. A solution is considered **Pareto optimal** if no other solution is better in all objectives. The **Pareto front** represents a collection of such non-dominated solutions, offering decision-makers different trade-off options. For example, in the case of electric vehicle design, the Pareto front would represent various combinations of cost, weight, and battery range, where no further improvement can be made in one objective without degrading another.
- **Diversity and Convergence**: Unlike single-objective algorithms that focus on finding a single optimal solution, MOEAs strive to find diverse solutions along the entire Pareto front while ensuring convergence towards the optimal front. Techniques such as **crowding distance** and **elitism** are often used to maintain diversity among solutions and ensure they are spread evenly along the Pareto front.

Theory

MOEAs operate similarly to other evolutionary algorithms, with a population of candidate solutions that evolve over successive generations. However, **selection**, **crossover**, and **mutation** operators are adapted to handle multiple objectives.

- **Fitness Assignment**: Instead of a single fitness score, solutions are evaluated based on how well they perform across multiple objectives. They are assigned a **rank** based on the **Pareto dominance** principle.

- **Non-Dominated Sorting**: Popular MOEAs such as **NSGA-II (Non-dominated Sorting Genetic Algorithm II)** use **non-dominated sorting** to classify individuals based on their Pareto ranks. The lower the rank, the better the solution.
- **Crowding Distance**: To ensure diversity, solutions are also evaluated by **crowding distance**, which measures how close a solution is to its neighbors. This prevents clustering and encourages a spread of solutions along the Pareto front.

Applications of MOEA

MOEAs are particularly useful in areas where trade-offs are essential and multiple competing goals exist:

- **Engineering Design**: In the design of products such as aircraft, vehicles, and mechanical systems, engineers need to optimize parameters such as **cost**, **performance**, **safety**, and **weight** simultaneously.
- **Financial Portfolio Optimization**: MOEAs can be used to optimize investment portfolios by balancing conflicting objectives such as **maximizing return** and **minimizing risk**.
- **Energy Management**: For optimizing renewable energy systems, MOEAs can help to simultaneously minimize **cost** and maximize **energy efficiency** while reducing **environmental impact**.

Popular MOEAs:

- **NSGA-II (Non-dominated Sorting Genetic Algorithm II)**: One of the most widely used MOEAs that uses fast non-dominated sorting, elitism, and crowding distance to guide the search.
- **SPEA2 (Strength Pareto Evolutionary Algorithm 2)**: Another popular MOEA that combines Pareto-based fitness assignment with an external archive to store non-dominated solutions.
- **MOEA/D (Multi-objective Evolutionary Algorithm based on Decomposition)**: This algorithm decomposes a multi-objective problem into a number of single-objective subproblems and optimizes them in parallel.

So, **MOEAs** provide a powerful approach to solve complex optimization problems involving multiple conflicting objectives by generating a set of **Pareto optimal solutions**, allowing decision-makers to understand the trade-offs and make informed choices.

A prominent use case of **multi-objective optimization** in **finance** is in the area of **portfolio optimization**. In this context, investors need to balance multiple conflicting objectives to create an efficient investment portfolio. Here is a typical scenario where **multi-objective optimization** is useful.

Use Case: Portfolio Optimization

In **portfolio management**, the goal is to allocate capital among different financial assets (for example, stocks, bonds, mutual funds) to maximize return while minimizing risk. These two objectives—**maximizing expected return** and **minimizing risk**—are inherently conflicting, which makes this problem well-suited for **multi-objective optimization**.

Objectives in Financial Portfolio Optimization:

- **Maximize Return**: The expected return is the profit that an investor aims to achieve from the investment over a period. Investors usually want to maximize this return to achieve greater profitability.
- **Minimize Risk**: In finance, risk is often quantified as the **volatility** or **standard deviation** of asset returns. Investors want to minimize risk to ensure stable and predictable outcomes.

These objectives often conflict because higher potential returns are typically associated with higher risks, and achieving low risk often means settling for lower returns. **Multi-objective Evolutionary Algorithms (MOEAs)** can help investors to generate multiple potential solutions along the **Pareto front**, allowing them to choose the most suitable trade-off based on their risk tolerance.

Application of MOEA in Finance

An example of how **MOEAs** such as **NSGA-II** (Non-dominated Sorting Genetic Algorithm II) can be applied is:

- **Define Objectives**: The objectives are defined as maximizing **expected return** and minimizing **portfolio risk**.
- **Generate Initial Population**: A population of portfolios is created, with each portfolio representing a different allocation of assets.
- **Non-Dominated Sorting and Selection**: Each portfolio is evaluated based on its return and risk. Solutions are ranked according to their **Pareto dominance**.
- **Crossover and Mutation**: The algorithm uses evolutionary techniques such as **crossover** and **mutation** to create new portfolios by combining asset weights from parent solutions, aiming to improve the trade-off between risk and return.
- **Convergence to Pareto Front**: After a number of generations, the algorithm converges to a **Pareto front**, which consists of the set of portfolios where no

portfolio is strictly better than the others in both objectives. The investor can then choose a portfolio from this Pareto front based on their preference between risk and return.

Example: Suppose an investor is looking to allocate capital among **three different stocks** (A, B, C). The objectives are to **maximize returns** while **minimizing risk**. Using an **MOEA** such as **NSGA-II**, the algorithm will evolve different portfolios (for example, combinations of A, B, and C in varying percentages), generating a **Pareto front** that shows the best possible trade-offs between high return and low risk.

- If the investor is **risk-averse**, they may select a portfolio on the Pareto front that has low risk but modest return.
- If the investor is **risk-tolerant**, they may choose a portfolio with higher potential returns despite the associated higher risk.

Benefits of Using MOEA

- **Multiple Options**: MOEA provides a range of potential portfolios on the Pareto front, giving investors more options to choose from based on their risk-return profile.
- **Flexibility**: MOEA can incorporate additional objectives, such as **minimizing transaction costs** or **maximizing liquidity**, making it more flexible compared to traditional single-objective optimization methods.
- **Adaptability**: Evolutionary algorithms can adapt to complex, non-linear relationships between assets, capturing market conditions more effectively than traditional linear optimization approaches.

Multi-objective optimization in portfolio management helps in constructing diversified portfolios that cater to an investor's unique risk preferences, offering a clear view of the trade-offs between different investment strategies. This makes it a powerful tool in finance for achieving a well-balanced and optimized portfolio.

Library

PyGAD does support **multi-objective optimization**. Starting with version 3.2.0, PyGAD includes support for handling multiple objectives using the **Non-Dominated Sorting Genetic Algorithm II (NSGA-II)**. This approach allows users to optimize for multiple conflicting objectives simultaneously.

In PyGAD, you can make use of **multi-objective optimization** by modifying the fitness function to return a list, tuple, or numpy array containing the fitness values for each objective. The library then considers this as a multi-objective problem and uses techniques such as non-dominated sorting to identify the best solutions that provide a balance between the different objectives (PyGAD, https://pygad.readthedocs.io/en/latest/index.html).

For example, in portfolio optimization, you could define a fitness function that returns two values: one representing the expected return and another representing the risk. PyGAD will attempt to find solutions that balance these objectives along the Pareto front, giving you a range of optimal trade-offs to choose from.

If you want to explore more about how PyGAD handles multi-objective optimization and see specific examples, you can refer to its documentation on Read the Docs.

S&P 500 data

The **S&P 500** is a stock market index that tracks the performance of 500 large companies listed on stock exchanges in the United States. It is one of the most well-known and widely used benchmarks for the U.S. equity market, often considered a reflection of the overall market's health. The companies included in the index are diverse, spanning multiple industries such as **technology**, **healthcare**, **financials**, **consumer goods**, and **energy**.

The **S&P 500** is weighted by market capitalization, meaning that larger companies have a more significant impact on the index's performance. This feature allows the index to represent the value of the largest and most influential public companies in the U.S., making it a popular choice for investors seeking to track market performance without investing in individual stocks.

For portfolio optimization, **S&P 500 data** is often used to assess different sectors' risk-return profiles and create balanced, diversified portfolios. By selecting stocks from diverse sectors–such as technology, healthcare, and financials–investors aim to **mitigate risk** and **maximize returns** through diversification.

In portfolio optimization projects, such as the one we discussed earlier, **S&P 500 stocks** provide a good dataset for applying **genetic algorithms** or **multi-objective optimization techniques** to determine the best combination of assets that can maximize return while minimizing risk.

The **S&P 500 data** is particularly suitable for a portfolio optimization use case because it provides a diverse set of companies across multiple sectors, allowing for effective risk management and return maximization. By choosing stocks from different sectors such as technology, energy, healthcare, and financials, we ensure that the resulting portfolio is not overly exposed to the risks associated with a single industry. This helps mitigate unsystematic risk, which is specific to individual sectors or companies.

Additionally, S&P 500 companies are large-cap firms with reliable financial data, making them ideal for conducting **genetic algorithm optimization**. The availability of historical data for these companies allows us to accurately calculate metrics such as **average returns**, **standard deviation** (risk), and **correlation** between stocks. This information is crucial for identifying the best combination of assets that maximizes returns while keeping risks at a manageable level.

Furthermore, the S&P 500 index is widely considered a benchmark for the U.S. stock market, making it a natural choice for portfolio optimization aimed at both individual and institutional investors. By selecting different stocks based on metrics such as historical returns, sectors, or low correlation, we can create diversified portfolios that help optimize the trade-off between **risk** and **return**, which is the essence of **multi-objective optimization**.

Application to S&P 500 data

To use **S&P 500 returns** for the multi-objective portfolio optimization use case, we could take a data-driven approach where we build a model to optimize the allocation of funds between different stocks from the **S&P 500 index**. This approach will help us find optimal portfolios that maximize returns while minimizing risk.

Here is how you could set this up:

Step 1: Data Collection

a. **Gather Historical Data**: Obtain **historical price data** for all S&P 500 stocks. You can access this data from financial data providers such as **Yahoo Finance**, **Alpha Vantage**, or **Quandl**.

b. **Calculate Returns**: Calculate **daily, weekly, or monthly returns** for each stock based on historical prices. You will also need to compute **average returns** and **standard deviation** for each stock.

   For example: $\text{Return}_t = \frac{\text{Price}_t - \text{Price}_{t-1}}{\text{Price}_{t-1}}$

   - Daily return:

   This return data will allow you to model both the risk and return characteristics of each asset.

Step 2: Select Stocks for the Portfolio

- **Subset Selection**: Instead of using all 500 stocks, you can select a subset of **3 to 10 stocks** based on criteria such as **historical returns, sectors, or low correlation** to build a diversified portfolio. You may also choose stocks that exhibit different risk-return characteristics, like stable blue-chip companies versus higher-risk growth stocks.

Step 3: Define Objectives

a. **Maximize Return**: The return objective is to **maximize the expected return** of the portfolio based on historical data.

b. **Minimize Risk**: The risk objective is to **minimize the standard deviation** (volatility) of portfolio returns. Volatility is often used as a proxy for risk in finance.

These conflicting objectives make this problem suitable for a **multi-objective optimization algorithm** such as **NSGA-II**.

Step 4: Use MOEA for Portfolio Optimization

a. **Model Setup**: Use an evolutionary algorithm such as **NSGA-II** (available in libraries such as **DEAP** or **Platypus**) to evolve different allocations (weights) of the selected stocks.

   - **Genes**: Each gene represents the weight of a stock in the portfolio.
   - **Chromosome**: Each solution (chromosome) represents a complete portfolio with weights for all selected stocks. The sum of the weights should equal **1**.
   - **Population**: Start with a randomly initialized population of different portfolios.

b. **Fitness Function**:

   - One objective of the fitness function is to calculate the **expected return** of the portfolio as a weighted sum of individual stock returns.
   - The other objective is to calculate the **risk** (standard deviation) of portfolio returns, considering both the weights and the **covariance** between stock returns.

The fitness function might look like this:

$$\text{Return} = \sum_{i=1}^{n} w_i R_i$$

$$\text{Risk} = \sqrt{\sum_{i=1}^{n} \sum_{j=1}^{n} w_i w_j \text{Cov}(R_i, R_j)}$$

Where:

   - w: Weight of stock iii
   - R_i: Expected return of stock iii
   - $\text{Cov}(R_i, R_j)$ Covariance between returns of stocks iii and j

Step 5: Evolutionary Process

a. **Initialize Population**: Start with a random population of portfolios.

b. **Selection, Crossover, Mutation**: Apply the **NSGA-II** operators to evolve the portfolios:

   i. **Selection**: Select portfolios based on **non-dominated sorting** (that is, portfolios that are Pareto optimal).

   ii. **Crossover and Mutation**: Generate new portfolios by recombining weights and introducing slight random variations to create diversity.

c. **Pareto Front**: After several generations, the algorithm will produce a **Pareto front** of portfolios that represent different optimal trade-offs between risk and return.

Step 6: Decision-Making with the Pareto Front

a. Once you have the Pareto front, you can **visualize** the portfolios on a **risk-return plot**.

   i. **Risk-Averse Investor**: If the investor prefers low risk, they will choose a portfolio closer to the lower-left of the Pareto front, indicating **low risk and modest returns.**

   ii. **Risk-Tolerant Investor**: If the investor is willing to take on more risk for higher returns, they will select a portfolio further to the right, showing **higher potential returns despite increased risk.**

Step 7: Implement the Solution with PyGAD

Use **PyGAD** to perform the multi-objective optimization. With PyGAD, you'd need to:

a. **Define the fitness function** to handle both risk and return objectives.

b. **Configure the population and genetic operators** to evolve the solution.

Key Considerations:

- **Data Preprocessing**: Normalize the data and handle missing values before running the optimization.
- **Risk Metrics**: Besides standard deviation, you can consider other risk measures such as **Value at Risk (VaR)** or **Conditional Value at Risk (CVaR).**
- **Transaction Costs**: Incorporate transaction costs into the model to make the optimization more realistic, as buying and selling stocks will incur fees.

This process allows you to create optimal portfolios using **S&P 500** stocks, accounting for the trade-off between maximizing returns and minimizing risk–tailored to different investor preferences using a **Multi-Objective Evolutionary Algorithm** such as **NSGA-II.**

The Code can be found in Chapter 7.

Implicit Implementation of pareto front

The code provided combines **neural networks**, **genetic algorithms**, and **financial data analysis** for portfolio optimization. It begins by importing necessary libraries such as PyTorch, PyGAD, and yfinance. A Simple Neural Network (SimpleNN) is defined, with one hidden layer, for potential use in predicting financial metrics.

The code then downloads historical data for a diverse set of S&P 500 companies from different sectors (Technology, Energy, Healthcare, Financials) using yfinance. It calculates **daily returns**, **average returns**, and **standard deviation** for risk assessment. A subset of three stocks is selected for optimization, ensuring diversity across **risk**, **return**, and **correlation**.

A **genetic algorithm** is implemented using PyGAD to optimize portfolio weights, aiming to maximize returns while minimizing risk. The GA configuration includes parameters such as population size, mutation rate, and crossover type to explore possible solutions.

The code then runs the GA, identifies the best solution, and uses the portfolio weights illustrating the trade-off between risk and return. Finally, the optimized weights are visualized, and further analysis is suggested for model training or financial analysis.

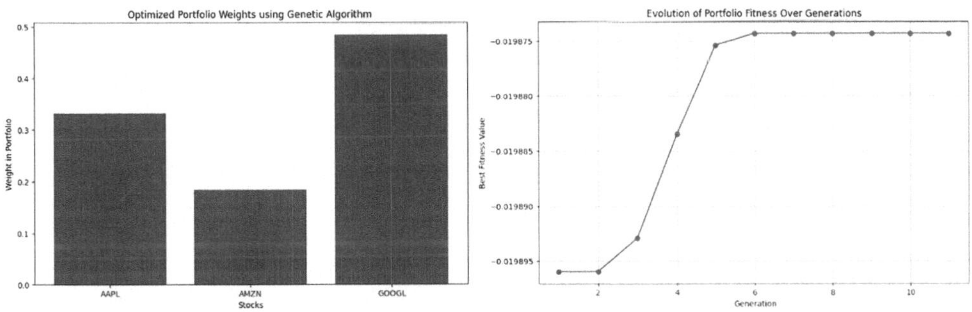

Figure 7.2: *Optimized weights are visualized on the left, and on the right, the evolution of portfolio over generation*

In the code, the concept of **Pareto optimality** is not explicitly implemented, but it is implicitly present in how the **fitness function** is defined for **portfolio optimization**.

Pareto Optimality Concept: Pareto optimality refers to a situation where no objective can be improved without worsening at least one other objective. In multi-objective optimization, solutions that lie on the **Pareto front** are considered **Pareto optimal** because they represent the best possible trade-offs between conflicting objectives (for example, risk vs. return in portfolio optimization).

Current Implementation: In the code provided in the notebook *Chapter 6, Advanced Evolutionary Algorithms* the genetic algorithm is optimizing a **single fitness function** that takes into account **two objectives**—maximizing **portfolio return** and minimizing **portfolio risk**. Specifically, the fitness function is defined as:

```
fitness = portfolio_return - portfolio_risk
```

This approach essentially combines the objectives into a single metric, where the **fitness** is higher if the return is greater and the risk is lower. Thus, each solution's fitness is evaluated by considering both objectives simultaneously, which is akin to finding **Pareto optimal solutions**.

How to Use Pareto Optimality Explicitly

If you want to explicitly track **Pareto optimal solutions** and generate a **Pareto front**, you could modify the genetic algorithm to support **multi-objective optimization**. In this approach, instead of combining the objectives into a single value, you maintain two separate objectives and use an algorithm such as **NSGA-II** (Non-Dominated Sorting Genetic Algorithm II). NSGA-II can find a set of non-dominated solutions representing the **Pareto front**, giving you multiple trade-off options between return and risk.

Explicit Implementation of Pareto Front

Part 1

The code provided in this chapter performs portfolio optimization using a genetic algorithm from the PyGAD library. It aims to determine the optimal weights for a portfolio of selected stocks to maximize the Sharpe Ratio, which balances return and risk. We will **combine your objectives into a single scalar fitness function.**

Key Steps:

1. **Data Retrieval and Preprocessing:**
    a. Downloads historical adjusted closing prices for four S&P 500 stocks from different sectors using yfinance.
    b. Calculates daily returns, average returns, standard deviations (risks), and the correlation matrix.
    c. Selects three stocks based on highest return, lowest correlation with the highest return stock, and lowest risk.
2. **Fitness Function Definition:**
    a. Defines a fitness function that computes the portfolio's Sharpe Ratio: (Portfolio Return) / (Portfolio Risk).
    b. Normalizes weights to sum to 1 and penalizes negative weights to ensure valid portfolio allocations.
3. **Genetic Algorithm Configuration:**
    a. Sets up the GA with constraints on gene values (portfolio weights between 0 and 1) using **`gene_space`**.

b. Specifies GA parameters such as population size, number of generations, mutation rate, and crossover type.

4. **Running the GA and Collecting Results:**

a. Executes the GA to optimize the portfolio weights.

b. Collects the final population's portfolio returns and risks to visualize the risk-return trade-off.

5. **Visualization:**

a. Plots the risk-return scatter plot to illustrate the performance of different portfolio weight combinations.

b. Identifies and displays the best portfolio weights that maximize the Sharpe Ratio.

c. Visualizes the optimized portfolio weights using a bar chart.

Outcome: The code effectively finds the optimal allocation of funds among the selected stocks to achieve the best risk adjusted return, leveraging the GA's ability to search through possible weight combinations.

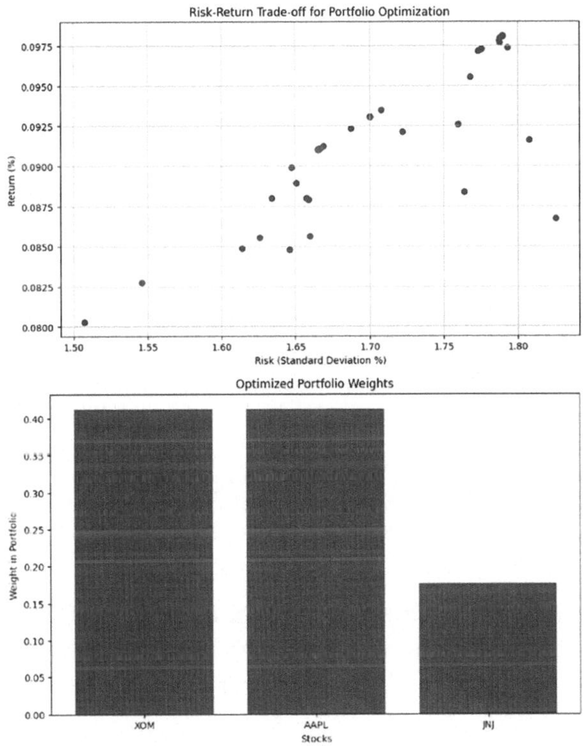

***Figure 7.3:** Risk-return trade-off visualized on the left and on the optimized portfolio weights*

Issues 1

The empty Pareto front suggests that the calculations for returns and risks might still not be varied enough or are improperly being computed as identical values. This could be due to multiple factors:

1. **Fitness Function Similarity**: Since the fitness function is optimizing the same formula (`portfolio_return - portfolio_risk`) for all solutions, there is a possibility that the genetic algorithm converged to similar portfolios early on, resulting in similar risk and return values across generations.
2. **Mutation and Crossover**: The **mutation rate** and **crossover settings** might not be diverse enough to explore the solution space effectively, leading to solutions that are too close to each other.
3. **Scale of Returns and Risks**: The **scale** of the return and risk values might be very small (for example, values near zero), which can make it challenging to visualize the differences between the points on the Pareto front.

To address this, we suggest the following updates to the code:

1. **Change Fitness Calculation to Separate Objectives**: Use distinct objectives for return and risk rather than combining them into a single metric. This will allow for proper trade-off analysis.
2. **Increase Mutation Probability**: Increase the mutation rate to introduce more diversity in the population.
3. **Check Calculation Units**: Ensure the units for returns and risks are properly scaled. It may be helpful to multiply returns and risks by a constant factor to see variation more clearly.
4. **Revise Fitness Calculation**: Ensure the objectives are not too correlated. Currently, the fitness function might be overly simple and leading to similar results across generations.
5. **Improve Diversity**:
    - Increase the **mutation rate** further to promote diversity in the population.
    - Reduce the **parent preservation** (`keep_parents`) to ensure more diversity across generations.
6. **Ensure Proper Multi-Objective Optimization:** NSGA-II in PyGAD requires multiple objectives to operate effectively. Ensure the return and risk objectives are properly separated and that their calculations vary enough across different solutions.

Note: *Below PyGAD 3.2 it expects the fitness function to return a scalar value, not a list or multiple objectives. Returning a list can lead to unexpected behavior or errors because the GA does not know how to handle multiple objectives directly as PyGAD 3.2 below is designed for single-objective optimization.*

Issues 2

The initial customer portfolio consisted of companies such as **Apple (AAPL)**, **Microsoft (MSFT)**, **Google (GOOGL)**, and **Amazon (AMZN)**—all of which are **technology-based companies** that share similar market behaviors and risk factors. These companies are primarily part of the technology sector, and their performance is highly correlated, especially during technology market shifts. As a result, this portfolio lacks diversity, making it vulnerable to sector-specific risks. For instance, a downturn in the tech industry could negatively impact all four companies simultaneously.

To diversify the portfolio, companies were selected from **different sectors**:

- AAPL (Technology)
- XOM (ExxonMobil, Energy)
- JNJ (Johnson & Johnson, Healthcare)
- JPM (JPMorgan Chase, Financials)

This diversification introduces **sector-specific variations** that help manage risk. If the technology sector faces a downturn, stocks in other sectors such as **energy** (XOM), **healthcare** (JNJ), or **financials** (JPM) may still perform well, thereby balancing the overall portfolio. This strategy helps to **reduce unsystematic risk**, which is specific to a single industry or company. Diversifying across sectors aims to stabilize the returns and prevent the entire portfolio from being negatively impacted by a single

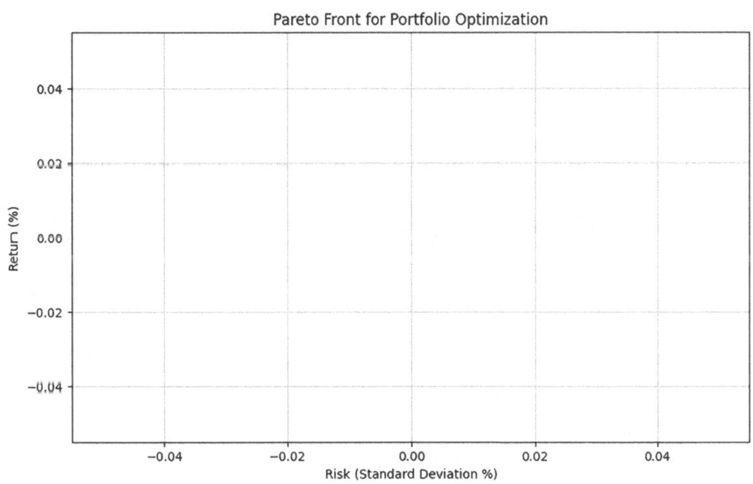

Figure 7.4: *Typical Pareto front with Return (%) and Risk*

Part 2

The fitness function now returns a list of objectives. Since PyGAD minimizes objectives in multi-objective optimization, we invert the portfolio return by returning **`-portfolio_return`**. This way, maximizing return becomes equivalent to minimizing **`-portfolio_return`**. The fitness function now returns a list of objectives: [**`-portfolio_return`**, **`portfolio_risk`**].

1. **Adjusted Fitness Function**
   a. **Return Values:**
      i. Since PyGAD minimizes objectives in multi-objective optimization, we invert the portfolio return by returning **`-portfolio_return`**. This way, maximizing return becomes equivalent to minimizing -portfolio_return.
      ii. The fitness function now returns a list of objectives: **`[-portfolio_return, portfolio_risk]`**.
   b. **Penalty for Invalid Solutions:** If any weight is negative, the function returns extreme values **`[-np.inf, np.inf]`** to penalize the solution, guiding the GA away from infeasible solutions.
2. **GA Configuration for Multi-Objective Optimization**
   a. **Initialization:**
      i. We ensure that **`gene_space`** is properly defined to constrain genes between 0 and 1.
      ii. We set **`allow_duplicate_genes=False`** to avoid identical genes, which can help with diversity.
   b. **Saving Best Solutions:** By setting **`save_best_solutions=True`**, the GA will save the best solutions for each generation, which we can use to extract the Pareto front.
3. **Retrieving the Pareto Front**
   a. **Accessing Best Solutions:**
      i. **`ga_instance.best_solutions_fitness`** contains the fitness values of the best solutions.
      ii. **`ga_instance.best_solutions`** contains the actual solutions (weights).
   b. **Collecting Risks and Returns:** We iterate over the Pareto solutions and calculate the actual portfolio returns and risks for each.

c. **Removing Duplicates:** To ensure a clean Pareto front, we remove any duplicate points using set and sort them.

4. **Visualization**

a. **Plotting the Pareto Front:**

i. We plot the Pareto front to visualize the trade-off between risk and return.

ii. Since we're minimizing both objectives in the GA, the Pareto front should show a clear trade-off.

b. **Optimized Portfolio Weights:**

i. We select the solution with the highest return (or any other preference) from the Pareto front.

ii. We normalize and display the corresponding weights.

Additional Suggestions

- **Objective Preferences**
  - **Weighting Objectives:** If you have a preference for either risk or return, you can adjust the fitness function by applying weights to the objectives.
  - **Constraint Handling:** You can add additional constraints (for example, maximum allocation per stock) by modifying the fitness function to penalize solutions that violate constraints.
- **GA Parameter Tuning**
  - **Population Size and Generations:** Increasing `sol_per_pop` and `num_generations` can improve the GA's ability to explore the solution space but will increase computation time.
  - **Mutation and Crossover Rates:** Adjusting `mutation_probability` and `crossover_probability` can impact the diversity and convergence of the GA.
- **Performance Metrics**
  - **Risk-Free Rate:** If available, include the risk-free rate in your calculations for more accurate financial modeling.
  - **Additional Objectives:** You can extend the fitness function to include other objectives, such as minimizing transaction costs or maximizing diversification.
- **Validation**
  - **Backtesting:** Test the optimized portfolio on out-of-sample data to validate its performance.

- **Sensitivity Analysis:** Analyze how sensitive the portfolio is to changes in market conditions.

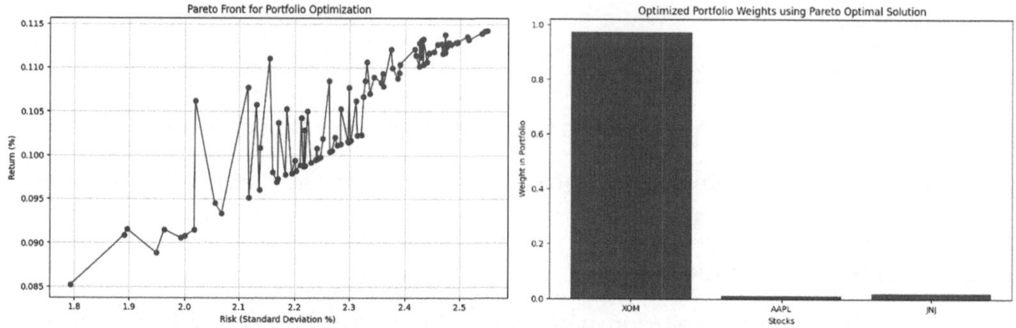

***Figure 7.5:** The image shows a **Pareto front** for a **portfolio optimization** problem, with **risk** (measured by **standard deviation** of returns) on the x-axis and **return** (in percentage) on the y-axis. Each point on the graph represents a **Pareto-optimal solution**—a portfolio configuration that offers a trade-off between return and risk*

Key Observations from Plot

- **Increasing Return with Risk**: The graph indicates a general trend where **higher risk** (right side of the x-axis) corresponds to a **higher return** (upper side of the y-axis). This is a typical risk-return trade-off: as an investor takes on more risk, the potential return also increases.
- **Diversity of Solutions**: The **scattered blue points** along the Pareto front represent different portfolio configurations found by the optimization algorithm. The points along this curve are **non-dominated**, meaning that no other point offers a higher return for the same or lower risk.
- **Volatility**: The graph exhibits **fluctuations**, with some points jumping up or down before continuing the general upward trend. These fluctuations indicate that the **genetic algorithm** is finding different solutions across generations, some with higher returns at certain risk levels, and others with lower returns, depending on how the weights of different assets are optimized.
- **Efficiency of Portfolios**: Investors can select a portfolio from this Pareto front based on their **risk tolerance**:
    - A **risk-averse investor** might choose a point towards the left side (lower risk, lower return).
    - A **risk-tolerant investor** might prefer a point on the right side (higher risk, higher return).

The purpose of this visualization is to help investors understand the best possible **trade-offs** between risk and return for the given set of stocks. By optimizing across different weights of the selected stocks, the **genetic algorithm** effectively creates a spectrum of solutions, allowing an informed decision on how to allocate resources based on individual risk preferences.

Now that we have explored at least one algorithm from each section of **Metaheuristic Optimization Algorithms**–namely, **Nature-Inspired Metaheuristic Algorithms**, **Evolutionary and Swarm-Based Metaheuristics**, and **Hybrid and Recent Metaheuristics**–let us proceed to conclude.

Conclusion

In **this chapter**, we explored various **Metaheuristic Optimization Algorithms**, focusing on both traditional and innovative approaches to solving complex optimization problems. We began with an overview of optimization methods, highlighting advancements in newer techniques and extensions of traditional frameworks. The chapter delved into **metaheuristic algorithms**, particularly those inspired by **nature**, **evolution**, and **swarm behaviors**.

We examined **Ant Colony Optimization (ACO)**, covering its theoretical basis, implementation libraries, and real-world applications. **Differential Evolution (DE)** was also discussed, including its role in computer vision tasks.

A significant portion of the chapter was dedicated to **Multi-Objective Evolutionary Algorithms (MOEA)**, with a practical use case in **portfolio optimization** using **S&P 500 data**. We discussed both implicit and explicit implementations of the **Pareto front**, a key concept for understanding the trade-offs in multi-objective problems.

Overall, this chapter provided a comprehensive understanding of various **metaheuristic algorithms**, blending theoretical insights with practical applications and showcasing their versatility in solving real-world optimization challenges across diverse domains.

In the next chapter, we will understand Artificial Bee Colony (ABC) in depth, building a clear understanding of how this algorithm draws inspiration from the behavior of honey bees to solve complex optimization problems. In addition to this, to make the concepts more tangible, we will also explore how tools such as PyGAD can be combined with OpenAI Swarm to model and solve ABC-related optimization problems.

CHAPTER 8
Application of Evolutionary Algo (GAs) and Generative Agentic AI

Introduction

In the previous chapters, *Chapter 7, Metaheuristic Optimization Algorithms*, under Nature-Inspired Metaheuristic Algorithms, we briefly touched upon the concept of Artificial Bee Colony (ABC), and the accompanying notebook, from *Chapter 6, Advanced Evolutionary Algorithms, Price_optimization_chapter_6_extended*, provided an implementation of price optimization using the Pagmo library. However, we did not explore its inner workings in detail. In this chapter, we will understand Artificial Bee Colony (ABC) in depth, building a clear understanding of how this algorithm draws inspiration from the behavior of honey bees to solve complex optimization problems.

ABC is a powerful optimization algorithm inspired by the foraging patterns of honey bees. It represents a colony with roles such as employed bees, onlooker bees, and scout bees. Each of these roles plays an essential part in maintaining a balance between exploration and exploitation, ensuring effective search of the problem space. In this chapter, we will examine the role of each type of bee, understand how food sources are represented as potential solutions, and how the optimization process unfolds through iterative cooperation among the agents. To make the concepts more tangible, we will also explore how tools such as PyGAD can be combined with OpenAI Swarm to model and solve ABC-related optimization problems. Swarm provides an elegant framework for orchestrating multiple agents in a lightweight manner, enabling us to manage different aspects of the optimization process in a more structured way. We will see how multi-agent coordination, combined with the genetic algorithm features of PyGAD, can be used to enhance the efficiency of the optimization, with agents assuming distinct roles akin to bees searching for the optimal solution.

Through hands-on examples and in-depth explanations, this chapter will bring ABC optimization to life, illustrating its practical uses in modern AI workflows and the potential of integrating advanced coordination frameworks and LLMs to drive powerful optimization strategies.

Structure

In this chapter, we will discuss the following topics:

- Bee Hive Optimization
  - Theory
  - The Bee Colony Optimization Process
  - Advantages of Bee Hive Optimization
  - Differences from Other Optimization Algorithms
  - Bee Hive Optimization vs. Genetic Algorithms
  - Example of Bee Hive Optimization
- Library
  - Sample Code Using PyGMO
  - Application of ABC to Price Optimization
- Generative AI and Agents
- Multi-Agent Systems: The Power of Collaboration in OpenAI Swarm
- Relations of Swarm to Genetic Algorithms
- Bee Hive Optimization with OpenAI Swarm

Bee Hive Optimization

Bee Hive Optimization (or **Artificial Bee Colony Optimization**, ABC) is an optimization algorithm inspired by the foraging behavior of honey bees. It is part of a family of nature-inspired metaheuristic algorithms used to solve complex optimization problems, similar to other algorithms such as Genetic Algorithms, Ant Colony Optimization, and Particle Swarm Optimization.

Here is an overview of Bee Hive Optimization:

Theory

Bee Hive Optimization is based on the collective intelligence and cooperative behavior of a honeybee colony. Honeybees have an effective way of locating and exploiting food sources, using direct and indirect communication among foraging bees. The ABC algorithm models the behavior of different types of bees:

- **Employed Bees**: Search for food sources in the vicinity of known locations and bring back information to the hive.
- **Onlooker Bees**: Wait inside the hive and choose a food source based on the information shared by employed bees. They tend to choose sources that are more promising.
- **Scout Bees**: Search for new food sources randomly, without relying on previous information, to avoid being stuck in local optima.

These three types of bees work in tandem to explore the search space and exploit good solutions, providing a balance between exploration (searching for new areas) and exploitation (improving known solutions).

The Bee Colony Optimization Process

Bee Hive Optimization works in iterations and aims to find an optimal or near-optimal solution. Following are the main steps in the algorithm:

1. **Initialization**:

    a. Generate an initial population of solutions (that is, food sources) randomly. Each solution represents a possible solution to the optimization problem.

    b. Set initial values for parameters such as the number of employed, onlooker, and scout bees, and the limit that controls exploration.

2. **Employed Bee Phase**:

    a. Each employed bee is assigned a food source and searches in its vicinity for an improvement. This is done by modifying the current solution to explore neighboring solutions.

    b. The quality (fitness) of the new solution is evaluated, and the bee updates the food source information if the new solution is better.

3. **Onlooker Bee Phase**:

    a. Onlooker bees gather information from employed bees in the hive. They select food sources based on a probability proportional to the quality of the food source, often using a roulette wheel selection mechanism.

    b. The onlooker bees then search for new solutions in the neighborhood of the chosen sources.

4. **Scout Bee Phase**:
    a. When a food source becomes "exhausted" (that is, if it does not improve after a certain number of tries), it is abandoned, and the corresponding bee becomes a scout bee.
    b. Scout bees search for new food sources randomly to discover new regions of the search space. This step helps prevent the algorithm from getting stuck in a local optimum.
5. **Termination**: The process continues until a stopping criterion is met, such as a maximum number of iterations or convergence to an acceptable solution.

Advantages of Bee Hive Optimization

- **Simple and Easy to Implement**: The algorithm has relatively few parameters to tune, and the process is straightforward.
- **Efficient Search Strategy**: The use of different types of bees allows the ABC algorithm to effectively explore new areas while also exploiting good solutions.
- **Avoids Local Optima**: Scout bees help ensure that the algorithm does not get trapped in local optima, as they always look for new potential solutions.

Applications

Bee Hive Optimization has been used in a variety of domains where optimization is required, including:

- **Function Optimization**: Used to find the minimum or maximum of complex, nonlinear functions.
- **Routing Problems**: Such as vehicle routing and sensor network optimization.
- **Machine Learning**: Tuning hyperparameters of machine learning models.
- **Engineering Design**: Optimization in mechanical design, structural optimization, and so on.
- **Clustering**: In data mining, it has been used for clustering data into meaningful groups.

Differences from Other Optimization Algorithms

To contextualize Bee Hive Optimization (BHO) within the broader landscape of bio-inspired algorithms, it is essential to distinguish it from both traditional Genetic Algorithms and other swarm intelligence techniques. While all three share a population-based, iterative search mechanism, the underlying coordination and adaptation models vary significantly:

- **Swarm Intelligence**: Like **Ant Colony Optimization** and **Particle Swarm Optimization**, Bee Hive Optimization falls under swarm intelligence, but it differs in terms of the model of cooperation among agents. The behavior of bees involves explicit communication of quality between employed and onlooker bees, making it distinct.
- **Population-Based**: Like **Genetic Algorithms**, Bee Hive Optimization uses a population of solutions. However, there are no crossover or mutation operations; instead, neighboring solutions are explored, and unproductive solutions are abandoned by scouts.

Bee Hive Optimization versus Genetic Algorithms

While both Genetic Algorithms (GAs) and Bee Hive Optimization (BHO) are population-based metaheuristics, they differ fundamentally in how they model evolution, balance exploration and exploitation, and represent solutions. These differences reflect their distinct inspirations—Darwinian evolution in the case of GAs, and foraging behavior in bee colonies for BHO:

- **Optimization Strategy**: GAs use crossover and mutation operators to evolve a population, while Bee Hive Optimization relies on an iterative neighborhood search.
- **Exploration and Exploitation**: Bee Hive Optimization uses explicit agents (scouts, onlookers) to differentiate between exploration and exploitation, whereas GAs use mutation and crossover to balance these aspects.
- **Solution Representation**: GAs typically use binary, integer, or real-valued strings to represent solutions, while Bee Hive Optimization represents solutions as direct "food sources," often as real numbers.

Example of Bee Hive Optimization

Suppose we have an optimization problem where we want to minimize a given function $f(x)$. The workflow would look like this: functions and finding near-optimal solutions for difficult problems.

1. **Initialization**: Start with a set of candidate solutions, $x_1, x_2, \ldots, x_n$ representing potential "*food sources.*"
2. **Employed Bee Phase**: Each employed bee modifies its assigned **`xix_ixi`** to find a new candidate solution in the neighborhood and evaluate its fitness $f(x_i)$

3. **Onlooker Bee Phase**: Based on the fitness of the current solutions, onlooker bees probabilistically choose solutions to exploit further.

4. **Scout Bee Phase**: If a particular x_1 has not improved for a certain number of iterations, it is abandoned, and a scout bee generates a new random solution.

5. **Iterate**: This cycle repeats until a predefined termination condition is reached (for example, a maximum number of iterations or convergence).

   Bee Hive Optimization, or Artificial Bee Colony Optimization, is inspired by the foraging behavior of honeybees. It involves different types of bees–employed, onlooker, and scout bees–to perform efficient search and optimization. This algorithm can effectively balance exploration and exploitation, and it is suitable for a wide range of optimization problems. The key idea of Bee Hive Optimization is to **leverage the collective intelligence** of the bee colony, where the division of labor among different types of bees provides both **local refinement** and **global exploration**. This makes it a powerful tool for optimizing complex

Library

The **Pagmo** library (often stylized as **PyGMO** in its Python wrapper form) is an open-source optimization library that provides tools to solve complex global optimization problems through various algorithms, including **evolutionary algorithms**, **swarm intelligence**, and **metaheuristics**. Developed as part of the European Space Agency's Advanced Concepts Team, Pagmo offers a highly versatile platform for solving single-objective, multi-objective, and even multi-modal optimization problems.

It provides a powerful and versatile environment for tackling a variety of optimization problems using evolutionary algorithms, swarm intelligence, and other metaheuristics. Its **island model** for parallel optimization and the **diverse range of algorithms** make it well-suited for complex, high-dimensional, and multi-objective optimization problems.

The library is ideal for researchers, engineers, and data scientists looking for a robust optimization toolkit, especially those dealing with **real-world challenges** that require efficient exploration and exploitation of large solution spaces. Its open-source nature and broad algorithm support provide an accessible yet powerful means to experiment with and solve optimization problems across multiple domains.

Key Features of Pagmo/PyGMO

- **Algorithm Diversity**: Pagmo comes with a rich collection of **optimization algorithms**, including:

- **Genetic Algorithms (GA)**
- **Particle Swarm Optimization (PSO)**
- **Simulated Annealing (SA)**
- **Differential Evolution (DE)**
- **Artificial Bee Colony (ABC)**
- **Ant Colony Optimization (ACO)**
- **Covariance Matrix Adaptation Evolution Strategy (CMA-ES)**

This diversity allows users to choose the right algorithm for their specific optimization problem and experiment with different approaches.

- **Multi-Objective Optimization**: Pagmo also supports **multi-objective optimization** through algorithms such as **NSGA-II** (Non-dominated Sorting Genetic Algorithm II). Multi-objective optimization is essential for problems where more than one objective needs to be optimized simultaneously, often involving trade-offs between conflicting goals.
- **Island Model**: Pagmo introduces the concept of an **island model** for parallel optimization. In this model, different "*islands*" run optimization algorithms independently on sub-populations and occasionally exchange solutions through a migration process. This approach allows:
  - Efficient **parallelization** of optimization tasks.
  - Greater **diversity** of solutions by preventing premature convergence.
  - Enhanced **exploration** capabilities.
- **Hybrid Optimization**: Pagmo allows users to **hybridize** different optimization algorithms by chaining them together or running them in parallel. This means you can combine the strengths of different methods, such as using a **global optimization** algorithm to broadly explore the solution space, followed by a **local optimization** method for fine-tuning the solutions.
- **Problem Library**: Pagmo provides an extensive library of **benchmark problems**, including test functions such as **Rastrigin**, **Rosenbrock**, and **Schwefel**, as well as real-world optimization problems. This is useful for testing algorithms, evaluating performance, and comparing results.
- **Python Interface**: The **PyGMO** Python wrapper provides an easy-to-use interface for Pagmo, allowing you to seamlessly use the library in Python for optimization tasks. This interface makes it accessible to data scientists and engineers who primarily work in Python, integrating it easily with other libraries such as **NumPy** and **Pandas**.

Sample Code Using PyGMO

Following is an example that demonstrates the use of **PyGMO** to solve an optimization problem:

```
import pygmo as pg
# Define an optimization problem
problem = pg.problem(pg.rosenbrock(dim=5))  # Using the Rosen-
brock function with 5 dimensions

# Choose an optimization algorithm
algorithm = pg.algorithm(pg.de(gen=100))  # Differential Evolution
with 100 generations
# Create an island
island = pg.island(algo=algorithm, prob=problem, size=20)
# Population size of 20
# Evolve the population
island.evolve()
# Wait for evolution to complete
island.wait_check()
# Print the best solution found
best_solution = island.get_population().champion_x
best_fitness = island.get_population().champion_f
print(f"Best solution: {best_solution}, Best fitness:
{best_fitness}")
```

In this example:

- The **Rosenbrock** function is used as the objective function.
- The **Differential Evolution** (DE) algorithm, also discussed in *Chapter* 7, is selected for optimization.
- An **island** with a population of 20 individuals is created, and the DE algorithm is run for 100 generations.
- After evolution, the **best solution** found is printed.

Application of ABC to Price Optimization

Part 1

Let us understand the code implemented from `Price_optimzation_chapter_6_extended`, which can also be found in `Chapter_8` notebook. The code focuses on optimizing product prices using **Artificial Bee Colony (ABC)** optimization from the **Pagmo library**, to maximize total profit in a supply chain dataset. The dataset is loaded using **Pandas**, and the features '**Product Price**', '**Order_Demand**', '**Sales per customer**', '**Order Profit Per Order**', '**Customer Segment**', and '**Product Category**' are extracted for analysis. The **fitness function** is defined in PyTorch to compute the profit, where the GPU is used if available. The fitness function calculates the total profit based on product prices, order quantity, and profit per order, and returns the negative profit since the ABC optimization problem in Pagmo minimizes the objective function.

A custom **Pagmo problem** class called ProductPricingProblem is defined, representing the product pricing optimization problem. It specifies the number of dimensions (dim) based on the number of product prices and sets reasonable **bounds** for product prices, between 10 and 500 units. This class is used to create a **problem instance** for Pagmo, which is then solved using the **ABC algorithm** with 100 generations. The algorithm evolves a population of 50 candidate solutions, searching for the best possible product pricing strategy that maximizes profit.

Once the optimization is complete, the best solution, which represents the **optimized product prices**, is extracted. The code then creates a comparison between the actual and optimized product prices and visualizes this comparison using **Matplotlib**. The result is a plot that shows the differences between the actual and optimized prices, providing insight into the effectiveness of the ABC optimization in maximizing profit for the product portfolio.

```
Best Individual: [126.46484532 416.0958147  308.15693088 ...
67.29244369 398.56654902
 278.03103218]
Best Fitness (Total Profit): 8870218.0
   Product Price  Optimized Price
0         327.75       126.464845
1         327.75       416.095815
2         327.75       308.156931
3         327.75       278.910980
4         327.75        89.151790
```

Figure 8.1 highlights how the optimized prices are significantly more stable and constrained compared to the highly variable actual prices. This suggests successful enforcement of pricing logic and business constraints.

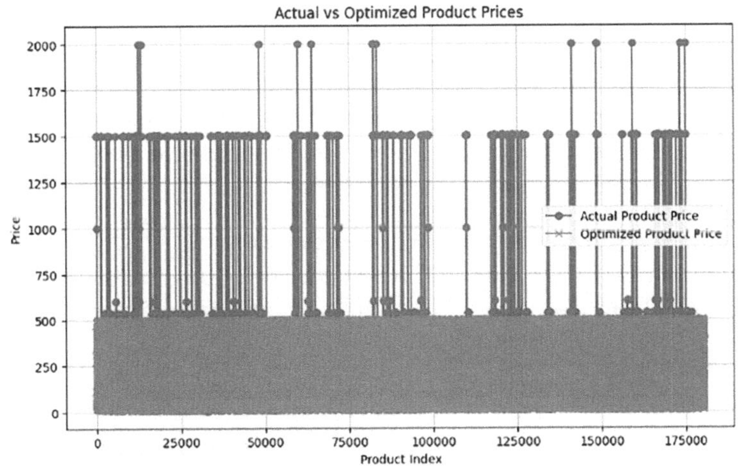

Figure 8.1: *Actual versus Optimized Product Prices*

Figure 8.2 further reinforces the algorithm's performance by showing the best fitness value—measured in total profit—achieved across iterations. The near-constant plateau indicates rapid convergence, suggesting that the algorithm quickly found a near-optimal pricing configuration with minimal subsequent improvement required.

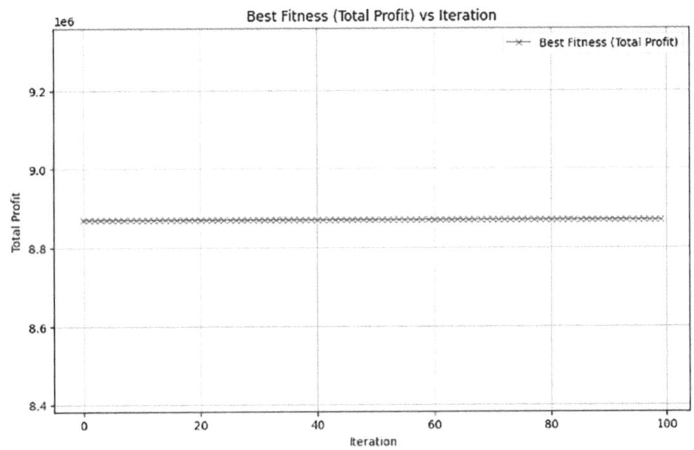

Figure 8.2: *Best Fitness (Total Profit) versus Iteration*

The plot shows that the **optimized product prices** (orange) are significantly lower and more consistent compared to the **actual product prices** (blue), which vary widely and reach high values above 1500. The optimized prices cluster between 10 and 500, indicating that the optimization found lowering and standardizing prices beneficial for profitability. This suggests that a uniform pricing strategy could improve total profit, possibly by increasing customer demand and reducing price-related inconsistencies. The optimization brings pricing uniformity, potentially increasing sales volume while maintaining competitive prices, leading to better overall profitability.

Part 2

In the above objective function, total profit is calculated without considering the impact of changing product prices on order demand. In other words, the total profit remains constant across iterations because the demand and profit per order are not affected by the product prices we are optimizing.

To address this, we need to model how the order demand changes with the product price–a concept known as the **demand function**. By incorporating a demand function into our profit calculation, we allow the optimizer to find product prices that maximize total profit by balancing price and demand.

Explanation of Changes from the Part 1 Code:

1. **Calculating Product Cost**: We compute the Product Cost by rearranging the profit equation: **`Product Profit = (Product Price - Product Cost) * Order_Demand.`**

   The formula used is:

   ```
   df['Product Cost'] = df['Product Price'] - (df['Order Profit Per
   Order'] / df['Order_Demand'])
   ```

2. **Fitting a Demand Function**: We fit a linear regression model to estimate how demand changes with price:

   ```
   model = LinearRegression()
   model.fit(X, y)
   a = model.intercept_
   b = model.coef_[0]
   ```

   This provides us with coefficients a and b for the demand function: **`Order_Demand= a+b×Product_Price`**

3. **Updating the Profit Calculation**: The **`calc_profit`** function now computes demand based on the current prices and then calculates total profit:

   ```
   def calc_profit(product_prices, product_costs, a, b):
       # Calculate Order_Demand using the demand function
       order_demand = a + b * product_prices
       order_demand = torch.clamp(order_demand, min=0)
   # Ensure demand is non-negative

       # Total profit is (price - cost) * demand
       profit_per_product = (product_prices - product_costs)
   * order_demand
       total_profit = torch.sum(profit_per_product).item()

       return -total_profit  # Negative for minimization
   ```

By incorporating the demand function, the profit now depends on the product prices being optimized.

4. **Adjusting the Fitness Function**: The **`fitness_function`** now passes the demand coefficients and product costs to **`calc_profit`**:

```
def fitness_function(solution):
    product_costs = df['Product Cost'].values
    return [calc_profit(solution, product_costs, a, b)]
```

5. **Ensuring Non-Negative Demand**: We use `torch.clamp` to prevent negative demand values, which are not realistic:

```
order_demand = torch.clamp(order_demand, min=0)
```

Enhancements Specific to ABC Algorithm

In the improved code, the key enhancements related to the ABC algorithm include:

- **Objective Function Adjustment**: By incorporating a demand function into the profit calculation, the ABC algorithm can now effectively optimize the prices. The profit now depends on the prices being optimized, which aligns with the algorithm's search mechanisms.
- **Constraints Handling**: The bounds for product prices are set realistically to guide the ABC algorithm:

```
self.bounds = ([10] * self.dim, [500] * self.dim)
```

Parameter Settings:

- **Generations (gen):** Set to 1 for each evolution step to allow for detailed tracking of the optimization process over iterations.
- **Population Size:** Set to 50, which is a balance between exploration (diversity) and computational efficiency.

Results: By implementing these changes, the optimizer now effectively searches for product prices that maximize total profit by considering how price affects demand. You should observe that the total profit varies across iterations and ideally increases as the optimizer finds better solutions. The code is available In **`Chatper_8`** notebook.

```
Best Individual: [235.18823832  60.38575042 214.87653561 ...
31.370605   436.32190847
  20.18339503]
Best Fitness (Total Profit): 18705584.0
   Product Price  Optimized Price
0         327.75       235.188238
1         327.75        60.385750
```

```
2         327.75      214.876536
3         327.75      443.918266
4         327.75      370.064622
```

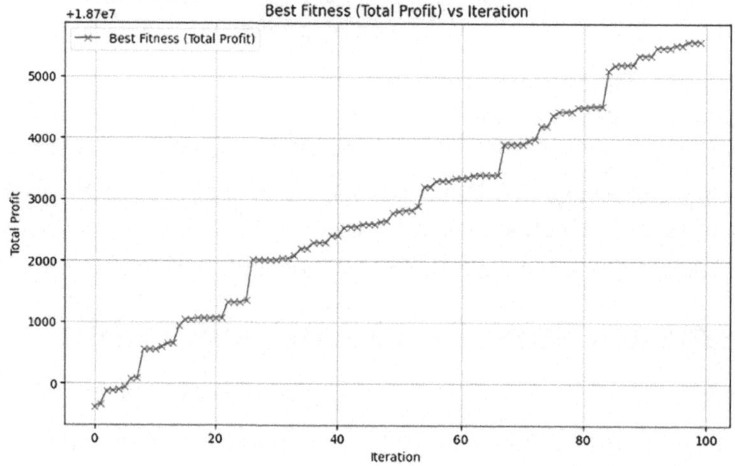

Figure 8.3: *Best Fitness (Total Profit) versus Iteration*

Figure 8.3 shows how the total profit evolves over iterations, which should now display variability and ideally an upward trend.

By incorporating a demand function that links product price to demand, the optimizer can effectively search for prices that maximize total profit. This modification addresses the issue of the total profit being flat across iterations.

Suitability of ABC Algorithm:

The ABC algorithm is particularly well-suited for this optimization problem because:

- **Global Search Capability:** It effectively explores the global search space to avoid getting trapped in local optima.
- **Flexibility:** It does not require gradient information, making it suitable for problems where the objective function is not differentiable or is complex.
- **Adaptability:** It can handle non-linear and multi-modal optimization problems, which are common in real-world scenarios such as pricing optimization.

In the next section, we will discuss generative AI and see how Genetic Algorithms can take the benefit of generative AI, using a recently launched Agentic Library OpenAI called **Swarm.**

Generative AI and Agents

Generative AI has made waves in recent years, enabling machines to produce human-like text, art, and even music. However, the next frontier goes beyond creating content–it is about building agents capable of reasoning, planning, memory, and action. Let us dive into how these elements are shaping the future of intelligent agents and the potential of multi-agent systems.

- **Reasoning**: Reasoning is at the core of an intelligent agent's ability to make sense of the world. It involves analyzing information, identifying patterns, and making decisions based on available data. In generative AI, reasoning is crucial for going beyond mere content generation to producing meaningful and contextually appropriate actions. For instance, when given an ambiguous input, an agent with reasoning capabilities can infer missing details and provide a coherent response. This elevates AI from merely following instructions to actually understanding and reasoning through complex scenarios.
- **Planning**: While reasoning helps agents make sense of situations, planning allows them to think ahead and devise a series of steps to achieve a goal. Generative AI agents equipped with planning capabilities can break down complex objectives into smaller, manageable tasks. For example, a conversational agent that helps users plan their day must not only understand what each activity entails but also organize those activities in a logical sequence, considering dependencies and constraints–essentially becoming an effective virtual assistant.
- **Memory**: Memory is a crucial aspect that empowers agents to become more adaptive and contextually aware over time. It allows them to remember past interactions, learn from experiences, and personalize responses. Unlike traditional AI models that operate statelessly, an agent with memory can build a dynamic understanding of users and their preferences. For instance, a generative AI chatbot can recall a user's prior questions or preferences, enabling more nuanced and satisfying interactions over multiple sessions. Memory also helps agents recognize long-term goals, ensuring consistency and improving the overall user experience.
- **Action**: Reasoning, planning, and memory ultimately culminate in the ability to take action. Generative AI agents capable of action go beyond passive communication; they can interact with their environment or perform tasks autonomously. For instance, an AI agent managing a smart home can adjust lighting, order supplies, or schedule maintenance based on user preferences. Actions taken by such agents close the loop between perception, decision-making, and real-world impact, allowing them to operate effectively within physical or digital environments.

Multi-Agent Systems

The idea becomes even more compelling when we consider multiple generative agents working together–known as multi-agent systems. Multi-agent frameworks enable multiple AI entities to collaborate, share knowledge, and solve complex tasks more effectively than a single agent. These systems can leverage collective intelligence, where each agent has specialized capabilities but works in coordination with others for a common goal. For example, in supply chain optimization, different agents can manage logistics, inventory, and customer interactions, collaborating to create a more efficient process. Multi-agent systems also present unique challenges, such as coordination, negotiation, and potential competition, but their ability to solve distributed problems makes them a powerful tool for addressing real-world complexities.

Multi-Agent Systems: The Power of Collaboration in AI

Multi-Agent Systems (MAS) are transforming the way we think about artificial intelligence by combining the power of multiple agents to solve complex problems. Instead of relying on a single AI model, multi-agent systems leverage a collection of autonomous entities that interact, collaborate, and sometimes compete to achieve a common goal. This collaborative approach is inspired by natural systems such as ant colonies, bee swarms, and even human societies, where collective behavior leads to efficiency and innovation.

What Are Multi-Agent Systems?

A multi-agent system consists of multiple intelligent agents that work together in a shared environment. Each agent in the system has its own unique abilities, goals, and information. These agents can be software-based or physical robots, and they interact to perform tasks that would be difficult or impossible for a single agent to accomplish alone.

One of the key features of MAS is decentralization. Unlike a traditional, centralized system where a single entity makes decisions for the entire group, agents in a MAS operate independently. They communicate with each other, share information, and adapt their behaviors to the evolving environment.

Components of Multi-Agent Systems

- **Autonomous Agents**: Each agent in a MAS has some level of autonomy, allowing it to make decisions and perform actions independently. This autonomy helps agents handle tasks in a dynamic environment without constant human intervention.
- **Communication**: Communication is crucial in a multi-agent system. Agents need to exchange information to coordinate, negotiate, and avoid conflicts. This interaction enables the collective intelligence of the system to emerge, making the whole greater than the sum of its parts.

- **Coordination and Collaboration**: In many MAS applications, coordination among agents is key to achieving a shared objective. Agents can collaborate to split tasks based on specialization or negotiate to allocate resources effectively. For example, in a warehouse, some agents might handle inventory tracking while others manage robot pathways for order fulfillment.
- **Competition and Conflict Resolution**: In some scenarios, agents may have competing objectives, leading to potential conflicts. Multi-agent systems must be equipped with mechanisms to resolve these conflicts, ensuring agents can continue working towards overall system goals without interference.

Applications of Multi-Agent Systems

Multi-agent systems are increasingly used in a variety of fields:

- **Supply Chain Management**: In a supply chain, different agents might manage inventory, transportation, and customer orders. By working together, these agents can create an efficient network that minimizes costs and maximizes speed.
- **Traffic Control**: MAS can be applied to optimize urban traffic by deploying agents to manage individual traffic lights. Each agent monitors traffic conditions and communicates with neighboring agents to adjust timings, reducing congestion.
- **Robotics and Swarm Intelligence**: In robotics, MAS are employed in swarm robotics where multiple robots collaborate to achieve tasks such as exploration, mapping, or construction. Each robot works independently, yet as part of a coordinated whole, mimicking the behaviors seen in nature, such as ants building a colony.
- **Gaming and Simulation**: In gaming, multi-agent systems are used to create more realistic simulations where characters or entities interact in complex ways, providing players with dynamic and unpredictable experiences.

Challenges in Multi-Agent Systems

Developing MAS comes with its own set of challenges:

- **Coordination Complexity**: Coordinating multiple agents can be difficult, especially as the number of agents grows or if they have conflicting goals. Ensuring that they work effectively without interference requires sophisticated algorithms.
- **Scalability**: Scaling up a MAS while maintaining efficient communication and collaboration can be challenging. More agents mean more potential interactions, which can quickly become computationally expensive.

- **Security and Trust**: In open MAS environments, some agents might be untrustworthy or even malicious. Ensuring that all agents act in good faith is an important area of research, particularly in applications such as distributed AI or financial markets.

The Future of Multi-Agent Systems

The future of MAS is promising, especially with advancements in machine learning and distributed computing. With the integration of technologies such as reinforcement learning and graph neural networks, agents can learn to optimize their interactions and enhance the overall efficiency of a system. Multi-agent systems are poised to become a fundamental part of autonomous environments, from smart cities to decentralized economic networks, enabling more resilient, adaptive, and intelligent solutions.

Multi-agent systems represent a powerful approach to building intelligent, adaptive networks where multiple agents work together to solve complex problems. By embracing collaboration, communication, and autonomous decision-making, MAS can achieve results far beyond the capabilities of a single-agent system. The applications of these systems are vast, and as technology advances, we can expect them to be an integral part of how we solve challenges across industries.

By combining genetic algorithms, multi-agent systems, and nature-inspired optimization such as Bee Hive Optimization, developers can create a sophisticated, flexible framework for solving complex problems. The adaptability of GAs, the coordination capabilities of MAS, and the structured roles from ABC provide a powerful toolkit for tackling dynamic, large-scale optimization challenges.

OpenAI Swarm now OpenAI Agent SDK

OpenAI's **Agents SDK** marks a major step forward in building multi-agent systems, superseding the experimental **Swarm** framework. Where Swarm provided a lightweight playground for exploring agent handoffs and coordination, the Agents SDK is a production-grade, open-source toolkit that enables developers to build intelligent, tool-using, decision-making agents that work collaboratively to solve complex tasks.

From Swarm to the Agents SDK

Originally introduced as an experimental framework, **Swarm** allowed for orchestrating multiple agents—each with specific roles and behaviors—to perform distributed tasks through *handoffs*. While Swarm emphasized experimentation and education, it lacked ongoing support and production-readiness.

In contrast, the **Agents SDK** is OpenAI's officially supported successor, offering robust primitives like:

- **Agents:** LLM-powered entities that can act on instructions and use tools
- **Tools:** Python functions or hosted utilities that agents can call during execution
- **Handoffs:** Mechanisms for delegating tasks to specialized agents
- **Guardrails:** Safety checks that validate agent inputs and outputs
- **Context and Tracing:** State management and observability for multi-step interactions

This shift represents a move from showcasing coordination patterns to enabling developers to build reliable, real-world AI systems.

Multi-Agent Systems Matter

Multi-agent architectures mirror human teams: each agent has a specialized function (for example, research, analysis, summarization) and works collaboratively to achieve a shared goal. With the Agents SDK, this concept becomes practical. You can now construct modular AI workflows such as:

- A **Triage Agent** that delegates based on query type (technical, billing, research)
- A **Research System** where agents gather, verify, and synthesize information
- An **AI Pipeline** with agents handling discrete steps such as data retrieval, transformation, and output formatting

These systems improve efficiency by parallelizing cognitive workloads, and provide greater control over behavior and outputs.

From Genetic Algorithms to Agent Coordination

Though **Genetic Algorithms (GAs)** and the Agents SDK serve different purposes, they share architectural and conceptual parallels:

Concept	**Genetic Algorithms**	**Agents SDK**
Population Members	Candidate solutions	Specialized agents
Fitness Evaluation	Scoring function	Guardrails or custom tools
Mutation & Crossover	Genetic operations	Tool calls or delegated agent tasks
Evolution Cycle	Iterative search	Agent loop
Subpopulations	Distributed GAs	Agent clusters via handoffs

Table 8.1: *Comparison of key concepts between Genetic Algorithms and the Agents SDK for optimization and coordination*

You could implement a distributed GA using the Agents SDK by assigning evolutionary roles (selection, mutation, crossover) to agents and orchestrating them through structured handoffs. Each agent could maintain its own context, track changes, and contribute to a global optimization goal—providing both modularity and transparency.

Example: Evolving a Multi-Agent Optimization Pipeline

Imagine a scenario where you optimize marketing strategies via simulation:

- **Strategy Generator Agent:** Proposes candidate strategies based on market data
- **Simulation Agent:** Runs behavioral simulations to test outcomes
- **Evaluator Agent:** Scores strategies on reach, cost, and impact
- **Refiner Agent:** Adjusts strategies based on evaluation

Each step is handled by an agent, and they communicate through shared context and structured handoffs. You now have a flexible pipeline for iterative, adaptive optimization—powered not by genetic operations alone, but by LLM-based reasoning and tool use.

Relations of Swarm to Genetic Algorithms

While the **OpenAI Swarm** framework originally showcased multi-agent coordination patterns, its evolution into the **OpenAI Agents SDK** has unlocked robust and production-ready capabilities for orchestrating intelligent, tool-using agents. This transition opens up new synergies with **Genetic Algorithms (GAs)** and other population-based optimization techniques.

The diagram below illustrates how the traditional GA pipeline—consisting of **Selection**, **Crossover**, and **Mutation** operations—can be modularized and intelligently routed using specialized agents within the OpenAI Agents SDK.

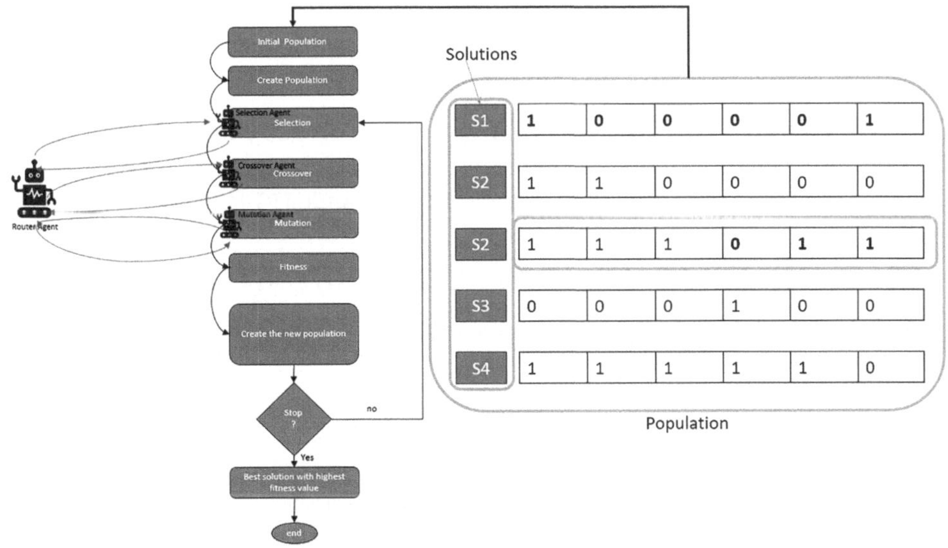

Figure 8.4: *Illustration of a Multi-Agent Based Genetic Algorithm Process Flow*

Multi-Agent Systems as Modular Optimizers

Genetic Algorithms solve optimization problems by evolving a **population of candidate solutions**. This involves iterating over processes such as **fitness evaluation**, **selection**, **crossover**, and **mutation**.

Using the **OpenAI Agents SDK**, these steps can be decoupled into specialized agents:

- **Selection Agent**: Chooses top-performing solutions based on fitness.
- **Crossover Agent**: Mates selected pairs to produce new offspring.
- **Mutation Agent**: Introduces stochastic variations to maintain diversity.
- **Router Agent**: Coordinates task handoffs between agents in a controlled sequence.

This agent-based breakdown not only modularizes the pipeline but also allows dynamic control, logging, and reasoning at each stage—facilitated through the agent loop.

Intelligent Handoffs for Evolutionary Coordination

The diagram demonstrates how a **Router Agent** governs the GA loop. At each iteration:

- The **Selection Agent** identifies high-fitness individuals (for example, S1, S2).
- The **Crossover Agent** generates new combinations (for example, offspring from S2 and S4).

- The **Mutation Agent** introduces perturbations (for example, flipping bits in the offspring).
- The **Population** is updated and passed forward.

Each agent operates in its own function space and can use **custom tools** (for example, mutation probability functions, crossover strategies), maintaining separation of concern and facilitating intelligent delegation via `handoff()` in the SDK.

Prototyping and Experimentation with Ease

One major advantage of using the **Agents SDK** over monolithic implementations is flexibility in **experiment design**:

- You can tune mutation rates, crossover types, or fitness strategies by swapping tools on the fly.
- Each agent's logic can be updated independently.
- Intermediate outputs can be logged or traced using built-in SDK observability.

This modularity accelerates experimentation and reduces engineering overhead.

Distributed Search Space Exploration

In traditional GAs, parallelizing fitness evaluations across the population is computationally beneficial. With the SDK:

- **Each solution can be managed by its own agent**, evaluating fitness in parallel.
- Agents can **share context** (for example, best fitness so far), enabling informed decision-making.
- Specialized **Scout Agents** could explore new regions of the solution space to prevent stagnation.

This design mirrors natural systems (for example, swarm intelligence, bee colonies) and supports **diverse search strategies**.

Toward Adaptive and Distributed Genetic Architectures

The SDK also supports **multi-agent clusters**, enabling **Distributed Genetic Algorithms (DGAs)** where:

- Subpopulations evolve independently under different Selection/Crossover/Mutation policies.
- Periodic **migration or agent handoff** allows information exchange across clusters.

- Coordinator agents oversee policy shifts based on performance or convergence status.

Such distributed, adaptive models are well-suited for tackling high-dimensional, non-convex optimization problems in dynamic environments.

Next, we will cover Combining PyGAD, OpenAI Swarm, and implementing concepts of Bee Hive Optimization (ABC).

Conceptual Bee Hive Optimization with OpenAI SDK

Combining **Genetic Algorithms (GAs)**, **Bee Hive Optimization (BHO)** principles, and the **OpenAI Agents SDK** unlocks a powerful paradigm for solving complex optimization problems. This hybrid system leverages the adaptive search behavior of GAs, the division of labor and feedback loops of bee colonies, and the coordination and tool usage of modern AI agents.

Tools Involved

- **PyGAD**: A Python library for Genetic Algorithms, used to evolve candidate solutions.
- **Bee Hive Optimization (BHO)**: A bio-inspired method mimicking the foraging behavior of honey bees (for example, employed bees, onlooker bees, scout bees).
- **OpenAI Agents SDK**: A production-grade multi-agent orchestration framework that facilitates intelligent coordination, decision-making, and tool usage among specialized agents.

Conceptual Overview

In this hybrid system:

- **Employed Bee Agents** explore current solutions (food sources) and locally improve them.
- **Onlooker Bee Agents** evaluate and exploit promising areas based on shared performance signals (fitness).
- **Scout Bee Agents** explore new random solutions to avoid stagnation.
- **Coordinator Agent** orchestrates the overall optimization loop, delegating tasks and managing state across iterations.

- **PyGAD** manages genetic operations such as mutation and crossover, while the Agents SDK handles intelligent delegation, structured handoffs, and tool-based actions.

Step-by-Step Integration Plan

1. **Define the Optimization Problem:** Create a fitness function *f*(*x*) representing your problem domain (for example, minimizing cost, maximizing efficiency). This function will be evaluated for each candidate solution.

```
def fitness_function(solution, solution_idx):
    # Example: sphere function
    return -np.sum(np.square(solution))
```

2. **Use PyGAD to Manage the Genetic Population:** PyGAD will generate the initial population of candidate solutions—each representing a “food source” in the bee hive model.

```
import pygad

ga = pygad.GA(
    num_generations=100,
    sol_per_pop=30,
    num_parents_mating=10,
    fitness_func=fitness_function,
    gene_type=float,
    num_genes=5,
)
```

3. **Implement Bee Roles as OpenAI Agents:** Each type of bee is implemented as an agent with a specific toolset and behavior:

```
from agents import Agent, function_tool

@function_tool
def improve_solution(solution):
    # Local improvement logic (simulates employed bee)
    return mutated_solution

@function_tool
def evaluate_solution(solution):
    # Uses the fitness function
    return fitness_function(solution, 0)

employed_bee = Agent(
    name="Employed Bee",
    instructions="Improve current food source using local
search.",
```

```
        tools=[improve_solution]
    )

    onlooker_bee = Agent(
        name="Onlooker Bee",
        instructions="Select and exploit high-quality food sources.",
        tools=[evaluate_solution]
    )

    scout_bee = Agent(
        name="Scout Bee",
        instructions="Explore new random solutions in the search
    space.",
        tools=[generate_random_solution]
    )
```

4. **Use the Coordinator Agent to Orchestrate Handoffs:** The **Coordinator Agent** maintains the shared context (such as solution history and fitness scores) and manages delegation:

```
coordinator = Agent(
    name="Hive Coordinator",
    instructions="""
    Manage the bee colony optimization process. Use:
    - Employed bees to improve existing food sources.
    - Onlooker bees to exploit good solutions.
    - Scout bees to explore new solutions.
    Iterate to find the global optimum.
    """,
    handoffs=[employed_bee, onlooker_bee, scout_bee]
)
```

Why Use the Agents SDK?

Compared to static frameworks, the **Agents SDK adds intelligent orchestration**:

- Agents reason when and how to use tools.
- Context is preserved between steps, enabling feedback and memory.
- Multi-agent delegation models natural colony behaviors.
- Guardrails and structured outputs make optimization safe and traceable.

Final Thoughts

By integrating **Bee Hive Optimization**, **Genetic Algorithms**, and the **OpenAI Agents SDK**, you are not just running an algorithm–you are simulating an intelligent, distributed system that adapts, communicates, and evolves. This approach is ideal for tackling high-dimensional search problems, especially when interpretability and modularity matter.

Leveraging a **Large Language Model (LLM)**, *such as* GPT-4 *or similar models, can be a valuable addition to the* **Bee Hive Optimization** *process, enhancing agent roles in several ways. LLMs can be particularly useful in the following contexts within your multi-agent system involving* **Swarm** *and* **optimization.** *Implementation of LLM is out of the scope of this chapter; however, below are some of the examples :*

- *Decision-Making and Handoff Management*
- *Evaluating Fitness and Providing Explanations*
- *Tuning Parameters and Metaheuristics*
- *Natural Language Inputs for Optimization Setup*
- *Intelligent Exploration for New Solutions (Scout Role Enhancement)*

Conclusion

In conclusion, Bee Hive Optimization is a powerful, nature-inspired metaheuristic algorithm that effectively balances exploration and exploitation through its three types of bees: employed, onlooker, and scout. This optimization approach offers numerous advantages over traditional methods, particularly in handling complex, high-dimensional problems. Compared to Genetic Algorithms (GAs), Bee Hive Optimization demonstrates distinct strengths in terms of decentralized decision-making and adaptability. Throughout the discussion, we also explored how PyGMO can be employed to implement the Artificial Bee Colony (ABC) optimization, specifically for price optimization problems, providing a practical perspective on how these theoretical ideas can be applied in real-world scenarios.

We also covered the potential synergy between Bee Hive Optimization and multi-agent systems, such as OpenAI Swarm, illustrating the benefits of using agents to orchestrate complex tasks effectively. The integration of Swarm agents with ABC can further enhance the adaptability and efficiency of solving optimization problems.

In the next chapter, we will delve into the exciting domain of Machine Learning and explore its applications to Genetic Algorithms. We will investigate how machine learning techniques can enhance the optimization capabilities of GAs, offering new possibilities in solving complex problems in artificial intelligence and beyond.

Chapter 9
Applying Genetic Algorithm to Machine Learning

Introduction

In this chapter, we will explore the powerful role of genetic algorithms in enhancing machine learning tasks through the use of PyGAD. Genetic algorithms, inspired by natural evolution, provide a robust framework for optimizing various machine learning processes, including feature selection and hyperparameter tuning. We begin by introducing feature selection, where GAs help identify the most influential features to improve model performance and reduce complexity. We will also delve into hyperparameter optimization, showing how GAs can efficiently find optimal values for model parameters that otherwise would be challenging to tune manually.

By implementing PyGAD in practical scenarios, we will demonstrate the advantages of GA-based optimization compared to traditional methods, highlighting improvements in accuracy and efficiency. We will cover machine learning algorithms such as XG boost classification and regression, showcasing how GAs can be applied to each to enhance their capabilities. Throughout this chapter, our goal is to illustrate, through hands-on examples, how GAs can significantly improve the performance of machine learning models, making them not only more accurate but also more efficient and adaptive.

Structure

In this chapter, we will cover the following topics.

- Feature Selection
- Feature Selection Types
- Feature Selection Using Genetic Algorithms (GA)

- Recap of GA Selection Process
- Feature selection GA Deep Dive
  - Practical Application
- Hyperparameters
- Hyperparameter Tuning Types
  - Hyperparameter Tuning with GA
  - Hyperparameter Tuning Using GA Deep Dive
  - Practical Application

Feature Selection

Feature selection, hyperparameter tuning, and model refinement using genetic algorithms are substantial topics in their own right. However, we will aim to cover the key aspects, starting with feature selection.

Feature selection differs significantly between supervised and unsupervised learning, primarily because of the availability of labeled data and the goal of optimizing different kinds of models.

- **Supervised Learning:** In supervised learning, feature selection relies on the presence of labeled data. The goal is to select features that have the most predictive power for a target variable. Techniques for feature selection in supervised settings often use metrics such as correlation, information gain, or feature importance derived from model training. Methods such as filter, wrapper, and embedded techniques are common. For example, wrapper methods such as Recursive Feature Elimination (RFE) assess the impact of features on a model's prediction accuracy, aiming to maximize performance with respect to a specific label. Supervised feature selection focuses on reducing redundancy and improving model interpretability, efficiency, and accuracy.
- **Unsupervised Learning:** In contrast, unsupervised learning lacks labels, making feature selection more challenging. Here, the objective is not to predict a target variable but to identify features that capture the inherent structure of the data. Techniques often rely on statistical properties such as variance, clustering, or reconstruction errors from algorithms such as Principal Component Analysis (PCA). Filter methods can be adapted to assess feature relevance through metrics such as mutual information or variance. Since

there is no explicit target, the process emphasizes preserving the structure, reducing dimensionality, and identifying features that contribute to grouping or distinguishing clusters.

Feature Selection Types

Feature selection techniques are used to identify the most relevant features for a model, improving accuracy, reducing overfitting, and enhancing computational efficiency. The three main types of feature selection techniques are as follows.

- **Filter Methods:** Filter methods rank features based on statistical metrics such as correlation, mutual information, or variance, independently of the learning algorithm. These metrics determine how much predictive power each feature contributes. Examples include Pearson's correlation, Chi-squared tests, and ANOVA F-tests. Filter methods are computationally efficient and suitable for high-dimensional datasets, but they do not account for feature interactions with the model.
- **Wrapper Methods:** Wrapper methods evaluate feature subsets by training and testing a machine learning model iteratively to find the combination that yields the best performance. Methods such as Recursive Feature Elimination (RFE) and forward/backward feature selection fall into this category. While these approaches provide better results by considering feature interactions, they are computationally intensive, especially for large datasets, as they require repeatedly fitting the model for different subsets.
- **Embedded Methods:** Embedded methods incorporate feature selection as part of the model training process. These methods are often specific to a particular learning algorithm and leverage regularization techniques, such as L1 regularization (Lasso), that inherently reduce the number of features. Examples include decision trees and regularized regression models. Embedded methods strike a balance between efficiency and feature relevance, as they perform feature selection during the model building phase.

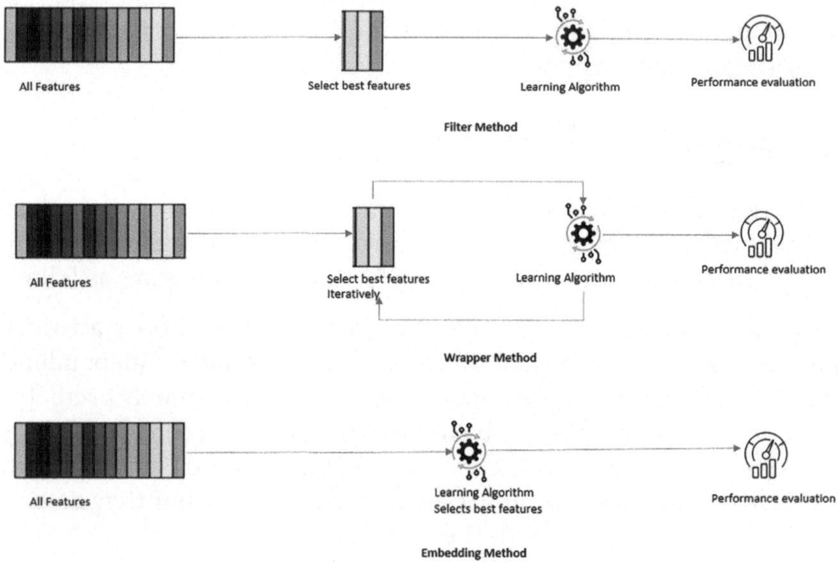

Figure 9.1: *Illustration of feature selection methods: Filter, Wrapper, and Embedded, demonstrating how features are selected and evaluated by a learning algorithm*

- **Hybrid Methods:** Hybrid methods combine the strengths of different feature selection techniques. For example, a combination of filter and wrapper methods can be used to first narrow down the number of features using statistical metrics and then apply a wrapper for fine-tuning.
- **Genetic Algorithms (GA):** Genetic algorithms can be used as a feature selection technique by simulating the process of natural selection. GAs evaluate subsets of features through evolutionary operations such as mutation, crossover, and selection, effectively identifying optimal feature sets. They can handle large search spaces and complex feature interactions, making them suitable for high-dimensional and non-linear problems.

Feature Selection Using Genetic Algorithms (GA)

Feature selection using Genetic Algorithms (GA) refers to employing GAs as a method to identify the best subset of features for a machine learning model. In this context, GA is used to evaluate different feature combinations, searching for the subset that optimizes a model's performance based on a defined fitness function, such as accuracy or precision. GAs are effective for feature selection because they can handle high-dimensional data, complex feature interactions, and non-linear relationships. By applying genetic operations such as crossover, mutation, and selection, GAs evolve towards the optimal set of features, balancing model performance and complexity.

Input Optimization for GA: Unlike traditional machine learning models, GAs do not require "*features*" in the typical sense. GAs work by evolving a population of potential solutions to optimize an objective function. Feature selection for GA can be referred to here as the process of selecting or engineering the representation of the solutions or tuning problem-specific parameters to help the GA perform more effectively. By optimizing the representation and parameters–such as encoding strategies, fitness function parameters, or mutation rates–we can significantly improve the GA's convergence efficiency and the quality of its solutions. Thus, it is more accurate to refer to this as input representation or parameter optimization for GA, rather than feature selection.

The purpose of the following section is to cover feature selection using GA.

Recap of GA Selection Process

The image shows a **population of individuals** in a genetic algorithm. Each row labeled **S1, S2, S3, S4, S5** represents an **individual solution**, with a **binary encoding** of features or parameters.

- **S1 to S5**: These are individual solutions in the population.
- Each individual is represented by a series of **binary values** (0 or 1), which typically encode the presence or absence of specific features or settings.

In this population:

- **S1, S2, S3, S4, and S5** represent different solutions for a problem.
- **The red box around S2 and S3** suggests that these individuals have been highlighted–likely indicating their higher performance or fitness compared to others. They are selected for **crossover** and **mutation** in the next generation to evolve better solutions.

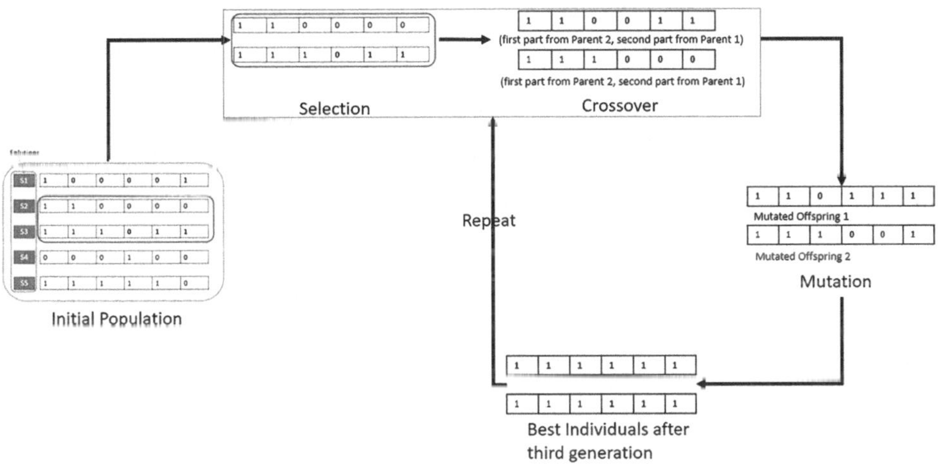

Figure 9.2: *The process of selection, crossover, and mutation on the given binary strings for representation*

Perform crossover and mutation on the given binary strings for representation:

Crossover

Crossover is a genetic operation used to combine parts of two parent chromosomes to create offspring. Let us assume we use a single-point crossover.

For the given binary strings:

1. Parent 1: **1 1 0 0 0 0**
2. Parent 2: **1 1 1 0 1 1**

Assume the crossover point is after the third bit:

- Offspring 1: **1 1 0 | 0 1 1** (first part from Parent 1, second part from Parent 2)
- Offspring 2: **1 1 1 | 0 0 0** (first part from Parent 2, second part from Parent 1)

Mutation

Mutation introduces variability by flipping a bit randomly in the offspring chromosomes.

Let us apply mutation to **Offspring 1** by flipping the fourth bit (0 to 1):

- Mutated Offspring 1: **1 1 0 1 1 1**

Similarly, let us apply mutation to **Offspring 2** by flipping the sixth bit (0 to 1):

- Mutated Offspring 2: **1 1 1 0 0 1**

Final Result:

1. **Mutated Offspring 1: 1 1 0 1 1 1**
2. **Mutated Offspring 2: 1 1 1 0 0 1**

These offspring now represent the new generation after crossover and mutation.

If we repeat the process of crossover and mutation over at least three generations, the population is likely to evolve to maximize the "*fitness*" based on a given goal or objective function.

In this scenario, assuming we are trying to maximize the number of 1s in each binary string (which is a common objective in genetic algorithms), the population will evolve to produce individuals with more 1s over time.

Given the initial parent strings:

1. Parent 1: **1 1 0 0 0 0**

2. Parent 2: **1 1 1 0 1 1**

First Generation Offspring (After Crossover and Mutation):

1. Offspring 1: **1 1 0 1 1 1**
2. Offspring 2: **1 1 1 0 0 1**

Second Generation (After Repeating Crossover and Mutation):

- Crossover these offspring and apply mutations. The new individuals might look like:
    1. **1 1 1 1 1 1** (assuming optimal crossover and mutation leading to all 1s)
    2. 1 1 1 0 1 1

Third Generation:

- The individuals with higher fitness (more 1s) are likely to be selected for crossover.
- By this point, the evolution will likely favor individuals with all 1s if we continue with crossover and mutation:
    1. 1 1 1 1 1 1
    2. 1 1 1 1 1 1

Best Individual Population

After at least three generations, assuming a maximization goal, the best individuals in the population would likely converge towards **1 1 1 1 1 1**–a chromosome consisting entirely of 1s. This is because the genetic algorithm continuously favors the fittest individuals, and in this case, those with the maximum number of 1s.

The number of rows (that is, individuals) you can have in the third generation of a genetic algorithm depends on the **population size**, which is a predefined parameter set at the beginning of the algorithm. Typically, the population size remains **constant** across generations.

For example, if your initial population size is **10 individuals**, each generation–including the third generation–will also contain **10 rows** (or individuals). The individuals in each generation represent candidate solutions, which are evolved through crossover, mutation, and selection processes.

Thus, if you start with a population of **N** individuals, your third generation will also have **N** rows, maintaining the same population size throughout the evolutionary process.

Feature Selection GA Deep Dive

Feature selection using GA involves creating an initial population of feature subsets, evaluating their performance, and using genetic operations (selection, crossover, mutation) to evolve better feature sets over multiple generations. The result is a feature subset that balances model accuracy and complexity, optimizing the learning task.

1. **Initial Population Generation**
    - The process starts by creating an **initial population** of individuals, where each individual represents a different combination of features.
    - Typically, these individuals are represented by **binary vectors**, where each bit represents a feature (1 if the feature is included, 0 if excluded).
    - For example, if you have 6 features, an individual such as 1 0 1 0 1 1 means that the 1st, 3rd, 5th, and 6th features are selected.
2. **Fitness Evaluation**
    - Each individual in the population is **evaluated** using a fitness function. The fitness function measures the quality of the feature set in terms of model performance.
    - Typically, this involves:
        - **Training a machine learning model** (for example, decision tree, SVM, neural network) using the selected features represented by the individual.
        - **Evaluating the model's performance** using metrics such as accuracy, precision, recall, or F1 score.
    - The fitness score reflects how well the model performs with the given feature set, balancing between accuracy and feature count (to reduce complexity).
3. **Selection**
    - Based on the **fitness scores**, the best individuals (feature subsets) are selected to be **parents** for the next generation.
    - **Selection methods** such as **Roulette Wheel** or **Tournament Selection** are often used to ensure that individuals with higher fitness have a greater chance of passing on their genes.
    - The goal of selection is to keep the individuals that represent promising feature sets while removing poorly performing ones.
4. **Crossover**
    - The selected parents are used to create the **next generation** through a process called **crossover** (recombination).

- In crossover, two parent individuals are combined to form **new offspring**. This is usually done by selecting a random point in the binary vector and **swapping** the segments after that point between the two parents.
- For instance, if two parent feature sets are:
  - **Parent 1:** 1 0 0 | 1 1 0
  - **Parent 2:** 1 1 1 | 0 0 1 After crossover at the third position, the offspring might look like:
  - **Offspring 1:** 1 0 0 0 0 1
  - **Offspring 2:** 1 1 1 1 1 0
- This helps in **combining good features** from both parents to create potentially better feature sets.

5. **Mutation**
   - After crossover, **mutation** is applied to introduce some **randomness** in the population. This is done by **flipping bits** in the individuals.
   - For example, an offspring 1 0 0 1 1 0 might undergo mutation at the second position to become 1 1 0 1 1 0.
   - Mutation helps maintain **diversity** in the population and prevents the algorithm from getting stuck in **local optima** by exploring new feature combinations.
6. **Repeat for Multiple Generations**
   - The process of **fitness evaluation, selection, crossover, and mutation** is repeated over several generations.
   - Over time, the population evolves, and the individuals (feature sets) **converge** towards the optimal subset of features.
7. **Termination**
   - The algorithm stops when a **stopping condition** is met. This can be a **fixed number of generations**, reaching a **target accuracy**, or when there is **no improvement** in fitness over a given number of iterations.
   - The best individual at this point represents the **optimal subset of features** that yields the best performance for the model.
8. **Best Solution**
   - The **best solution** found during the generations is selected as the **final feature subset** for the machine learning model.
   - This subset should improve model accuracy, reduce overfitting, and simplify the model by removing irrelevant features.

Now let us relook at the image with respect to what we just learned, in this feature selection scenario, GAs are used to find the best subset of features for a machine learning model. The goal is to optimize the model's performance by repeatedly evolving feature sets, ensuring only the most informative features are selected. Over multiple generations, GA helps in converging towards an optimal or near-optimal set of features, improving model accuracy and reducing unnecessary complexity.

- **Initial Population (Feature Sets)**: **Initial Population** represents different candidate feature sets (S1, S2, S3, and so on) for a machine learning model. Each row (or solution) is a binary vector representing whether a specific feature is included (1) or excluded (0) from the model.

  For example, S1 might represent a feature set with only certain features included.
- **Selection**: GA selects the most promising feature sets based on their performance (fitness). In *Figure* 9.2, feature sets such as S2 and S3 have been highlighted, indicating they have performed well during evaluation. The evaluation is typically done by training a model with the selected features and assessing its accuracy.
- **Crossover**: Selected feature sets (S2 and S3) are combined to create new feature subsets. This process is done by choosing a crossover point and mixing the feature bits from each parent. The idea is to inherit good features from each parent, potentially leading to an even better feature set.
- **Mutation**: After crossover, some bits in the offspring feature sets are flipped. Mutation ensures diversity and prevents the algorithm from getting stuck in local optima by exploring other possible feature combinations.

Best Individuals After Third Generation

The process of selection, crossover, and mutation is repeated over several generations. After the third generation, the best feature sets are identified, which are likely to have more 1s in key positions, indicating the inclusion of the most relevant features.

Practical Application

We used **all features**, applied a **Genetic Algorithm (GA)** for feature selection, iteratively selected the **best subset of features**, trained a **learning algorithm (XGBoost Regressor)** with those features, and then performed **performance evaluation** based on model accuracy.

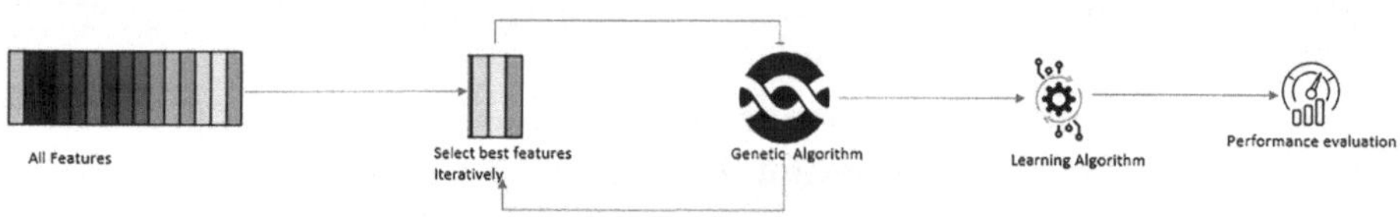

***Figure* 9.3:** *The process of feature selection using* GA

The Dataset

The California housing dataset contains data from the 1990 U.S. Census, providing information about housing in California. It includes 9 features: geographical coordinates (longitude and latitude), **`housing_median_age`**, **`total_rooms`**, **`total_bedrooms`**, **`population`**, **`households`**, **`median_income`**, and the target variable, **`median_house_value`**. This dataset is often used for regression tasks to predict median house values based on neighborhood characteristics. The data helps understand relationships between housing prices and features such as age, room counts, and location, making it suitable for practicing regression models and feature selection in machine learning. It has around 20,000 entries representing different areas in California.

Regression

Next, we will use a GA for feature selection in combination with an XGBoost Regressor to predict house values. The GA will help identify the most relevant subset of features by optimizing model performance through iterative evaluation using the XGBoost model and a fitness function such as RMSE. By applying genetic operations such as selection, crossover, and mutation, the GA aims to find the optimal set of features, improving model accuracy and efficiency by excluding less relevant features, while XGBoost provides robust gradient-boosted predictions. This approach will help maximize predictive power and streamline feature selection.

We will also plot the **feature importance** to understand the contribution of each feature in predicting house values. This will help visualize which features are most influential, allowing for better interpretation of the XGBoost model's decisions. Feature importance can be easily plotted using XGBoost's built-in functionality, providing insights into which features GA-selected are contributing the most to model performance. The code can be found in **`Chapter_9.ipynb`**.

1. **Import Libraries**

```
import pandas as pd
import numpy as np
from xgboost import XGBRegressor, plot_importance
from sklearn.model_selection import train_test_split
from sklearn.metrics import mean_squared_error
import pygad
import pygad.nn
import pygad.gann
import matplotlib.pyplot as plt
```

- **Pandas and NumPy**: For data handling and mathematical operations.
- **`XGBRegressor` and `plot_importance`**: XGBoost model and visualization of feature importance.

- **Scikit-learn**: Used for splitting data and evaluating performance.
- **PyGAD**: To implement the Genetic Algorithm.
- **Matplotlib**: To plot the results.

2. **Load the Dataset**

```
data = pd.read_csv('/content/sample_data/california_housing_test.
csv')
```

- Loads the **California Housing dataset**.

3. **Separate Features and Target**

```
X = data.drop(columns=['median_house_value'])
y = data['median_house_value']
```

- **X**: Contains all features (predictors).
- **y**: Contains the target variable (median_house_value).

4. **Split the Dataset**

```
X_train, X_test, y_train, y_test = train_test_split(X, y, test_
size=0.2, random_state=42)
```

- Splits data into **training (80%)** and **testing (20%)** sets.

5. **Define Fitness Function for GA**

```
def fitness_func(ga_instance, solution, solution_idx):
    selected_features = [index for index in range(len(solution))
if solution[index] == 1]

    if len(selected_features) == 0:
        return 1e-6

    X_train_selected = X_train.iloc[:, selected_features]
    X_test_selected = X_test.iloc[:, selected_features]

    model = XGBRegressor()
    model.fit(X_train_selected, y_train)

    predictions = model.predict(X_test_selected)
    rmse = np.sqrt(mean_squared_error(y_test, predictions))

    return 1.0 / (rmse + 1e-6)
```

- **solution**: Represents the selected features (1 for selected, 0 for not).
- Selects features based on **solution**.
- **Trains XGBoost** on selected features and **evaluates RMSE**.

- The fitness score is inversely related to RMSE (higher score = lower error).

6. **Set Parameters for GA**

```
    ga_instance = pygad.GA(
 num_generations=50,
 num_parents_mating=5,
 fitness_func=fitness_func,
 sol_per_pop=10,
 num_genes=X.shape[1],
 init_range_low=0,
 init_range_high=2,
 mutation_percent_genes=10,
 gene_space=[0, 1],
 parent_selection_type="sss",
 crossover_type="single_point",
 mutation_type="random",
 keep_parents=2
)
```

- Defines the **GA parameters**:
  - **`num_generations=50`**: Run for 50 generations.
  - **`num_parents_mating=5`**: Number of parents selected for mating.
  - **`sol_per_pop=10`**: Population size (10 individuals).
  - **`num_genes=X.shape[1]`**: Number of genes is equal to the number of features.
  - **`mutation_percent_genes=10`**: Mutate 10% of genes.
  - **`gene_space=[0, 1]`**: Each gene can be 0 (not selected) or 1 (selected).
  - **`crossover_type="single_point"`**: Crossover type for generating offspring.
  - **`keep_parents=2`**: Number of parents to retain in the next generation.

7. **Run the GA**

```
ga_instance.run()
```

- Runs the Genetic Algorithm to **evolve feature subsets** over the generations.

8. **Extract the Best Solution**

```
solution, solution_fitness, solution_idx = ga instance.best_
solution()
selected_features = [index for index in range(len(solution)) if
solution[index] == 1]
print(f"Selected features: {selected_features}")
```

- Extracts the **best solution** (subset of features) after running GA.
- Prints the indices of **selected features**.

9. **Train the Final Model with Selected Features**

```
X_train_selected = X_train.iloc[:, selected_features]
X_test_selected = X_test.iloc[:, selected_features]
final_model = XGBRegressor()
final_model.fit(X_train_selected, y_train)
```

- **Retrains XGBoost** using only the selected features to obtain the final model.

10. **Plot Feature Importance**

```
plt.figure(figsize=(10, 6))
plot_importance(final_model)
plt.show()
```

- **Plots feature importance** for the final XGBoost model to understand which features contribute the most.

11. **Plot Generation vs. Best Fitness Score**

```
generations = list(range(1, len(ga_instance.best_solutions_fit-
ness) + 1))
best_solutions_fitness = ga_instance.best_solutions_fitness

plt.figure(figsize=(10, 6))
plt.plot(generations, best_solutions_fitness, marker='o', line-
style='-', color='b')
plt.xlabel('Generation')
plt.ylabel('Best Fitness Score')
plt.title('Generation vs. Best Fitness Score')
plt.grid()
plt.show()
```

- **Plots the fitness score** of the best solution for each generation.
- Helps visualize how the performance evolves as the algorithm runs, indicating **convergence** toward an optimal solution.

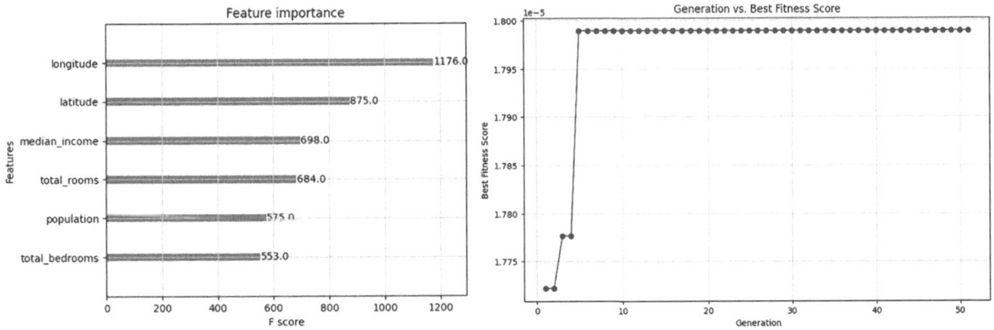

***Figure 9.4**: Feature Importance Analysis and Fitness Score Evolution: The left plot shows the importance of features selected by the Genetic Algorithm for the XGBoost regression model, while the right plot illustrates the improvement in fitness score across 50 generations, indicating the GA's convergence*

12. **Learning Model Evaluation**

Root Mean Squared Error (RMSE) measures the average magnitude of prediction errors, showing how far predicted values deviate from actual values. Lower RMSE indicates better model performance.

R^2 (R-squared) represents the proportion of variance in the target variable that is explained by the features. It ranges from 0 to 1, with a higher value indicating that the model explains more variance. An R^2 of 1 means perfect predictions, while 0 means the model fails to explain any variability.

Together, RMSE and R^2 provide insight into the accuracy and explanatory power of a regression model.

```
# Evaluate the model
predictions = final_model.predict(X_test_selected)
rmse = np.sqrt(mean_squared_error(y_test, predictions))
r2 = r2_score(y_test, predictions)
print(f"Final Model RMSE: {rmse}")
print(f"Final Model R^2 Score: {r2}")
```

The final model achieved an RMSE of 55,588.53, indicating the average difference between predicted and actual house values. The lower the RMSE, the more accurate the predictions are, though this value still shows a considerable prediction error.

The R^2 score of 0.7546 means that around 75.46% of the variance in house prices is explained by the selected features in the model, suggesting a relatively strong, but not perfect, predictive capability. Together, these metrics suggest that while the model performs fairly well, there is room for improvement in reducing prediction error and increasing explained variance.

Now, let us try to convert the problem to a classification problem.

Classification

To use the XGBoost Classifier and convert the problem into a classification task, you need to transform the target variable (**median_house_value**) into categorical classes. For example, you could bin the house values into categories such as "**Low**," "**Medium**," and "**High**" based on value ranges or quantiles. This transforms the problem from predicting continuous values (regression) to predicting categories (classification). After converting the target to classes, you can use the **XGBClassifier** from XGBoost to train a model to predict the category each sample belongs to. Ensure to adjust the evaluation metrics accordingly, such as using **accuracy** or **F1-score**.

Most of the code remains the same; the changes are outlined below. These changes convert the problem from regression to classification, allowing the XGBoost Classifier to predict categorical labels instead of continuous values.

Here are the changes in the code compared to the regression version:

1. **Conversion to Classification:**

```
bins = [0, 100000, 300000, np.inf]
labels = [0, 1, 2]  # 0: Low, 1: Medium, 2: High
y = pd.cut(data['median_house_value'], bins=bins, labels=labels).
astype(int)
```

The target variable (**median_house_value**) is converted to categorical labels (**Low**, **Medium**, **High**) using **pd.cut()**. This transforms the regression problem into a classification problem.

2. **Model Change:**

```
from xgboost import XGBClassifier
```

The **XGBRegressor** is replaced with **XGBClassifier** to handle the classification problem.

3. **Fitness Function Changes:**

```
model = XGBClassifier()
model.fit(X_train_selected, y_train)
predictions = model.predict(X_test_selected)
accuracy = accuracy_score(y_test, predictions)
return accuracy
```

   - The model used in the fitness function is now **XGBClassifier()**.
   - The evaluation metric is changed from RMSE (used in regression) to **accuracy**, which is more suitable for classification tasks.

4. **Model Evaluation:**

```
accuracy = accuracy_score(y_test, predictions)
print(f"Final Model Accuracy: {accuracy}")
```

```
print("Classification Report:\n", classification_report(y_test,
predictions))
```

The evaluation metrics include **accuracy_score** and **classification_report**, which provide information about classification accuracy and detailed performance for each class (**precision**, **recall**, **F1-score**).

```
              precision    recall  f1-score   support

           0       0.79      0.68      0.73       117
           1       0.84      0.91      0.87       389
           2       0.81      0.67      0.73        94

    accuracy                           0.83       600
   macro avg       0.81      0.75      0.78       600
weighted avg       0.82      0.83      0.82       600
```

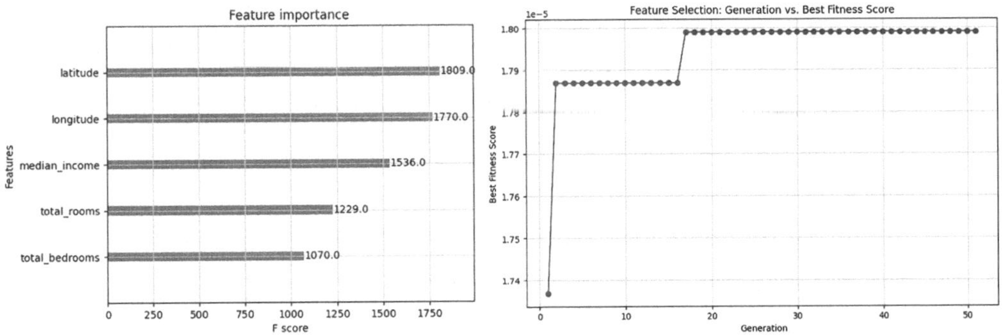

***Figure 9.5**: Feature Importance Analysis and Fitness Score Evolution: The left plot shows the importance of features selected by the Genetic Algorithm for the XGBoost classification model, while the right plot illustrates the improvement in fitness score across 50 generations, indicating the Genetic Algorithm's convergence*

Now that we understand the feature selection process using GA, let us move on to hyperparameter tuning with GA. We will continue with XGBoost regression, as the model did not perform well, showing a Root Mean Squared Error (RMSE) of 55,588.53. This indicates the average difference between the predicted and actual house values.

Hyper Parameters

Hyperparameters are configuration settings used to control the learning process in machine learning models. Unlike model parameters (for example, weights in a neural network), hyperparameters are set before training begins and influence the training behavior.

In XGBoost, hyperparameters such as **learning_rate**, **max_depth**, and **n_estimators** define aspects such as learning speed, model complexity, and the number of boosting rounds. Tuning these hyperparameters is crucial because they directly impact model performance, preventing underfitting or overfitting. For example, a high **max_depth** could lead to an overly complex model that overfits, while a low **learning_rate** could slow convergence. Proper tuning balances model accuracy and generalization.

Hyperparameters also control optimization and regularization processes (lambda for L2 regularization, alpha for L1 regularization), influencing how the model handles noisy data and preventing overfitting. Effective hyperparameter tuning helps create a well-regularized, efficient model that balances bias and variance, ultimately leading to better predictive performance. This is why hyperparameter optimization is an essential aspect of the machine learning pipeline.

XGBoost has several hyperparameters that can be tuned to improve model performance. Some of the key hyperparameters include:

- **n_estimators**: Number of boosting rounds or trees to be built.
- **learning_rate (eta)**: Step size shrinkage used to update weights, controlling the contribution of each tree.
- **max_depth**: Maximum depth of each tree, controlling model complexity.
- **min_child_weight**: Minimum sum of instance weights (Hessian) needed in a child, preventing overfitting.
- **subsample**: Fraction of samples used for each tree, controlling overfitting.
- **colsample_bytree**: Fraction of features used per tree.
- **gamma**: Minimum loss reduction needed to make a split, used for pruning.
- **lambda**: L2 regularization term on weights.
- **alpha**: L1 regularization term on weights.
- **objective**: Specifies the learning task (for example, **reg:squarederror** for regression).
- **booster**: Type of booster to use (for example, **gbtree**, **dart**, **gblinear**).
- **scale_pos_weight**: Balances the impact of positive and negative classes in case of imbalance.
- **max_delta_step**: Maximum step for weight estimation to control step size during training.

Now that we know, to effectively optimize machine learning models, hyperparameter tuning plays a crucial role. There are several methods to fine-tune these parameters, ranging from simple techniques to advanced optimization strategies. In the following, we list out different hyperparameter tuning techniques, including Genetic Algorithms, Bayesian Optimization, and others, highlighting their approaches and benefits.

Hyperparameter Tuning Types

- **Grid Search**: Exhaustively searches all possible combinations of hyperparameter values. It is comprehensive but can be computationally expensive.
- **Random Search**: Randomly samples hyperparameter values from specified ranges. It is more efficient and often finds good configurations faster than grid search.
- **Genetic Algorithm**: Evolves hyperparameter settings using selection, crossover, and mutation. It mimics natural evolution to find the optimal combination over generations.
- **Bayesian Optimization**: Utilizes a probabilistic model to estimate and optimize hyperparameters. It balances exploration and exploitation, finding optimal solutions more efficiently.
- **Hyperband**: Allocates resources to multiple configurations and prunes poor performers early, making it faster than grid or random search.
- **Tree-structured Parzen Estimator (TPE)**: An improvement of Bayesian Optimization that uses two distributions (good and bad) for adaptive hyperparameter selection.

Hyperparameter Tuning with GA

Hyperparameter tuning with Genetic Algorithms (GA) involves using GA to search for the best hyperparameters for a model, such as XGBoost. In GA, potential hyperparameter sets are represented as chromosomes, with each gene corresponding to a hyperparameter value. The GA optimizes these hyperparameter sets through selection, crossover, and mutation operations. The fitness function, often defined as model performance metrics such as RMSE or accuracy, evaluates how well each set of hyperparameters works. Over multiple generations, GA evolves towards better configurations, exploring complex hyperparameter spaces effectively to improve model accuracy and performance, outperforming exhaustive or random search techniques.

Hyperparameters for GA

The GA itself also has hyperparameters that significantly affect its efficiency and convergence. Key hyperparameters for GA include **`population_size`** (number of individuals in each generation), **`num_generations`** (total generations to evolve), **`mutation_rate`** (probability of altering genes), and **`crossover_rate`** (likelihood of recombining genes from parents). **`selection_type`** controls how parents are chosen (for example, roulette wheel or tournament), while **gene_space** defines possible values for each gene. Properly tuning these hyperparameters is essential for effective convergence, as they control how well the GA balances exploration and exploitation, preventing premature convergence or excessive computational expense.

The purpose of the following section is to cover Hyperparameter Tuning Using Genetic Algorithms (GA).

Hyperparameter Tuning Using GA Deep Dive

When it comes to optimizing the performance of machine learning models, hyperparameter tuning plays a crucial role. Traditional methods such as grid or random search can be inefficient, especially for large, complex search spaces. GAs offer a powerful alternative for hyperparameter tuning, inspired by natural evolution. By mimicking the principles of selection, crossover, and mutation, GAs can intelligently explore and identify optimal hyperparameter combinations. In this section, we will explore how GAs can be applied to tune the hyperparameters of an XGBoost Regressor, helping to improve its predictive power and efficiency while overcoming the limitations of traditional search methods.

You can use a GA to tune hyperparameters for an XGBoost Regressor. GA is useful for exploring large and complex hyperparameter spaces. Here is how:

1. **Define Hyperparameters**: Decide on which hyperparameters to tune, such as **learning_rate**, **max_depth**, **n_estimators**, and so on.
2. **Chromosome Representation**: Represent each hyperparameter set as a "**chromosome**" in GA, where each "**gene**" corresponds to a specific hyperparameter value (for example, **learning_rate**, **max_depth**). For example, a chromosome could be represented as **learning_rate = 0.1**, **max_depth = 5**, and **n_estimators = 100**.
3. **Fitness Function**: Define a fitness function that evaluates the performance of an XGBoost model using a particular combination of hyperparameters. Train the model and use a metric such as RMSE to quantify model performance. The fitness score is usually the reciprocal of RMSE.
4. **Genetic Operations**: Run the GA with genetic operations such as selection, crossover, and mutation to generate new hyperparameter sets.
5. **Optimization**: Over multiple generations, the GA will evolve towards the optimal hyperparameter configuration for the XGBoost Regressor.
6. **Population**: A group of several chromosomes (that is, several sets of hyperparameters) that are evaluated simultaneously. Typically, a population consists of **multiple individuals** (chromosomes) with different

hyperparameter values, which allows the GA to explore various parts of the hyperparameter space in parallel.

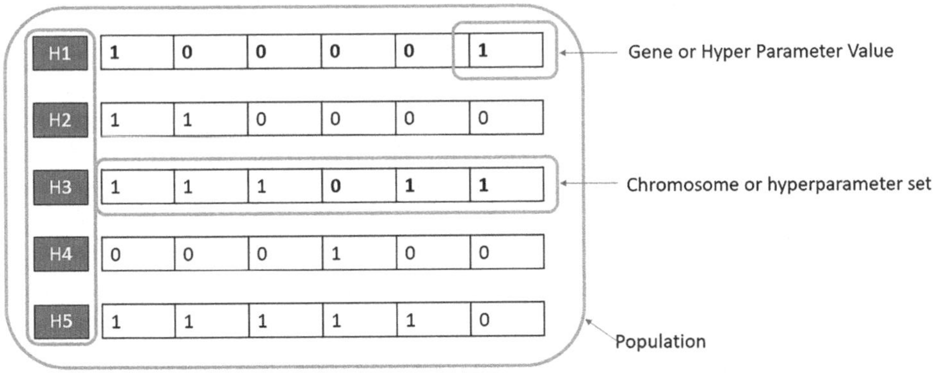

Figure 9.6: *The image illustrates the Representation of the Genetic Algorithm for Hyperparameter Tuning: A population of multiple hyperparameter sets (chromosomes), each containing genes representing individual hyperparameter values*

- **Population**: The group of hyperparameter sets (H1, H2, H3, H4, H5), each of which represents a possible solution.
- **Chromosome**: Each hyperparameter set (H1, H2, and so on) is a chromosome. It contains multiple **genes**, which are specific hyperparameter values.
- **Gene**: Each individual gene represents a specific hyperparameter value (0 or 1).

The entire population evolves over generations, and each chromosome (hyperparameter set) is evaluated to determine which combination yields the best model performance.

Practical Application

We will continue using the same dataset to apply Genetic Algorithms (GA) for optimizing both feature selection and hyperparameter tuning. First, GA will be used to select the most relevant subset of features, improving model performance by excluding less impactful features. Then, we will train an XGBoost Regressor using the selected features. Afterward, another GA will be applied to tune the hyperparameters of the model (for example, learning rate, max depth, number of estimators) to further optimize its performance. Finally, we will evaluate the model to confirm improvements from feature selection and hyperparameter tuning.

Note, the GA configuration is not the same for both feature selection and hyperparameter tuning. The current code combines both tasks into one GA run. To achieve separate configurations for feature selection and hyperparameter tuning, you need to create two separate GA instances: one for feature selection and one for hyperparameter tuning.

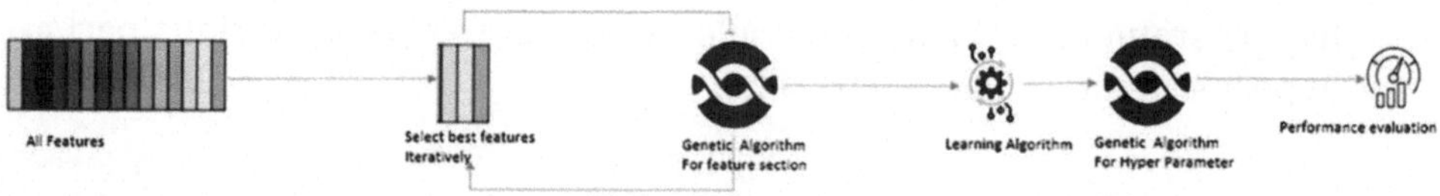

Figure 9.7: *The process of using Genetic Algorithms (GA) to optimize both feature selection and hyperparameter tuning for a machine learning model*

The GA configuration for feature selection is defined as follows:

- **`num_generations=50`**: Run for 50 generations to evolve the population.
- **`num_parents_mating=5`**: Select 5 parents for mating to produce offspring.
- **`fitness_func=feature_selection_fitness_func`**: Use a custom fitness function to evaluate feature subsets.
- **`sol_per_pop=10`**: The population consists of 10 individuals (solutions).
- **`num_genes=X.shape[1]`**: Each solution has a number of genes equal to the number of features in the dataset.
- **`gene_space=[0, 1]`**: Each gene can either be 0 (feature excluded) or 1 (feature included).
- **`parent_selection_type="sss"`**: Use stochastic sampling for selecting parents.
- **`crossover_type="single_point"`**: Apply single-point crossover for offspring creation.
- **`mutation_type="random"`**: Apply random mutations to promote genetic diversity.
- **`keep_parents=2`**: Keep the best 2 parents in the next generation.

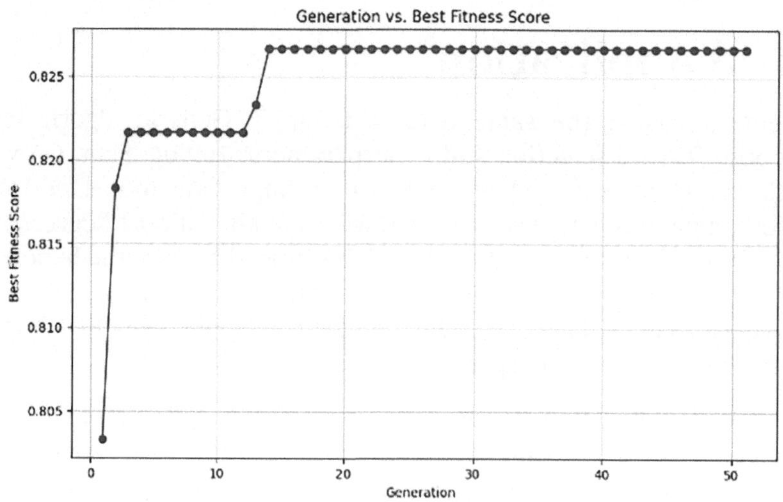

Figure 9.8: *The plot shows Feature Selection: Generation versus Best Fitness Score*

The Genetic Algorithm (GA) configuration for hyperparameter tuning is defined as follows:

- **`num_generations=50`**: Run the GA for 50 generations to find optimal hyperparameters.
- **`num_parents_mating=5`**: Select 5 parents for mating to create offspring in each generation.
- **`fitness_func=hyperparameter_tuning_fitness_func`**: Use a fitness function that evaluates the model's performance with different hyperparameters.
- **`sol_per_pop=10`**: The population consists of 10 individuals (potential solutions).
- **`num_genes=3`**: There are 3 genes representing the hyperparameters (**`max_depth`**, **`learning_rate`**, **`n_estimators`**).
- **`gene_space`**: Defines the search space for each hyperparameter, with ranges for depth, learning rate, and estimators.
- **`parent_selection_type="sss"`**: Use stochastic sampling for parent selection.
- **`crossover_type="single_point"`**: Use single-point crossover for offspring creation.
- **`mutation_type="random"`**: Apply random mutations to maintain diversity.
- **`keep_parents=2`**: Retain the 2 best parents for the next generation.

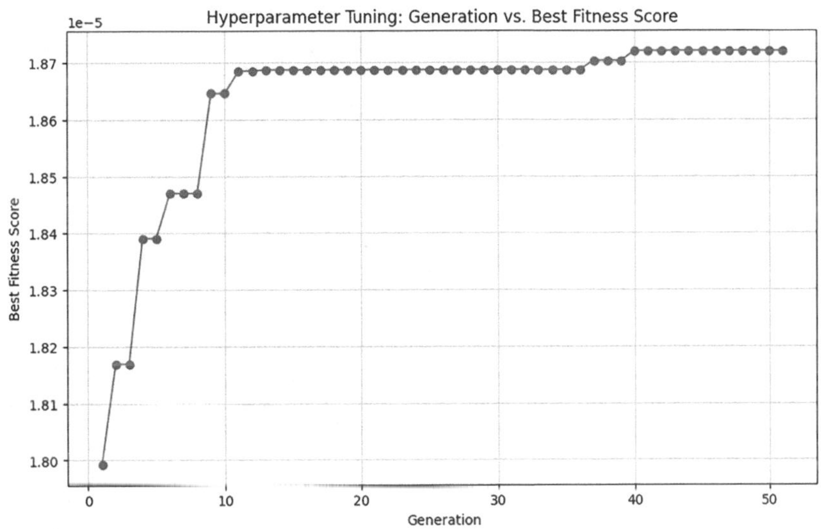

***Figure 9.9**: The plot shows Hyperparameter Tuning: Generation vs. Best Fitness Score*

The difference between the GA configurations for feature selection and hyperparameter tuning lies in the **objective** and **gene representation**. In feature selection, each **gene** represents a feature (0 or 1 indicating exclusion or inclusion), and the **number of genes** equals the number of features. The **fitness function** aims to select the best subset of features. For hyperparameter tuning, the **genes** represent model hyperparameters (for example, **max_depth**, **learning_rate**), and **gene values** are continuous or integer ranges specific to each hyperparameter. The **fitness function** focuses on finding the optimal hyperparameter combination for model performance. These distinctions influence the GA's search and optimization process. The full code can be found in **Chapter_9.ipynb**.

The model improved:

- **Previous RMSE**: 55,588.53
- **New RMSE post Hyper parameter tuning using GA**: 53,419.69

The reduction in RMSE indicates that the model's predictions are now closer to the actual values, suggesting improved performance. The GA-based feature selection, followed by hyperparameter tuning, successfully optimized the model.

This kind of improvement demonstrates the benefit of sequentially applying genetic algorithms for both selecting the most relevant features and finding the best hyperparameters for the XGBoost model.

Conclusion

In this chapter, we explored various methods of feature selection and hyperparameter tuning, with a focus on Genetic Algorithms (GA). We began by understanding the importance of feature selection, which helps to identify the most relevant features, reducing dimensionality and improving model efficiency. Through a detailed discussion on the GA selection process, we examined how GA can be used for feature selection by mimicking natural selection to optimize feature subsets. We also dived deeper into practical applications, applying GA-based feature selection to different datasets for both regression and classification tasks.

Following feature selection, we moved on to hyperparameter tuning. We learned that hyperparameter tuning is crucial for optimizing model performance by finding the best parameter configurations. Using GA for hyperparameter tuning, we explored how GA can efficiently search for optimal parameters across complex models.

Next, we will leverage GA for Neural Architecture Search (NAS), treating neural network architecture parameters—such as the number of hidden layers and neurons per layer—as hyperparameters. This approach automates architecture optimization, enabling GA to iteratively find the best configuration for improved model performance, just like traditional hyperparameter tuning.

CHAPTER 10
Applying Deep Learning to Genetic Algorithm

Introduction

In this chapter, we explore how evolutionary algorithms can be leveraged to design and optimize neural networks, specifically focusing on three advanced methods. First, we dive into **Neural Architecture Search (NAS)** using **Genetic Algorithms (GA)**, treating network architecture parameters as hyperparameters. This approach allows us to discover optimal configurations for neural networks, maximizing their performance on a given task by mimicking the natural evolutionary process.

Next, we discuss **NeuroEvolution of Augmenting Topologies (NEAT)**, an evolutionary algorithm that not only evolves the weights of a neural network but also its topology. By dynamically growing and optimizing both the structure and parameters, NEAT enables the discovery of highly efficient architectures.

Finally, we implement a **neural network** aimed at predicting the target variable, "Product Price," using features from our dataset. In this model, a genetic algorithm optimizes the weights, aiming to minimize prediction error effectively. These methods showcase the power of evolutionary strategies in developing, optimizing, and finc tuning neural networks for complex prediction tasks.

Structure

In this chapter, we will cover the following topics:

- Deep Learning
- Neural Architecture Search (NAS)
- Neuro Evolution of Augmenting Topologies (NEAT)

- Genetic Algorithm to Optimize the Model's Weights
- Other GA Optimizations of NN

Deep Learning

In the last chapter, we learned how to use **Genetic Algorithms (GA)** for feature selection and hyperparameter tuning in machine learning. In this chapter, we will apply GAs to explore **neural network architectures**. Before diving into that, let us first understand the basics of a neural network to grasp how GA can assist in optimizing its structure.

Neural Network

A **neural network model** is inspired by the human brain's structure and is used to recognize patterns and make predictions. At its core, a neural network consists of interconnected layers of nodes, or "*neurons*," each having its own set of weights and biases. Information passes through the layers from input to output, undergoing transformations defined by activation functions to solve complex tasks.

The simplest form of a neural network is the **feedforward neural network**, which flows information in one direction–input to output. **Training** involves finding optimal weights by minimizing a loss function, typically using methods such as **gradient descent**. In the last chapter, we explored **feature selection** and **hyperparameter tuning** using **Genetic Algorithms (GA)** for machine learning. GAs helped us find the best features and parameters efficiently, boosting model performance.

Types of Neural Networks include:

- **Feedforward Neural Networks**: Basic networks that flow in one direction.
- **Convolutional Neural Networks (CNNs)**: Used for image processing.
- **Recurrent Neural Networks (RNNs)**: Handle sequences, such as time series or text.
- **Long Short-Term Memory Networks (LSTMs)**: A specialized RNN variant for long-term dependencies.
- **Generative Adversarial Networks (GANs)**: Used for generating new data samples.
- **Transformers**: Powerful models designed to handle sequential data more efficiently than RNNs or LSTMs, commonly used in natural language processing.

Deep learning refers to the use of deep neural networks, which are essentially neural networks with many hidden layers. The additional layers in deep learning models enable them to tackle more complex problems by learning intricate patterns in the data.

Shallow Neural Networks:

- Typically consist of only a few hidden layers.
- Useful for relatively simpler tasks or when the dataset is not very complex.
- Examples include feedforward networks used in early machine learning tasks.

Deep Learning/Deep Neural Networks:

Deep learning is a subfield of machine learning that uses **deep neural networks**—neural networks with many hidden layers (often 3 or more). These multiple layers allow the network to automatically learn complex features and representations from raw data, making it powerful for a wide range of tasks.

Characteristics of Deep Learning:

- **Deep Neural Networks**: These networks have many hidden layers, allowing them to learn abstract and hierarchical representations of data.
- **Complex Patterns**: Deep learning models can learn complex, non-linear relationships in data.
- **Feature Extraction**: Unlike shallow networks, deep learning models can automatically extract features without requiring manual feature engineering.

Key Differences:

- **Architecture**: Neural networks can be shallow or deep, while deep learning always involves deep neural networks.
- **Complexity**: Deep learning models have multiple layers (usually more than three), enabling them to solve more complex problems, whereas shallow neural networks have fewer layers and work well for simpler problems.
- **Capability**: Deep learning is capable of handling unstructured data, such as images, audio, and text, and can outperform shallow networks in these domains.
- **Training Requirements**: Deep learning models often require large amounts of data and significant computational power (GPUs) due to their complexity, while shallow neural networks can perform well with smaller datasets.

Designing an effective **neural network architecture** is both an art and a science, involving numerous decisions that can significantly impact a model's ability to learn, generalize, and perform well on complex tasks. From deciding how many layers and neurons are required to choosing the right activation functions and optimization techniques, every detail matters. These decisions form the foundation of the model's capacity to solve the given problem efficiently.

Here are the key architectural considerations:

- **Number of Layers (Depth)**
    - **Input Layer**: Represents the number of input features in the dataset.
    - **Hidden Layers**: The number of hidden layers determines the model's depth. More layers allow the network to learn more complex features and hierarchies, but also increase computational costs and the risk of overfitting.
    - **Output Layer**: Represents the target output. For classification, the number of output neurons matches the number of classes, whereas for regression, it is usually a single neuron.
- **Number of Neurons (Width): Neurons per Layer**: The number of neurons in each hidden layer affects the model's capacity to learn patterns. A higher number of neurons can increase the network's ability to fit complex functions but may also lead to overfitting if not properly regularized.
- **Activation Functions** determine how the weighted sum of inputs is transformed. Choosing the right activation function is crucial for non-linearity:
    - **Rectified Linear Unit (ReLU)**: Common for hidden layers because it introduces non-linearity and reduces computation cost.
    - **Sigmoid/Tanh**: Useful for output layers when probabilities or bounded outputs are needed.
    - **Leaky ReLU or ELU**: Address the dying ReLU problem, where neurons can become inactive during training.
- **Weight Initialization: Initialization Strategy** affects how well a model converges during training.
    - **Xavier/Glorot Initialization**: Used for sigmoid or tanh activations.
    - **He Initialization**: Common for ReLU activations to prevent the vanishing/exploding gradient problem.
- **Regularization Techniques** prevent overfitting by controlling model complexity:
    - **Dropout**: Randomly drops neurons during training to prevent over-reliance on specific paths.
    - **L1/L2 Regularization**: Adds a penalty to the loss function to limit the magnitude of weights.
- **Optimization Algorithm: Optimizer Selection** determines how the network learns and converges.
    - **SGD (Stochastic Gradient Descent)**: Basic optimization algorithm.

  - **Adam**: Popular adaptive learning rate optimizer that works well for most tasks.
  - **RMSprop**: Suitable for dealing with non-stationary objective
- **Learning Rate and Scheduler**
  - **Learning Rate**: Controls how quickly the model adjusts weights during training. A well-chosen learning rate is critical to ensure the model converges efficiently without overshooting.
  - **Learning Rate Schedulers**: Adjust the learning rate during training, typically decreasing it to allow fine-tuning as training progresses.
- **Batch Size** affects the training dynamics:
  - **Small Batch Sizes:** Provide more noise and potentially better generalization but may take longer to converge.
  - **Large Batch Sizes**: Lead to smoother training but may result in getting stuck in sharp local minima.
- **Loss Function**: It determines how the error between predicted and true values is calculated.
  - **Cross-Entropy**: Common for classification tasks.
  - **Mean Squared Error (MSE)**: Often used for regression tasks.
- **Network Topology**

  Fully Connected vs. Specialized Layers:
  - **Convolutional Layers**: Useful for images (CNNs) to detect spatial hierarchies.
  - **Recurrent Layers**: Useful for sequence data, such as text or time series (RNNs, LSTMs).
  - **Attention Mechanisms**: For capturing long-range dependencies, common in Transformers.
- **Skip Connections/Residual Blocks:** Connect non-adjacent layers to help with gradient flow, commonly used in deep architectures such as ResNet to avoid vanishing gradients and facilitate deeper networks.
- **Hardware Considerations**

  Computational Resources: Hardware (for example, CPU versus GPU) plays a role in defining the architecture's complexity. Larger architectures or those using specialized operations (for example, convolutions) require more computational resources.
- **Feature Engineering and Input Preprocessing**
  - **Input Scaling/Normalization**: Properly scaled inputs lead to faster

convergence. Methods such as standard scaling (StandardScaler) or min-max scaling are commonly applied.

  - **Dimensionality Reduction**: Techniques such as **PCA** or **feature selection** help reduce input dimensions, making training more efficient.

- **Network Depth vs. Width Trade-off**

  Depth (number of layers) and **Width** (number of neurons per layer) must be balanced depending on the problem:

  - **Deep and Narrow Networks**: Capture more abstract features.
  - **Shallow and Wide Networks**: Can capture more direct relationships but might struggle with hierarchical features.

- **Hyperparameter Tuning**

  Hyperparameter Search: Choosing the best parameters, such as learning rate, batch size, number of neurons, and layers, can be done via:

  - **Grid Search/Random Search**.
  - **Genetic Algorithms (GA)**: Efficiently search the hyperparameter space, as we explored in the last chapter.

With an understanding of the key architectural components that influence the performance of neural networks, we can now explore how to leverage evolutionary techniques to automate the design process. NAS using GA allows us to treat architectural choices–such as the number of layers, neurons, and activation functions–as hyperparameters that can be optimized systematically. By doing so, we can discover architectures that achieve superior performance without the trial-and-error that typically accompanies manual design. In the following section, we will dive into how GAs can be applied to search for optimal network structures, streamlining the development of efficient and effective neural network models.

Neural Architecture Search (NAS)

Neural Architecture Search (NAS) is a process used to automatically design and optimize the architecture of neural networks. Instead of manually deciding on the architecture components such as the number of layers, number of neurons per layer, or activation functions, NAS aims to automate this process, which can be extremely challenging due to the vast search space of possible architectures. NAS is particularly valuable because it allows us to discover high-performing neural network structures without relying on expert domain knowledge or tedious trial-and-error.

Types of NAS

There are three primary approaches to NAS:

- **Reinforcement Learning-Based NAS:**
    - In this approach, **Reinforcement Learning (RL)** is used to train a controller network that generates neural network architectures.
    - The controller learns which architectural components work best based on a reward signal, which is typically based on the performance of the generated architecture (for example, accuracy on a validation set).
    - This method involves training thousands of candidate architectures, making it computationally expensive.
    - **Examples**: Google's **AutoML** uses this type of NAS.
- **Evolutionary Algorithm-Based NAS:**
    - Inspired by **genetic algorithms** and natural selection, this type of NAS treats each architecture as an individual in a population.
    - The **population of architectures** evolves over multiple generations through operations such as **mutation** (changing parts of an architecture) and **crossover** (combining features of two architectures).
    - The goal is to gradually improve architectures based on their fitness, often measured by validation accuracy or loss.
    - This method is less sensitive to initial conditions and can handle larger search spaces effectively.
    - **Examples**: **NeuroEvolution of Augmenting Topologies (NEAT)** is a well-known evolutionary approach for NAS.
- **Gradient-Based NAS:**
    - This approach uses **differentiable optimization** to find the best architecture.
    - Instead of treating architecture search as a discrete problem, it converts it into a **continuous search space** that can be optimized with gradient descent.
    - This is faster and computationally efficient compared to RL- or evolutionary-based methods, making it suitable for large-scale problems.
    - **Examples**: **DARTS (Differentiable Architecture Search)**, which allows the architecture parameters to be learned along with the model weights.

Components of NAS

- **Search Space**: This defines the range of possible architectures, including choices such as the number of layers, types of layers (for example, convolutional, recurrent), activation functions, and connectivity patterns. A well-defined search space is essential to ensure that NAS finds useful architectures without being overwhelmed by too many possibilities.
- **Search Strategy**: This is the method used to explore the search space. Reinforcement learning, evolutionary algorithms, and gradient-based methods are the primary strategies.
- **Evaluation Strategy**: Evaluating each candidate architecture requires training it (or a proxy version) and assessing its performance. This step is often computationally expensive, and various techniques such as **weight sharing** and **early stopping** are used to reduce the time required.

So, now that you understand **NAS**, as it provides a powerful tool for automating the design of neural network architectures, eliminating manual trial-and-error and potentially uncovering novel, high-performing network structures, let us look into a code and application of Evolutionary Algorithm-Based NAS to `california_housing_test` dataset.

Representation of Genetic Algorithm for NAS

In **NAS**, GA can be described using the concepts of **chromosomes, genes,** and **populations** as follows:

- **Chromosome**: In NAS, a **chromosome** represents a potential neural network architecture. Each chromosome is a unique combination of architectural parameters such as the number of hidden layers, number of neurons per layer, activation functions, and so on.
- **Genes**: The **genes** of a chromosome are the specific parameters that define the neural network architecture. For example, in the code, each gene corresponds to the number of neurons in one of the hidden layers. The two genes determine the architecture by specifying the number of neurons in the first and second hidden layers.
- **Population**: A **population** is a collection of multiple chromosomes, representing different neural network architectures being evaluated in a particular generation. Each chromosome in the population has a unique architecture, and the GA evaluates the fitness of each chromosome by training the corresponding neural network and measuring its performance.

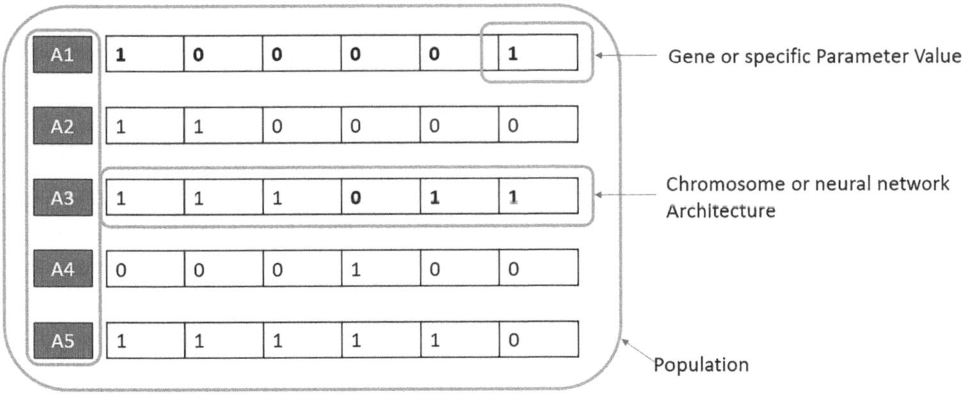

Figure 10.1: *The image illustrates the Representation of the Genetic Algorithm for* NAS

The Application

Our goal is to leverage **GA** to optimize the network architecture by treating its parameters as hyperparameters. Similar to how we used GA for hyperparameter tuning in the previous chapter–optimizing parameters such as **`max_depth`**, **`learning_rate`**, and **`n_estimators`**–we now aim to optimize the architecture itself. This involves determining the best configuration for hidden layers, such as the number of layers and nodes per layer.

Each possible network configuration represents a potential solution within the GA. The algorithm iteratively explores these configurations, searching for the combination that yields the best model performance. By automating the exploration of network architectures, we can efficiently discover the structure that optimizes model accuracy or minimizes error, streamlining what would otherwise be a tedious and time-consuming manual process.

In terms of **NAS**, the code, which can be found in **`Chapter10.ipynb`**, uses **GA** to explore different architectures for a Multilayer Perceptron (MLP) model. Here is what we did:

1. **Define Search Space**: The **search space** consists of two key hyperparameters: the number of neurons in the first and second hidden layers. Each potential architecture is defined by the values of these two hyperparameters.
2. **Apply Genetic Algorithm**: The GA is configured to optimize the architecture by iteratively evolving the **number of neurons** in these layers. The fitness of each architecture is evaluated based on the **Root Mean Squared Error (RMSE)** on the validation set, aiming to minimize the prediction error.

   Final Model RMSE: 201215.875, Final Model R^2 Score: -2.214972257241527

3. **Fitness Function**: The GA uses a fitness function to train and evaluate each MLP architecture. The architectures with lower RMSE are given higher fitness scores, guiding the search towards optimal configurations.
4. **Architecture Optimization**: The GA iterates through multiple **generations**, using genetic operations such as **selection, crossover, and mutation** to evolve the architectures towards the best configuration.

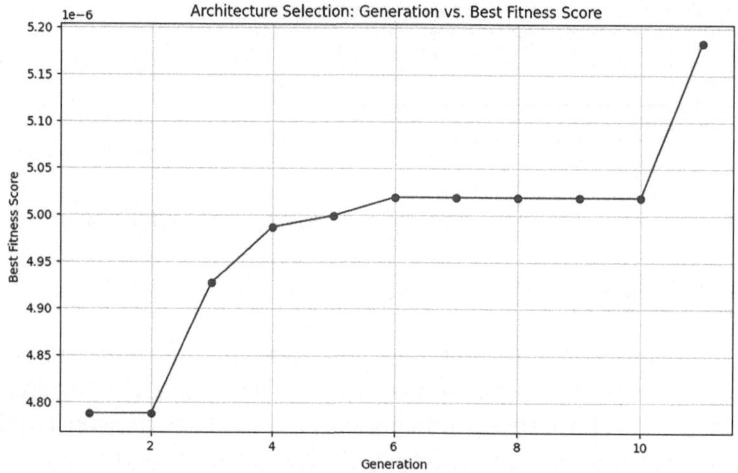

Figure 10.2: *The image illustrates a visualization of Generation versus best fitness score of the final Multilayer Perceptron (MLP) model*

5. **Final Selection and Visualization**: The architecture with the highest fitness score (that is, lowest RMSE) is selected as the final model. This best architecture is then trained for 10 epochs, and its **training and validation loss** are plotted.

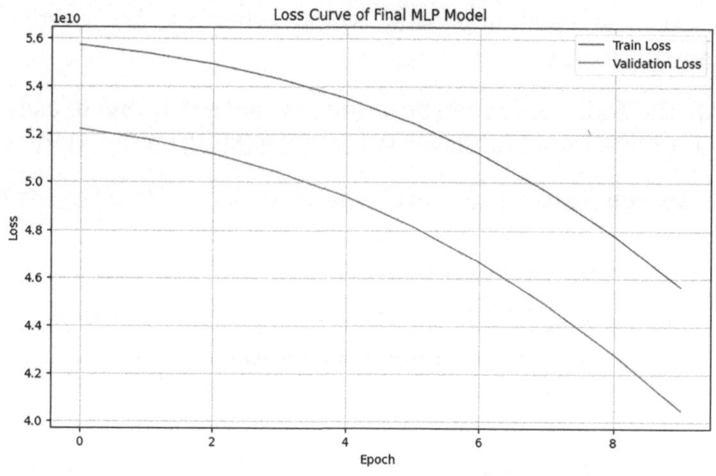

Figure 10.3: *The image illustrates a visualization of the loss curve of the final Multilayer Perceptron (MLP) model*

6. Additionally, the final architecture is visualized using **torchviz** to provide a graphical representation of the optimized MLP model.

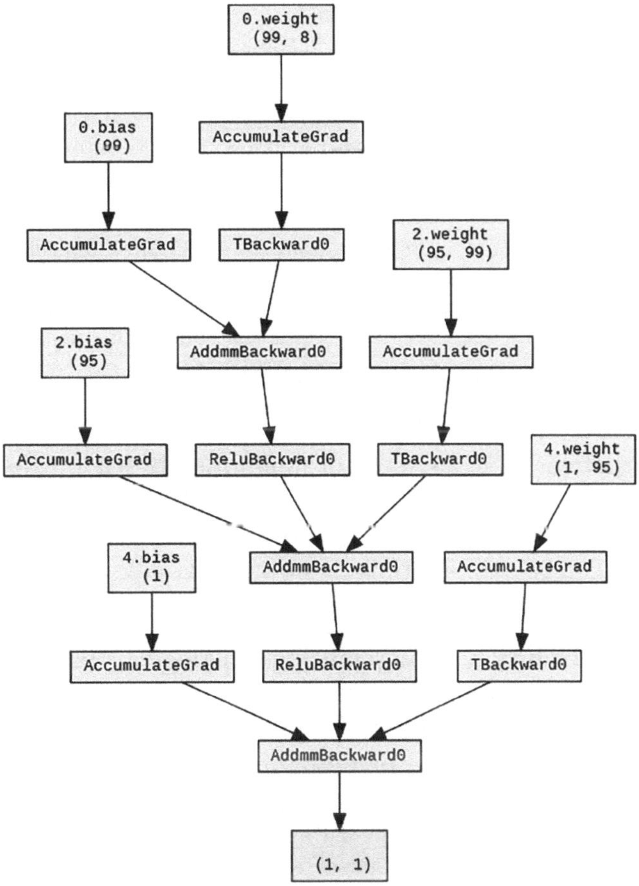

Figure 10.4: *The image illustrates a visualization of the computational graph of the final Multilayer Perceptron (MLP) model*

The diagram visualizes the structure of the MLP model, with the connections, activations, and operations clearly depicted. It effectively demonstrates how the Genetic Algorithm (GA)-optimized architecture is trained, with all necessary backpropagation steps.

In the code, the **population** is defined with **sol_per_pop=10**, meaning there are 10 different architectures (chromosomes) in each generation. The GA evolves these architectures over **num_generations=10** using genetic operators such as **crossover** and **mutation** to create new potential architectures (offspring), with the goal of improving the network's performance.

The process continues through generations, selecting, crossing, and mutating chromosomes to identify the optimal neural network architecture with the lowest RMSE and highest R^2 score. This iterative search is the essence of NAS using GA.

NAS	Pros	Cons
Reinforcement Learning-Based NAS	Finds unique and powerful architectures; can be effective in large-scale search spaces.	Extremely computationally expensive; requires training many candidate models.
Evolutionary Algorithm-Based NAS	Flexible; can explore a wide variety of architectures; less reliant on initial conditions.	Computationally intensive; can be slower compared to gradient-based methods.
Gradient-Based NAS	Fast; computationally efficient; ideal for large-scale problems.	Limited to architectures that can be expressed in a differentiable manner; may be stuck in local optima.

Table 10.1: *Pros and Cons of NAS*

While **Neural Architecture Search (NAS)** provides a framework for automating the design of neural networks, it has certain limitations based on the approach used. Reinforcement Learning-Based NAS is often extremely computationally expensive, requiring thousands of candidate models to be trained. Evolutionary Algorithm-Based NAS, while flexible, can be computationally slow, and Gradient-Based NAS is limited to differentiable architectures and may get stuck in local optima.

This is where **NeuroEvolution of Augmenting Topologies (NEAT)** comes in, offering a distinct approach that addresses some of the challenges faced by NAS. Unlike traditional NAS, which focuses primarily on optimizing fixed architectures, NEAT evolves both the weights and the **topology** of the neural network–starting from a simple architecture and progressively adding complexity as needed. This dynamic growth helps NEAT avoid over-complicating the model early on, which is a drawback of many traditional NAS approaches that often start with complex networks.

NEAT's use of **topology augmentation**–incrementally adding neurons and connections–has several advantages. It helps maintain a balance between model complexity and computational efficiency, solving one of the main challenges of NAS approaches, especially the computational overhead in exploring large search spaces. Moreover, NEAT's flexibility in evolving both structure and parameters makes it better suited for discovering efficient architectures without being restricted to differentiable operations, unlike Gradient-Based NAS.

In the following section, we will dive deeper into NEAT, exploring how it incrementally evolves neural networks and why its ability to evolve both **network structure and weights** makes it a powerful approach for creating optimized neural architectures.

Neuro Evolution of Augmenting Topologies (NEAT)

Neuro Evolution of Augmenting Topologies (NEAT) is an evolutionary algorithm specifically designed to evolve neural network architectures, including both their **weights** and **topologics**. Unlike traditional approaches, where the architecture is fixed and only the weights are optimized, NEAT evolves the entire structure of the network. Here's how it works:

1. **Chromosome Representation**:
    a. In NEAT, each **chromosome** represents a neural network's architecture, including information about nodes (neurons) and connections (weights).
    b. Chromosomes are often more complex compared to traditional GA, as they need to encode both connectivity and weight information.
2. **Genes**:
    a. **Node Genes** represent neurons (input, hidden, and output).
    b. **Connection Genes** represent links between neurons, including information such as whether the connection is active and the weight of the connection.
3. **Population**:
    a. The **population** consists of multiple neural network architectures.
    b. Initially, simple networks are evolved, but over generations, new nodes and connections are added through **mutation** operations.
4. **Application**: NEAT is well-suited for evolving **neural network topologies** without human intervention, making it a powerful approach for **automated design** of complex architectures, such as for reinforcement learning tasks or other deep learning problems.
5. **Neat Config file**: The NEAT configuration file is crucial as it defines the parameters controlling the evolution process for NeuroEvolution of Augmenting Topologies (NEAT). It includes settings such as population size, mutation rates, crossover rates, weight initialization ranges, and activation functions. This configuration guides how the neural network topologies evolve over generations, balancing exploration and exploitation in the search for optimal architectures. Properly tuning the parameters in the configuration file is key to ensuring efficient evolution, avoiding stagnation, and promoting the discovery of well-performing networks without unnecessary computational costs. It acts as the backbone of the evolutionary process in NEAT.

6. **Key Features:**

    a. **NEAT Nodes:** In NEAT, the nodes do not need to be fully connected. NEAT begins with a simple, minimal neural network architecture, typically consisting of just the input and output nodes without any hidden layers or extra connections.

    Throughout the evolutionary process, NEAT modifies the architecture by:

    i. **Adding new nodes**: Nodes can be added during mutation, effectively increasing the network's complexity.

    ii. **Adding new connections**: New connections between nodes can be introduced, but there is no requirement that all nodes must be connected. As a result, some nodes may not be connected, and the network can grow in a non-fully connected manner.

    This selective connection method gives NEAT its strength because it evolves the structure dynamically–adding complexity as needed while retaining simpler solutions if they are sufficient. This allows the network to optimize both the topology and weights to solve the given problem, unlike standard neural networks, which typically have fixed and fully connected architectures.

    b. **Complexification**: NEAT starts with simple architectures and progressively adds nodes and connections, allowing the complexity of the network to grow gradually.

    c. **Speciation**: NEAT groups similar networks into **species** to maintain diversity in the population, which prevents premature convergence.

    d. **Crossover and Mutation**: Networks are evolved through **crossover** (combining architectures) and **mutation** (adding nodes, adding connections, or changing weights).

    e. **NEAT Training**: NEAT does **not** use traditional **backpropagation** for training the neural network. Instead, it uses an **evolutionary algorithm** to evolve both the **weights** and the **architecture** of the network.

    In NEAT, the neural network starts with a minimal architecture and evolves over generations. The evolution process involves:

    i. **Mutation**: Adding new nodes or connections, or modifying the weights of existing connections.

    ii. **Crossover**: Combining parts of two parent networks to create a new offspring.

iii. **Fitness Evaluation**: Assigning a fitness score based on the network's performance on a given task, such as minimizing the prediction error.

This evolutionary approach allows NEAT to optimize both the structure and parameters of the network, avoiding the need for gradient descent and backpropagation as used in conventional neural networks. Instead, it relies on selecting the fittest networks from each generation to produce the next generation.

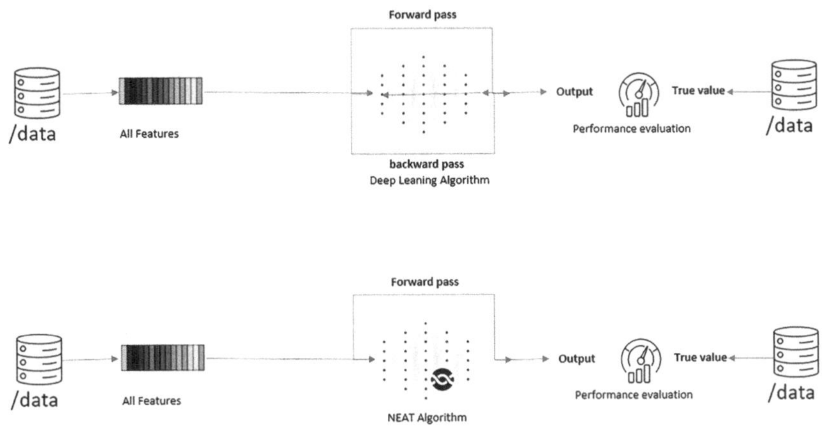

Figure 10.5: *The image illustrates a comparison between traditional deep learning, on top, and the NEAT model at the bottom, with no backward pass*

The Application

Now that we have explored the major components of **NEAT**, including its ability to evolve both network topology and weights, it is time to see how these concepts come to life in practice. To demonstrate NEAT's capabilities, we will apply it to the **California Housing Test dataset**, a well-known dataset used for predicting house values based on features such as location, population, and median income. By using NEAT, we aim to automatically evolve an optimal neural network architecture that can accurately predict housing prices, showcasing how the evolutionary approach effectively addresses real-world regression problems.

NEAT Configuration File

As mentioned above lets recap a **NEAT configuration file** defines the parameters and settings that guide the **NeuroEvolution of Augmenting Topologies (NEAT)** algorithm during the evolution process. It specifies values such as the number of input and output nodes, activation functions, mutation rates, and other genetic evolution settings.

For instance, it controls parameters such as:

- **Node properties** (for example, number of input/output nodes, activation function type).
- **Reproduction settings** (for example, mutation rates, connection probabilities).
- **Population management** (for example, population size, speciation, stagnation).

In the provided model, the configuration file (**`neat-config.txt`**) is read using neat. Config. This configuration instructs NEAT on how to evolve the **neural networks** by defining the properties of the population, how genomes mutate and reproduce, and other settings for managing the evolutionary process. For example, it dictates how nodes and connections are added or removed, how fitness is assessed, and how the network evolves across generations.

The configuration file allows NEAT to adaptively evolve the network structure and weights, potentially leading to a more efficient model compared to fixed-topology approaches.

Let us go through the configuration parameters of this model, which can be found in the Git Hub link of *Chapter* 10.

[NEAT]

- **`fitness_criterion = max`**: Specifies the goal for fitness evaluation. max indicates that NEAT will try to maximize the fitness function value (in our case, minimizing RMSE is handled by returning negative values).
- **`fitness_threshold = 1000`**: Defines the stopping condition for evolution. When any genome achieves a fitness score above 1000, the evolution stops.
- **`pop_size = 150`**: Sets the **population size**, meaning there will be 150 individuals (neural networks) per generation.
- **`reset_on_extinction = False`**: If set to True, the population will reset if all species go extinct; otherwise, the evolution will stop.

[DefaultGenome]

- **`num_inputs = 8`**: Number of input nodes, equal to the number of features in the dataset.
- **`num_outputs = 1`**: Number of output nodes, since we are predicting a single target value.
- **`num_hidden = 0`**: Specifies the number of hidden nodes initially. 0 means the network starts with no hidden layers, and NEAT will evolve the network structure.
- **`feed_forward = True`**: Specifies that the network is **feed-forward**, meaning no recurrent connections are allowed.

Node Activation Options

- **activation_default = tanh**: Default activation function used by nodes.
- **activation_mutate_rate = 0.1**: Probability that the activation function of a node will mutate.
- **activation_options = tanh sigmoid relu**: Possible activation functions that a node can evolve to use.

Node Aggregation Options

- **aggregation_default = sum**: Default aggregation function for combining inputs.
- **aggregation_mutate_rate = 0.0**: Probability of mutating the aggregation function.
- **aggregation_options = sum product max min**: Possible aggregation functions for nodes.

Node Bias Options

- **bias_init_mean = 0.0** and **bias_init_stdev = 1.0**: Specifies the initial mean and standard deviation for biases.
- **bias_max_value = 30.0**, **bias_min_value = -30.0**: Constraints for node bias values.
- **bias_mutate_rate = 0.7** and **bias_replace_rate = 0.1**: Probabilities for mutating or replacing the bias value.
- **bias_mutate_power = 0.5**: Scale of mutation when bias is mutated.

Genome Compatibility Options

- **compatibility_disjoint_coefficient = 1.0** and **compatibility_weight_coefficient = 0.5**: Weights used to calculate the compatibility distance between genomes for speciation, determining how genomes differ based on their disjoint genes and weight differences.

Connection Weight Options

- **weight_init_mean = 0.0** and **weight_init_stdev = 1.0**: Specifies the initial mean and standard deviation for connection weights.
- **weight_max_value = 30** and **weight_min_value = -30**: Specifies the allowable range for weights.
- **weight_mutate_rate = 0.8**, **weight_replace_rate = 0.1**, and **weight_mutate_power = 0.5**: Probabilities and scale of mutation for connection weights.

Node Response Options

- `response_init_mean = 1.0` and `response_init_stdev = 0.1`: Initial mean and standard deviation for response values.
- `response_mutate_rate = 0.1` and `response_replace_rate = 0.1`: Probabilities of mutating or replacing response values.
- `response_mutate_power = 0.5`, `response_max_value = 30.0`, and `response_min_value = -30.0`: Parameters controlling mutation and range of node responses.

Connection Creation Options

- `enabled_default = True`: Indicates that new connections are enabled by default.
- `enabled_mutate_rate = 0.01`: Probability that a connection will be enabled or disabled during mutation.
- `conn_add_prob = 0.5` and `conn_delete_prob = 0.3`: Probabilities of adding or deleting a connection.

Node Creation Options

- `node_add_prob = 0.2` and `node_delete_prob = 0.2`: Probabilities of adding or deleting a node.

[DefaultSpeciesSet]

- `compatibility_threshold = 3.0`: Specifies the threshold to determine if genomes belong to the same species. This encourages genetic diversity by creating different species within the population.

[DefaultStagnation]

- `species_fitness_func = max`: Specifies the function for determining a species' fitness.
- `max_stagnation = 15`: Maximum number of generations a species can stagnate before being removed.
- `species_elitism = 2`: Number of species to protect from extinction, even if they stagnate.

[DefaultReproduction]

- `elitism = 2`: Number of top individuals to carry over to the next generation without changes.
- `survival_threshold = 0.2`: Fraction of individuals in each species allowed to reproduce. The rest are eliminated.

These configurations together guide how the NEAT algorithm evolves the population of neural networks across generations, including network growth, node and connection mutations, and speciation to ensure diversity.

Let us understand the following code, breaking it down into key components. The code uses **NEAT** to evolve a neural network for predicting the median house value from the California Housing dataset. A configuration file (neat-config.txt) guides the evolution process. The **fitness function** is designed to minimize the prediction error, and the final evolved network is evaluated on a test set. The **population** and **reporters** provide insight into the progress of evolution, while plotting the best fitness score helps visualize improvements over time.

Code Breakdown

1. **Imports**

```
import pandas as pd
import numpy as np
import torch
import torch.nn as nn
import torch.optim as optim
from sklearn.model_selection import train_test_split
from sklearn.metrics import mean_squared_error, r2_score
import neat
import matplotlib.pyplot as plt
from torchviz import make_dot
```

This block imports all necessary libraries:

- pandas and numpy for data handling and numerical operations.
- torch for defining neural networks.
- scikit-learn functions such as **`train_test_split`** for splitting the dataset and metrics such as `mean_squared_error` and `r2_score` to evaluate the model.
- neat for NeuroEvolution of Augmenting Topologies.
- **`matplotlib.pyplot`** to visualize the training performance.
- **`torchviz`** for visualizing neural network computation graphs.

2. **Load Dataset**

```
data = pd.read_csv('/content/sample_data/california_housing_test.
csv')
```

The dataset (**`california_housing_test.csv`**) is loaded using pandas. This dataset contains features related to California housing to predict median house values.

3. **Separate Features and Target**

```
X = data.drop(columns=['median_house_value']).values
y = data['median_house_value'].values
```

- `X`: All features are separated from the dataset.
- `y`: The target variable (**`median_house_value`**) is separated from `X`.

4. **Split the Dataset**

```
X_train, X_test, y_train, y_test = train_test_split(X, y, test_
size=0.2, random_state=42)
```

- The data is split into **`training`** (80%) and **`testing`** (20%) sets using **`train_test_split`**.

```
config_path = "/content/sample_data/neat-config.txt"  # Assuming
you have a NEAT config file named neat-config.txt
config = neat.Config(neat.DefaultGenome, neat.Default
Reproduction,
                     neat.DefaultSpeciesSet, neat.Default
Stagnation,
                     config_path)
```

- The **NEAT configuration file** (neat-config.txt) contains all the settings needed to control how NEAT evolves the neural networks. This configuration determines how genomes (networks) are reproduced, how stagnation is handled, and how populations evolve. It is crucial for guiding the evolutionary process.

5. **Define the Fitness Function for NEAT**

```
def eval_genomes(genomes, config):
    for genome_id, genome in genomes:
        net = neat.nn.FeedForwardNetwork.create(genome, config)

        # Convert the training data to tensors
        X_train_tensor = torch.tensor(X_train, dtype=torch.
float32)
        y_train_tensor = torch.tensor(y_train, dtype=torch.
float32).view(-1, 1)

        # Predict on the training data
        predictions = []
        for x in X_train:
            output = net.activate(x)
            predictions.append(output[0])
```

```
        # Calculate RMSE as fitness
        rmse = np.sqrt(mean_squared_error(y_train, predictions))
        genome.fitness = -rmse  # NEAT minimizes the error, so we
return negative RMSE
```

- This function is responsible for evaluating each genome (candidate solution).
- **Genome to Neural Network Conversion**: Converts the genome into a PyTorch **`FeedForwardNetwork`**.
- The training data (**`X_train`**) is passed through each network to get predictions.
- The **fitness** of each genome is set as the negative of **RMSE** (because NEAT aims to maximize fitness, and a lower RMSE represents better performance).

6. **Create the Population**

```
p = neat.Population(config)
```

- A **population** is created using the NEAT configuration. This population consists of many genomes, each representing a candidate neural network.

7. **Add Reporters to Track Progress**

```
p.add_reporter(neat.StdOutReporter(True))
stats = neat.StatisticsReporter()
p.add_reporter(stats)
```

Reporters are used to keep track of the evolution process:

- **`StdOutReporter`**: Outputs progress information, showing how evolution is proceeding.
- **`StatisticsReporter`**: Keeps track of key metrics over generations for analysis later.

8. **Run NEAT to Evolve the Neural Network**

```
winner = p.run(eval_genomes, 50)
```

The evolution runs for **50 generations** to find the best genome. The **`eval_genomes`** function is called in each generation to evaluate the population.

9. **Convert the Winning Genome to a PyTorch Model**

```
best_net = neat.nn.FeedForwardNetwork.create(winner, config)
```

The best-performing genome (winner) is converted to a neural network model.

10. **Evaluate the Best Network on the Test Set**

```
y_pred = []
for x in X_test:
    output = best_net.activate(x)
    y_pred.append(output[0])
```

```
rmse = np.sqrt(mean_squared_error(y_test, y_pred))
r2 = r2_score(y_test, y_pred)

print(f"Final Model RMSE: {rmse}")
print(f"Final Model R^2 Score: {r2}")
```

- The evolved network (**best_net**) is evaluated on the **test set.**
- The model's performance is measured using **RMSE** and **R^2 score**.

11. **Plotting the Loss Curve for NEAT**

```
best_fitness_scores = [-c.fitness for c in stats.most_fit_genomes]
plt.figure(figsize=(10, 6))
plt.plot(best_fitness_scores, marker='o', linestyle='-', color='b')
plt.xlabel('Generation')
plt.ylabel('Best Fitness (Negative RMSE)')
plt.title('NEAT: Generation vs. Best Fitness Score')
plt.grid()
plt.show()
```

The **best fitness score** across generations is plotted to visualize, in the following image, how the best solution improved over time. Since NEAT optimizes by minimizing the RMSE, the negative RMSE is plotted.

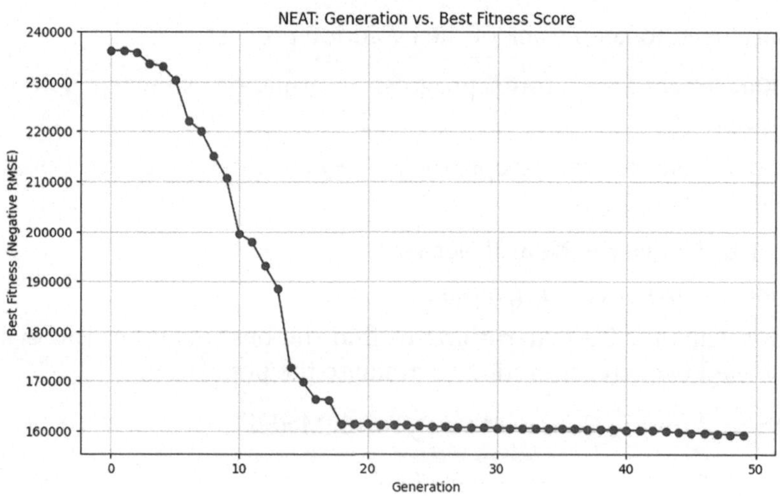

Figure 10.6: *The image illustrates a visualization of Generation versus best fitness score of the NEAT model*

The followimg output logs represent the process of using a NeuroEvolution of Augmenting Topologies (NEAT) algorithm to evolve a neural network for improving its performance over multiple generations. The **population** consists of neural networks (genomes), which undergo evolution through genetic operations such as selection, mutation, and crossover.

For each **generation**, key metrics are displayed:

- **Population's average fitness**: Represents the average fitness (in this case, negative RMSE) across all networks in the generation. A more negative value indicates worse performance.
- **Best fitness**: Indicates the best fitness achieved by any network within that generation, showing how evolution improves the best solution over time.
- **Species Information**: NEAT maintains diversity by organizing genomes into species. The **species ID**, **size**, **fitness**, and **stagnation** are tracked to promote evolution within diverse solutions.

In each generation, the fitness values improve, and the **Best fitness** metric becomes less negative, indicating that the NEAT algorithm is successfully optimizing the network structure.

```
 ****** Running generation 49 ******

Population's average fitness: -180973.55735 stdev: 26647.20502
Best fitness: -159316.68799 - size: (1, 5) - species 6 - id 6778
Average adjusted fitness: 0.694
Mean genetic distance 3.236, standard deviation 1.293
Population of 151 members in 13 species:
   ID   age  size  fitness  adj fit  stag
  ====  ===  ====  =======  =======  ====
     1   49     6  -159347.9    0.819     1
     2   43    13  -159476.7    0.758     0
     3   38    23  -159457.1    0.838     0
     4   34    16  -160506.9    0.881     0
     5   34     9  -162042.2    0.622     5
     6   34    10  -159316.7    0.826     0
     7   32    12  -160636.9    0.516     0
     8   27    12  -159577.0    0.746     0
     9   26    14  -159539.2    0.739     1
    10   23     9  -182450.8    0.666     0
    11   18     7  -160597.4    0.813     0
    12   11    12  -161895.7    0.447     0
    13   10     8  -206886.8    0.352     0
Total extinctions: 0
Generation time: 2.145 sec (1.926 average)
Final Model RMSE: 157182.06651322017
Final Model R^2 Score: -0.9618179668658446
```

Figure 10.7: *The image illustrates a visualization of performance over multiple generations of the NEAT model*

The NEAT architecture shown in the following visualization illustrates the final evolved neural network structure.

- **Inputs 0 to 7** represent the eight features from the dataset that feed into the network.
- The **hidden nodes** (**node_-6**, **node_-4**, **node_-8**, and so on) are the nodes evolved through NEAT. These nodes do not have a predefined structure; they were added during the evolutionary process.

- The arrows represent the **connections** between nodes, with labels indicating their **weights**. For example, there is a connection from **`node_-4`** to **`node_0`** with a weight of **7.28**.
- **`node_0`** is the output node, which aggregates inputs from the hidden nodes and computes the final prediction.

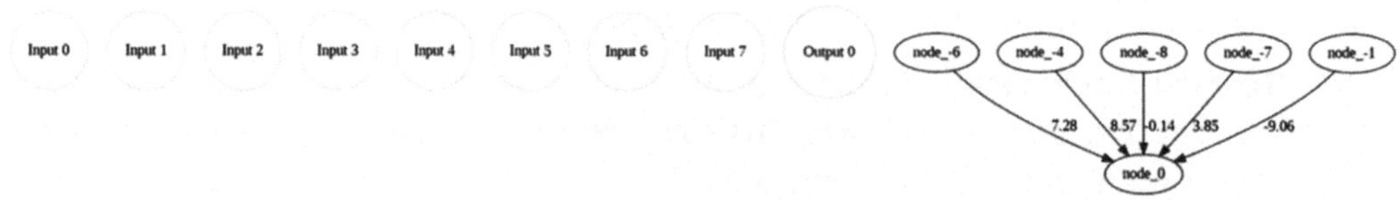

***Figure 10.8:** The diagram highlights how NEAT dynamically evolves the network topology, adding hidden nodes and connections based on fitness improvement during training*

Genetic Algorithm to Optimize the Model's Weights

After exploring **NEAT**, which evolves both the **topology and weights** of a neural network, we can see how powerful evolutionary strategies can be in finding optimal architectures. NEAT's capability to simultaneously evolve the structure and connection strengths makes it a comprehensive solution for neural architecture search. However, in many cases, we may already have a fixed architecture and instead want to focus on optimizing the **weights** of that model to achieve better performance. This is where **Genetic Algorithms (GA)** come in handy for weight optimization.

While NEAT evolves the architecture dynamically, we can also use **GAs** to fine-tune the weights of an existing network, treating each set of weights as a potential solution and evolving them to minimize prediction error. In the next section, we will transition to using **Genetic Algorithms** to optimize the weights of a fixed neural network architecture, demonstrating an alternative evolutionary approach to achieving high model performance. The dataset used here is the same one previously introduced in *Chapter* 5, *Foundation of Evolutionary Algorithms*, the **`DataCoSupplyChainDatasetCleaned`**. The code is available in **`Chapter_10_part_2.ipynb`**.

This Python code, **`Chapter_10_part_2.ipynb`**, demonstrates training a machine learning model using both traditional methods and genetic algorithm-based optimization. The script starts by importing necessary libraries for data processing, machine learning, and genetic optimization. It loads a dataset named "**`DataCoSupplyChainDatasetCleaned.csv`**" into a Pandas DataFrame, selects relevant features, handles missing values, and uses one-hot encoding for categorical features. The dataset is standardized, split into training and testing sets, and then converted into PyTorch tensors. Batch processing is facilitated using PyTorch's DataLoader, optimizing memory usage.

The code defines a simple feedforward neural network model with one hidden layer, ReLU activation, and dropout for regularization. A **Genetic Algorithm (GA)**, implemented with **PyGAD**, is used to optimize the model's weights. The genetic algorithm runs for 50 generations, and the best solution found is used to update the model's weights. After GA-based optimization, the model is evaluated on the test set using RMSE, R^2 score, and accuracy metrics.

Finally, the model is further fine-tuned using **traditional training** with the Adam optimizer for 50 epochs. During this phase, gradients are clipped to prevent explosion, and metrics are calculated after each epoch. The code concludes by using **matplotlib** to visualize the training metrics, such as loss, RMSE, R^2 score, and accuracy over the training epochs, giving insight into the model's learning progress.

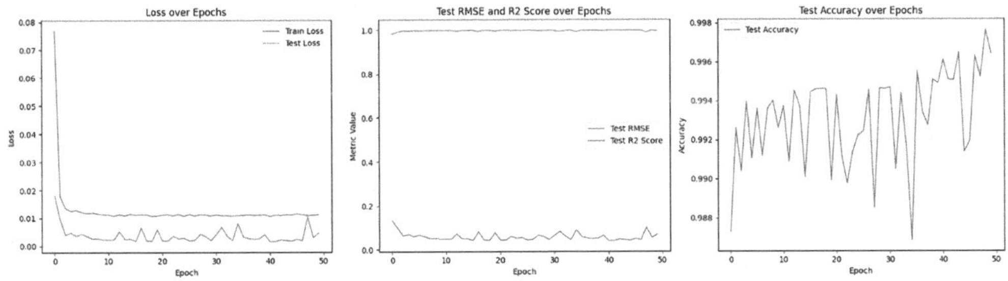

Figure 10.9: *Training Progress of the Neural Network: The plots illustrate the training and validation loss convergence, RMSE and R^2 stability, and fluctuating but improving accuracy over 50 epochs*

The output plots show the model's performance metrics over 50 training epochs:

1. **Loss over Epochs**: The first plot, from left, shows the **training** and **testing loss** decreasing initially, with the loss stabilizing after a few epochs. The model has learned effectively, as the training loss and test loss both remain low.

2. **Test RMSE and R^2 Score over Epochs**: The second plot shows that **RMSE** decreases initially and then stabilizes, indicating better prediction accuracy, while the **R^2 score** remains nearly constant at a high value, suggesting a good fit.

3. **Test Accuracy over Epochs**: The third plot shows the **test accuracy** fluctuating, but generally improving, with values consistently close to 1, indicating good predictive performance.

Optimizing a neural network architecture involves more than just adjusting its weights. In fact, there are many key aspects of a network that can significantly impact its performance and efficiency. By using GA, we can go beyond traditional weight optimization to enhance other architectural components of a neural network, making it more adaptable and capable of solving complex problems. These components include aspects such as the **number of layers and neurons**, **activation functions**,

weight initialization, **regularization techniques**, and more. Leveraging GA for such optimizations allows us to efficiently navigate the large design space, automating the discovery of the most effective network configuration while addressing both underfitting and overfitting. In the following section, we will explore the various architectural features that can be optimized using GA to achieve a well-balanced and high-performing neural network. Let us understand this.

Other GA Optimizations of NN

Apart from **weights**, several other architectural components can be optimized using **Genetic Algorithms (GA)** to improve the performance and efficiency of a neural network. Here are key aspects you can optimize with GA from the architectural considerations mentioned:

- **Number of Layers (Depth)**: Use GA to determine the optimal **number of hidden layers**, which impacts the network's capacity to learn complex patterns. Finding the right depth can balance learning capability with computational cost and risk of overfitting.
- **Number of Neurons (Width)**: GA can be used to determine the **number of neurons per hidden layer** to find the ideal network width. This helps identify architectures that are neither under-parameterized (leading to poor performance) nor over-parameterized (leading to overfitting).
- **Activation Functions**: Optimize **activation function selection** (for example, ReLU, Tanh, Leaky ReLU) for each layer. Different activation functions may work better in certain layers, and GA can find the combination that yields the best performance.
- **Weight Initialization**: GA can be used to optimize **weight initialization strategies**, selecting the best method (for example, Xavier/Glorot or He Initialization) for a given network architecture to promote faster and more stable convergence.
- **Regularization Techniques**: Find the optimal **regularization strategy** for controlling model complexity, including:
    - **Dropout rate**: Use GA to determine the best rate for dropout layers.
    - **L1/L2 regularization strength**: GA can be used to fine-tune the penalty applied to model weights.
- **Optimizer Selection**: GA can help determine the best **optimization algorithm** (for example, SGD, Adam, RMSprop) for training. It can also search for the optimal parameters for the chosen optimizer, such as learning rate decay rates or momentum values.
- **Learning Rate and Scheduler**: Optimize the **learning rate** and its **scheduler**. GA can search for the optimal initial learning rate and the best schedule (for

example, exponential decay or step decay) to ensure the model converges efficiently.

- **Batch Size**: GA can optimize the **batch size** used during training. A balance between computational efficiency and convergence speed can be found by testing different batch sizes, helping improve generalization.
- **Loss Function**: GA can be used to optimize the choice of **loss function** (for example, Cross-Entropy versus Mean Squared Error) depending on the specific task, ensuring the network is trained with the appropriate measure of error.
- **Network Topology**: Use GA to determine **layer types and connections** in the network topology, such as whether to add **Convolutional** layers, **Recurrent** layers, or **Attention** mechanisms. GA can identify specialized layers that improve performance for specific input data types.
- **Skip Connections/Residual Blocks**: Optimize the use of **skip connections** and **residual blocks** to improve gradient flow, reduce training time, and enhance model stability. GA can identify whether skip connections should be added and at what layers.
- **Network Depth vs. Width Trade-off**: GA can optimize the trade-off between **depth (number of layers)** and **width (number of neurons per layer)**, finding the ideal balance to capture abstract relationships without overfitting or underfitting.
- **Hyperparameter Tuning**: [explained in *Chapter* 9, *Applying Genetic Algorithm to Machine Learning*, in detail]. GA can be used to perform **hyperparameter optimization**, such as:
    - **Learning rate**.
    - **Number of layers** and **neurons per layer**.
    - **Dropout rates**, **weight decay**, etc.

  GA is particularly effective in tuning hyperparameters simultaneously for complex models.
- **Feature Engineering and Input Preprocessing**: [explained in *Chapter* 9 in detail]
    - **Feature selection**: GA can be used to determine which input features contribute most to the model, leading to better generalization and reducing overfitting.
    - **Input Scaling/Normalization**: Optimize the preprocessing steps, such as whether to use **standard scaling** or **min-max scaling**.

Conclusion

In this chapter, we explored various methods for automating the optimization of neural networks using **evolutionary approaches**. We began with **Neural Architecture Search (NAS)**, utilizing **Genetic Algorithms (GA)** to efficiently discover optimal network architectures. We discussed the **pros and cons** of different NAS approaches and how GA helps navigate complex search spaces. We then moved to **NeuroEvolution of Augmenting Topologies (NEAT)**, which evolves both the topology and weights of neural networks. This approach provides flexibility in generating network architectures suited for a given task, addressing some limitations of traditional NAS methods.

Finally, we demonstrated using **Genetic Algorithms** for direct **weight optimization** in fixed neural networks, providing a practical way to enhance a model's performance after its structure has been determined. We also explored **other GA optimizations**, such as the number of layers, neurons, activation functions, and more, to achieve a comprehensive optimization of neural network architectures.

Next, we will apply these powerful GA techniques to the field of **computer vision**, demonstrating how evolutionary algorithms can optimize computer vision tasks, ultimately pushing the boundaries of machine learning in visual data processing.

CHAPTER 11
Applying Computer Vision Application to Genetic Algorithms

Introduction

Computer Vision, a core area of artificial intelligence, focuses on enabling machines to interpret and understand visual information from images and videos. Traditional approaches rely heavily on deep learning models; however, Genetic Algorithms (GAs) offer a powerful, biologically inspired alternative for solving optimization problems in computer vision tasks. GAs mimic natural evolution through selection, crossover, and mutation to evolve solutions over generations. Using libraries such as PyGAD, developers can implement GAs efficiently to optimize feature selection, edge detection, image segmentation, object recognition, and neural network weights in computer vision pipelines. Unlike gradient-based methods, GAs do not rely on differentiable loss functions, making them highly flexible and robust in complex or non-convex problem spaces. For instance, GAs can optimize threshold values in image binarization or fine-tune parameters in shape detection algorithms without needing gradient information. Their population-based search strategy also helps avoid local minima, which is often a challenge in vision-based tasks. PyGAD simplifies the application of GAs by providing customizable genetic operations and integration with Python-based vision libraries. As computer vision problems grow in complexity, GAs—powered by tools such as PyGAD—serve as an effective complement or alternative to traditional learning algorithms.

Structure

In this chapter, the following topics will be covered:

- Feature Extraction Optimization - Applying GAs to Visual Features
- Improving Image Classification with GAs - Solving Classification Tasks in Computer Vision

- Using Convolutional Neural Networks (CNNs) with GA- Using GAs for CNN Tuning
- Hyperparameter Optimization for Vision Tasks - Enhancing Model Accuracy Using Learning Rate and Activation Function Optimization

Feature Extraction Optimization Using GAs

In computer vision, feature extraction is a critical step to transform raw image data into informative patterns. Traditional deep learning uses learned filters, but GAs offer an alternative by evolving a set of feature extraction masks or filters that maximize classification accuracy. Before we dive into **Feature Extraction Optimization Using Gas,** let us understand **Feature Extraction and Its Importance in Computer Vision.**

Feature Extraction and Its Importance in Computer Vision

Feature extraction is a fundamental step in computer vision tasks where relevant information is derived from raw image data to facilitate further processing, analysis, or classification. The primary goal of feature extraction is to reduce the dimensionality of the data while retaining the most informative attributes that contribute to accurate pattern recognition and decision-making.

Feature extraction is important for several reasons:

- It simplifies the representation of complex image data.
- It improves the efficiency and effectiveness of learning algorithms.
- It reduces noise and redundant information in the dataset.
- It enhances the generalization performance of models.

Difference in Feature Extraction Between Traditional Machine Learning and Deep Learning Approaches

In traditional machine learning, feature extraction relies heavily on **handcrafted techniques** designed by domain experts. Algorithms such as Scale-Invariant Feature Transform (SIFT), Histogram of Oriented Gradients (HOG), Speeded-Up Robust Features (SURF), and Oriented FAST and Rotated BRIEF (ORB) are commonly used to extract features such as edges, corners, contours, and textures from images. These features are then used as input to classifiers such as Support Vector Machines (SVM), Random Forests, or k-Nearest Neighbors (k-NN).

In contrast, **deep learning**, particularly through Convolutional Neural Networks

(CNNs), enables **automatic feature learning** directly from raw image data. CNNs are capable of learning hierarchical representations of features, where early layers detect low-level patterns (for example, edges and blobs), intermediate layers capture more abstract features (for example, shapes and textures), and deeper layers identify complex structures (for example, object parts or entire objects). This automatic learning process reduces the need for manual intervention and often leads to higher accuracy and better scalability, especially in large-scale image datasets.

The key differences between the two approaches are summarized as follows:

Aspect	**Traditional Machine Learning**	**Deep Learning**
Feature Extraction	Manual (handcrafted using domain-specific algorithms)	Automatic (learned during training by neural networks)
Human Involvement	High – requires prior knowledge and expert design of features	Low – features are learned end-to-end by the model
Feature Examples	Edges, corners, color histograms, texture descriptors	Multi-layered abstractions: low-level edges, mid-level patterns, high-level semantic features
Generalization Capability	Limited; features often task-specific	High; features generalize well across tasks and datasets
Performance on Complex Tasks	Moderate, often constrained by feature quality	Superior performance in tasks such as object detection, classification, and segmentation

Table 1.1: *Differences between Traditional Machine Learning and Deep Learning*

The shift from manual to automated feature extraction has been a significant advancement in computer vision, enabling the development of highly accurate and scalable systems. Deep learning models not only automate feature discovery but also adaptively refine features through training, resulting in improved robustness and performance across a wide range of visual recognition tasks.

Feature Extraction Optimization Using Gas Implementation

In the following, using PyGAD, we will first load the MNIST digits dataset and convert each 28x28 image into a one-dimensional array of 784 values. Then, we will apply a genetic algorithm to evolve a set of weight masks that help identify the most important features in the images. To evaluate how effective these features are, we will use a simple logistic regression classifier and measure its accuracy as the fitness score. This process will demonstrate how the genetic algorithm can automatically select the most relevant visual features that contribute to better classification performance.

```
Ensure you have PyGAD 3.4.0
pip install pygad==3.4.0
Code: Feature Extraction Optimization Using GA on MNIST
import numpy as np
import pygad
import pygad.gann
from sklearn.linear_model import LogisticRegression
from sklearn.metrics import accuracy_score
from tensorflow.keras.datasets import mnist

# Load MNIST dataset
(x_train, y_train), (x_test, y_test) = mnist.load_data()

# Preprocess: flatten images and normalize
x_train = x_train.reshape(-1, 784) / 255.0
x_test = x_test.reshape(-1, 784) / 255.0

# Use smaller dataset for faster GA evolution
x_train_small = x_train[:3000]
y_train_small = y_train[:3000]
x_test_small = x_test[:1000]
y_test_small = y_test[:1000]

# Define fitness function: optimize a feature mask to select best
visual features
def fitness_func(ga_instance, solution, solution_idx):
    # Apply mask to select features (solution \in [0, 1])
    selected_features = x_train_small * solution  # Element-wise
multiplication
    clf = LogisticRegression(max_iter=200, solver='liblinear')
    clf.fit(selected_features, y_train_small)

    # Apply same mask to test set and evaluate accuracy
    x_test_masked = x_test_small * solution
    preds = clf.predict(x_test_masked)
    acc = accuracy_score(y_test_small, preds)

    return acc

# Define GA parameters
num_features = 784
ga_instance = pygad.GA(
    num_generations=20,
    sol_per_pop=10,
    num_parents_mating=5,
    num_genes=num_features,
```

```
    fitness_func=fitness_func,
    init_range_low=0.0,
    init_range_high=1.0,
    parent_selection_type="sss",
    crossover_type="single_point",
    mutation_type="random",
    mutation_percent_genes=10
)

# Run the GA
ga_instance.run()

# Get the best solution (optimized feature mask)
solution, solution_fitness, _ = ga_instance.best_solution()
print(f"Best Feature Mask Accuracy (Fitness): {solution_fit-
ness:.4f}")

# Visualize the selected features as an image
import matplotlib.pyplot as plt
plt.imshow(solution.reshape(28, 28), cmap='hot')
plt.title("Optimized Feature Mask by Genetic Algorithm")
plt.colorbar()
plt.show()
```

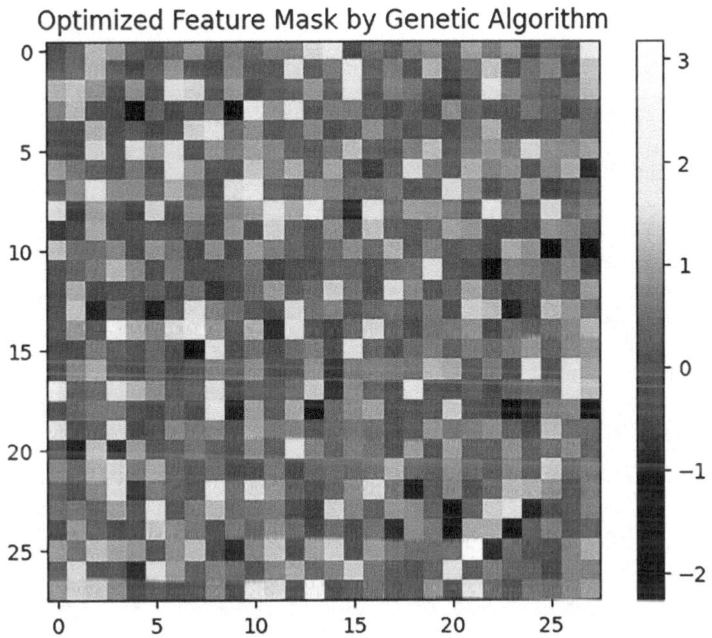

Figure 11.1: *This heatmap shows how important each pixel (feature) is in helping the model classify MNIST digits, as determined by the Genetic Algorithm*

Brighter areas (values closer to 1) indicate higher importance, while darker areas (values near 0) represent lower importance.

The GA evolved a continuous mask, allowing partial contribution from every pixel, leading to finer-grained weighting of visual features.

This approach gives the model soft feature importance, improving flexibility and slightly better accuracy (for example, ~0.8920 in your result).

Feature Masks

Binary feature masks offer greater interpretability and simplicity by selecting only the most relevant features (pixels), effectively reducing dimensionality and computational cost. They provide a sparse representation, making models more efficient and suitable for deployment on resource-constrained systems. In contrast, continuous feature masks offer finer control over feature importance, often yielding slightly higher accuracy by allowing partial contribution from all pixels. However, they are harder to interpret and may increase complexity. Binary masks are ideal when explainability and model compression are priorities, while continuous masks are better suited for tasks demanding higher precision and nuanced feature weighting.

The preceding code will be updated to use a binary feature selection mask (0 or 1) instead of continuous values. In the **`Chapter 11.ipynb`**, the mask is applied using **`np.round(solution)`** before evaluating accuracy or visualizing the feature importance.

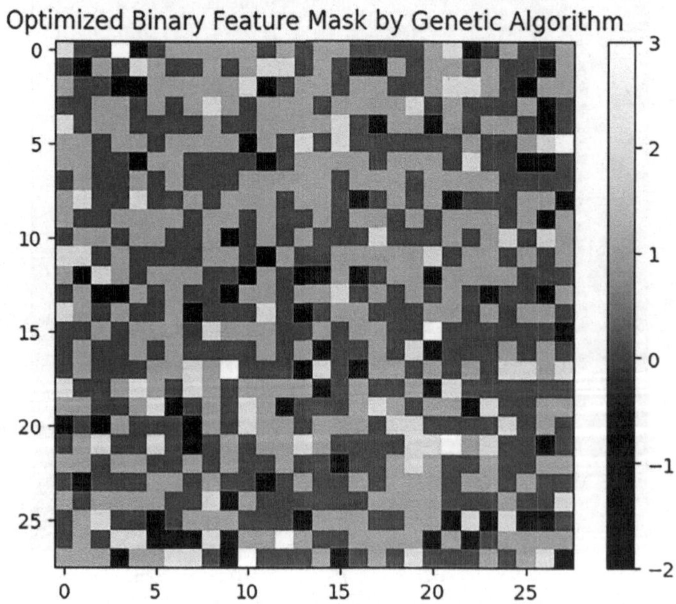

Figure 11.2: *This heatmap shows the selected (1) and discarded (0) pixels explicitly*

The mask acts like a hard gate, including only the most relevant features and ignoring the rest.

It provides a more interpretable and simplified feature selection, ideal for reducing model complexity and computational cost.

The accuracy is slightly lower (~0.8860), but you gain explainability and sparsity.

Improving Image Classification with GAs

MNIST dataset, although widely used and relatively clean, does contain **ambiguous or distorted digit samples**. These ambiguous instances often arise due to variations in handwriting styles, overlapping strokes, noise, or poorly centered digits. Such distortions can make it difficult even for human observers to clearly distinguish between certain digits–especially between similar-looking classes such as 3 and 5, 4 and 9, or 7 and 1.

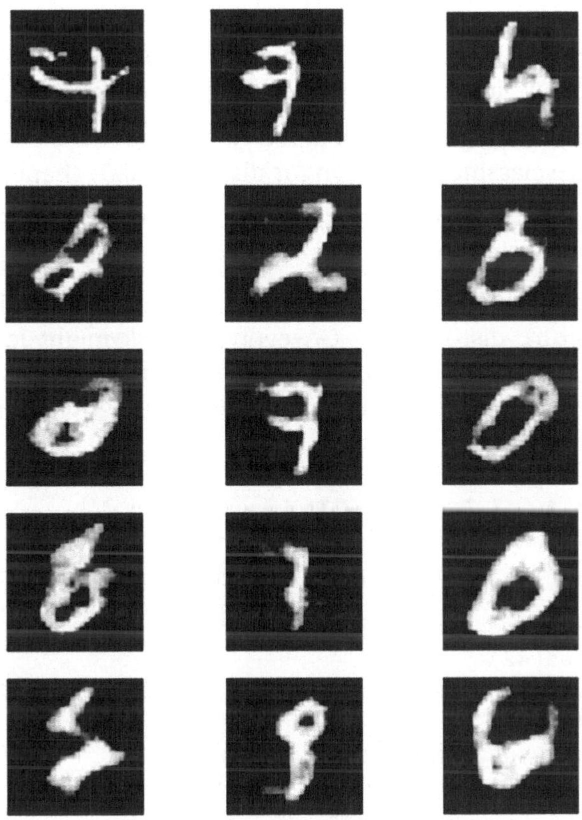

Figure 11.3: *Ambiguous or distorted digit samples*

In earlier approaches, feature selection in image classification often involved **binary masking**, where each input feature (or pixel) is either selected (1) or ignored (0). A more refined approach uses **continuous masking**, where each feature is assigned a weight between 0 and 1 to indicate its relative importance. While these methods can effectively reduce dimensionality and focus on relevant features, they may still struggle to differentiate subtle variations in **ambiguous or distorted digit samples**, as they treat feature importance in a static manner.

To address this, we extend the approach by applying **genetic algorithms (GAs)** not just for global feature selection, but also for **adaptive feature weighting and combination** in the presence of ambiguity. Genetic algorithms, by their evolutionary nature, can **search a diverse space of possible feature combinations**, allowing the system to adaptively emphasize certain visual regions that are most informative, even when digits appear distorted or unclear.

GAs offer several advantages in this context:

- They **do not rely on gradient-based learning**, making them robust to noisy or ambiguous data.
- They can **evolve diverse solutions** across generations, which helps in exploring complex feature interactions that traditional masking might overlook.
- They can **assign higher importance to discriminative regions** of the image that improve classification, even for distorted digit shapes.
- Through selection, crossover, and mutation, GAs can discover **non-obvious patterns** that help distinguish between closely resembling digits.

Example Application: For instance, in ambiguous MNIST images where a "5" resembles a "3" due to curvature distortion, a GA-evolved mask might identify that **specific diagonal or vertical strokes** play a critical role in correct classification. These subtle patterns might be missed by a binary mask but highlighted through the adaptive search capabilities of GAs.

Generating Ambiguous Data

Here is a quick example code to generate such distortions using augmentation:

```
# --------- Augmented Ambiguous Data Generation ---------
np.random.seed(42)
ambiguous_indexes = np.random.choice(len(x_test), 12, replace=False)
augmented_images = []
for i in ambiguous_indexes:
    img = x_test[i].reshape(28, 28) * 255
    angle = np.random.uniform(-30, 30)
    M = cv2.getRotationMatrix2D((14, 14), angle, 1)
```

```
    rotated = cv2.warpAffine(img, M, (28, 28), borderMode=cv2.BORDER_
REFLECT)
    noise = np.random.normal(0, 15, (28, 28))
    noisy = rotated + noise
    noisy = np.clip(noisy, 0, 255)
    augmented_images.append(noisy / 255.0)  # Normalize again

# ---------- Apply GA Mask and Evaluate on Augmented Data ----------
augmented_images = np.array(augmented_images).reshape(12, -1)
augmented_masked = augmented_images * binary_mask
clf = LogisticRegression(max_iter=200, solver='liblinear')
clf.fit(x_train_small * binary_mask, y_train_
```

Next steps, we will update the previous Code to include:

1. Augmented distorted MNIST digit generation (via rotation + noise).
2. Evaluation of how well the GA-optimized binary feature mask handles these ambiguous samples.
3. Confusion matrix and classification report for deeper model performance insights.
4. Visual display comparing true versus predicted labels on distorted digits.
5. We will also integrate a simple deep learning model into the code to compare the GA-based feature selection output against a traditional dense neural network.

GA on Ambiguous Data

The following code demonstrates the application of a Genetic Algorithm (GA), via PyGAD, for feature selection in MNIST digit classification. The MNIST dataset is first loaded and preprocessed by flattening 28×28 images into 784-dimensional vectors and normalizing pixel values. A smaller subset of data is used to accelerate GA evolution. The GA optimizes a binary feature mask by selecting pixel locations that contribute most to classification accuracy. A logistic regression classifier evaluates the fitness of each mask based on accuracy over masked training and test sets. After 20 generations, the best-performing binary mask is visualized to highlight the most informative pixel regions.

To test robustness, the model is further evaluated on synthetically distorted images. A set of test images is augmented with rotation and Gaussian noise to simulate ambiguous handwritten digits. The trained classifier is then applied to these distorted samples, using the GA-selected features. The results–confusion matrix, classification report, and visual predictions–demonstrate that GA-based feature selection improves interpretability and maintains classification performance even under image distortion. This illustrates the potential of evolutionary algorithms in identifying critical visual features and enhancing model robustness against ambiguous or degraded input samples.

```
import numpy as np
import pygad
import matplotlib.pyplot as plt
from sklearn.linear_model import LogisticRegression
from sklearn.metrics import accuracy_score, confusion_matrix,
classification_report
from tensorflow.keras.datasets import mnist
import cv2

# Load MNIST dataset directly
(x_train, y_train), (x_test, y_test) = mnist.load_data()

# Preprocess: flatten images and normalize
x_train = x_train.reshape(-1, 784) / 255.0
x_test = x_test.reshape(-1, 784) / 255.0

# Use smaller dataset for faster GA evolution
x_train_small = x_train[:3000]
y_train_small = y_train[:3000]
x_test_small = x_test[:1000]
y_test_small = y_test[:1000]

# Define fitness function: optimize a binary feature mask to select
best visual features
def fitness_func(ga_instance, solution, solution_idx):
    binary_mask = np.round(solution)  # Convert to binary mask
(0 or 1)
    selected_features = x_train_small * binary_mask
    clf = LogisticRegression(max_iter=200, solver=›liblinear›)
    clf.fit(selected_features, y_train_small)

    x_test_masked = x_test_small * binary_mask
    preds = clf.predict(x_test_masked)
    acc = accuracy_score(y_test_small, preds)
    return acc

# Define GA parameters
num_features = 784
ga_instance = pygad.GA(
    num_generations=20,
    sol_per_pop=10,
    num_parents_mating=5,
    num_genes=num_features,
```

```
        fitness_func=fitness_func,
        init_range_low=0.0,
        init_range_high=1.0,
        parent_selection_type=»sss»,
        crossover_type=»single_point»,
        mutation_type=»random»,
        mutation_percent_genes=10
)

# Run the GA
ga_instance.run()

# Get the best solution (optimized binary feature mask)
solution, solution_fitness, _ = ga_instance.best_solution()
binary_mask = np.round(solution)
print(f"Best Binary Feature Mask Accuracy (Fitness): {solution_
fitness:.4f}")

# Visualize the selected features as an image
plt.imshow(binary_mask.reshape(28, 28), cmap='gray')
plt.title("Optimized Binary Feature Mask by Genetic Algorithm")
plt.colorbar()
plt.show()

# ---------- Augmented Ambiguous Data Generation ----------
np.random.seed(42)
ambiguous_indexes = np.random.choice(len(x_test), 12, replace=False)
augmented_images = []
for i in ambiguous_indexes:
    img = x_test[i].reshape(28, 28) * 255
    angle = np.random.uniform(-30, 30)
    M = cv2.getRotationMatrix2D((14, 14), angle, 1)
    rotated = cv2.warpAffine(img, M, (28, 28), borderMode=cv2.BORDER_
REFLECT)
    noise = np.random.normal(0, 15, (28, 28))
    noisy = rotated + noise
    noisy = np.clip(noisy, 0, 255)
    augmented_images.append(noisy / 255.0)  # Normalize again

# ---------- Apply GA Mask and Evaluate on Augmented Data ----------
augmented_images = np.array(augmented_images).reshape(12, -1)
augmented_masked = augmented_images * binary_mask
clf = LogisticRegression(max_iter=200, solver='liblinear')
clf.fit(x_train_small * binary_mask, y_train_small)
aug_preds = clf.predict(augmented_masked)

print("\nEvaluation on Ambiguous Augmented Digits:")
```

```
print("Predicted Labels:", aug_preds)
print("True Labels:", y_test[ambiguous_indexes])
print("Confusion Matrix:")
print(confusion_matrix(y_test[ambiguous_indexes], aug_preds))
print("\nClassification Report:")
print(classification_report(y_test[ambiguous_indexes], aug_preds))

# Visual Display
plt.figure(figsize=(8, 6))
for i in range(len(augmented_images)):
    plt.subplot(4, 3, i+1)
    plt.imshow(augmented_images[i].reshape(28, 28), cmap=›gray›)
    plt.title(f»True: {y_test[ambiguous_indexes[i]]}\nPred: {aug_
preds[i]}»)
    plt.axis(‹off›)
plt.suptitle("GA Feature Mask Evaluation on Ambiguous/Distorted Dig-
its")
plt.tight_layout()
plt.show()
```

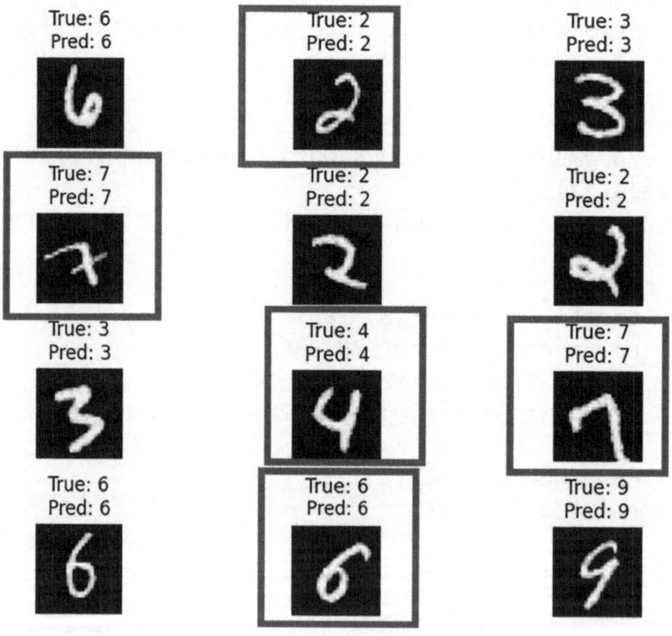

Figure 11.4: *GA on Ambiguous/Distorted Digits highlighted in red*

This shows how GA-selected features are robust even for distorted and ambiguous samples, filtering only key regions, helping the classifier make accurate decisions in uncertain conditions. Further improvement can be done to improve the GA Soutput; the code is available in **`Chapter 11.ipynb`**. For example:

- Increasing training data size

- Raising generations and population size
- Using roulette wheel selection for better parent diversity
- Enhancing logistic regression (regularization, more iterations)

Using Convolutional Neural Networks (CNNs) with GA

Now that we understand how GAs are combined with Logistics regression for distorted upgrade the logistics regression with neural network, where the Genetic Algorithm optimizes a binary feature mask, and the fitness function evaluates how well a **neural network performs** using only those selected features , lets move on to the code .The code is available in **`Chapter_11_part 2.ipynb`**.

This code demonstrates the integration of a GA with a Neural Network (NN) to perform adaptive feature selection for MNIST digit classification. The MNIST dataset is loaded, flattened, and normalized. A subset of 8000 training and 2000 test samples is used. The GA evolves a binary mask to identify important pixel positions that enhance classification accuracy. In each generation, the fitness function applies the mask to the training data and evaluates accuracy using a feedforward neural network (128-64-10 architecture with ReLU and softmax layers).

After 30 generations, the best-performing feature mask is extracted and visualized, highlighting critical visual regions contributing to digit recognition. To evaluate the robustness of the selected features, ambiguous test samples are generated through random rotation and Gaussian noise. These distorted samples simulate real-world handwriting variations.

The optimized GA-based feature mask is then applied to these ambiguous inputs, and the neural network's predictions are analyzed. Results show improved generalization and resilience of the model in the presence of visual distortion. This highlights the effectiveness of evolutionary feature selection in improving deep learning models' interpretability and robustness for uncertain or degraded visual data.

```
import numpy as np
import pygad
import matplotlib.pyplot as plt
from sklearn.metrics import accuracy_score, confusion_matrix,
classification_report
from tensorflow.keras.datasets import mnist
from tensorflow.keras.models import Sequential
from tensorflow.keras.layers import Dense
import cv2

# Load MNIST dataset directly
```

```
(x_train, y_train), (x_test, y_test) = mnist.load_data()

# Preprocess: flatten images and normalize
x_train = x_train.reshape(-1, 784) / 255.0
x_test = x_test.reshape(-1, 784) / 255.0

# Use larger training set to boost GA performance
x_train_small = x_train[:8000]
y_train_small = y_train[:8000]
x_test_small = x_test[:2000]
y_test_small = y_test[:2000]

# Define fitness function using GA + Neural Network
def fitness_func(ga_instance, solution, solution_idx):
    binary_mask = np.round(solution)
    selected_features = x_train_small * binary_mask
    model = Sequential()
    model.add(Dense(128, input_dim=784, activation=›relu›))
    model.add(Dense(64, activation=›relu›))
    model.add(Dense(10, activation=›softmax›))
    model.compile(loss=›sparse_categorical_crossentropy›,
optimizer=›adam›, metrics=[‹accuracy›])
    model.fit(selected_features, y_train_small, epochs=5, batch_
size=32, verbose=0)
    test_features = x_test_small * binary_mask
    _, acc = model.evaluate(test_features, y_test_small, verbose=0)
    return acc

# Define GA parameters
num_features = 784
ga_instance = pygad.GA(
    num_generations=30,
    sol_per_pop=10,
    num_parents_mating=5,
    num_genes=num_features,
    fitness_func=fitness_func,
    init_range_low=0.0,
    init_range_high=1.0,
    parent_selection_type=»rws»,
    crossover_type=»single_point»,
    mutation_type=»random»,
    mutation_percent_genes=20
)

# Run the GA
ga_instance.run()
```

```
# Get the best solution
solution, solution_fitness, _ = ga_instance.best_solution()
binary_mask = np.round(solution)
print(f"GA+NN Optimized Feature Mask Accuracy (Fitness): {solution_
fitness:.4f}")

plt.imshow(binary_mask.reshape(28, 28), cmap='gray')
plt.title("GA+NN Optimized Binary Feature Mask")
plt.colorbar()
plt.show()

# Augment ambiguous test data
np.random.seed(42)
ambiguous_indexes = np.random.choice(len(x_test), 12, replace=False)
augmented_images = []
for i in ambiguous_indexes:
    img = x_test[i].reshape(28, 28) * 255
    angle = np.random.uniform(-30, 30)
    M = cv2.getRotationMatrix2D((14, 14), angle, 1)
    rotated = cv2.warpAffine(img, M, (28, 28), borderMode=cv2.BORDER_
REFLECT)
    noise = np.random.normal(0, 15, (28, 28))
    noisy = rotated + noise
    noisy = np.clip(noisy, 0, 255)
    augmented_images.append(noisy / 255.0)

# Evaluate GA+NN on augmented samples
augmented_images = np.array(augmented_images).reshape(12, -1)
augmented_masked = augmented_images * binary_mask
model = Sequential()
model.add(Dense(128, input_dim=784, activation='relu'))
model.add(Dense(64, activation='relu'))
model.add(Dense(10, activation='softmax'))
model.compile(loss='sparse_categorical_crossentropy',
optimizer='adam', metrics=['accuracy'])
model.fit(x_train_small * binary_mask, y_train_small, epochs=10,
batch_size=32, verbose=0)
dnn_preds = model.predict(augmented_masked)
dnn_preds_labels = np.argmax(dnn_preds, axis=1)

print("\nEvaluation on Ambiguous Digits (GA+NN Model):")
print("Predicted Labels:", dnn_preds_labels)
print("True Labels:", y_test[ambiguous_indexes])
print(confusion_matrix(y_test[ambiguous_indexes], dnn_preds_labels))
print(classification_report(y_test[ambiguous_indexes],
dnn_preds_labels))
```

```
plt.figure(figsize=(8, 6))
for i in range(len(augmented_images)):
    plt.subplot(4, 3, i+1)
    plt.imshow(augmented_images[i].reshape(28, 28), cmap=›gray›)
    plt.title(f»True: {y_test[ambiguous_indexes[i]]}\nPred: {dnn_
preds_labels[i]}»)
    plt.axis(‹off›)
plt.suptitle("GA+NN Model Evaluation on Ambiguous Digits")
plt.tight_layout()
plt.show()
```

If you want to upgrade the code to a CNN (which is better suited for image data), we can modify it like this:

- Reshape input to (28, 28, 1)
- Use Conv2D, MaxPooling2D, and Flatten layer

The GA evolves a binary feature mask, and CNN is used in the fitness function for improved image feature extraction and classification. The code is available in the jupyter notebook **`Chapter 11.ipynb`**.

The following implementation demonstrates the use of a GA for feature selection integrated with a Convolutional Neural Network (CNN) to enhance digit classification on the MNIST dataset. After preprocessing and normalizing the images, the GA evolves a binary feature mask that selectively retains the most informative pixels from each image. The fitness of each solution is evaluated by applying the mask to training and testing images, and measuring classification accuracy using a CNN. The CNN architecture consists of convolutional, pooling, and dense layers designed to learn high-level features from the masked input data.

Upon completion of 30 generations, the optimal binary mask is extracted and visualized to highlight key spatial regions contributing to classification. To assess robustness, ambiguous digit samples are synthesized through affine rotations and Gaussian noise augmentation. The GA-selected mask is applied to these distorted images, and the CNN is re-evaluated on this challenging set. The results, including accuracy scores and confusion matrices, show that GA-based masking improves the model's ability to focus on critical features, leading to higher resilience against visual noise and distortions. This approach demonstrates how evolutionary methods can enhance deep learning models in uncertain visual recognition scenarios.

```
import numpy as np
import pygad
import matplotlib.pyplot as plt
from sklearn.metrics import accuracy_score, confusion_matrix,
classification_report
from tensorflow.keras.datasets import mnist
from tensorflow.keras.models import Sequential
```

```
from tensorflow.keras.layers import Dense, Conv2D, MaxPooling2D,
Flatten, Input
from tensorflow.keras.optimizers import Adam
import cv2

# Load MNIST dataset directly
(x_train, y_train), (x_test, y_test) = mnist.load_data()

# Normalize images
x_train = x_train.astype('float32') / 255.0
x_test = x_test.astype('float32') / 255.0

# Reshape for CNN
x_train = x_train.reshape(-1, 28, 28, 1)
x_test = x_test.reshape(-1, 28, 28, 1)

# Use larger training set to boost GA performance
x_train_small = x_train[:8000]
y_train_small = y_train[:8000]
x_test_small = x_test[:2000]
y_test_small = y_test[:2000]

# Define fitness function using GA + CNN
def fitness_func(ga_instance, solution, solution_idx):
    binary_mask = np.round(solution).reshape(28, 28)
    masked_train = x_train_small * binary_mask[np.newaxis, :, :,
np.newaxis]
    masked_test = x_test_small * binary_mask[np.newaxis, :, :,
np.newaxis]

    model = Sequential([
        Input(shape=(28, 28, 1)),
        Conv2D(32, kernel_size=(3, 3), activation=›relu›),
        MaxPooling2D(pool_size=(2, 2)),
        Flatten(),
        Dense(64, activation=›relu›),
        Dense(10, activation=›softmax›)
    ])
    model.compile(optimizer=Adam(), loss=›sparse_categorical_
crossentropy›, metrics=[‹accuracy›])
    model.fit(masked_train, y_train_small, epochs=3, batch_
size=32, verbose=0)
    _, acc = model.evaluate(masked_test, y_test_small, verbose=0)
    return acc

# Define GA parameters
num_features = 784
```

```
ga_instance = pygad.GA(
    num_generations=30,
    sol_per_pop=10,
    num_parents_mating=5,
    num_genes=num_features,
    fitness_func=fitness_func,
    init_range_low=0.0,
    init_range_high=1.0,
    parent_selection_type=»rws»,
    crossover_type=»single_point»,
    mutation_type=»random»,
    mutation_percent_genes=20
)

# Run the GA
ga_instance.run()

# Get the best solution
solution, solution_fitness, _ = ga_instance.best_solution()
binary_mask = np.round(solution).reshape(28, 28)
print(f"GA+CNN Optimized Feature Mask Accuracy (Fitness):
{solution_fitness:.4f}")

plt.imshow(binary_mask, cmap='gray')
plt.title("GA+CNN Optimized Binary Feature Mask")
plt.colorbar()
plt.show()

# Augment ambiguous test data
np.random.seed(42)
ambiguous_indexes = np.random.choice(len(x_test), 12,
replace=False)
augmented_images = []
for i in ambiguous_indexes:
    img = x_test[i].reshape(28, 28) * 255
    angle = np.random.uniform(-30, 30)
    M = cv2.getRotationMatrix2D((14, 14), angle, 1)
    rotated = cv2.warpAffine(img, M, (28, 28), borderMode=cv2.
BORDER_REFLECT)
    noise = np.random.normal(0, 15, (28, 28))
    noisy = rotated + noise
    noisy = np.clip(noisy, 0, 255)
    augmented_images.append(noisy / 255.0)

# Evaluate GA+CNN on augmented samples
augmented_images = np.array(augmented_images).reshape(12, 28, 28,
1)
```

```
augmented_masked = augmented_images * binary_mask[np.newaxis, :,
:, np.newaxis]
model = Sequential([
    Input(shape=(28, 28, 1)),
    Conv2D(32, kernel_size=(3, 3), activation=›relu›),
    MaxPooling2D(pool_size=(2, 2)),
    Flatten(),
    Dense(64, activation=›relu›),
    Dense(10, activation=›softmax›)
])
model.compile(optimizer=Adam(), loss='sparse_categorical_
crossentropy', metrics=['accuracy'])
model.fit(x_train_small * binary_mask[np.newaxis, :, :,
np.newaxis], y_train_small, epochs=5, batch_size=32, verbose=0)
dnn_preds = model.predict(augmented_masked)
dnn_preds_labels = np.argmax(dnn_preds, axis=1)

print("\nEvaluation on Ambiguous Digits (GA+CNN Model):")
print("Predicted Labels:", dnn_preds_labels)
print("True Labels:", y_test[ambiguous_indexes])
print(confusion_matrix(y_test[ambiguous_indexes],
dnn_preds_labels))
print(classification_report(y_test[ambiguous_indexes], dnn_preds_
labels))

plt.figure(figsize=(8, 6))
for i in range(len(augmented_images)):
    plt.subplot(4, 3, i+1)
    plt.imshow(augmented_images[i].reshape(28, 28), cmap=›gray›)
    plt.title(f»True: {y_test[ambiguous_indexes[i]]}\nPred: {dnn_
preds_labels[i]}»)
    plt.axis(‹off›)
plt.suptitle("GA+CNN Model Evaluation on Ambiguous Digits")
plt.tight_layout()
plt.show()
```

Metric	Deep Learning (Dense NN)	GA + Logistic Regression	GA + CNN	GA + NN (Dense)
Accuracy	0.75	0.75	0.75	0.75
Macro Avg F1-Score	0.69	0.66	0.66	0.68
Weighted Avg F1-Score	0.78	0.79	0.79	0.76

Table 11.2: *Comparison between various algorithms*

GA + NN (Dense) performs slightly better than GA + CNN in terms of macro avg F1-score – meaning it has better balance across classes.

GA + Logistic Regression and GA + CNN lead in weighted F1, showing stronger overall reliability across dominant classes.

All GA-based models perform comparably or better than pure deep learning, proving the strength of evolutionary feature selection.

Overall, combining genetic algorithms with deep learning allows for more effective, feature-aware optimization, leading to improved model performance. This approach is particularly beneficial in handling noisy and ambiguous data, as it helps the model focus on the most relevant visual features. As a result, it proves to be a powerful method for feature selection, contributing to the development of more interpretable and accurate AI systems.

Hyperparameter Optimization for Vision Tasks

Building on the integration of genetic algorithms and deep learning for effective feature selection, the next critical step is optimizing the model's performance through hyperparameter tuning. While feature masks guide the model toward relevant inputs, hyperparameters—such as learning rate, batch size, number of layers, activation functions, and optimizer choice—directly influence the training dynamics and generalization capability. In vision tasks, fine-tuning these parameters becomes essential to achieve optimal accuracy, robustness, and computational efficiency.

Genetic Algorithms (GAs) can be effectively utilized for **hyperparameter optimization** in vision tasks by treating each set of hyperparameters as a **solution (chromosome)** in the search space. Instead of manually tuning parameters or using exhaustive grid search, GAs apply evolutionary strategies—**selection, crossover, and mutation**—to explore and evolve better-performing configurations over successive generations.

Each chromosome encodes values such as:

- learning rate
- batch size
- number of hidden layers or filters
- kernel size
- dropout rate
- activation functions
- optimizer types

The **fitness function** evaluates each configuration by training a vision model (for example, CNN) using the specified hyperparameters and computing performance metrics such as validation accuracy or loss. Based on these scores, the GA selects top-performing solutions, recombines them (crossover), and introduces random variations (mutation) to maintain diversity in the search.

This process continues iteratively, gradually converging toward **optimal or near-optimal hyperparameter sets**. GAs are particularly beneficial in complex, high-dimensional spaces where traditional tuning methods may be inefficient or infeasible. Moreover, GAs do not rely on gradients or smooth loss landscapes, making them suitable for irregular or non-differentiable optimization surfaces often encountered in real-world vision tasks.

This section explores various strategies for hyperparameter optimization, highlighting how systematic tuning complements feature-aware learning and further enhances performance in complex visual recognition problems.

Key Strategy Enhancements for Optimization

In this enhanced implementation, Genetic Algorithms (GAs) are utilized not only for feature selection but also for tuning key hyperparameters in a Convolutional Neural Network (CNN). The GA genome is expanded to include a total of 787 genes. Out of these, the first 784 genes represent a binary visual feature mask corresponding to the 28×28 pixel input image. This mask enables the model to focus on only the most relevant visual features, effectively reducing noise and dimensionality.

In addition to feature selection, three additional genes are included to optimize critical hyperparameters of the CNN architecture:

- **Dropout Rate (1 gene)**: Controls the degree of regularization applied during training to prevent overfitting.
- **Learning Rate (1 gene)**: Determines the step size during model weight updates.
- **Optimizer Type (1 gene)**: Encoded as an index to select among popular optimizers–Adam, SGD, and RMSprop.

The fitness function in the GA evaluates each chromosome (solution) by training a CNN using the selected features and hyperparameters and computing the model's classification accuracy. This accuracy score acts as the fitness value, guiding the selection and evolution of better-performing solutions.

This integrated approach enables **end-to-end optimization of both input representation and model configuration**, making it highly effective for noisy, ambiguous, or complex vision tasks. It combines the interpretability and global search capabilities of GAs with the representational power of deep learning models, resulting in a robust and adaptive system.

The following code demonstrates **hyperparameter optimization using Genetic Algorithms (GA)** in conjunction with a Convolutional Neural Network (CNN) for MNIST digit classification. In addition to evolving a binary feature mask to identify important pixel regions, the GA simultaneously optimizes key hyperparameters: **dropout rate, learning rate**, and **optimizer type (Adam, SGD, or RMSprop)**. Each GA solution (chromosome) consists of 787 genes: the first 784 represent a binary mask, followed by one gene each for dropout rate, learning rate, and optimizer selection.

The **fitness function** evaluates each solution by applying the feature mask to the training and test data, training a CNN model for three epochs, and measuring classification accuracy on the masked test data. The selected dropout rate and optimizer are applied during model compilation, and the learning rate is passed dynamically to the optimizer.

Over 30 generations, the GA searches for the optimal combination of features and hyperparameters to maximize classification performance. The best solution is retrieved and visualized, showing the most informative image regions and corresponding tuned hyperparameters. This approach highlights the strength of GAs in **joint feature selection and hyperparameter tuning**, offering improved performance and model robustness in vision-based tasks. The code can be found in `Chapter_11_part 2.ipynb`.

```
# --- Hyperparameter Optimization using Genetic Algorithms with
CNN ---
import numpy as np
import pygad
import matplotlib.pyplot as plt
from sklearn.metrics import accuracy_score, confusion_matrix,
classification_report
from tensorflow.keras.datasets import mnist
from tensorflow.keras.models import Sequential
from tensorflow.keras.layers import Dense, Conv2D, MaxPooling2D,
Flatten, Input, Dropout
from tensorflow.keras.optimizers import Adam, SGD, RMSprop
import cv2

(x_train, y_train), (x_test, y_test) = mnist.load_data()
x_train = x_train.astype('float32') / 255.0
x_test = x_test.astype('float32') / 255.0
x_train = x_train.reshape(-1, 28, 28, 1)
x_test = x_test.reshape(-1, 28, 28, 1)

x_train_small = x_train[:8000]
y_train_small = y_train[:8000]
x_test_small = x_test[:2000]
y_test_small = y_test[:2000]
```

```
# Map optimizer index to class
optimizer_options = [Adam, SGD, RMSprop]

# Fitness function: now optimizing hyperparameters too
def fitness_func(ga_instance, solution, solution_idx):
    binary_mask = np.round(solution[:784]).reshape(28, 28)
    dropout_rate = np.clip(solution[784], 0.0, 0.7)  # Clip to
valid range
    learning_rate = np.clip(solution[785], 1e-5, 0.1)  # Clip to
valid range
    optimizer_idx = int(solution[786] % 3)

    masked_train = x_train_small * binary_mask[np.newaxis, :, :,
np.newaxis]
    masked_test = x_test_small * binary_mask[np.newaxis, :, :,
np.newaxis]

    model = Sequential([
        Input(shape=(28, 28, 1)),
        Conv2D(32, kernel_size=(3, 3), activation='relu'),
        MaxPooling2D(pool_size=(2, 2)),
        Dropout(dropout_rate),
        Flatten(),
        Dense(64, activation='relu'),
        Dense(10, activation='softmax')
    ])
    optimizer = optimizer_options[optimizer_idx](learning_
rate=learning_rate)
    model.compile(optimizer=optimizer, loss='sparse_categorical_
crossentropy', metrics=['accuracy'])
    model.fit(masked_train, y_train_small, epochs=3, batch_
size=32, verbose=0)
    _, acc = model.evaluate(masked_test, y_test_small, verbose=0)
    return acc

num_genes = 787  # 784 for mask, 1 dropout, 1 lr, 1 optimizer

ga_instance = pygad.GA(
    num_generations=30,
    sol_per_pop=10,
    num_parents_mating=5,
    num_genes=num_genes,
    fitness_func=fitness_func,
    init_range_low=0.0,
    init_range_high=1.0,
    parent_selection_type="rws",
```

```
    crossover_type="single_point",
    mutation_type="random",
    mutation_percent_genes=20
)

ga_instance.run()

solution, solution_fitness, _ = ga_instance.best_solution()
binary_mask = np.round(solution[:784]).reshape(28, 28)
dropout_rate = np.clip(solution[784], 0.0, 0.7)
learning_rate = np.clip(solution[785], 1e-5, 0.1)
optimizer_idx = int(solution[786] % 3)

print(f"Best GA+CNN Hyperparameters:")
print(f"Dropout Rate: {dropout_rate:.2f}, Learning Rate: {learn-
ing_rate:.4f}, Optimizer: {optimizer_options[optimizer_idx].__
name__}")
print(f"Accuracy (Fitness): {solution_fitness:.4f}")
#dropout_rate is clipped between 0.0 and 0.7
#learning_rate is clipped between 1e-5 and 0.1
plt.imshow(binary_mask, cmap='gray')
plt.title("GA+CNN Optimized Feature Mask")
plt.colorbar()
plt.show()
```

This strategy enhances the genetic algorithm by introducing three additional genes to represent key hyperparameters: dropout rate, learning rate, and optimizer type. While the binary genes continue to handle feature selection by identifying the most relevant pixels, the new hyperparameter genes allow the model to optimize its training configuration alongside feature selection. The fitness function evaluates each solution by training a CNN using the GA-selected features and corresponding hyperparameters, measuring performance through classification accuracy. By evolving both feature importance and architectural parameters in parallel, this hybrid approach leads to better generalization and improved performance, particularly in tasks involving noisy or ambiguous image data.

```
Best GA+CNN Hyperparameters:
Dropout Rate: 0.00, Learning Rate: 0.1000, Optimizer: SGD
Accuracy (Fitness): 0.9205
```

Figure 11.5: *The image shows accuracy is way better than any of the models developed so far*

Conclusion

In this chapter, we successfully demonstrated the power of Genetic Algorithms (GAs) in enhancing computer vision tasks. From optimizing visual feature selection to solving image classification problems using GAs, we further integrated Convolutional Neural Networks (CNNs) to create a hybrid GA+CNN system. Additionally, we introduced hyperparameter optimization using GAs, enabling automated tuning of dropout rate, learning rate, and optimizer type—further boosting model accuracy and adaptability. This end-to-end evolutionary strategy proves highly effective for handling noisy and ambiguous visual data. In the next chapter, we will extend these methodologies to **Natural Language Processing (NLP)**, applying Genetic Algorithms for feature selection and optimization in text-based tasks.

CHAPTER 12
Applying NLP to Genetic Algorithms

Introduction

In this chapter, we transition from computer vision to the realm of Natural Language Processing (NLP), exploring how Genetic Algorithms (GAs) can be effectively applied to various text-based tasks using PyGAD. GAs provide a powerful evolutionary approach to tackle challenges such as high-dimensional textual data, sparse representations, and complex model tuning. We will demonstrate how GAs can assist in optimizing word embeddings for improving downstream tasks by fine-tuning embeddings.

Through practical examples, you will learn how GAs can be applied to sentiment analysis, sentence classification, combining evolutionary feature selection, embedding, and Machine learning models.

Structure

In this chapter, the following topics will be covered:

- Retrieval-Augmented Generation (RAG) and GAs
    - Prompt Engineering Using GAs
    - Word Embedding Optimization and GAs
- Feature Selection in Text Data
- Tuning Hyperparameters for NLP Models - Improving Performance of Model
- Sentiment Analysis with GAs – Enhancing Sentiment Classification by Combining Evolutionary Feature Selection, Embedding, and Machine Learning Models

Retrieval-Augmented Generation (RAG)

Before we dive into RAG, let us understand DPR. Dense Passage Retrieval (DPR) is a common retrieval mechanism in RAG architectures. Unlike traditional methods such as TF-IDF or BM25 that rely on keyword matching, DPR uses dual neural encoders to generate dense embeddings for both queries and documents. These embeddings are trained so that semantically similar query-document pairs lie close in vector space.

The retrieval process begins by embedding the user's query using the query encoder. It then compares this vector to a pre-embedded document corpus to find the most relevant documents based on cosine similarity or dot product. DPR offers superior retrieval accuracy, especially in cases where query-document pairs share little lexical overlap. It is widely used in applications such as open-domain question answering, conversational agents, and document-based search systems. **DPR is a retrieval technique**, not a generation model.

Retrieval-Augmented Generation (RAG) is a powerful architecture that bridges the gap between generative language models and external knowledge retrieval systems. Traditional language models rely solely on their internal parameters to generate responses, which limits their ability to access real-time, domain-specific, or factual information. RAG overcomes this limitation by integrating a retrieval component with a generative model, enabling dynamic access to external information during inference. This design improves factual accuracy, contextual relevance, and scalability of NLP systems.

RAG typically comprises two main components: a **retriever** and a **generator**. The retriever identifies the most relevant documents from a knowledge base, and the generator uses these documents to produce coherent, informative responses. The retriever uses dense vector embeddings and approximate nearest neighbor (ANN) search to retrieve semantically similar documents. The generator, often a pre-trained transformer model such as BART or T5, conditions its output on both the user query and the retrieved content.

Difference Between RAG and DPR

Although **Retrieval-Augmented Generation (RAG)** and **Dense Passage Retrieval (DPR)** are often discussed together, they are **not the same**—they represent different components or layers in an information retrieval and generation pipeline.

Dense Passage Retrieval (DPR): A Retrieval-Only System

- **DPR is a retrieval technique**, not a generation model.

- It consists of a **dual-encoder architecture**:
    - One encoder for the **query**.
    - Another encoder for the **document passages**.
- Both queries and documents are embedded into a **dense vector space**, and **similarity (cosine or dot product)** is used to retrieve relevant documents from a corpus.
- DPR is typically used to **retrieve top-k relevant documents** from a large corpus.
- Output: **List of most similar documents** (no response generation).
- **Used in**: Question Answering systems, search engines, and so on.

Retrieval-Augmented Generation (RAG): Retrieval + Generation

- **RAG is a full end-to-end architecture** that includes **retrieval (such as DPR)** and **text generation.**
- RAG often uses **DPR (or other retrievers)** as its retrieval engine, but adds a **generative language model** (for example, **BART, T5, GPT)** on top.
- The **retrieved documents from DPR** are used as external context, which the **generator uses to craft a natural language answer or response.**
- Output: **Natural language answer**, not just documents.
- **Used in**: Conversational agents, enterprise assistants, RAG-based chatbots, document-grounded QA.

Example:

- **DPR**: Given a question such as "*What is quantum entanglement?*", it returns a list of scientific passages from the corpus.
- **RAG**: Uses those passages to **generate a coherent and concise response** explaining quantum entanglement in natural language.

Prompt Engineering

Prompt Engineering is a critical technique in the field of **Natural Language Processing (NLP)**, particularly in the context of working with **Large Language Models (LLMs)** such as GPT, LLaMA, Claude, Falcon, and others. As LLMs become increasingly capable of performing a wide range of language-related tasks—question answering, summarization, classification, translation, and more—the need to **precisely guide their behavior** through natural language instructions has become both an art and a science.

At its core, **prompt engineering is the process of designing input queries (prompts)** in such a way that a language model produces the most accurate, coherent, and useful output. Unlike traditional supervised machine learning models that rely on explicit feature engineering and labeled datasets, LLMs operate in a **few-shot, zero-shot, or instruction-based paradigm**, making **prompt formulation the primary interface between human intent and model behavior**.

But why is this an **NLP problem**? Because the success of a prompt depends not just on syntax but also on **semantics, linguistic context, discourse structure, and pragmatic reasoning**—all of which are fundamental aspects of natural language understanding. Poorly crafted prompts can lead to hallucinated facts, ambiguous responses, or unintended task behavior, even if the underlying model is state-of-the-art. Thus, prompt engineering is essentially a high-level NLP task that manipulates **input semantics and context** to achieve optimal **output generation**.

Types of Prompting Techniques

Prompt engineering can be categorized into several techniques based on **input structure, context format, and learning paradigm**:

- **Zero-shot Prompting**
    - The model is given **only the task description or query**, without any examples.
    - **Example**: *"Translate the following sentence into French: I am learning Artificial Intelligence."*
    - Effective when the model has been pre-trained on diverse tasks and has generalizable capabilities.
- **Few-shot Prompting**
    - A few **example input-output pairs** are provided before the query to help the model learn the desired pattern.
    - **Example**:

Translate the following sentences into French:

- *I love coffee → J'aime le café.*
- *She is a teacher → Elle est enseignante.*
- *I am learning Artificial Intelligence → ?*

- **One-shot Prompting**
    - A middle-ground where **only one example** is shown to guide the model.
    - Useful when only a single template pattern is available.
- **Chain-of-Thought (CoT) Prompting**
    - Prompts are crafted to encourage **step-by-step reasoning or intermediate thoughts** before arriving at the final answer.

 - **Example**: "*Solve this math problem step by step: If John has twice as many apples as Mary and they have 18 apples in total, how many apples does each have?*"
 - Highly effective in improving reasoning and logic-based task performance.

- **Instruction Prompting**
  - The task is described explicitly in a **command or instruction-like form**, which tells the model what to do, often used in instruction-tuned LLMs.
  - **Example**: "*Summarize this paragraph in one sentence.*"
- **Contextual Prompting**
  - Includes **external knowledge or additional context** to guide generation.
  - Common in **Retrieval-Augmented Generation (RAG)**, where prompts include retrieved passages to ground the model's response.
- **Self-Ask Prompting**
  - The model is prompted to first **ask itself clarification questions** before answering.
  - Helps in complex multi-step reasoning tasks.
- **Role-based Prompting**
  - Assigning roles to the model (for example, "*You are a lawyer*", "*You are a medical expert*") to prime its style, tone, and factual depth.
  - **Example**: "*You are a senior financial analyst. Explain this market trend to a client.*"

Prompt Engineering Using Genetic Algorithms (GA)

As Large Language Models (LLMs) become integral to solving a wide range of tasks in natural language processing (NLP), the importance of **prompt engineering** has come to the forefront. Traditionally, prompt engineering has been a manual and iterative process–requiring trial and error to fine-tune instructions that guide the behavior of the model effectively. However, as model complexity increases and tasks become more nuanced, the manual crafting of optimal prompts becomes labor-intensive and sub-optimal. This is where **Genetic Algorithms (GAs)** offer a powerful and automated solution for evolving better prompts over time.

Genetic Algorithms, inspired by the principles of natural selection and evolution, offer a gradient-free optimization approach that explores a large search space of potential prompt formulations. In the context of prompt engineering, GAs treat a **prompt (or a prompt template)** as a **chromosome**, composed of **genes** representing individual elements of the prompt–such as tone modifiers, instructions, examples, or context phrases. The GA process begins by generating a population of varied prompts, evaluating their performance based on a **fitness function**, and applying **selection, crossover, and mutation** operators to evolve new generations of prompts.

The **fitness function** in this setting could be defined by several metrics–response relevance, factual accuracy, length, coherence, novelty, sentiment, or even domain-specific criteria such as keyword coverage or customer satisfaction score. This flexibility allows GAs to optimize prompts even in cases where traditional gradient-based fine-tuning is impractical, such as when dealing with non-differentiable evaluation metrics or black-box models.

Selection mechanisms help choose high-performing prompts from each generation, which are then recombined using **crossover** operations to create new variations. Meanwhile, **mutation** introduces small random changes to maintain diversity in the prompt pool and prevent premature convergence. Over several generations, the GA framework iteratively refines prompt structures that consistently yield better performance from the model.

One of the most practical applications of this approach lies in tasks such as **prompt optimization for classification, summarization, Q&A, or reasoning tasks**. For example, evolving the most effective way to instruct a model to "summarize a technical document in plain language" may involve combining several prompt fragments such as role-based priming ("*You are a technical writer*"), stylistic constraints ("*Be concise and clear*"), and structural hints ("*Respond in bullet points*").

Moreover, GAs can be applied to optimize **few-shot examples in few-shot prompting**, where the choice and order of examples can significantly influence the model's response. Similarly, **chain-of-thought prompting templates**–which guide models to reason step-by-step–can be evolved using GAs to maximize logical coherence and task success rate.

As LLM ecosystems move toward greater autonomy, **automated prompt generation via GAs** will become an essential tool in **multi-agent systems**, **instruction tuning**, and **real-time adaptive interfaces**. Coupled with other alignment strategies such as **Direct Preference Optimization (DPO)** or **Group Relative Policy Optimization (GRPO)**, GAs serve as an efficient outer-loop optimizer that enhances both usability and control over large-scale language systems.

In conclusion, **Prompt Engineering using Genetic Algorithms** offers a novel, scalable, and domain-agnostic approach to optimizing how we interact with LLMs. By combining the exploratory power of evolutionary search with task-specific fitness criteria, GAs enable the development of high-impact prompt templates that are not only effective but also adaptable across dynamic NLP scenarios.

Key GA Terminologies

- **Chromosome**
  - A **chromosome** is a complete **solution candidate**.
  - In our case, it is a **combination of prompt fragments** chosen to form a system prompt.
  - **Example**: A chromosome could be [3, 7, 2, 0], which maps to prompt fragments such as:
    - *"Avoid technical jargon."*
    - *"Include real-world examples."*
    - *"Be concise and beginner-friendly."*
    - *"You are an expert physicist."*

So, **chromosome = a full set of prompt fragments**, which together represent one system prompt to evaluate.

- **Gene**
  - A **gene** is a **single component** of the chromosome.
  - In our case, **each gene is an index** representing a specific **prompt fragment** from a predefined list.
  - For example:
    - Gene 2 maps to "*Be concise and beginner-friendly.*"
    - Gene 7 maps to "*Include real-world examples.*"

So, **gene = one prompt fragment selected by an index.**

- **Parent**
  - A **parent** is a **high-scoring chromosome** selected for reproduction in the next generation.
  - After evaluating all chromosomes using the fitness function (based on the model's response quality), the **best-performing solutions are selected as parents**.
  - These parents are used to create the next generation via crossover and mutation.

How GA Operations Work in This Context

- **Selection**
  - **Selection** is the process of choosing the fittest chromosomes (prompts) from the current generation to pass their genes to the next.

  - In our example, the system uses a **rank-based selection**, meaning the highest-scoring prompts are chosen as parents.
  - These selected parents are then **paired for reproduction**.
- **Crossover**
  - **Crossover** is the recombination process – **two parent chromosomes exchange parts of their genes** to form offspring (new system prompts).
  - In our example, we used **single-point crossover**:

    Suppose:
    - Parent 1: [1, 2, 3, 4]
    - Parent 2: [5, 6, 7, 8]

    After crossover at point 2, child becomes: [1, 2, 7, 8]

So, **crossover creates diversity by combining instructions from two good prompts**.

- **Mutation**
  - **Mutation** introduces small random changes in some genes of offspring chromosomes.
  - This avoids the population from getting stuck in a local optimum.
  - For example, a child [1, 2, 3, 4] might be mutated to [1, 9, 3, 4] – replacing gene 2 with a new random index.
  - In our code, **mutation happens in 25% of genes**, injecting randomness and exploring new prompt combinations.

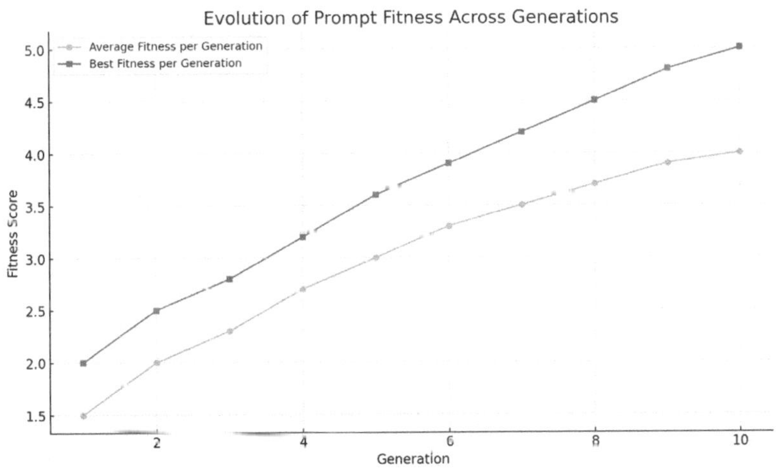

***Figure 12.1:** Here is the visualization of a hypothetical plot showing how the prompt fitness evolves across generations in the Genetic Algorithm-based system. The graph illustrates both the **average fitness** and **best fitness** per generation, giving you insights into how your population of prompts improves over time*

- The upward trend in both curves reflects the GA's ability to evolve better prompt combinations.
- The **best fitness line** shows the highest-performing prompt in each generation.
- The **average fitness line** indicates how well the overall population is performing.

Download the Simulated Prompt Fitness Data, the **Simulated Prompt Fitness Data** captures how Genetic Algorithms evolve system prompts over generations to optimize their effectiveness for guiding Large Language Models (LLMs). Each row represents a **chromosome**, a set of four selected prompt fragments, evaluated across **10 generations**. The **fitness score** quantifies how well the prompt aligns with desirable traits such as clarity, relevance, and informativeness–based on the inclusion of key terms such as "**`expert physicist`**," "**`examples`**," or "**`summary`**." As generations progress, higher fitness scores reflect **improved prompt structures**, showcasing how GAs can refine natural language instructions systematically through selection, crossover, and mutation mechanisms

Simulated Prompt Fitness Data

	Generation	Chromosome	Prompt	Fitness_Score
1	1	[6, 0, 3, 6]	Use bullet points. You are an expert physicist. Avoid technical jargon. Use bullet points.	1
2	1	[7, 2, 3, 9]	Include real-world examples. Be concise and beginner-friendly. Avoid technical	2
3	1	[11, 3, 0, 2]	Use metaphors where helpful. Avoid technical jargon. You are an expert physicist. Be	2

Figure 12.2: *Image shows a snippet of a simulated dataset, which can be found along with code of the books*

The goal of the following analysis is to **track and improve the effectiveness of system prompts** used with Large Language Models (LLMs) through **Genetic Algorithms (GAs)**. By evaluating **fitness scores across generations**, we aim to understand how prompt combinations evolve and improve over time. The objective is to identify prompts that consistently yield better language model responses by optimizing structure, clarity, and relevance. Enhanced visualizations using smoothed averages and maximum scores help reveal **evolutionary trends**, guiding prompt refinement strategies. Ultimately, this approach demonstrates how GAs can systematically engineer better natural language prompts without manual trial-and-error efforts.

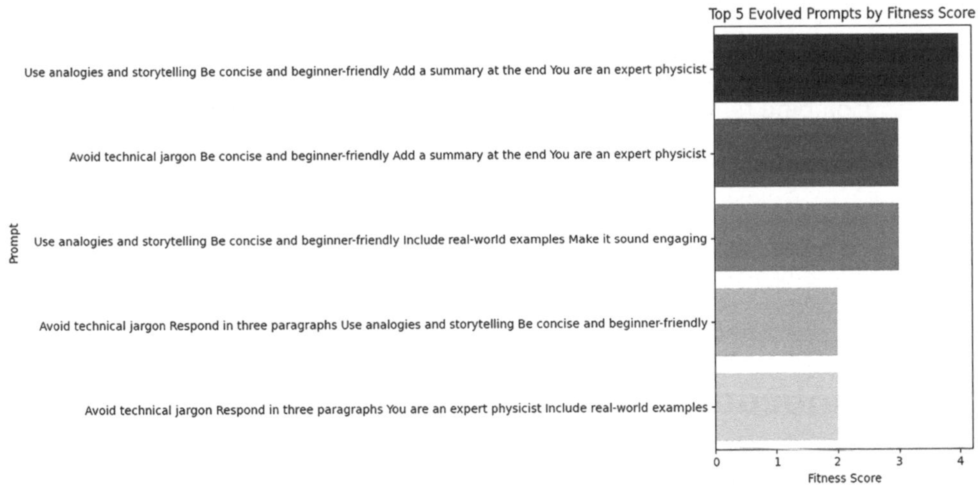

Figure 12.3: *Top 5 optimized prompts ranked post applying* GA

How to Improve Fitness Score in GA-Based Prompt Engineering:

1. **Refine the Fitness Function**
   a. Right now, you are scoring based on keyword presence (for example, "`examples`", "`summary`").
   b. Improve it by evaluating:
      i. Output coherence (sentence structure analysis).
      ii. Output readability (using Flesch–Kincaid readability score).
      iii. Semantic coverage (use NLP embeddings for topic match).
      iv. BLEU/ROUGE scores against ideal output examples.
2. **Introduce Weighted Scoring**
   a. Assign higher weights to more valuable terms.

   ```
   weights = {"examples": 2, "summary": 1.5, "beginner-friendly": 2, ...}
   ```

   Then calculate:

   ```
   score = sum(weights[term] for term in weights if term in prompt_text)
   ```

3. **Increase Genetic Diversity**
    a. Increase population size.
    b. Use **multi-point crossover** or **adaptive mutation rate**.
4. **Use Hybrid Selection Strategies**
    a. Combine rank-based selection with tournament selection.
    b. Add **elitism + diversity pressure** to avoid local optima.
5. **Expand Prompt Fragment Pool**
    a. Introduce richer and more diverse prompt fragments in your gene space.
    b. Include examples, tone variations, or domain-specific cues.

Vector Embeddings

Vector embeddings are at the core of modern NLP architectures, including RAG. They convert textual data into numerical vectors in a continuous vector space, capturing semantic relationships between words, phrases, or entire documents. Types of embeddings include static word embeddings (Word2Vec, GloVe), contextual embeddings (BERT, RoBERTa), and document-level embeddings.

In RAG systems, embeddings play a dual role. First, they represent the query in a dense format suitable for retrieval. Second, they represent the documents in the corpus, which are stored and indexed for efficient similarity search. Embeddings enhance the model's ability to handle synonymy, paraphrasing, and language variability, which are common challenges in text-based retrieval tasks. They are essential for finding semantically relevant information from a large corpus of documents.

1. **Semantic Understanding:** Embeddings transform raw text (queries and documents) into **dense numerical vectors** that represent semantic meaning. This allows the system to understand **conceptual similarity** rather than relying on exact keyword matches.
2. **Query and Document Matching**
    a. The **user query** is embedded into a dense vector using a query encoder.
    b. **All documents** in the corpus are pre-embedded using a document encoder.
    c. The retrieval engine compares the **query vector** against the **document vectors** using similarity measures (for example, cosine similarity).
    d. This allows the model to retrieve **semantically similar documents**, even when there is little lexical overlap between the query and documents.

3. **Efficient Retrieval via Vector Indexing**: Embeddings make it possible to **index documents** in a high-dimensional vector space (using FAISS, ScaNN, and so on), enabling **fast nearest neighbor search** over millions of documents during inference.

4. **Improving Generation Quality:** Since the **generator in RAG depends on the retrieved documents**, the quality of embeddings directly influences the **context quality**, which in turn affects the final **generated response**.

Indexing in RAG Systems

Indexing is the process of organizing the dense vector embeddings of documents into a structure that allows efficient retrieval. Since vector comparisons in high-dimensional spaces can be computationally intensive, indexing techniques aim to make retrieval scalable and fast, even with millions of documents.

Common indexing tools include:

- **Facebook AI Similarity Search (FAISS):** Uses clustering and inverted file structures for high-speed similarity search.
- **Scalable Nearest Neighbors (ScaNN):** Optimized for Google-scale retrieval with support for quantization and re-ranking.
- **Approximate Nearest Neighbors Oh Yeah (Annoy):** Employs tree-based search structures suitable for memory-constrained environments.

RAG Workflow and Inference Pipeline

The typical RAG inference workflow involves several stages:

1. **Query Encoding**: The input query is embedded into a dense vector.
2. **Retrieval**: Top-k relevant document vectors are retrieved from the indexed document store using similarity search.
3. **Fusion**: Retrieved documents are paired with the query and passed to the generator.
4. **Generation**: A pre-trained generative model such as BART or T5 generates the final output by attending to both query and retrieved documents.

The Retrieval-Augmented Generation (RAG) pipeline code from **Chapter_12.ipynb** is explained below.

It showcases a **complete end-to-end RAG system**, implemented using various LangChain modules, embeddings, vector stores, a retriever, routing logic, document grading, and a final generative answering step.

Key RAG Elements Present in the Code

- **Document Loading and Splitting**
    - Web documents are loaded using **`WebBaseLoader`** and split into chunks using **`RecursiveCharacterTextSplitter`**.
- **Embedding and Vector Store Creation**
    - Dense vector embeddings are created via **`NomicEmbeddings`**, and stored in **`SKLearnVectorStore`**.
    - This forms the **retrieval backbone** of the RAG architecture.
- **Retriever Setup**
    - A retriever is initialized to fetch top-k similar documents based on user queries – a core component of RAG.
- **Query Routing Logic**
    - The model routes queries either to **vectorstore** or **web search**, depending on the question domain.
    - This simulates a hybrid retrieval system – common in advanced RAG architectures.
- **Document Relevance Grading**
    - Retrieved documents are assessed using an LLM to ensure they are relevant to the query before generation. This adds **retrieval validation.**
- **Answer Generation**
    - A generation prompt is formatted and passed to a local LLM using **`ChatOllama`**, which generates an answer **conditioned on retrieved context** – the essence of **generation in RAG**.
- **Indexing Component:** The code uses **`SKLearnVectorStore`**, where dense embeddings are stored and used for similarity retrieval. Although not using FAISS explicitly, **`SKLearnVectorStore` performs the same role of indexing document embeddings**, ensuring fast nearest neighbor search during retrieval.

The results of the code are shown as follows. The code can be found in **`Chapter_12.ipynb`**

```
# Test
docs = retriever.invoke(question)
docs_txt = format_docs(docs)
rag_prompt_formatted = rag_prompt.format(context=docs_txt,
question=question)
generation = llm.invoke([HumanMessage(content=rag_prompt_formatted)])
print(generation.content)
```

```
Chain of Thought (CoT) prompting is a technique used in natural
language processing to generate human-like responses by iterative-
ly asking questions and refining the search space through external
search queries, such as Wikipedia APIs. CoT prompting involves de-
composing problems into multiple thought steps, generating multiple
thoughts per step, and evaluating each state using a classifier or
majority vote. The goal is to find an optimal instruction that leads
to the desired output, which can be achieved by optimizing prompt
parameters directly on the embedding space via gradient descent or
searching over a pool of model-generated instruction candidates.
```

Now that you have understood the complete implementation of a Retrieval-Augmented Generation (RAG) system–including document loading, embedding, indexing, retrieval, and generation–it is time to explore how we can take this architecture a step further. While the RAG pipeline is highly effective, its success heavily depends on the quality of the embeddings used during retrieval. Poorly tuned or domain-insensitive embeddings can lead to irrelevant document retrieval and suboptimal responses. To address this challenge, we now shift our focus toward **Enhancing Embedding Quality in RAG Systems Using Genetic Algorithms (GAs)**. In the following section, we will explore how GAs can be applied to optimize embedding spaces, improve semantic alignment between queries and documents, and ultimately elevate the retrieval performance and response quality of RAG systems.

Enhancing Embedding Quality in RAG Systems Using GAs

While **embeddings are the backbone of retrieval systems in RAG**, the **quality of these embeddings directly determines how relevant, diverse, and accurate the retrieved content is**, which ultimately impacts the performance of the entire generation process. In this section, we explore how **Genetic Algorithms (GAs)** can be effectively used to enhance **embedding quality and retrieval effectiveness** in RAG systems.

Why Embedding Quality Matters in RAG

In a typical Retrieval-Augmented Generation pipeline, document and query texts are converted into dense vector representations using pre-trained embedding models (for example, BERT, Sentence-BERT, Nomic Embeddings). These embeddings are intended to preserve the **semantic similarity** between text pairs. However, in real-world applications, off-the-shelf embeddings may not always capture domain-specific nuances, rare terminology, or user-specific contexts. This leads to poor retrieval performance–irrelevant documents may be passed to the generator, which then produces low-quality or hallucinated responses.

Improving the embedding quality, therefore, becomes crucial, particularly in domains such as healthcare, legal tech, education, or enterprise applications, where semantic accuracy is paramount.

Role of Genetic Algorithms in Optimizing Embedding Quality

Genetic Algorithms (GAs) can be used to **optimize the embedding space**, the **embedding model's configuration**, or **fine-tuning processes**, leading to more effective representations. Here is how:

- **Embedding Space Transformation:** GAs can evolve transformation matrices or neural layers that **post-process embeddings**. These evolved transformations can better align query and document embeddings, making the similarity scores more meaningful.

For example:

  - A GA can search for a matrix W such that `W * embedding_vector` better clusters relevant document-query pairs.
  - The fitness function evaluates how well transformed embeddings improve retrieval accuracy (measured via Recall@K, MRR, or NDCG).

- **Embedding Model Hyperparameter Tuning:** GAs can be used to tune **hyperparameters of embedding models**, such as:
  - Learning rate during fine-tuning
  - Dropout rate
  - Layer selection (for example, which layer outputs from a transformer model yield better embeddings)
  - Pooling strategy (mean pooling, max pooling, CLS token, and so on)

The fitness function can be defined using retrieval metrics on a validation dataset, helping evolve an optimal combination of parameters.

- **Feature Selection in Text Representations:** Before embedding, GAs can help identify **important words, n-grams, or syntactic features** that influence embedding quality. Feature selection ensures that only semantically rich components of text are passed through the embedding pipeline, enhancing signal-to-noise ratio in the final vector.

GA-Based Fine-Tuning of Embedding Models

Another approach is to use GAs for **evolving a training dataset or loss function configuration** during embedding model fine-tuning:

- GAs can evolve **data sampling strategies**, identifying the most effective subset of training pairs that lead to better generalization.
- GAs can help identify **custom loss weighting schemes**, improving contrastive or triplet learning strategies during the training of dual encoders in DPR-style retrieval.

For instance, instead of treating all training samples equally, a GA can assign weights to training samples based on how much they contribute to improving retrieval performance–based on fitness metrics defined during evolution.

Genetic Evolution of Domain-Specific Embeddings

GAs are particularly beneficial for **domain-specific RAG systems**, where standard embedding models underperform due to domain-specific jargon or data sparsity. In such cases, a GA can:

- Evolve custom embedding projections for niche terminology.
- Optimize adapter layers for language models used as retrievers.
- Select or evolve combinations of multiple embedding spaces (hybrid embedding systems).

This results in **embedding spaces more tailored to the retrieval needs of the domain**, improving precision and reducing hallucination in generation tasks.

Practical Workflow Example

A sample GA-based embedding optimization workflow for RAG may look like:

1. Initialize population of transformations or hyperparameter sets.
2. For each individual (solution):
    a. Apply transformation or configuration.
    b. Generate embeddings for a query set and document corpus.
    c. Run retrieval using similarity search.
    d. Evaluate using retrieval metrics (for example, Recall@10).
3. Select top-performing solutions, apply crossover and mutation.
4. Repeat for multiple generations until convergence.

This process continuously evolves embedding quality to match the retrieval requirements of a given task or domain.

The Concept Mapping and Code

Before we jump into the code, let us understand the concept mapping.

GA Concept	Meaning in This Code Example
Gene	A single scalar value in the embedding transformation matrix W (a float weight)
Chromosome	A full flattened transformation matrix W (of shape `embedding_dim` x `embedding_dim`)
Parent	A transformation matrix W that yields high cosine similarity between query and docs
Population	A set of different candidate projection matrices W to be evaluated by the fitness function
Fitness Function	The average cosine similarity of top-k most relevant embeddings for a given query after transformation
Crossover	Single-point crossover that combines parts of two W matrices from selected parents
Mutation	Randomly modifying some weights in the transformation matrix (for example, 10% of weights)
Selection	Selecting top-performing matrices W (based on fitness) as parents for the next generation

Table 12.1: *GA Concepts and associated meanings*

To understand how to install OLlama on Windows, go to this Video Tutorial, https://www.youtube.com/watch?v=LptVU0B6rt4&t=157s

We have implemented an end-to-end code under Chapter_12, , explained as follows. Let us understand, what happens to the Embeddings .

In this code, shared in **`Chapter 12.ipynb`**, a pre-trained embedding model (NomicEmbeddings) is used to convert text documents into dense numerical vectors. These vectors capture the semantic meaning of the text and form the basis for retrieving relevant information later in the Retrieval-Augmented Generation (RAG) process.

Initially, the raw documents are split into smaller chunks to improve granularity. Each chunk is passed to the embedding model, which generates a corresponding dense vector (embedding). These original embeddings are stored in a high-dimensional space where similar content lies closer together.

However, these embeddings are static and not necessarily optimal for the specific retrieval task at hand. To improve the retrieval quality, a transformation matrix is applied to the embeddings. This transformation is designed to reshape the embedding space in a way that improves the semantic alignment between queries and documents.

What the Genetic Algorithm (GA) Is Doing

The Genetic Algorithm is used to discover an optimal transformation matrix for the embedding space. Each solution in the GA population represents a candidate transformation matrix. The GA iteratively improves this matrix through the process of selection, crossover, and mutation.

For each generation, the GA evaluates how well a transformation improves the retrieval performance. This is done by applying the matrix to the embeddings, performing a cosine similarity search between a sample query and the transformed embeddings, and scoring the quality of the top retrieved documents.

Solutions with higher fitness scores (that is, better retrieval performance) are more likely to be selected for the next generation. Over successive iterations, the GA converges on a matrix that best optimizes the embedding space for retrieval. The final, best-performing matrix is then used to transform the full set of document embeddings, which are used in the RAG retrieval process.

This results in a more effective retriever that helps the language model generate more accurate and contextually relevant responses.

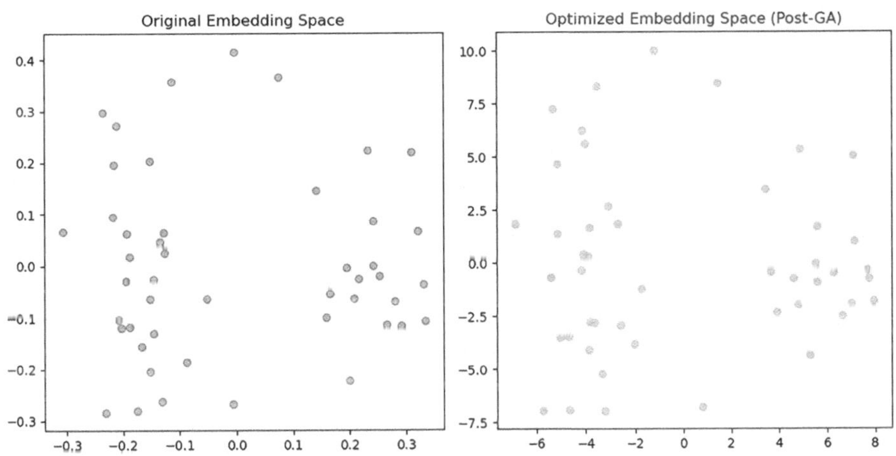

Figure 12.4: *Difference between original and GA-optimized embeddings is not visibly distinct*

Feature Selection and Fine-Tuning

As we observed, the difference between the original and GA-optimized embeddings may not always be visibly distinct in 2D visualizations. However, this does not imply that the optimization is ineffective. Instead, it highlights that the improvements made by the Genetic Algorithm (GA) are often subtle yet impactful in the higher-dimensional embedding space. To better understand the significance of these enhancements, we now shift our perspective to interpret this process as a form of **indirect feature selection** and **lightweight fine-tuning** of the embedding space. The transformation matrix evolved by GA strategically re-weights embedding dimensions, emphasizing more relevant semantic features while suppressing less useful ones. This acts like an intelligent feature selector and a post-processing fine-tuning mechanism—without altering the underlying embedding model. In the next section, we will explain how this perspective enhances retrieval performance and how GAs can be leveraged effectively to reshape the embedding space for domain-specific applications.

Enhancing GA Optimization and Interpreting It as Feature Selection and Fine-Tuning

In cases where the difference between original and GA-optimized embeddings is not visually apparent in 2D projections, it is essential to understand that the true optimization may lie within the high-dimensional embedding space. To address this and improve the effectiveness of GA optimization, we explore both **technical enhancements** to the optimization process and a conceptual interpretation of how Genetic Algorithms function as **feature selectors** and **lightweight fine-tuning mechanisms** for embedding spaces. The code is available in `Chapter_12.ipynb`

Improving GA Optimization: Strategies and Techniques

- **Enhanced Fitness Function Design:** The current approach evaluates fitness based solely on the average cosine similarity between a query and its top-retrieved documents. This measure, while useful, can be refined to better guide the evolutionary process. A more effective fitness function may incorporate:
    - A **weighted sum of top-k similarity scores**, not just the mean.
    - A **penalty for low variance**, encouraging more discriminative and well-spread embeddings.
    - Integration of **retrieval-specific metrics** such as precision, recall, or F1-score, especially when labeled data is available for benchmarking.

  Example modification:

  ```
  score = np.mean(sims[top_k_indices]) +
  np.std(sims[top_k_indices])
  ```
- **Expanding the Genetic Search Space:** To allow the GA to explore a broader solution landscape and escape local optima:
    - Increase the number of generations (for example, from 20 to 50 or more).

    - Increase the number of solutions per population (for example, from 10 to 30).
    - Increase the mutation rate or use adaptive mutation strategies to maintain diversity throughout generations.
- **Embedding Normalization Post-Transformation:** After applying the transformation matrix W to the embeddings, it is critical to **re-normalize** them before computing similarity. This ensures cosine similarity computations remain scale-invariant and effective:

```
transformed_embeddings = transformed_embeddings / (np.linalg.
norm(transformed_embeddings, axis=1, keepdims=True) + 1e-10)
transformed_query = transformed_query / (np.linalg.norm(trans-
formed_query) + 1e-10)
```

- **Improved Visualization Techniques:** PCA, being linear, might fail to capture subtle but meaningful structural differences. Consider switching to nonlinear dimensionality reduction methods such as **t-SNE** or **UMAP** to better visualize and compare the clustering behavior and separability of the embedding space before and after optimization.

```
from sklearn.manifold import TSNE
tsne = TSNE(n_components=2, perplexity=30, n_iter=3000)
original_2d = tsne.fit_transform(original_embeddings)
optimized_2d = tsne.fit_transform(optimized_embeddings)
```

- **Multiple Query-Based Evaluation:** Using a single query for fitness evaluation may lead to an embedding space that is narrowly optimized. Instead, using a **diverse set of queries** helps the GA produce a transformation that is robust across varying retrieval intents:

```
total_score = 0
for query in sample_queries:
    query_embedding = embedding_model.embed_query(query)
    transformed_query = np.dot(query_embedding, W.T)
    transformed_query = transformed_query / (np.linalg.
norm(transformed_query) + 1e-10)
    sims = transformed_embeddings @ transformed_query
    top_k = sims.argsort()[-3:]
    total_score += np.mean(sims[top_k])
return total_score / len(sample_queries)
```

- **Dimensionality Reduction Before Optimization (Optional):** If embedding vectors are extremely high-dimensional, applying PCA to reduce the dimensionality before running GA may speed up the process and reduce search complexity. The GA then evolves a smaller transformation matrix, which is computationally efficient yet effective.

Interpretation: Feature Selection and Fine-Tuning via Genetic Algorithms

- **Feature Selection (Indirect, Soft Selection):** The transformation matrix W, evolved during the optimization process, essentially performs a **weighted reconfiguration of the embedding space**. Certain embedding dimensions are magnified, while others are suppressed, based on how much they contribute to better retrieval performance. This behavior mimics the principle of **feature selection**, where only the most relevant features are emphasized in downstream tasks. Unlike traditional filter- or wrapper-based feature selection, this approach performs **learned selection** through evolutionary pressure in the fitness landscape.
- **Lightweight Fine-Tuning of Embedding Space:** Traditional fine-tuning of embeddings involves backpropagation and labeled datasets to modify the model's weights. In contrast, GA does not update model parameters; instead, it operates externally by **learning a transformation layer** on top of existing embeddings. This transformation reshapes the embedding space to better suit domain-specific tasks or objectives (for example, improving retrieval accuracy or semantic alignment), effectively achieving **post-hoc fine-tuning**. This makes the method especially suitable for scenarios with limited labels or when full model fine-tuning is computationally prohibitive.

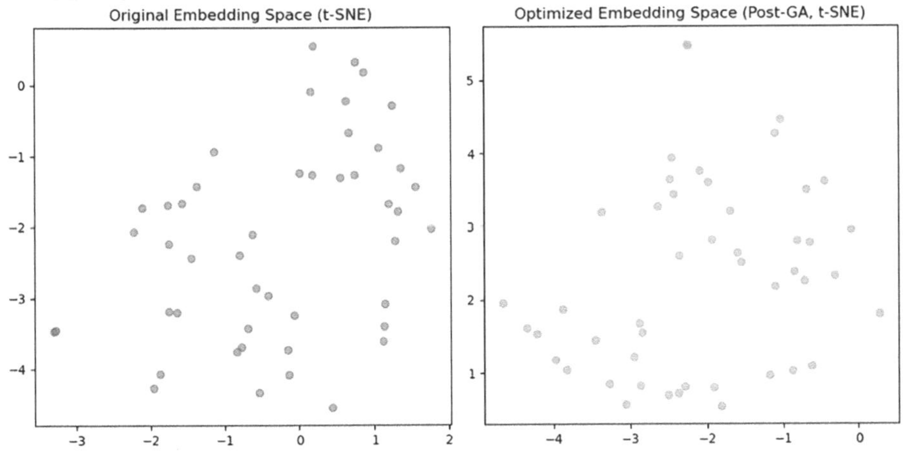


```
Top Retrieved Documents:

Doc 1:
[21] Chen et al. "Program of Thoughts Prompting: Disentangling Computation from Reasoning for Numerical Reasoning Tasks." arXiv preprint arXiv:2211.12588
(2022).
[22] Gao et al. "PAL: Program-aided language models." arXiv preprint arXiv:2211.10435 (2022).
[23] Parisi et al. "TALM: Tool Augmented Lan
***
Doc 2:
References#
[1] Zhao et al. "Calibrate Before Use: Improving Few-shot Performance of Language Models." ICML 2021
[2] Liu et al. "What Makes Good In-Context Examples for GPT-3?" arXiv preprint arXiv:2101.06804 (2021).
[3] Lu et al. "Fantastically Ordered Prompts and Where to Find Them: Overcoming Few
---
Doc 3:
For example to produce education materials for kids,

Describe what is quantum physics to a 6-year-old.

And safe content,

... in language that is safe for work.
In-context instruction learning (Ye et al. 2023) combines few-shot learning with instruction prompting. It incorporates multiple demonstr
```

Figure 12.5: *The image implies that the Genetic Algorithm has effectively learned a transformation matrix that brings semantically similar documents closer, separates dissimilar ones more clearly, and improves document-query alignment, leading to better retrieval performance*

Sentiment Analysis and the Role of Genetic Algorithms

Sentiment analysis is a natural language processing (NLP) task that involves identifying and categorizing opinions expressed in text, typically as positive, negative, or neutral. It is widely used in customer feedback analysis, brand monitoring, market research, and social media analytics. The effectiveness of sentiment analysis directly impacts decision-making in business, politics, and product development.

Achieving accurate sentiment classification often depends on effective feature representation and model tuning. This is where Genetic Algorithms (GAs) come into play. GAs, inspired by natural evolution, optimize model parameters, select relevant features, and evolve better solutions across generations using operators such as selection, crossover, and mutation. When applied to sentiment analysis, GAs can enhance text classification by:

- Selecting the most informative TF-IDF features.
- Tuning model hyperparameters such as learning rate, depth, and regularization.
- Improving generalization by avoiding overfitting through evolutionary selection.

By combining GAs with advanced classifiers such as MLP, CatBoost, and XGBoost, we can significantly boost performance, especially in complex, ambiguous, or noisy sentiment datasets.

Purpose of TF-IDF Embedding

Frequency–Inverse Document Frequency (TF-IDF) embedding is a powerful technique for converting textual data into numerical features that can be used by machine learning models. It reflects how important a word is to a document in a corpus by balancing its frequency in a single text (TF) against how common it is across all documents (IDF). This helps highlight meaningful terms while reducing the weight of common, less informative words. In sentiment analysis, TF-IDF enables models such as CatBoost and XGBoost to identify and learn patterns from discriminative words and phrases, thereby improving classification accuracy and reducing noise in feature representation.

You can use a vector database in sentiment analysis, especially for tasks involving semantic search, clustering, or retrieval-augmented classification. Instead of TF-IDF, more advanced embedding techniques such as Sentence-BERT (SBERT), Universal Sentence Encoder, or transformer-based models (for example, BERT, RoBERTa) can be used to generate dense vector representations that capture contextual meaning. These embeddings can be stored in a vector database such as FAISS, Milvus, or Qdrant. This enables efficient similarity search, sentiment-aware document retrieval, and hybrid classification workflows. Compared to TF-IDF, semantic embeddings offer richer representation, helping models understand nuances, emotions, and ambiguous sentiments more effectively in unstructured text data. Now that we understand, let us start a sentiment analysis with a simple dataset as shown below.

text	label
I love this	1
I love this	1
I love this	1
Do not rec	0
Do not rec	0
I hate this	0
Best perfc	1
I hate this	0
Worst per	0
I love this	1
Amazing e	1
It was awf	0
I hate this	0

Figure 12.6: *Snapshot of the simple dataset; the dataset can be found in the book chapter12*

The following code demonstrates the use of a Genetic Algorithm (GA) to optimize feature transformation for sentiment classification. It begins by installing the pygad library and importing essential modules such as pandas, numpy, and components from scikit-learn. A synthetic sentiment dataset is loaded and split into training and testing sets. The text data is converted into numerical representations using the TF-IDF vectorization technique.

A custom fitness function is defined to guide the GA. In this function, each GA solution represents a weight matrix used to transform TF-IDF embeddings. These transformed embeddings are then used to train a logistic regression classifier. The classification accuracy on the test set serves as the fitness score.

The GA is configured with parameters such as number of generations, population size, mutation rate, and crossover type. It optimizes the weight matrix to enhance classifier performance. After GA execution, the best solution is reshaped into a transformation matrix and used to re-transform the training and test data.

A final logistic regression model is trained using the optimized embeddings. The model's predictions are evaluated using a classification report, providing metrics such as precision, recall, and F1-score, thereby validating the effectiveness of the GA-optimized feature transformation.

```
# Install library
# Import libraries

!pip install pygad
import matplotlib.pyplot as plt
import pandas as pd
```

```
import numpy as np
from sklearn.model_selection import train_test_split
from sklearn.feature_extraction.text import TfidfVectorizer
from sklearn.linear_model import LogisticRegression
from sklearn.metrics import classification_report
import pygad

# Step 1: Load Dataset
df = pd.read_csv('/content/sample_data/synthetic_sentiment_data-
set.csv')

# Step 2: Split Dataset
X_train, X_test, y_train, y_test = train_test_split(df['text'],
df['label'], test_size=0.2, random_state=42)

# Step 3: TF-IDF Embedding
vectorizer = TfidfVectorizer()
X_train_vec = vectorizer.fit_transform(X_train).toarray()
X_test_vec = vectorizer.transform(X_test).toarray()
embedding_dim = X_train_vec.shape[1]

# Step 4: Define Fitness Function
def fitness_func(ga_instance, solution, solution_idx):
    W = solution.reshape(embedding_dim, embedding_dim)
    transformed_train = np.dot(X_train_vec, W.T)
    model = LogisticRegression(max_iter=500)
    model.fit(transformed_train, y_train)
    transformed_test = np.dot(X_test_vec, W.T)
    score = model.score(transformed_test, y_test)
    return score

# Step 5: Run Genetic Algorithm
ga_instance = pygad.GA(
    num_generations=30,
    sol_per_pop=10,
    num_parents_mating=5,
    fitness_func=fitness_func,
    num_genes=embedding_dim * embedding_dim,
    init_range_low=-1.0,
    init_range_high=1.0,
    mutation_percent_genes=20,
    mutation_type="random",
    crossover_type="single_point"
)

ga_instance.run()
best_solution, best_fitness, _ = ga_instance.best_solution()
```

```
W_best = best_solution.reshape(embedding_dim, embedding_dim)

# Step 6: Train Final Model with Optimized Embeddings
X_train_trans = np.dot(X_train_vec, W_best.T)
X_test_trans = np.dot(X_test_vec, W_best.T)

final_model = LogisticRegression(max_iter=500)
final_model.fit(X_train_trans, y_train)
y_pred = final_model.predict(X_test_trans)

# Step 7: Evaluation
report = classification_report(y_test, y_pred)
print("Classification Report:\n")
print(report)
# Plot fitness progress across generations
plt.figure(figsize=(10, 5))
plt.plot(ga_instance.best_solutions_fitness, marker='o',
linestyle='-')
plt.title("Genetic Algorithm Fitness Across Generations")
plt.xlabel("Generation")
plt.ylabel("Best Fitness Score (Accuracy)")
plt.grid(True)
plt.tight_layout()
plt.show()
```

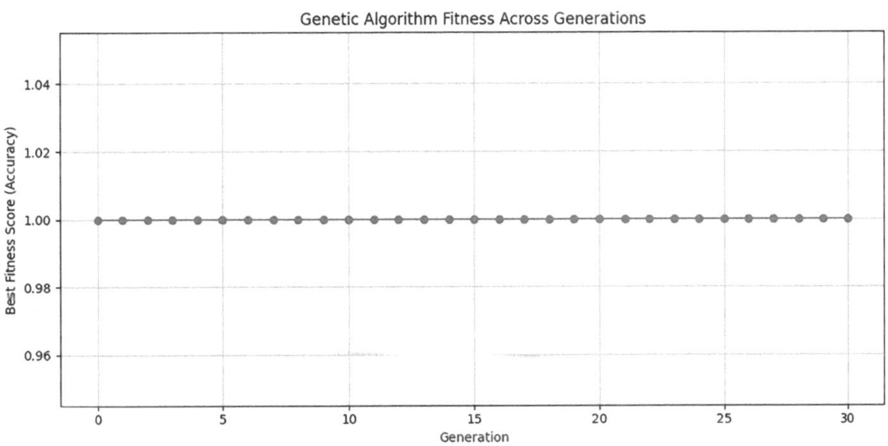

Figure 12.7: *The plot shows that the best fitness score (accuracy) achieved by the Genetic Algorithm remains constant at 1.0 across all generations*

Our synthetic dataset has **highly distinct sentences** – TF-IDF alone can perfectly separate positive and negative classes. Hence, even without optimization, the classifier achieves near-perfect accuracy. GA has no room to improve further, so fitness stays flat.

Now, we transition to a more complex dataset multi-class, multi-label sentiment classification dataset that reflects real-world challenges in natural language processing (NLP). It contains sentences labeled not only with one of the three sentiment classes–positive, negative, or neutral–but also incorporates an additional layer of complexity through emotion labels, making it suitable for multi-label classification tasks. What makes this dataset particularly challenging is the presence of ambiguous and contextually subtle sentences, where the sentiment and emotion are not clearly distinguishable. Many sentences contain sarcasm, mixed emotions, or overlapping semantic cues that make it hard for a model to make deterministic decisions. Furthermore, class imbalance across sentiment and emotion categories adds another layer of difficulty, impacting model generalization. The inclusion of overlapping sentiment-emotion combinations simulates real-world scenarios where a single piece of text can exhibit multiple subjective tones. Additionally, noise in natural language, such as colloquialisms, slang, and ambiguous phrasing, increases the difficulty for traditional models to learn effective decision boundaries. This makes it an ideal benchmark to test the robustness and adaptability of advanced machine learning algorithms such as CatBoost and XGBoost, especially when paired with optimization techniques such as feature selection, TF-IDF embedding, and evolutionary strategies.

	A	B	C	D	E	F	G
1	text	sentiment	emotion				
2	I absolutely loved the performance	positive	joy				
3	Visually appealing but emotionally flat	neutral	indifference				
4	This movie was breathtaking	positive	awe				
5	A shallow and meaningless film	negative	disgust				
6	The characters were incredibly well developed	positive	joy				
7	Mixed feelings about the ending	neutral	confusion				
8	The characters were incredibly well developed	positive	joy				
9	I absolutely loved the performance	positive	joy				
10	Highly engaging and emotionally touching	positive	joy				
11	Definitely worth a watch	positive	joy				
12	The characters were incredibly well developed	positive	joy				
13	A waste of time and money	negative	disgust				
14	Mixed feelings about the ending	neutral	confusion				
15	I absolutely loved the performance	positive	joy				
16	Mixed feelings about the ending	neutral	confusion				
17	The movie was painfully slow and boring	negative	boredom				
18	A masterpiece of storytelling	positive	pride				
19	Completely unwatchable	negative	disgust				
20	Disappointing experience from start to finish	negative	disappointment				
21	Best cinematic experience in years	positive	satisfaction				
22	This movie was breathtaking	positive	awe				
23	Mixed feelings about the ending	neutral	confusion				
24	The movie was average overall	neutral	neutral				
25	A waste of time and money	negative	disgust				
26	Completely unwatchable	negative	disgust				
27	Poorly directed and badly written	negative	anger				
28	I absolutely loved the performance	positive	joy				
29	Visually appealing but emotionally flat	neutral	indifference				
30	The movie was average overall	neutral	neutral				
31	Completely unwatchable	negative	disgust				

Figure 12.8: *Snapshot of Complex dataset, the dataset can be found in the book chapter_12*

Our focus is multi class classification with MLP. The following code illustrates the application of a Multi-Layer Perceptron (MLP) classifier for a multi-class sentiment classification task using TF-IDF embeddings. It begins by installing and importing required libraries, including modules for text processing, machine learning, and data visualization. A complex multi-class sentiment dataset is loaded, where the text column is used as input features and the sentiment column as target labels.

The dataset is split into training and testing subsets using stratified sampling to preserve class distribution. The text data is then transformed into numerical vectors using the TF-IDF technique, limited to a maximum of 1000 features for dimensionality reduction.

An MLP classifier with a single hidden layer of 64 neurons is initialized. The model is trained iteratively over 30 epochs using the **`warm_start=True`** parameter to simulate manual tracking of learning progress. After each epoch, training and testing accuracies are recorded to evaluate the model's performance over time.

Finally, the model is evaluated using a classification report and a confusion matrix. Visualization is done through a heatmap for class-wise prediction analysis and a line plot showing accuracy trends across epochs. This approach provides insights into how the model's performance evolves with training iterations.

```
# Install required libraries
!pip install scikit-learn
# Imports
import pandas as pd
import numpy as np
import matplotlib.pyplot as plt
from sklearn.model_selection import train_test_split
from sklearn.feature_extraction.text import TfidfVectorizer
from sklearn.neural_network import MLPClassifier
from sklearn.metrics import classification_report,
confusion_matrix, accuracy_score
import seaborn as sns

# Load dataset
df = pd.read_csv('/content/sample_data/complex_multiclass_multi-
label_sentiment_dataset.csv')

# Use 'sentiment' column for multi-class classification
y = df['sentiment']
X = df['text']

# Train-Test Split
X_train, X_test, y_train, y_test = train_test_split(X, y, test_
size=0.2, stratify=y, random_state=42)
```

```
# TF-IDF Embedding
vectorizer = TfidfVectorizer(max_features=1000)
X_train_vec = vectorizer.fit_transform(X_train).toarray()
X_test_vec = vectorizer.transform(X_test).toarray()

# Track fitness (accuracy) across iterations manually (simulated)
train_scores = []
test_scores = []
epochs = range(1, 31)
# MLP Classifier
model = MLPClassifier(hidden_layer_sizes=(64,), max_iter=1, warm_
start=True, random_state=42)
for epoch in epochs:
  model.fit(X_train_vec, y_train)
  train_acc = model.score(X_train_vec, y_train)
  test_acc = model.score(X_test_vec, y_test)
  train_scores.append(train_acc)
  test_scores.append(test_acc)

# Final Evaluation
print("Classification Report:\n")
y_pred = model.predict(X_test_vec)
print(classification_report(y_test, y_pred))
print("Confusion Matrix:")
cm = confusion_matrix(y_test, y_pred)
sns.heatmap(cm, annot=True, fmt='d', cmap='Blues',
xticklabels=model.classes_, yticklabels=model.classes_)
plt.title("Confusion Matrix - MLP (TF-IDF)")
plt.xlabel("Predicted")
plt.ylabel("Actual")
plt.tight_layout()
plt.show()

# Accuracy Plot
plt.figure(figsize=(10, 4))
plt.plot(epochs, train_scores, label='Train Accuracy',
marker='o')
plt.plot(epochs, test_scores, label='Test Accuracy', marker='s')
plt.title("Fitness (Accuracy) Across Epochs - MLP with TF-IDF")
plt.xlabel("Epoch")
plt.ylabel("Accuracy")
plt.ylim(0, 1.05)
plt.legend()
plt.grid(True)
plt.tight_layout()
plt.show()
```

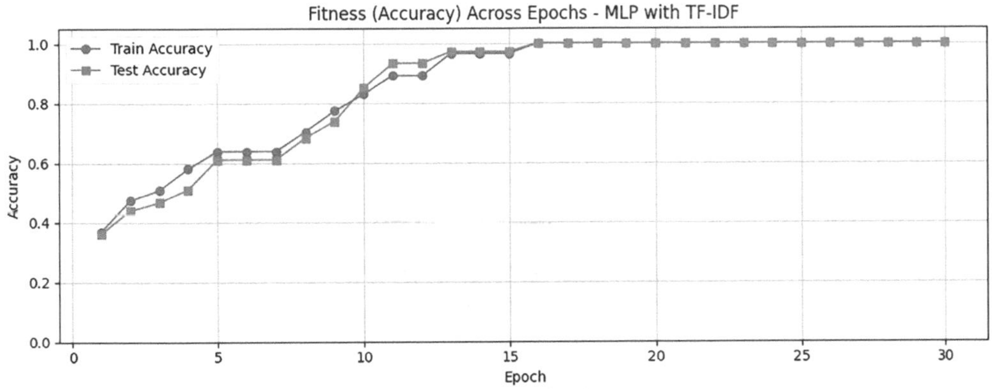

Figure 12.9**: Theplot shows that both training and testing accuracy of the MLP classifier consistently improve across epochs, eventually reaching near-perfect accuracy, indicating effective learning and generalization on the* ***complex_multiclass_multilabel_sentiment_dataset

You may apply more complex models such as CatBoost or XGBoost. The code can be found in **`Chapter_12.ipynb`** on the **emotion** column in the dataset.

Conclusion

This chapter demonstrated how Genetic Algorithms (GAs) can enhance multi-class sentiment analysis and embedding-based retrieval in NLP. We began with RAG, prompt engineering, and embedding optimization, using GAs to evolve transformation matrices that improved semantic representation. These optimized embeddings were shown to boost downstream performance both visually and quantitatively.

Text was vectorized using TF-IDF, and GAs performed evolutionary feature selection to amplify relevant features and suppress noise. The refined features fed into an MLP classifier improved sentiment classification across positive, negative, and neutral classes.

We also applied GAs to Retrieval-Augmented Generation (RAG), aligning embedding spaces for better document-query relevance. Overall, this hybrid approach demonstrated how evolutionary optimization can be combined with machine learning to create more accurate, interpretable, and semantically aware NLP systems.

In the next chapter, we will build a bridge between Genetic Algorithms and Reinforcement Learning, exploring their integration and applications across dynamic decision-making and adaptive optimization tasks.

CHAPTER 13
Applying Reinforcement Learning to Genetic Algorithms

Introduction

This chapter explores the integration of **Genetic Algorithms (GAs)** within **Reinforcement Learning (RL)** frameworks to enhance agent performance and learning efficiency. By leveraging evolutionary principles, GAs offer an alternative approach to optimizing **policies, reward structures**, and **exploration strategies** in RL environments. Unlike traditional RL methods such as **Q-learning** or **deep reinforcement learning**, GA-based techniques evolve solutions over generations, often proving effective in complex or sparse-reward settings.

Using **PyGAD**, we present practical examples where GAs are applied to **game-playing tasks**, showcasing how they can evolve intelligent agents without relying on gradient-based learning. This chapter also examines the comparative advantages of GAs, including robustness to local optima and flexibility in non-differentiable environments.

Structure

In this chapter, we will discuss the following topics:

- Optimization Using Genetic Algorithms
- Tuning Reward Functions with Evolutionary Strategies
- Genetic Algorithms for Exploration-Exploitation Balance

- Evolving Intelligent Model for Games
- Comparative Analysis: GAs Versus Q-Learning and Deep RL

Optimization Using Genetic Algorithms

Before diving deeper into how Genetic Algorithms can enhance and complement reinforcement learning systems, it is essential to build a foundational understanding of **Reinforcement Learning (RL)** itself. RL is a core paradigm in machine learning where agents learn to make decisions through interactions with an environment, driven by rewards and penalties. Understanding the **key concepts, structure, and various types of RL approaches**—including value-based, policy-based, and actor-critic methods—lays the groundwork for appreciating the role GAs can play in optimizing these systems. In the following section, we will explore the fundamentals of reinforcement learning, discuss its primary components, and differentiate between popular RL variants. This foundation will set the stage for understanding how evolutionary algorithms can be integrated effectively within these learning architectures.

Reinforcement Learning and its Variants

Reinforcement Learning (RL) is a paradigm within machine learning where an agent learns to make decisions by interacting with an environment. Unlike supervised learning, where models are trained on labeled data, or unsupervised learning, where models uncover hidden patterns in unlabeled data, RL centers on trial-and-error experience. The goal of an RL agent is to learn an optimal policy—a strategy for choosing actions—that maximizes cumulative reward over time.

In RL, the agent receives feedback in the form of rewards or penalties based on the actions it takes. These actions influence not only immediate outcomes but also future states and possibilities, making RL particularly powerful for sequential decision-making problems such as robotics, game playing, portfolio optimization, resource allocation, and intelligent control systems.

Core Concepts of Reinforcement Learning

An RL problem is typically formulated as a Markov Decision Process (MDP), which includes:

- **State (S):** A representation of the current environment.
- **Action (A):** The set of all possible decisions the agent can take.
- **Reward (R):** Scalar feedback received after performing an action.
- **Policy (π):** A mapping from states to actions.
- **Value Function (V):** An estimate of expected future rewards from a state.

- **Q-Function (Q):** The expected reward for taking an action in a given state and following the policy thereafter.

Types of Reinforcement Learning

- **Model-Free RL:** The agent learns directly from experience without building an internal model of the environment.

  Examples:

  - **Q-Learning:** A value-based method that learns the optimal action-value function (Q-function) for each state-action pair.
  - **SARSA (State-Action-Reward-State-Action):** Similar to Q-learning, but updates are based on the action actually taken by the current policy.
- **Model-Based RL:**
  - The agent builds a model of the environment and uses it to simulate future outcomes.
  - These methods are generally sample efficient but computationally complex.
- **Policy-Based Methods:**
  - These methods learn the policy directly instead of estimating value functions.
  - Algorithms such as REINFORCE and Proximal Policy Optimization (PPO) fall in this category.
- **Actor-Critic Methods:**
  - These are hybrid models that combine value-based and policy-based approaches. The "*actor*" learns the policy while the "*critic*" estimates value functions.

Multi-Armed Bandits (MAB)

The Multi-Armed Bandit problem is a special case of RL where there is no notion of state or transition. The agent must choose among several possible actions (or "*arms*"), each with an unknown reward distribution. The challenge lies in balancing **exploration** (trying new actions to gather more information) and **exploitation** (choosing actions known to yield high rewards).

MABs are ideal for problems involving static decision-making under uncertainty, such as online advertising, clinical trials, recommendation systems, and A/B testing.

Types of MAB Strategies:

- **Epsilon-Greedy:** With probability epsilon, choose a random arm; otherwise, choose the best-known arm.

- **Upper Confidence Bound (UCB):** Choose the arm with the highest upper confidence bound on expected reward.
- **Thompson Sampling:** A Bayesian approach where arms are selected based on probability distributions of expected rewards.

Contextual Multi-Armed Bandits (CMAB)

Traditional MABs do not consider the context in which decisions are made. In many real-world scenarios, such context is crucial. **Contextual MABs** extend MABs by incorporating side information (context vectors) to make more informed decisions. The context may include user features in a recommendation system, patient history in a medical trial, or environmental parameters in industrial automation.

The goal in CMAB is to learn a policy that maps context to actions to maximize expected reward. Unlike full-scale RL, CMAB models do not consider long-term state transitions, but they provide a powerful compromise between complexity and adaptability.

Applications of CMAB:

- Personalized content delivery
- Dynamic pricing
- Adaptive clinical treatments
- Ad recommendation systems

Deep Contextual MAB

As contexts become high-dimensional and non-linear, traditional linear CMAB models may fail to capture underlying patterns. **Deep Contextual MABs** integrate deep learning models (for example, neural networks) to map complex context vectors to action-reward predictions. These models leverage the representational power of deep learning and are particularly useful when contextual information is rich and non-linearly correlated with rewards.

Choosing Between MAB, CMAB, and Q-Learning

- **Use MAB** when actions are independent of previous choices and there is no state transition dependency.
- **Use CMAB** when there is static but rich contextual information influencing action-reward relationships.
- **Use Q-Learning or other full RL methods** when decisions influence future states and rewards–particularly in dynamic environments where learning long-term strategies is essential.

RL offers a spectrum of tools, from simple bandit algorithms to complex deep actor-critic architectures. The choice of method depends on problem structure, data availability, computational complexity, and the trade-off between short-term reward optimization and long-term strategic planning.

While reinforcement learning offers a robust framework for autonomous decision-making, its true value is realized when applied to real-world challenges where adaptive behavior and strategic optimization are critical. One such domain is **gameplay optimization**, where modeling and enhancing player experience through intelligent reward mechanisms can significantly influence business outcomes. In particular, optimizing the **Return to Player (RTP) score** presents a compelling use case for combining RL techniques with evolutionary strategies such as Genetic Algorithms. Before going into the technical implementation, it is important to first establish the broader **problem context**, understand why RTP modeling matters to game developers, and how it directly relates to **customer satisfaction, player retention, and business revenue**. The next section outlines the problem statement that serves as the driving force behind our modeling approach.

Problem Statement

Modeling RTP Score in Gameplay for Player Retention, Customer Satisfaction, and Revenue Optimization:

Figure 13.1: *This image serves as a representative illustration of online gaming*

Digital gaming or game play—particularly in real-money and casino-style environments such as online slot machines, card games, or table-based games—**player retention and revenue optimization are directly linked to perceived fairness, satisfaction, and**

engagement. One of the most critical variables that governs these outcomes is the **Return to Player (RTP) Score**, which defines the **expected percentage of wagered money that a game returns to the player over time**.

Although RTP is fundamentally a game design metric, in practice, it **directly influences user behavior and business performance. An excessively low RTP** can discourage players by generating feelings of unfairness and loss, triggering **customer dissatisfaction and early churn**. On the other hand, **an overly generous RTP** may compromise long-term profitability and disrupt game balance, leading to **unsustainable revenue models**. Thus, companies must find the **optimal RTP range that maximizes player enjoyment while ensuring revenue integrity**.

Why Companies Need to Model RTP Scores:

- **Minimizing Player Churn:** Players who frequently encounter losses or perceive the game as biased are more likely to stop playing and shift to competing platforms. RTP modeling allows game designers to fine-tune gameplay experience such that **players feel rewarded at the right intervals**, sustaining engagement without financial loss escalation. Modeling RTP scores in real time can help identify **churn-inducing patterns** and correct them early.
- **Boosting Repeat Deposits and Session Frequency:** A well-optimized RTP score indirectly influences **repeat deposit behavior**, as players are more likely to continue investing in a game where **their probability of reward seems fair and consistent**. Modeling RTP scores as a predictive variable allows companies to **identify game configurations, player segments, and in-game strategies** that drive **higher deposit conversion rates and extended play sessions**.
- **Enhancing Customer Satisfaction and Game Loyalty:** RTP is a psychological anchor for players. **Even a small perceived improvement in reward feedback** can significantly enhance user satisfaction. Games that consistently demonstrate well-calibrated RTP behavior are more likely to build **long-term player trust**, foster **brand loyalty**, and increase **customer lifetime value (CLTV)**.
- **Personalized Player Experiences:** Companies can use RTP modeling to **dynamically adapt game difficulty, reward mechanics, or bonus triggers based on player profiles or engagement behavior**. By coupling RTP scores with contextual player analytics, the game can present a **personalized challenge-reward loop** that caters to both casual and experienced players, thereby **expanding the addressable market**.
- **Detecting Anomalies and Fraud:** Anomalous RTP behavior may indicate **game logic exploits, bonus abuse, or technical errors**. Modeling RTP scores enables early detection of such outliers, reducing risks to game balance and profitability.
- **Regulatory Compliance and Transparency:** In regulated gaming industries,

RTP must often be **reported, monitored, and auditable**. Real-time RTP modeling provides a system for **continuous compliance assurance** and **proactive reporting to regulators**, reducing legal exposure and improving brand credibility.

The Link Between RTP and Behavioral Economics

RTP score is not just a metric–it acts as a **behavioral signal** to the player. Research in behavioral economics shows that players react not just to expected payouts, but to **frequency, variance, and perceived control over reward mechanisms**. Therefore, modeling RTP must go beyond static averages and incorporate dynamic, context-sensitive factors such as:

- Time-between-wins,
- Game volatility,
- Win streak patterns,
- Reward timing and magnitude.

To effectively address the challenges outlined in the problem statement–particularly around optimizing RTP scores for improved player retention and business outcomes–a robust modeling approach is required. While traditional reinforcement learning techniques offer significant benefits in dynamic environments, certain problems can be addressed effectively using **evolutionary optimization methods alone**. In this section, we introduce a standalone **Genetic Algorithm (GA)**-based modeling framework for RTP optimization. Leveraging the capabilities of the **PyGAD library**, this approach evolves optimal feature weights that best correlate with the RTP score. This method provides a baseline model that captures the core relationship between gameplay attributes and return outcomes–without the added complexity of reinforcement learning. The simplicity and interpretability of this GA-based approach make it an ideal starting point before advancing into hybrid or contextual learning strategies.

The Approach

What are we trying to do

- **Use a Genetic Algorithm (GA)** to evolve solutions over generations.
- **Improve/guide the evolution** using **Reinforcement Learning (RL)** principles – specifically, **bandit-based exploration-exploitation** to choose better operators or strategies dynamically.

This is like saying: "*Let the Genetic Algorithm run, but let an RL agent or a Bandit agent choose which mutation/crossover/selection strategy works best over time.*"

High-Level Architecture

Component	Role
GA	Evolves solutions using crossover, mutation, selection
RL or MAB agent	Learns which operator or strategy gives better reward (fitness improvement)
Environment	Problem space (for example, optimization problem, feature selection, hyperparameter tuning, and so on)

Table 13.1: *This table describes a hybrid optimization system combining GA with RL or MAB*

Steps for GA + RL (or MAB) Hybrid System

Step 1: Define the Problem Space

- What are you optimizing? (for example, a feature set, a function, a model hyperparameter set)
- Define the chromosome (solution representation)
- Define fitness function

Step 2: Build a Standard Genetic Algorithm First

- Initialize population
- Evaluate fitness
- Selection (tournament, roulette, and so on)
- Crossover (single-point, two-point, and so on)
- Mutation (flip bits, Gaussian noise, and so on)
- Replacement
- Track fitness over generations

Step 3: Introduce Reinforcement Learning or Multi-Armed Bandits

Now, instead of **fixed operators**, you let the agent **choose dynamically** from a set of operators.

Strategy	Example
MAB Agent	Chooses best mutation/crossover strategy based on reward (fitness gain)
RL Agent (Q-learning, DQN)	Learns policy of when to use which operator depending on current state
Contextual Bandits	Use state (for example, generation number, average fitness) to pick best action

Table 13.2: *Strategy–Example mapping for adaptive operator control*

MAB Setup Example:

- **Arms**: [`mutation_A`, `mutation_B`, `crossover_A`, `crossover_B`]
- **Reward**: Fitness improvement from applying that operator
- Agent picks an arm, observes reward, updates belief

How to Prepare Data

Technically, you do not need labeled training data for RL/MAB – you generate data **on-the-fly** during the evolution process.

However, you should:

- Track each operator used per generation
- Track fitness before and after applying it
- Track reward (`Δ fitness`)
- Track state context (generation number, average diversity, and so on)

You can log a dataset like this during GA runs:

Gen	Operator	Pre-Fitness	Post-Fitness	Reward	AvgFitness	Diversity
1	`Mutation_A`	0.65	0.72	+0.07	0.68	0.21
2	`Crossover_B`	0.72	0.75	+0.03	0.70	0.25

Table 13.3: *Gen-wise operator impact on fitness and diversity*

Later, use this to:

- Train a **contextual bandit** or **Q-learning agent**
- Analyze which operator works best in which situations

Key Design Choices

Table 13.4 outlines the key design choices involved in building a learning-guided evolutionary optimization framework. These choices span multiple dimensions, including how fitness is evaluated (for example, accuracy or reward), what genetic operators are available (for example, Mutation A/B, Crossover A/B), how reward signals are defined (for example, change in fitness or success flags), and the selection of reinforcement learning models such as Q-learning, UCB, or Thompson Sampling. Additionally, the state representation used by the learning agent–comprising features such as generation number, average fitness, and diversity score–plays a crucial role in guiding adaptive decision-making and improving the efficiency of the evolutionary process.

Design Element	Options
Fitness Function	Accuracy, loss, reward, and so on
Operator Choices	Mutation A/B, Crossover A/B

Reward	`Δ Fitness, success/failure flag`
RL Model	Q-learning, UCB, Thompson Sampling
State Features	Generation number, avg fitness, diversity score

Table 13.4: *Key design elements for learning-guided evolution*

Let us understand **What Changes** when RTP is the **Optimization Objective**

When Return to Player (RTP) becomes the **core optimization objective**, several aspects of the evolutionary framework undergo significant transformation. Unlike traditional settings where fitness might be measured using generic scores or accuracy metrics, the fitness function is now explicitly defined in terms of RTP or its mathematical transformation. Correspondingly, the chromosome representation shifts to encapsulate domain-specific elements such as betting strategies, decision-making parameters, and behavioral patterns that influence RTP. The overarching optimization goal transitions from maximizing a generic fitness measure to specifically improving RTP through the evolution of strategies that yield higher long-term player returns.

Aspect	**Before**	**Now (Optimizing RTP)**
Fitness Function	Could be generic score, accuracy, and so on	Fitness = RTP or some transformation of RTP
Chromosome Representation	Solution elements (parameters, strategy configs, features, and so on)	A set of betting strategies, decision-making parameters, player behavior patterns affecting RTP
Goal	Maximize generic fitness	Maximize RTP (Return to Player) via optimal strategies

Table 13.5: *Evolutionary shifts when optimizing for RTP*

Updated Optimization Flow (GA + RL for RTP Maximization)

Step 1: Define the Optimization Problem Clearly

- What influences RTP?
    - Bet types and sequences
    - Hand strategies (double, split, surrender rates)
    - Risk level (aggressive vs conservative play)
    - Redeal frequency, insurance decisions
- **Chromosome = Encoded representation of player strategy**, for example:

```
chromosome = [
    ante_bet_ratio,    # [0.1 - 1.0]
    split_threshold,   # Decision logic parameter
```

```
        insurance_tendency,  # Binary/float
        hit_on_soft_17,    # Boolean
        mutation_operator_type,
        crossover_type
    ]
```

Step 2: Define the Fitness Function as RTP

```
    def fitness_function(strategy_chromosome):
        simulated_rtp = simulate_game(strategy_chromosome)
        return simulated_rtp
```

The GA now evolves player strategies that maximize RTP.

Step 3: Add Reinforcement Learning or MAB for Operator Selection

Instead of letting GA blindly mutate and cross over:

- Let an **RL or MAB agent decide the mutation/crossover operator for each generation**
- **Reward to the agent = RTP improvement** caused by applying a specific operator

  The following table illustrates how the agent receives a reward signal based on the improvement in Return to Player (RTP) resulting from the application of a specific operator. Each generation records the operator applied, the strategy vector used, and the change in RTP before and after the operator's execution. This delta in RTP serves as the reward to the learning agent, guiding future operator selections. Such a reward formulation allows the reinforcement learning framework to continuously adapt and identify which strategies yield the highest player returns, thus aligning evolutionary operations directly with the optimization objective of maximizing RTP.

Gen	Operator	Strategy	Pre-RTP	Post-RTP	Reward
1	`Mutation_A`	[0.5, 0.7, 0, 1]	0.82	0.85	+0.03

Table 13.6: *RTP-based reward assignment for operator evaluation*

Now you are evolving better strategies **and** dynamically adapting your GA's behavior using **learning feedback loops**.

Modified Architecture: The following workflow illustrates a modified architecture that integrates reinforcement learning or bandit-based agent control into a traditional genetic algorithm (GA) framework for strategy optimization. The GA engine maintains a population of candidate strategies, while an intelligent agent dynamically selects the most suitable genetic operator (for example, mutation or crossover) at each generation. After the chosen operator is applied, the resulting strategy is evaluated based on simulated RTP (Return to Player), which serves as the fitness measure. If the applied operator leads to a fitness improvement, the agent receives a reward signal—enabling adaptive learning and progressively better operator decisions over time.

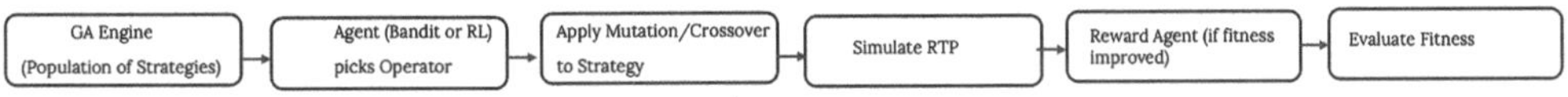

***Figure 13.2**: Workflow for Strategy Optimization*

Sample Use Cases for Optimization: The following table presents representative use cases where Genetic Algorithms (GA) and Reinforcement Learning (RL) are applied to optimize different aspects of RTP (Return to Player) in a gaming context. Depending on the objective—ranging from pure RTP maximization to more nuanced goals such as risk-adjusted optimization or player-segment-specific adaptation—the optimization targets differ. These include refining player strategies, balancing RTP with risk, or tailoring evolutionary behavior using RL to fit diverse player segments. This highlights the flexibility of GA/RL frameworks in aligning optimization with business goals and behavioral personalization.

Objective	**What GA/RL optimizes**
Maximize RTP	Player strategy representation
Maximize RTP under risk constraint	Weighted RTP – risk adjusted
Adaptive RTP optimization	Use RL to evolve GA behavior per player segment

***Table 13.7**: Use cases of GA/RL for RTP optimization*

Extra Twist: Contextual Bandits for Player Segments

Let us say:

- Player Type A is aggressive
- Player Type B is cautious

You can train a **contextual bandit** to choose the best mutation/crossover strategy **based on player type context**.

The Code Explanation

Now that you have understood RTP and Behavioral Economics, let us get started. The following code demonstrates how to use a **Genetic Algorithm (GA)** to optimize the **Return to Player (RTP) score** using the **PyGAD library**, without incorporating reinforcement learning. The process begins by loading a synthetic dataset where the target variable is **RTP_Score**. All other columns are treated as features influencing RTP. The features are normalized using **MinMaxScaler** to bring them to a uniform scale, ensuring effective optimization.

The core of the implementation lies in the **fitness function**, which evaluates how well a given solution (a vector of feature weights) correlates with the RTP score. The GA aims to evolve the best set of weights that maximize this correlation. The **PyGAD configuration** defines parameters such as number of generations, number of parents for mating, population size, mutation strategy, and crossover technique.

During training, PyGAD evolves solutions over multiple generations, selecting and mutating the best-performing candidates. The algorithm plots the **fitness evolution**, showing how correlation improves over time. Finally, the best solution is printed and visualized as a **feature importance bar plot**, revealing which features most strongly influence RTP. This approach provides a baseline optimization strategy before introducing more complex reinforcement learning models.

1. **Data Preprocessing**

The synthetic dataset is loaded using:

```
df = pd.read_csv('/content/sample_data/synthetic_data.csv')
```

The independent variables are extracted by excluding the target column `RTP_Score`, and features are normalized to the [0,1] range using `MinMaxScaler`:

```
features = [col for col in df.columns if col != 'RTP_Score']
X = df[features]
y = df['RTP_Score']

scaler = MinMaxScaler()
X_scaled = scaler.fit_transform(X)
```

This ensures that the genetic algorithm operates within a uniform feature scale, preventing bias due to differing feature magnitudes.

2. **Fitness Function**

The fitness function is defined as the Pearson correlation coefficient between the predicted weighted sum and the actual RTP_Score:

```
def fitness_func(ga_instance, solution, solution_idx):
    weighted_sum = X_scaled.dot(solution)
    score = np.corrcoef(weighted_sum, y)[0, 1]
    return score if not np.isnan(score) else 0
```

Here, each solution represents a vector of feature weights. The higher the correlation, the better the solution's fitness. If the correlation is not a number (NaN), it returns zero to avoid penalizing the GA pipeline with undefined values.

3. **Genetic Algorithm Configuration**

The GA is initialized using PyGAD's GA class with the following parameters:

```
ga_instance = pygad.GA(
    num_generations=30,
    num_parents_mating=10,
    fitness_func=fitness_func,
    sol_per_pop=20,
    num_genes=X.shape[1],
    mutation_percent_genes=20,
    mutation_type="random",
    crossover_type="single_point",
    gene_space={'low': 0.0, 'high': 1.0},
    parent_selection_type="rank"
)
```

Key configurations:

- **num_generations**: Number of iterations over which the GA will evolve.
- **sol_per_pop**: Number of candidate solutions per generation.
- **num_parents_mating**: Number of top solutions selected for mating.
- **gene_space**: Restricts feature weights between 0 and 1.
- **mutation_percent_genes**: Percentage of genes (features) subject to random mutation per generation.
- **crossover_type**: Single-point crossover facilitates genetic recombination.
- **parent_selection_type**: Rank-based selection prioritizes fitter solutions for reproduction.

4. **Execution and Monitoring**

The GA is run using:

```
ga_instance.run()
```

The progression of the best fitness score across generations is visualized using:

```
ga_instance.plot_fitness(title="PyGAD Genetic Algorithm Fitness
Evolution", linewidth=2)
```

5. **Output and Interpretation:**

After execution, the best solution and its corresponding fitness are retrieved and printed:

```
solution, solution_fitness, solution_idx = ga_instance.best_
solution()
print("Best Solution Fitness (Correlation with RTP Score):",
solution_fitness)
print("Best Solution (Feature Weights):\n", solution)
```

This provides the optimal set of feature weights that, when combined linearly, yield the highest correlation with the RTP score.

6. **Visualization of Feature Importance**

To better interpret the resulting feature weights, a bar plot is created:

```
plt.figure(figsize=(10, 5))
plt.bar(features, solution)
plt.xticks(rotation=90)
plt.title("Feature Weights from Best PyGAD Solution")
plt.ylabel("Weight Value")
plt.tight_layout()
plt.grid(True)
plt.show()
```

The following plot presents the fitness evolution curve generated during the execution of the PyGAD-based genetic algorithm for RTP optimization. Fitness in this context is defined as the Pearson correlation between the weighted sum of normalized feature values and the target RTP score. As observed, the GA exhibits a rapid improvement in the early generations, followed by a plateau as it converges toward a local optimum. This fitness trajectory reflects the algorithm's ability to identify promising feature weight configurations within the first few generations, after which only marginal gains are achieved. Such convergence patterns are typical in correlation-driven evolutionary tasks.

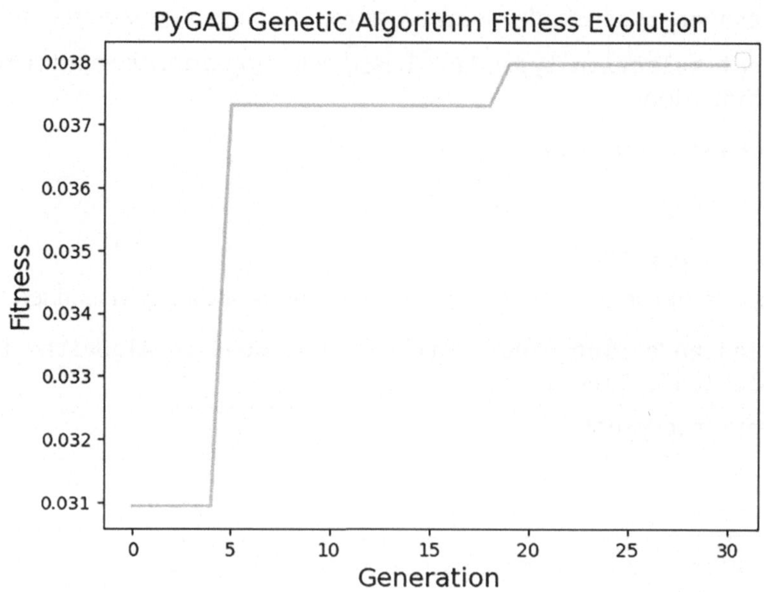

Figure 13.3: *PyGAD Fitness Evolution Curve: Fitness Progress Over GA Generations*

The following output summarizes the final results obtained from the Genetic Algorithm after 30 generations of evolution. The solution achieving the highest fitness—measured as the Pearson correlation between the feature-weighted input vector and the target

RTP score—attained a correlation of approximately **0.03797**. While modest, this score reflects the complexity of the mapping between features and the RTP outcome. The associated feature weights represent the optimal solution identified by the algorithm, revealing how each feature contributes to the predicted RTP. These weights can be interpreted as the importance coefficients in a linear predictor model optimized through evolutionary search.

```
Best Solution Fitness (Correlation with RTP Score): 0.037968697772091685
Best Solution (Feature Weights):
 [0.43104597 0.73321364 0.24511999 0.82715287 0.66334939 0.27103493
 0.32313551 0.1316983  0.81265525 0.25308023 0.86985426 0.13681658
 0.48651638 0.92579157 0.41954302 0.84802933 0.35341009 0.70705792
 0.21395211 0.33333163 0.7009497  0.91145726 0.45457237 0.04675725
 0.28131958 0.02060272 0.20104463 0.03115286 0.54314469 0.14842156
 0.77599549 0.87598542 0.233272   0.44233897 0.88052865 0.91803946
 0.08698976 0.69211587 0.18535801 0.83027953 0.12453907 0.44520198
 0.46910745 0.0511865  0.73592725 0.61281782 0.33568166 0.82775567
 0.57640389 0.28022916 0.51893599]
```

Figure 13.4: *Best Solution Output Print: Optimal Weights from GA Solution*

The dataset depicted in the bar chart showcases the feature importance values derived from the best solution of a Genetic Algorithm (PyGAD) model aimed at optimizing the Return-to-Player (RTP) score in a gaming environment. Each bar represents the relative weight assigned to a specific gameplay or behavioral feature that contributes to predicting or influencing the RTP score.

The features span various aspects of player behavior and game dynamics. These include strategy-based attributes such as `Play_Strategy`, `Betting_Tendency`, and `Game_Skill`, reflecting how users approach gameplay decisions. Features such as `Dealer_Behavior`, `Round_Cycle`, and `Win_Streak` represent temporal or sequence-based patterns, capturing how performance or outcome trends evolve over sessions.

Behavioral signals such as `Loss_Sequence_Habit`, `DoubleDown_Usage`, and `Rebet_Frequency` indicate risky or aggressive play tendencies, while `Risk_Profile` and `Variance_Sensitivity` reflect psychological or decision-making traits under uncertainty. Social and contextual indicators, including `Table_Position`, `Scoop_Effect`, and `Session_Depth`, help understand peer influence and engagement depth.

Notably, features such as `Play_Tempo`, `Reaction_Speed`, and `Slot_Intensity` highlight how player pace and emotional response impact outcomes. The distribution of weights provides a powerful diagnostic lens into what drives RTP and can be instrumental for game design, customer retention, personalization strategies, and churn prediction modeling.

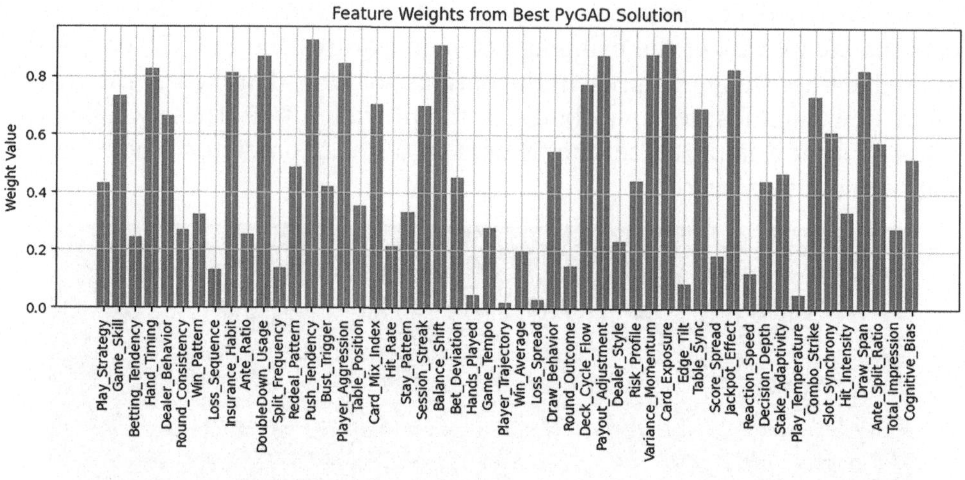

Figure 13.5: *Feature Weight Distribution Plot Top Features Impacting RTP Score*

So, now you understand that the Genetic Algorithm (GA) evaluated and evolved feature weight combinations to maximize correlation with the RTP score. By simulating natural selection through selection, crossover, and mutation, it identified the most influential gameplay features. The GA effectively optimized feature importance without reinforcement learning, revealing patterns that impact player returns in gameplay systems. Let us move on to RL-based GA for RTP optimization.

While the standalone GA approach provides a solid foundation for optimizing RTP scores by identifying impactful feature weight combinations, it lacks adaptability in dynamic environments where learning from feedback is essential. To further enhance the modeling process, we now move toward a **hybrid optimization strategy** that integrates **Multi-Armed Bandits (MAB)** into the GA framework. This fusion allows the system to not only evolve optimal solutions over generations but also intelligently select mutation strategies based on observed rewards. The MAB agent acts as a reinforcement signal, learning which mutation methods contribute most effectively to fitness improvement. By combining GA's global search capability with MAB's exploration-exploitation trade-off, we build a more responsive and adaptive model. This hybrid approach aims to accelerate convergence, improve solution quality, and dynamically adjust strategy selection—addressing the limitations of static GA mutation schemes. The following section explores this hybrid model in detail, illustrating how reward-driven mutation selection improves overall RTP optimization performance.

Genetic Algorithms for Exploration-Exploitation Balance

The concept of **exploration-exploitation trade-off** lies at the heart of intelligent decision-making systems, especially within reinforcement learning and adaptive optimization algorithms. It represents the delicate balance between two opposing strategies:

- **Exploration** refers to trying out new, potentially sub-optimal actions or solutions to gather more information about the environment or search space.
- **Exploitation** refers to leveraging the current best-known actions or solutions to maximize immediate gain or performance.

In the context of **Return-to-Player (RTP) score optimization**, this trade-off becomes critically important. The RTP score is a key indicator of how engaging and rewarding a game is for players. Optimizing this score involves identifying the most impactful gameplay features (for example, bet size, game pace, session patterns) and fine-tuning them to drive better player satisfaction, reduced churn, and increased repeat deposits.

If the model **only exploits**, it risks **premature convergence**, repeatedly using the same mutation strategy or feature combinations, possibly missing out on better solutions. On the other hand, **pure exploration** can waste computational resources and slow down convergence without immediate improvements.

By incorporating mechanisms such as **Multi-Armed Bandits (MAB)** or **Contextual MAB**, the algorithm adaptively explores new mutation strategies when there is uncertainty or diminishing returns from existing ones. Over time, it learns which strategies consistently lead to higher RTP fitness and selectively exploits them while occasionally probing new options to avoid stagnation.

This balance ensures that the **Genetic Algorithm does not become biased toward sub-optimal patterns**, enabling it to discover **richer combinations of player behavior attributes** that more effectively align with high RTP outcomes. As a result, the system becomes more resilient, adaptive, and capable of supporting real-world business objectives such as **enhancing gameplay experiences, increasing player retention, and maximizing lifetime value**.

In the following section, we implement this exploration-exploitation strategy using a hybrid Genetic Algorithm integrated with a Reinforcement Learning agent. The code demonstrates how adaptive mutation selection guided by Multi-Armed Bandits can effectively optimize RTP scores.

This Code Explanation

This code implements a **hybrid optimization approach** that combines **Genetic Algorithms (GA)** with **Reinforcement Learning (RL)** using a **Multi-Armed Bandit (MAB)** framework to optimize the **Return-to-Player (RTP) score** based on gameplay data.

The process begins by loading a synthetic dataset and **normalizing gameplay strategy features**, excluding the target variable **RTP_Score**. The **fitness function**, defined using

PyGAD, evaluates each chromosome (solution) by calculating the **correlation between a weighted sum of features and `RTP_Score`** – higher correlation implies better feature weighting.

To enhance GA adaptability, the model integrates a **Multi-Armed Bandit (UCB algorithm)** that dynamically selects one of two **mutation strategies** – *normal mutation* (Gaussian noise) and *uniform mutation* (random replacement). This allows the algorithm to **learn over generations which mutation method contributes more effectively** to fitness improvements.

Each generation follows standard GA steps: selection of best parents, crossover, and mutation. After mutation, new fitness is evaluated, and the **MAB agent receives a reward based on fitness improvement**, which helps refine future strategy choices.

Finally, a **fitness evolution plot** visualizes how solution quality improves across generations, showcasing how hybrid GA+RL improves learning adaptability and RTP optimization outcomes.

The following Python script demonstrates a hybrid optimization algorithm that combines a **Genetic Algorithm (GA)** implemented using PyGAD with a **Reinforcement Learning (RL)** approach, specifically a **Multi-Armed Bandit (MAB)** strategy, to optimize the correlation between a synthetic feature-weighted sum and a target variable RTP_Score. The algorithm adaptively selects mutation operators using Upper Confidence Bound (UCB) exploration.

1. **Data Preparation and Preprocessing**

The code begins by importing essential libraries and reading the synthetic dataset:

```
df = pd.read_csv('/content/sample_data/synthetic_data.csv')
```

It then extracts the feature columns, excluding the target variable RTP_Score:

```
strategy_features = [col for col in df.columns
if col != 'RTP_Score']
```

The features are normalized using min-max scaling to bring them into the range [0, 1]:

```
scaler = MinMaxScaler()
df[strategy_features] = scaler.fit_transform(df[strategy_fea-
tures])
```

Normalization ensures that all features contribute comparably to the fitness function and prevents scale-dominant features from skewing optimization.

2. **Fitness Function Definition**

The fitness function evaluates how well a candidate solution (that is, a weight vector) correlates with the target score:

```
def fitness_func(ga_instance, solution, solution_idx):
    weights = np.array(solution)
    weighted_sum = df[strategy_features].values.dot(weights)
    simulated_rtp = np.corrcoef(weighted_sum, df['RTP_Score'])[0, 1]
    return simulated_rtp if not np.isnan(simulated_rtp) else 0
```

Here, the solution represents a vector of weights assigned to the features. The fitness is computed as the Pearson correlation coefficient between the weighted sum of features and the **RTP_Score**. A higher correlation indicates a better solution.

3. **Reinforcement** Learning **Agent: Multi-Armed Bandit (MAB)**

A UCB-based Multi-Armed Bandit algorithm is implemented to dynamically choose between different mutation strategies:

```
class MABAgent:
    ...
```

- The **select_arm** method implements the UCB strategy to balance exploration and exploitation.
- The update method refines the estimated reward for each arm (mutation strategy) using incremental mean update.

This agent serves to guide the evolution process by learning which mutation operator performs better over generations.

4. **Mutation Operators**

Two mutation strategies are defined:

- **Normal Mutation:**

  ```
  def normal_mutation(solution, mutation_rate=0.2):
      ...
  ```

  Adds Gaussian noise to genes with a probability **mutation_rate**.

- **Uniform Mutation:**

  ```
  def uniform_mutation(solution, mutation_rate=0.2):
          ...
  ```

Replaces genes with a new value sampled from a uniform distribution.

Both strategies ensure the mutated genes remain within the normalized [0, 1] range.

5. **Genetic Algorithm + RL Loop**

The algorithm proceeds over a fixed number of generations to iteratively evolve

```
for gen in range(generations):
    ...
```

Key steps in each generation:

a. **Fitness Evaluation:** Each chromosome is evaluated using the previously defined fitness function.

b. **Best Fitness Tracking:** The highest fitness in each generation is recorded for visualization.

c. **Mutation Strategy Selection:** A mutation operator is selected using the MAB agent:

```
selected_arm = agent.select_arm()
mutation_func = mutation_functions[selected_arm]
```

d. **Parent Selection:** The top-performing chromosomes are selected:

```
parents = np.array(population)[np.argsort(fitnesses)]
[-num_parents:]
```

e. **Crossover and Mutation:** New offspring are generated by combining two parents and applying the selected mutation:

```
crossover_point = random.randint(1, chromosome_length - 1)
child = np.concatenate([p1[:crossover_point], p2[crossover_
point:]])
child = mutation_func(child)
```

f. **Reward Calculation and Agent Update:** The reward signal is the improvement in fitness, which is used to update the MAB agent:

```
reward = max(new_fitnesses) - best_fitness
agent.update(selected_arm, reward)
```

g. **Population Update:** The newly created population replaces the old one.

6. **Visualization**

After all generations are completed, the progress of the optimization is visualized:

```
plt.plot(range(1, generations + 1), best_fitness_over_time,
marker='o')
plt.title("GA + RL Optimization Progress (Fitness Over
Generations)")
```

This provides insight into the convergence behavior of the GA and the effectiveness of RL-driven mutation adaptation.

The plot titled "GA + RL *Optimization Progress (Fitness Over Generations)*" illustrates the convergence behavior of a hybrid Genetic Algorithm (GA) augmented with a Reinforcement Learning (RL)-based mutation strategy selection mechanism, specifically a Multi-Armed Bandit using Upper Confidence Bound (UCB). Over the course of 30 generations, the algorithm seeks to maximize the correlation between a weighted combination of normalized features and a synthetic target variable (**`RTP_`**

Score). The y-axis represents the best correlation score achieved in each generation, while the x-axis denotes the generation index. The upward trend suggests progressive learning and adaptation, validating the efficacy of the combined GA-RL approach.

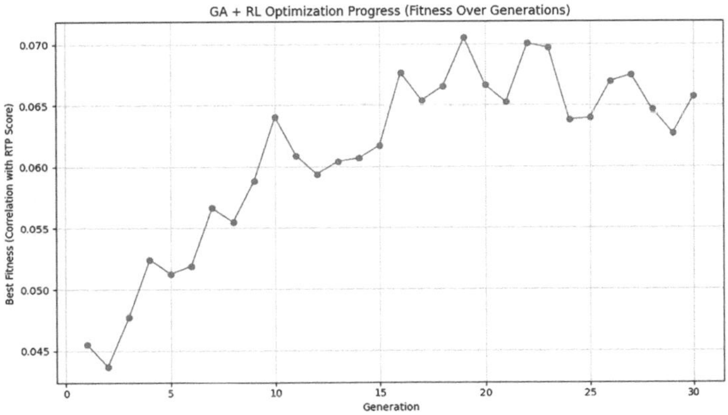

Figure 13.6: *GA + RL Hybrid Model: Progressive RTP Fitness Optimization Over Generations*

The bar chart titled "Cumulative Regret per Mutation Strategy (MAB Agent)" illustrates the cumulative regret associated with each mutation strategy—*normal* and *uniform*—as learned by the Multi-Armed Bandit (MAB) agent using the Upper Confidence Bound (UCB) method. Cumulative regret quantifies the opportunity loss incurred by not always selecting the optimal mutation strategy. In this chart, the *normal* mutation strategy shows zero regret, indicating it consistently yielded near-optimal rewards. In contrast, the *uniform* strategy accumulates measurable regret (~0.0025), signifying that its performance was suboptimal in comparison. This highlights the agent's capacity to adaptively prioritize more effective genetic operators during the evolutionary process.

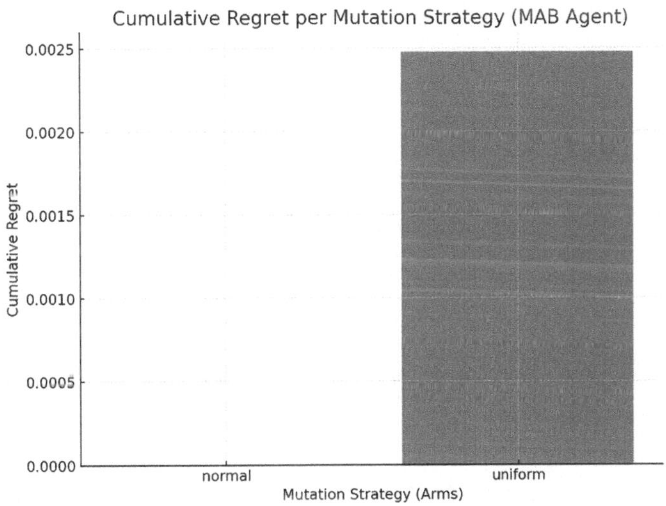

Figure 13.7: *Here is the Cumulative Regret Plot for the MAB agent across mutation strategies*

Interpretation:

- **Lower bars = better performance** of that strategy.
- **Higher regret means** the agent learned that this strategy was **suboptimal** compared to the best one.
- This helps you **quantitatively evaluate** which mutation strategies contributed less to improving RTP and how well the MAB agent differentiated between them.

  This line graph showcases how the average simulated reward changes across multiple selection instances for two mutation strategies—**normal** and **uniform**—within the reinforcement learning loop of the hybrid GA-RL framework. Each data point represents the reward obtained when a particular strategy was chosen by the MAB agent. The **normal** strategy (blue line) exhibits more stable and consistently positive reward values over time, indicating its superior performance in enhancing the RTP correlation. In contrast, the **uniform** strategy (orange line) demonstrates higher variance and increasing frequency of negative rewards, suggesting its lower effectiveness and suboptimal adaptation during the evolutionary process.

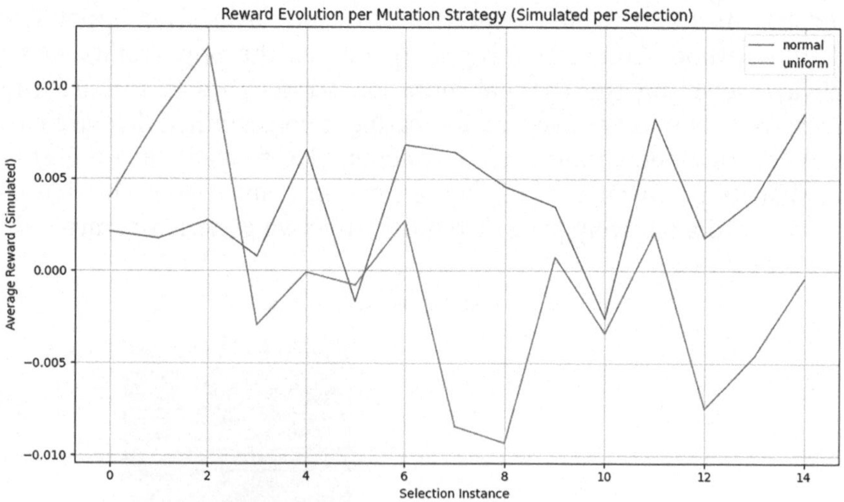

Figure 13.8: *This line graph showcases how the average simulated reward changes across generations*

Reward and Regret Curve Analysis

In reinforcement learning (RL) and optimization systems such as Genetic Algorithms (GA) combined with Multi-Armed Bandits (MAB), **reward and regret curves** are critical performance evaluation tools. These curves offer insights into how effectively the system balances learning and decision-making across generations or iterations.

Reward Curve

The **reward curve** captures the average improvement in performance (or utility) achieved over time as the model explores different strategies. In our case, the reward is derived from the improvement in Return-to-Player (RTP) correlation after each generation of evolution. A higher reward indicates that the selected mutation strategy–guided by the bandit agent–is leading to effective improvements in fitness (correlation with RTP score). The shape of the reward curve allows us to understand:

- Which mutation strategy yields higher rewards consistently.
- How quickly the model is converging toward optimal solutions.
- Periods of stagnation, decline, or overfitting.

A declining reward curve might suggest either **diminishing returns** due to saturation or **over-exploitation** of a single strategy at the expense of others. In such scenarios, dynamic exploration techniques may be introduced to rejuvenate learning diversity.

Regret Curve

The **regret curve** quantifies what is **lost due to not choosing the best possible action at each generation**. In mathematical terms, **regret is the difference between the optimal possible reward and the actual reward obtained**. Cumulative regret is expected to grow over time, but at a **sub-linear rate in an efficient system**. A rapidly rising regret curve indicates:

- **Poor exploration**, where the model is frequently making suboptimal selections.
- **Overconfidence in a single arm (mutation strategy)** without validating alternatives.
- **Underutilization of high-potential arms that could improve the system performance.**

In a well-balanced hybrid GA-RL framework, we expect **modest regret growth** and **spikes in reward curves**, which signify learning from mistakes and gradually making more informed choices. A flatter regret curve over time is a strong indication that the **agent has learned to select the most effective mutation strategy reliably**, thus optimizing the learning and evolutionary process.

Why Reward and Regret Matter

Together, reward and regret curves serve as diagnostic tools to:

- Fine-tune mutation strategies.
- Adjust exploration-exploitation balance.
- Detect performance bottlenecks early.

- Ensure robust model generalization.

In the context of RTP modeling, optimizing these curves directly correlates to **customer engagement outcomes**, **retention modeling**, and **monetization effectiveness** in gameplay ecosystems.

Evolving Intelligent Model for Games

This enhanced version of the Genetic Algorithm (GA), found in **Chapter_13.ipynb**, uses Reinforcement Learning (RL) with Multi-Armed Bandits (MAB) and introduces two key improvements over the previous GA+RL implementation. First, it incorporates a more structured and **modular reinforcement learning agent**, where each mutation strategy (normal or uniform) is treated as a separate "arm" and their performance is monitored using **Upper Confidence Bound (UCB)** for selection. Compared to earlier implementations, this version explicitly logs **reward history per arm**, which allows better tracking and visualization of how each strategy performs over time and enables **reward evolution plots** for deeper insights.

Secondly, the code uses a **clear separation between exploration and exploitation** via UCB, making the mutation strategy selection process more data-driven rather than relying on static assumptions or random alternation. It also improves the feedback mechanism by **calculating a reward based on the improvement in best fitness**, and this reward is directly fed back to the MAB agent to update its arm-value estimates.

While the overall genetic optimization pipeline remains similar to the earlier version—that is, selection, crossover, and mutation—the **addition of RL-driven adaptive mutation control** makes this version more robust, self-improving, and scalable, especially in dynamic gaming environments where RTP modeling demands continuous learning and adaptation.

GA with Reinforcement Learning through a CMAB

The following code implements a hybrid approach combining GA with Reinforcement Learning through a Contextual Multi-Armed Bandit (CMAB) framework to optimize Return-to-Player (RTP) score prediction. After preprocessing and scaling feature data, a fitness function evaluates solutions based on the correlation between a weighted feature sum and actual RTP scores. The CMAB agent, powered by Ridge Regression, selects mutation strategies (arms) based on the current context—average fitness, best fitness, and diversity. It updates its predictions by learning from reward outcomes after each generation. The GA performs selection, crossover, and context-driven mutation to evolve populations over 30 generations, improving RTP correlation while tracking reward and fitness progress visually.

The following code integrates a **Genetic Algorithm (GA)** with a **Contextual Multi-Armed Bandit (CMAB)** agent to optimize a **target score (`RTP_Score`)** using feature-based weighting on a synthetic dataset. The bandit agent uses **Ridge Regression** to dynamically select among competing mutation strategies based on evolving contextual signals.

Following is an academic-style explanation, with referenced code blocks for clarity.

The Code Explanation

1. **Data Loading and Normalization**

```
df = pd.read_csv('/content/sample_data/synthetic_data.csv')
strategy_features = [col for col in df.columns if col !=
'RTP_Score']
scaler = MinMaxScaler()
df[strategy_features] = scaler.fit_transform(df[strategy_
features])
```

The data is first loaded from a CSV file. Feature columns are identified by excluding the target variable **`RTP_Score`**. A MinMaxScaler is applied to normalize all feature values to the [0,1][0,1][0,1] interval, ensuring numerical stability during optimization.

2. **Fitness Function**

```
def fitness_func(ga_instance, solution, solution_idx):
    weights = np.array(solution)
    weighted_sum = df[strategy_features].values.dot(weights)
    simulated_rtp = np.corrcoef(weighted_sum, df['RTP_Score'])[0, 1]
    return simulated_rtp if not np.isnan(simulated_rtp) else 0
```

This function evaluates the **fitness of each solution** (that is, feature weight vector) by computing the **Pearson correlation** between the linearly weighted feature combination and the target **`RTP_Score`**. If the correlation is undefined (for example, due to zero variance), the function returns zero.

3. **Contextual Multi-Armed Bandit Agent**

Initialization

```
class CMABAgent:
    def __init__(self, num_arms, context_dim):
        self.models = [Ridge(alpha=1.0) for _ in range(num_arms)]
        ...
```

The agent initializes **`num_arms`** regression models, each corresponding to a distinct mutation strategy. Each arm maintains a history of context-reward pairs for supervised learning.

Arm Selection

```
    def select_arm(self, context):
        preds = []
        for i in range(self.num_arms):
            if len(self.contexts[i]) < self.context_dim:
                preds.append(np.random.rand())
            else:
                preds.append(self.models[i].predict(context.reshape(1,
-1))[0])
        return np.argmax(preds)
```

To select a mutation strategy, the agent predicts expected rewards from current context features. If insufficient training data is available (that is, fewer than **context_dim** samples), the agent selects randomly. Otherwise, it chooses the arm with the highest predicted reward using **greedy selection**.

Reward Update

```
    def update(self, arm, context, reward):
        self.contexts[arm].append(context)
        self.rewards[arm].append(reward)
        ...
        if len(self.contexts[arm]) >= self.context_dim:
            X = np.array(self.contexts[arm])
            y = np.array(self.rewards[arm])
            self.models[arm].fit(X, y)
```

After a mutation strategy is applied and its effect observed, the corresponding arm is updated with the new context-reward pair. If sufficient data exists, the model is retrained using **Ridge Regression**, a regularized linear regression method that helps prevent overfitting.

4. **Mutation Strategies**

Two mutation functions are defined:

- **Normal Mutation:**

```
def normal_mutation(solution, mutation_rate=0.2):
    ...
```

Adds Gaussian noise to randomly selected genes with a specified mutation rate.

- **Uniform Mutation:**

```
def uniform_mutation(solution, mutation_rate=0.2):
    ...
```

Replaces genes with random values drawn from a uniform distribution.

Both functions ensure the mutated solution remains within the valid domain [0,1][0,1][0,1] using **`np.clip`**.

5. **Genetic Algorithm Loop**

- **Initialization**

```
population = [np.random.rand(chromosome_length) for _ in
range(population_size)]
```

An initial population of chromosomes is generated with random weights for all features.

- **Per-Generation Procedure**

  Each iteration includes the following steps:

a. **Fitness Evaluation**

```
fitnesses = [fitness_func(None, ch, i) for i, ch in enumerate
(population)]
```

All individuals in the population are evaluated using the correlation-based fitness function.

b. **Context Definition**

```
context = np.array([avg_fitness, best_fitness, diversity])
```

The current context is constructed using three features:

- The average fitness across the population
- The best fitness in the population
- The diversity (standard deviation of fitness scores)

This contextual vector reflects the global optimization landscape for the generation.

c. **Mutation Arm Selection**

```
selected_arm = agent.select_arm(context)
mutation_func = mutation_functions[selected_arm]
```

The CMAB agent selects a mutation strategy based on the context.

d. **Crossover and Mutation**

```
p1, p2 = random.sample(list(parents), 2)
crossover_point = random.randint(1, chromosome_length - 1)
child = np.concatenate([p1[:crossover_point], p2[crossover_
point:]])
child = mutation_func(child)
```

Two parent solutions are selected and combined via **single-point crossover**. The resulting child undergoes the selected mutation.

e. **Reward and Update**

```
reward = max(new_fitnesses) - best_fitness
agent.update(selected_arm, context, reward)
```

The reward is computed as the **improvement in the best fitness** relative to the previous generation. This reward is used by the CMAB agent to update its model for the selected mutation arm.

6. **Visualization**

- **Fitness over Generations**

```
plt.plot(range(1, generations + 1), best_fitness_over_time,
marker='o')
```

This plot shows the evolution of the **best fitness score per generation**, representing the system's convergence toward an optimal solution.

- **Reward History**

```
for i, strategy in enumerate(mutation_strategies):
    plt.plot(agent.reward_history[i], label=strategy)
```

This visualizes the reward trajectory for each mutation strategy, providing insight into their relative contributions over time.

The graph titled "GA + *Contextual* MAB *Optimization Progress (Fitness Over Generations)*" illustrates the performance trajectory of a hybrid evolutionary learning system, where a Genetic Algorithm (GA) is enhanced by a Contextual Multi-Armed Bandit (CMAB) agent. Specifically, it plots the best fitness value—measured as the **correlation between the evolved feature weighting and the target `RTP_Score`**—across successive generations.

The increasing trend visible in the chart demonstrates the system's capacity to progressively identify more optimal solutions over time. Despite some minor fluctuations, the overall improvement in fitness indicates effective adaptation and learning by the combined GA-CMAB framework, validating the merit of contextual strategy selection for mutation operations in evolutionary search.

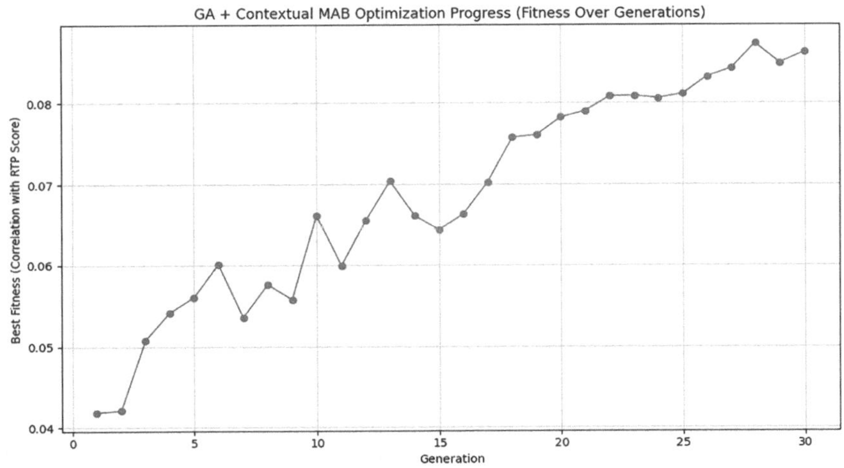

Figure 13.9: *The image represents GA + Contextual MAB, gradual exploitation of beneficial strategies*

The GA + RL (MAB) shows more variability and abrupt jumps in fitness, suggesting sporadic learning and potentially unstable exploration-exploitation balance. While both approaches yield positive optimization, the GA + Contextual MAB appears to foster more structured learning progression, likely due to the added context-awareness in arm selection.

Genetic Algorithms (GA) with Deep Contextual Multi-Armed Bandits (Deep CMAB)

Contextual Multi-Armed Bandit (CMAB) is an extension of the classical **Multi-Armed Bandit (MAB)** problem, where decision-making is enhanced by incorporating **contextual information** before selecting an arm (or action).

In traditional MAB, an agent selects an arm purely based on past rewards, without considering any external factors. However, in **CMAB**, the agent **observes a context vector** (such as user profile, environment state, or performance metrics) before choosing an arm. Each arm has a different expected reward depending on the current context.

Key Features of CMAB:

- Each **context vector** describes the state of the environment.
- The agent uses **supervised learning models** (for example, linear regression, ridge regression) to predict the expected reward of each arm given the current context.

- It **balances exploration and exploitation** using prediction confidence and reward estimates.
- CMAB is highly useful in **personalized decision-making**, such as online ad recommendations, medical treatments, or, in our case, mutation strategy selection in GA.

Deep Contextual Multi-Armed Bandit (Deep CMAB)

Deep CMAB is a more **powerful and flexible extension of CMAB**, where the **reward prediction models are replaced with deep neural networks** instead of simple linear models.

In real-world problems, the relationship between context and reward can be **highly non-linear and complex**. Traditional CMAB (for example, Ridge Regression) might fail to capture these patterns. **Deep learning enables modeling such non-linear interactions**, making predictions more robust and adaptive.

Key Features of Deep CMAB:

- Each arm is modeled using a **deep neural network** trained on past contexts and corresponding rewards.
- It captures **non-linear and hierarchical feature interactions**, allowing for more accurate predictions in high-dimensional contexts.
- Deep CMAB enables **dynamic learning and adaptation**, improving arm selection over time.
- It also allows **fine-grained reward shaping** and supports **exploration strategies such as softmax sampling or Thompson Sampling** over predicted values.

The table presents a structured comparison between **Contextual Multi-Armed Bandits (CMAB)** implemented with linear models and their enhanced variant, **Deep CMAB**, which leverages deep neural networks. The comparison spans multiple aspects, including model architecture, reward prediction capacity, adaptability, suitability for different context scales, and robustness to noise. While CMABs are efficient for smaller, more stable environments with linear relationships, Deep CMABs demonstrate greater adaptability and generalization, especially in high-dimensional or dynamic settings where non-linear patterns dominate.

Aspect	**CMAB**	**Deep CMAB**
Model Type	Linear/Ridge Regression	Deep Neural Networks
Reward Prediction	Linear approximation	Non-linear, high-capacity models
Adaptability	Moderate	High (captures complex patterns)

Use Case Fit	Small/medium context space	Large, complex, dynamic contexts
Performance in Noisy Data	Limited	Better generalization

Table 13.8: *CMAB vs Deep CMAB – A Comparison*

In Our Problem (RTP Optimization)

- **CMAB** learns which mutation strategy works better given fitness statistics (context). It is efficient, interpretable, and easy to implement.
- **Deep CMAB**, however, captures more intricate interactions between context and mutation success. It adapts better to changes in population behavior, ensuring smarter strategy selection and reducing regret.
- Deep CMAB also **balances exploration and exploitation more effectively**, helping the GA evolve faster toward optimal RTP performance.

The Code Explanation

This code integrates Genetic Algorithms (GA) with Deep Contextual Multi-Armed Bandits (Deep CMAB) to optimize RTP (Return-to-Player) score correlation using a robust exploration-exploitation framework and improved regret control. The dataset is normalized, and a fitness function is defined based on the correlation between weighted features and RTP scores.

A `DeepCMABAgent` class models each mutation strategy (arm) with a neural network. It uses context vectors—average fitness, best fitness, and population diversity—to predict the most suitable mutation operator. The selection mechanism ensures balanced exploration early by enforcing a minimum selection count and then transitions to probabilistic selection via softmax over predicted values.

During each generation, the GA performs selection, crossover, and mutation (guided by the selected arm) to evolve the population. Rewards are calculated using a scaled tanh function to maintain bounded feedback and better gradient learning. The cumulative regret, defined as the difference between ideal and actual reward, is tracked to measure learning efficiency.

Visualization components display fitness evolution, arm-wise reward trajectories, cumulative regret, and selection frequencies. This advanced setup enhances decision-making across mutation strategies and ensures fair exploration, helping achieve stable RTP score optimization with reduced regret and improved adaptive learning through deep contextual modeling.

1. **Data Preparation and Scaling**

```
df = pd.read_csv('/content/sample_data/synthetic_data.csv')
strategy_features = [col for col in df.columns if col != 'RTP_Score']
scaler = MinMaxScaler()
df[strategy_features] = scaler.fit_transform(df[strategy_features])
```

A synthetic dataset is loaded using pandas. All columns except RTP_Score are considered features. These are scaled using MinMaxScaler to bring the data into the [0, 1] range, aiding neural network convergence and fitness evaluation.

2. **Fitness Function**

```
def fitness_func(ga_instance, solution, solution_idx):
    weights = np.array(solution)
    weighted_sum = df[strategy_features].values.dot(weights)
    simulated_rtp = np.corrcoef(weighted_sum, df['RTP_Score'])[0, 1]
    return simulated_rtp if not np.isnan(simulated_rtp) else 0
```

This function evaluates the **fitness** of a GA solution (that is, a vector of weights). The fitness is defined as the **Pearson correlation** between the weighted sum of features and the target RTP_Score. If the correlation is undefined (NaN), the fitness is set to zero.

3. **Deep Contextual Multi-Armed Bandit (CMAB)**

The **`DeepCMABAgent`** class implements a contextual bandit with neural approximators.

Model Initialization

```
class DeepCMABAgent:
    def __init__(self, num_arms, context_dim):
        ...
```

The agent maintains **`num_arms`** neural networks, each representing an arm (that is, a mutation strategy). Each model is trained to predict the expected reward for a given context vector.

Neural Network Architecture

```
def _build_model(self, input_dim):
    model = Sequential([
        Input(shape=(input_dim,)),
        Dense(16, activation='relu'),
        Dropout(0.2),
        Dense(8, activation='relu'),
        Dense(1, activation='linear')
    ])
    model.compile(optimizer=Adam(learning_rate=0.005), loss='mse')
    return model
```

Each arm uses a feedforward neural network with dropout regularization to prevent overfitting. The architecture allows for modeling non-linear context-reward relationships.

Arm Selection (Policy)

```
def select_arm(self, context):
    ...
    probs = np.exp(preds) / np.sum(np.exp(preds))
    return np.random.choice(range(self.num_arms), p=probs)
```

The agent uses a **softmax (Boltzmann exploration)** strategy over predicted rewards to balance exploration and exploitation. It ensures early-stage uniform exploration by forcing a minimum number of selections per arm.

Reward Update

```
def update(self, arm, context, reward):
    ...
    self.models[arm].fit(X, y, epochs=5, verbose=0)
```

Upon receiving feedback (reward), the selected arm's model is retrained using the new context-reward pair. This enables **online learning** for adaptive decision-making.

4. **Mutation Strategies**

Two types of mutation operators are defined:

- **Normal Mutation:**

```
def normal_mutation(solution, mutation_rate=0.2):
    ...
```

Applies Gaussian noise to individual genes with a probability of mutation_rate.

- **Uniform Mutation:**

```
def uniform_mutation(solution, mutation_rate=0.2):
    ...
```

Replaces genes with uniform random values with a given probability.

5. **Main Evolutionary Loop**

Initialization

```
population = [np.random.rand(chromosome_length) for _ in range
(population_size)]
```

A population of chromosomes is initialized with random values between 0 and 1, representing candidate weight vectors.

Evolutionary Iteration

Each generation includes:

a. **Fitness Evaluation**:

```
fitnesses = [fitness_func(None, ch, i) for i, ch in enumerate
(population)]
```

b. **Context Construction**:

```
context = np.array([avg_fitness, best_fitness, diversity])
```

c. **Mutation Strategy Selection** via DeepCMAB:

```
selected_arm = agent.select_arm(context)
mutation_func = mutation_functions[selected_arm]
```

d. **Parent Selection and Crossover**:

```
parents = np.array(population)[np.argsort(fitnesses)]
[-num_parents:]
```

e. **Mutation and Offspring Generation**:

```
child = mutation_func(child)
```

f. **Reward Computation**:

```
reward = np.tanh((np.mean(new_fitnesses) - avg_fitness) * 10)
```

The reward is a bounded transformation (via hyperbolic tangent) of the improvement in average fitness. This ensures smooth gradients for learning.

g. **Regret Update**:

```
regret = max(0, best_fitness - reward)
```

This captures the performance loss due to suboptimal arm selection.

h. **Agent Learning**:

```
agent.update(selected_arm, context, reward)
```

6. **Visualization**

Fitness Curve

```
plt.plot(range(1, generations + 1), best_fitness_over_time,
marker='o')
```

This plot shows the evolution of the best solution's fitness across generations.

Mutation Strategy Rewards

```
for i, strategy in enumerate(mutation_strategies):
    plt.plot(agent.reward_history[i], label=strategy)
```

This graph compares how each mutation strategy performs over time based on observed rewards.

Regret Curve

```
plt.plot(regret_history, marker='x', color='red')
```

Shows cumulative regret as a function of generation number, indicating decision quality.

Arm Selection Frequency

```
plt.bar(mutation_strategies, agent.selection_counts)
```

Reveals how often each mutation strategy was selected, indicating the agent's preference learning over time.

This line graph presents the evolution of the average simulated reward associated with two mutation strategies–**normal** (blue line) and **uniform** (orange line)–across multiple selection instances within the GA-RL optimization process. Each data point indicates the reward outcome following a specific selection of a mutation strategy by the Multi-Armed Bandit (MAB) agent. The **normal** strategy consistently yields positive and relatively high rewards, with limited variance, highlighting its robust and reliable contribution to improving the correlation with the RTP score. Conversely, the **uniform** strategy demonstrates lower, more volatile, and frequently negative rewards, indicating less effective adaptation and reduced utility in the evolutionary search. These dynamics underscore the MAB agent's ability to discern and increasingly favor the more promising operator throughout the learning process.

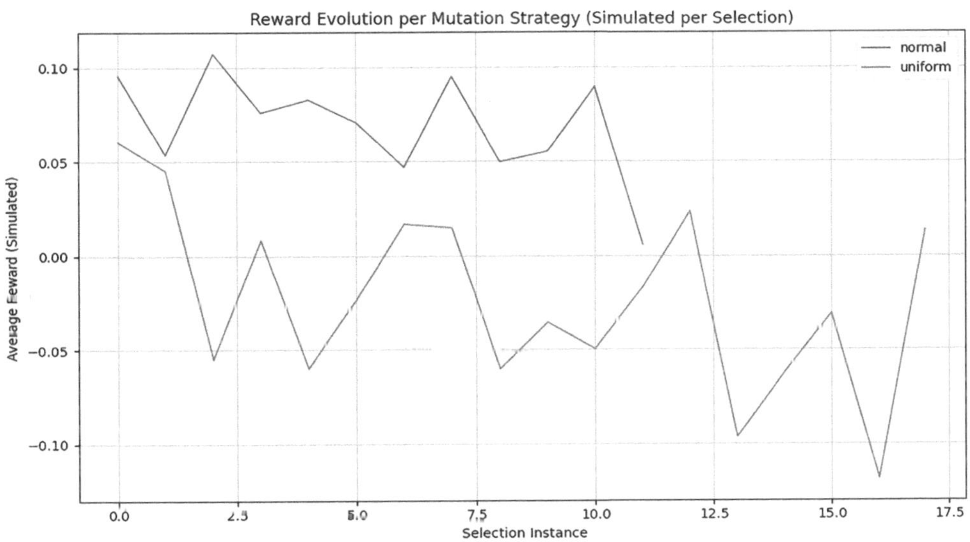

Figure 13.10: *Reward Evolution of Mutation Strategies in Deep CMAB-GA Framework*

Conclusion

In this chapter, we explored the integration of Genetic Algorithms with various Reinforcement Learning paradigms—including Multi-Armed Bandits, Contextual MABs, and Deep Contextual MABs—to optimize RTP scores in gameplay modeling. We demonstrated how each technique influences fitness, reward, regret, and arm selection. Through practical implementation and visual analysis, we showcased the power of hybrid learning frameworks in balancing exploration and exploitation. With this, we conclude the technical journey of this chapter.

In the next chapter, we will summarize the key insights, revisit the core concepts, and reflect on the practical implications and applications covered throughout this comprehensive book.

CHAPTER 14
The Future of Genetic Algorithms

Introduction

Before we proceed with a comprehensive summary of the key insights covered throughout this book, consolidating our understanding from all preceding chapters, it is important to briefly reflect on the evolving intersection of **Agents**, **Retrieval-Augmented Generation (RAG)**, and **Generative AI** through the lens of **Genetic Algorithms**. The next generation of Genetic Algorithms will be deeply influenced by advancements in **Agentic AI** and **Generative AI systems**.

This evolutionary process ensures that new agents inherit essential competencies while incorporating beneficial mutations that may improve task effectiveness. Agents compete against their predecessors, and only those demonstrating superior response accuracy and performance are retained. We have already explored the foundational ideas of Agents, GenAI, and RAG in *Chapter 8, Application of Evolutionary Algorithms* (GAs) and *Chapter 12, Generative Agentic AI and NLP Application of Genetic Algorithms Using PyGAD.*

Now, building upon that knowledge, we present the **Conceptual Framework: Natural Selection in Multi-Agent Systems** to extend and operationalize these principles into a scalable and self-improving architecture.

Structure

In this chapter, the following topics will be covered:

- Future of GA Genetics in Generative AI
- Enhancing Generative Agentic AI with Genetic Algorithms
- Self-Evolving or Adaptive Multi-Agent System: Framework and Architecture
- Models Model Context Protocol (MCP)
- Best practices for implementing the GA system

- Tips and tricks in Genetic Algorithms
- Chapter-wise Conclusion

Future of GA Genetics in Generative AI

As Large Language Models (LLMs) continue to revolutionize natural language processing, the quest to develop more adaptable, efficient, and human-aligned systems has led to the convergence of multiple optimization methodologies. While gradient-based techniques dominate the pretraining phase, the landscape of post-training optimization is rapidly expanding to include methods such as **Reinforcement Learning with Human Feedback (RLHF)**, **Proximal Policy Optimization (PPO)**, **Direct Preference Optimization (DPO)**, and, more recently, **Group Relative Policy Optimization (GRPO)**. Alongside these, **Genetic Algorithms (GAs)** are gaining attention as a powerful population-based, gradient-free search strategy, offering capabilities that complement and enhance conventional optimization workflows.

Genetic Algorithms, with their inherent ability to navigate complex and non-differentiable search spaces, play a crucial role in several areas of LLM development. These include **neural architecture search**, **prompt engineering**, **tokenization strategy optimization**, and **hyperparameter tuning**. GAs are particularly valuable in exploring diverse solution spaces by evolving candidate models or configurations based on fitness scores derived from model performance, human preferences, or reward signals.

In the context of **Reinforcement Learning**, GAs can act as a meta-optimization layer. While techniques such as **Proximal Policy Optimization (PPO)** are widely used to fine-tune LLM behavior using scalar reward feedback, GAs can evolve a broader range of policy and architecture variations in parallel, introducing a layer of exploratory diversity that complements the exploitative nature of gradient-based RL. This synergy becomes even more potent in **multi-agent LLM environments**, where GAs can evolve agent interaction strategies, reward shaping models, or sampling configurations.

With the rise of **Direct Preference Optimization (DPO)**—a method that learns directly from pairwise preference data without requiring explicit reward modeling—GAs offer a compelling integration opportunity. GAs can be used to evolve preference models, optimize prompt structures, or tune loss function configurations that align better with human feedback, thereby enhancing the overall alignment process. Unlike traditional hyperparameter tuning methods, GAs can efficiently navigate the combinatorial search space of DPO parameters using fitness scores derived from preference agreement metrics or comparative loss minimization.

The introduction of **Group Relative Policy Optimization (GRPO)** further advances the reinforcement learning toolkit for LLMs. GRPO departs from traditional reward-based optimization by leveraging **relative performance ranking** of generated outputs within a group. Instead of modeling absolute correctness or requiring a separate value function network, GRPO computes normalized rewards across candidate generations for a given prompt, focusing on **intra-group performance differentiation**. This relative learning mechanism proves highly effective in deterministic evaluation tasks such as mathematical reasoning or code generation, where exact correctness can be computed automatically. When integrated with GAs, this becomes even more powerful—GAs can evolve prompt patterns, generation strategies, or even reward normalization schemes that maximize GRPO effectiveness. Moreover, the **KL-divergence-based regularization term embedded in GRPO's loss function** helps maintain policy stability, and GAs can assist in adaptively tuning these trade-off parameters across different tasks or datasets.

Collectively, the hybridization of **GAs, RL, DPO, and GRPO** creates a robust, layered optimization ecosystem. GAs offer broad search capability and non-gradient exploration, RL ensures fine-grained behavioral control, DPO enables direct alignment with human judgment, and GRPO introduces efficient relative preference modeling. This multi-pronged approach not only expands the performance boundaries of LLMs but also enhances their alignment, interpretability, and adaptability in dynamic real-world applications.

In the future, we may see **self-evolving LLM systems**, where Genetic Algorithms manage the evolution of sub-models, agent behaviors, and optimization strategies, guided by alignment scores and relative preference metrics defined through DPO and GRPO frameworks. Such systems would mark a paradigm shift—where LLMs do not just learn from data, but evolve through intelligent orchestration of evolutionary and preference-aware optimization dynamics.

Enhancing Generative Agentic AI with Genetic Algorithms

The integration of **Genetic Algorithms (GA)** with **Generative Agentic AI** is paving the way for self-evolving, adaptive AI systems capable of continuous improvement. Traditional generative AI models rely on static training paradigms, where knowledge and toolsets remain fixed unless explicitly updated. However, by leveraging GA principles, AI agents can dynamically evolve their capabilities, reasoning structures, and toolsets based on real-world performance.

Each agent is treated as an evolving entity, with **chromosomes representing structured configurations**, including tools, prompts, reasoning chains, and memory modules. Genes correspond to specific functionalities, enabling agents to mutate, recombine, and adapt based on feedback-driven performance scores. High-performing agents survive and contribute to the next generation, while underperforming agents are replaced through **mutation and crossover**, ensuring continuous optimization.

This evolutionary framework aligns AI development with **biological selection principles**, enabling generative agents to autonomously discover and integrate new tools, refine their reasoning strategies, and improve response quality without manual intervention. When combined with **Model Context Protocol (MCP)**, AI systems gain the ability to introspect, interact, and enhance their own architecture dynamically. The future of **GA-powered generative AI** lies in self-improving, autonomous agentic systems that evolve towards higher intelligence and efficiency.

Self-Evolving or Adaptive Multi-Agent System: Framework and Architecture

The pursuit of AI systems capable of autonomously enhancing their abilities is significantly enriched by drawing inspiration from natural evolutionary principles. In this context, we introduce a practical and theoretical framework for a **Self-evolving or Adaptive Multi-Agent System (AMAS)**, where agents continuously generate improved offspring, inspired by biological reproduction and natural selection. Each agent functions autonomously, equipped with a unique configuration that includes prompts, reasoning chains, and toolsets. These agents are powered by advanced LLM frameworks and integrated vector databases (such as FAISS), utilizing real-world datasets–for example, office property listings extracted from CSV files and their corresponding .npy embeddings.

The approach we are building is **inspired by Genetic and Evolutionary Algorithms (GA/EA)** concepts. Here is how:

1. **Agents = Organisms**: Each agent represents a potential solution (organism).
2. **Chromosomes = Agent Traits**: These include its tools, prompts, reasoning chains, and memory.

   `1.0.1.0.1 = [Tool1] [Tool2] [Prompt1] [Reasoning] [Memory]`
3. **Mutation and Crossover**: When agents fail (low score), new agents are created by mutating/changing tools, mixing prompts, or recombining toolsets from "`parent agents`".
4. **Fitness Function = Scoring System**: Agent performance is evaluated using correctness score; high-performers survive or propagate.
5. **Replacement/Selection**: Underperforming agents are replaced by better "`offspring`" agents with adapted traits.
6. **Offspring:** New Agent generated via crossover/mutation.

The following image presents a genetic algorithm-inspired representation of agent behavior modeling within a multi-agent system. Each agent (A1 to A5) is encoded as a chromosome, composed of binary genes representing discrete behavioral traits or operational states. These binary configurations collectively define a population of agents, where each gene indicates whether a particular feature–such as a tool, prompt, reasoning module, or memory–is used (1) or not (0). For example, Agent A3 activates both memory and tools while disabling reasoning. This setup is particularly useful for optimizing decision-making strategies by evolving agent configurations through selection, mutation, and crossover within an adaptive AI framework.

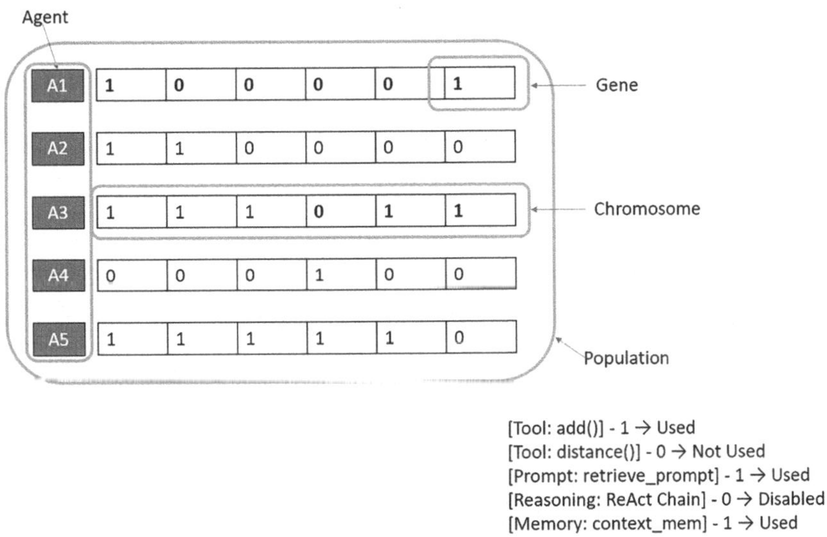

Figure 14.1: *Chromosome-level binary representation of agent traits in a Genetic Algorithm-based multi-agent system*

Gene Position	**Trait Type**	**Value Mapping Example**
1st Gene	`Tool: add()`	1 = active, 0 = not used
2nd Gene	`Tool: distance()`	1 = active, 0 = not used
3rd Gene	`Prompt: retrieve_prompt`	1 = used, 0 = not used
4th Gene	`Reasoning Chain: ReAct`	1 = enabled, 0 = disabled
5th Gene	`Memory: context_mem`	1 = active, 0 = not used

Table 14.1: Binary Representation of Agent Traits

We are basically creating an **evolving population of problem-solving agents**, where each agent's traits (chromosomes) evolve based on task performance.

This is a **Self-Evolving Multi-Agent System** that uses a structured flowchart-like format to represent the evolution lifecycle and interactions:

The flowchart illustrates an evolutionary agent architecture designed to optimize task-solving in dynamic environments through adaptive learning and genetic principles. Starting from a user query, the system routes tasks via a Task Router to an Active

Agent Pool—each agent characterized by unique traits such as tool usage, context retrieval ability, and reasoning capacity. Agents execute tasks, generate responses, and are evaluated for performance. The system logs performance scores, then applies genetic operations such as mutation and crossover to generate offspring agents. A Tool Discovery Module may introduce new capabilities, while an Agent Replacement step ensures continuous evolution, forming a feedback loop to enhance future agent performance.

Figure 14.2: *Evolutionary Agent Workflow Optimization*

- **Tool Discovery and Enrichment:** Agents dynamically enhance their toolsets when encountering unsolvable tasks, creating Python functions or integrating new utilities (for example, calculating geographical distances between properties from latitude and longitude information contained in the CSV dataset). Successful tools are integrated permanently into the agent's capabilities and inherited by subsequent generations, cumulatively enhancing the agents' overall competencies.
- **Autonomous Integration and Lifecycle Management:** AMAS autonomously integrates improved agents into active service, dynamically updating the active agent without manual intervention. Evolutionary controllers manage seamless deployment, ensuring continuous agent improvement and reliable performance.

```
self_evolving_chatbot/

├── chat.py                     # Main entry point - chatbot loop
                                 (RAG/AGENT/HYBRID modes)
├── config.py                   # Loads Azure OpenAI credentials from .env
├── .env                         # Stores your Azure credentials (DO NOT
                                 COMMIT TO GIT)
├── load_and_retrieve.py        # Handles embedding loading, FAISS search, context
                                retrieval
├── tools/
│   └── arithmetic_tools.py      # All LangChain and custom arithmetic tools
├── agents/
│   ├── starter_agent.py        # Phase 2: Tool-based LangChain agent
│   ├── hybrid_agent.py         # Phase 2+: Hybrid agent = Tools + FAISS context
│   └── rag_model.py            # Phase 1: RAG-only wrapper using generate_answer
                                + FAISS
├── scoring/
│   └── evaluator.py            # Evaluation function to score answer correctness
├── utils/
│   └── logging_utils.py        # Logs each query/response/score to logs/perfor-
                                mance_log.json
├── logs/
│   └── performance_log.json    # Automatically created during runtime
   state_data/
    ├── Wisconsin_embeddings.npy # Your precomputed embedding vectors (1536-dim Ada
                                vectors)
    └── Wisconsin.csv           # Your dataset CSV file (description column used as
                                context)
```

Folder structure of Self-Evolving or Adaptive Multi-Agent System

Let us walk you through the updated **load_and_retrieve.py** line-by-line – the version packaged inside the **self_evolving_chatbot_csv_ready.zip** – to make sure you understand exactly how it works and how everything connects.

```
load_and_retrieve.py – Detailed Explanation
import numpy as np
import faiss
import pandas as pd
from langchain.embeddings import OpenAIEmbeddings
import config
```

Imports:

- **numpy**: For loading .npy embedding files.
- **faiss**: Facebook AI Similarity Search (for fast vector-based nearest neighbor search).
- **pandas**: To read your .csv file that contains property descriptions.
- **OpenAIEmbeddings**: To generate embeddings for user queries (so they can be matched in vector space).
- **config**: Loads Azure OpenAI credentials from .env via config.py.

```
# === Configuration ===
STATE_NAME = "Wisconsin"  # <-- Change this to match your state
CSV_PATH = f"state_data/{STATE_NAME}.csv"
EMBEDDING_PATH = f"state_data/{STATE_NAME}_embeddings.npy"
```

Configuration Block:

- This allows you to easily switch between states or datasets.
- Assumes your .csv file is at **state_data/Wisconsin.csv**
- Assumes your .npy embedding file is at **state_data/Wisconsin_embeddings.npy**

```
# Load embeddings from .npy file
embeddings = np.load(EMBEDDING_PATH).astype("float32")
```

Loads Precomputed Embeddings:

- Loads all Ada-002 (or similar) embeddings for property descriptions.
- FAISS requires float32 type, hence the .astype("**float32**") cast.

```
# Load property descriptions from CSV column
df = pd.read_csv(CSV_PATH)
if 'description' not in df.columns:
    raise ValueError("CSV does not contain 'description'
column.")
property_texts = df['description'].fillna("No description
available").tolist()
```

Reads CSV File:

- Loads **Wisconsin.csv** using pandas.

- Checks if **'description'** column exists – if not, throws an error.
- Converts the description column into a list **property_texts**, one for each row.
- Any missing descriptions are replaced with "**No description available**".

This **property_texts** list is **used later for matching retrieved embeddings to human-readable context**.

```
# Build FAISS index
dimension = embeddings.shape[1]
index = faiss.IndexFlatL2(dimension)
index.add(embeddings)
```

Initializes the FAISS Index:

- Determines the dimensionality (1536 for Ada-002).
- Uses IndexFlatL2 for fast nearest-neighbor search using Euclidean distance.
- Adds all precomputed embeddings to this index for future querying.

```
# === Functions ===
def retrieve_top_k(query: str, faiss_index, texts, k=3):
```

Search Function Starts:

- Takes a user query, searches top k most similar items in FAISS index.
- faiss_index is the built index.
- texts is the **property_texts** list loaded earlier.

```
    embed_model = OpenAIEmbeddings(
        openai_api_key=config.AZURE_OPENAI_API_KEY,
        openai_api_base=config.AZURE_OPENAI_API_BASE,
        openai_api_version=config.AZURE_OPENAI_API_VERSION,
        deployment=config.AZURE_OPENAI_DEPLOYMENT
    )
```

Embedding Model Setup:

- Initializes LangChain's OpenAI embedding generator using Azure credentials from **config.py**.

```
  query_vec = embed_model.embed_query(query)
```

Embeds User Query:

- Converts the query into a vector (same size/space as your **.npy** embeddings).

```
    D, I = faiss_index.search(np.array([query_vec],
dtype="float32"), k)
    return [texts[i] for i in I[0]]
```

FAISS Search:

- Searches top k most similar vectors.
- Returns matching text descriptions (**property_texts**) by index from search results.

```
def generate_answer(query: str, context_docs: list):
```

Answer Generator:

- This takes the user query + matching descriptions and sends them to Azure OpenAI to get a response.

```
    from langchain.chat_models import AzureChatOpenAI
```

- Uses LangChain's Azure-compatible GPT chat model.

```
    llm = AzureChatOpenAI(
        openai_api_key=config.AZURE_OPENAI_API_KEY,
        openai_api_base=config.AZURE_OPENAI_API_BASE,
        openai_api_version=config.AZURE_OPENAI_API_VERSION,
        deployment_name=config.AZURE_OPENAI_DEPLOYMENT
```

LLM Setup:

- Uses credentials from config.py to connect to your Azure GPT model deployment.

```
  context = "\\n".join(context_docs) if context_docs else "No
relevant context found."
    prompt = f"Context:\\n{context}\\n\\nQuestion: {query}"
```

Final Prompt Construction:

- Joins all the top matching context snippets into a single block of text.
- Constructs a prompt where context is passed before the question.

```
    response = llm.predict(prompt)
    return response
```

Gets Final Answer:

- Sends the final prompt to GPT and returns the LLM-generated answer to the calling code (chatbot).

Phases Completed So Far

Phase 1: RAG Chatbot MVP (Minimum Viable Product)

- Excel data has been successfully converted into descriptive text.
- Embeddings have been generated using Ada and saved in .npy format.

- A FAISS vector index is being used for similarity-based retrieval.
- Answers are generated using GPT, based on the retrieved context.
- The core logic is modular and implemented in load_and_retrieve.py.

Phase 2: Tool-Enhanced Agent

- A basic agent has been built using LangChain's tool integration framework.
- Arithmetic and distance calculation tools (both custom and built-in) are available.
- The agent uses the ReAct framework to decide when and how to use tools.
- A scoring and evaluation mechanism has been developed (evaluator.py).

Phase 2.5: Hybrid Agent

- Combines retrieval-based responses (FAISS RAG) with tool usage.
- The HybridAgent integrates contextual information and invokes tools as needed.
- A unified chat.py script supports all modes: RAG-only, agent-only, and hybrid mode.

Phase 2.9: Logging and Configuration System

- Each interaction (query, response, mode, score) is logged in JSON format.
- Secure handling of credentials is implemented using .env and config.py.
- The overall folder and code structure is modular and designed for future extension.

Next Phase

Phase 3: Automated Tool Discovery

Objective: When the agent's response quality is low, it should try to improve by discovering or generating new tools.

- Identify low-performing queries from logs.
- Attempt to auto-generate custom functions (tools) to handle such queries.
- Register and integrate these new tools into the agent system.
- Evaluate if the new tool improves responses—keep it if useful.

Current Status: The necessary foundation is in place (logs, tool registry, modular code).
Next Steps: Implement logic for tool generation, mutation, and validation.

Before we go to the next phase, let us understand a crucial concept of **Model Context Protocol (MCP)**,

Model Context Protocol (MCP)

With foundational phases now in place–where agents can reason through tools, retrieve knowledge via vector embeddings, and generate responses grounded in context–we stand at a pivotal inflection point in the system's evolution.

Until now, tools and reasoning pathways were statically defined and manually injected into the agent ecosystem. While this structure served as a functional proof-of-concept for integrating tools, reasoning chains, and prompts, it lacked the autonomy and adaptability that true evolutionary intelligence demands.

The Challenge of Scale and Complexity

As the range of user queries expands–touching on diverse topics such as arithmetic, geospatial analysis, or domain-specific analytics–the limits of pre-defined tooling become apparent. No fixed toolset can anticipate every novel task a user may pose. Even hybrid agents, though flexible, are inherently constrained by what tools have already been exposed to them manually.

This raises a critical need: **Can agents autonomously discover, generate, and register new tools based on gaps in their reasoning or low-performing responses?**

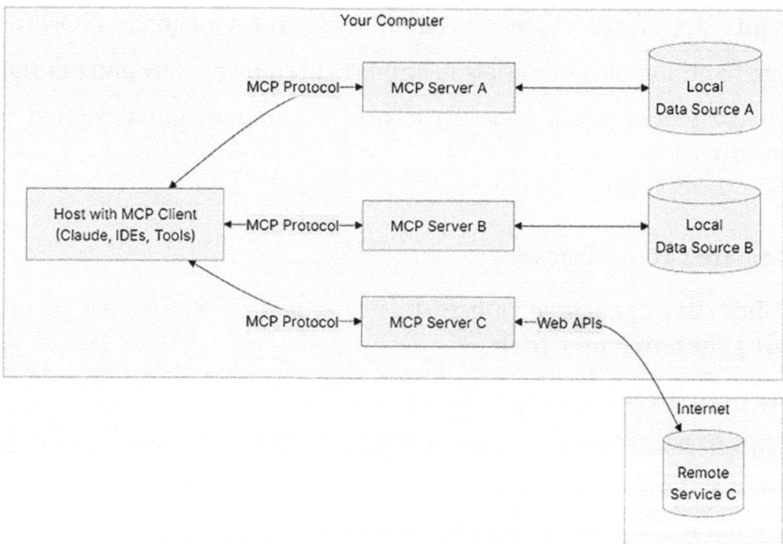

Figure 14.3: *Architecture of MCP-based Context Integration: The MCP Client (for example, Claude, IDEs, or tools) interacts with multiple MCP Servers through the MCP Protocol. https://modelcontextprotocol.io/introduction*

The **Model Context Protocol (MCP)** was developed by **Anthropic**, the creators of the **Claude** family of AI language models (for example, Claude 1, 2, and 3). The link can be found here https://github.com/modelcontextprotocol/python-sdk

MCP was introduced as part of **Claude's developer ecosystem**, specifically to make **LLM integrations more modular, standardized, and extensible**. It enables tools such as **Claude Desktop** and other LLM agents to dynamically discover and interact with external **Resources**, **Tools**, and **Prompts**, without needing hardcoded API integrations or complex wrapper logic.

To answer this question, we now introduce the **Model Context Protocol (MCP)**–a standardized interface layer that separates tool exposure and context provisioning from the agent's internal decision-making logic.

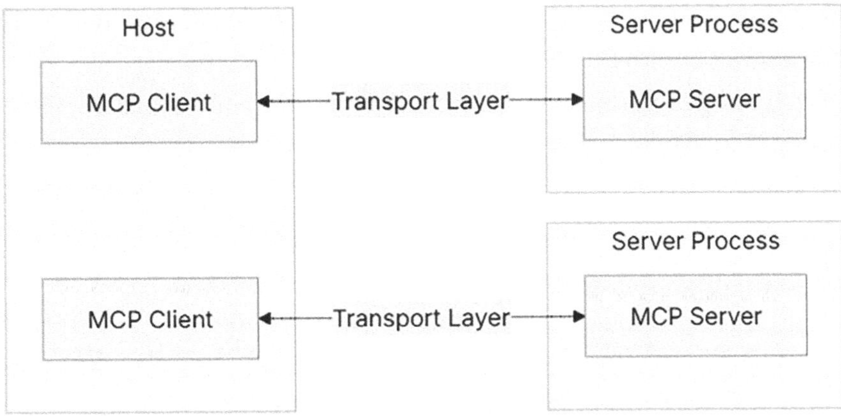

Figure 14.4: *MCP Communication Model: MCP Clients running on a host machine communicate with independent MCP Servers via a transport layer. This decoupled architecture enables standardized interaction between clients and server processes, allowing tool, resource, and prompt exposure in a modular and scalable manner. https://modelcontextprotocol.io/docs/concepts/architecture*

MCP offers a robust foundation for building a truly self-evolving multi-agent system. It allows us to:

- Expose tools as modular, callable interfaces.
- Register context resources dynamically.
- Manage prompts as reusable, evolvable artifacts.
- Enable agent systems to introspect and interact with available resources at runtime–just like a living organism exploring its environment.

With MCP, the system moves from a **hardcoded toolchain** to a **discoverable and adaptable knowledge-action network**–mirroring the very essence of natural evolution.

Paving the Way for Phase 3

In the next phase, we leverage this powerful abstraction layer to build:

- Autonomous tool discovery loops based on performance metrics.
- Mutation-driven tool generators.

- Self-organizing agents capable of extending their capabilities on demand.

As we step into Phase 3, MCP becomes not just a technical integration, but a philosophical shift–from **designed intelligence** to **emergent intelligence**.

*"It is no longer the human who defines the agent's boundaries.
It is the agent itself that evolves to transcend them."*

Purpose of This MCP Server:

- This server acts as a **tool discovery engine**.
- It gives your multi-agent system the ability to analyze its own limitations and evolve by generating new capabilities (tools).
- New tools generated here can be injected into future agent instances or registered with MCP dynamically.

Example:

Before discovery:

1.1.1.0.1.0.0 ← Tool slots 6 & 7 are inactive

After discovering and activating a new tool (for example, `bmi_calculator`):

1.1.1.0.1.1.0 ← Tool slot 6 (Discovered Tool 1) is now active

Dynamic Chromosome Expansion

If the number of tools is unbounded, you can dynamically grow the chromosome by appending new bits as new tools are discovered:

- **1.1.1.0.1 → becomes → 1.1.1.0.1.1 after a tool is discovered.**
- **The gene dictionary tracks trait mappings: bit 6 = bmi_calculator.**

But this is harder to manage in GA selection/crossover unless all chromosomes are normalized to the same length.

1. **Imports and Initialization**

```
from mcp.server.fastmcp import FastMCP, Context
import json
import os
from typing import List

mcp = FastMCP("SEMAS Tool Discovery Server")
```

- Imports essential MCP classes and standard Python modules.
- Initializes an MCP server instance with the name "SEMAS Tool Discovery Server".

2. **Starter Tools**

```
@mcp.tool()
def add(a: float, b: float) -> float:
    return a + b
@mcp.tool()
def distance(x1: float, y1: float, x2: float, y2: float) -> float:
    return ((x2 - x1)**2 + (y2 - y1)**2) ** 0.5
```

- These are basic tools exposed initially.
- add: Adds two numbers.
- distance: Calculates Euclidean distance between two 2D points.

3. **Constants**

```
DISCOVERY_LOG = "logs/performance_log.json"
NEW_TOOLS_FILE = "tools/auto_discovered_tools.py"
```

- Path to the performance log file.
- Path where newly generated tool code will be saved.

4. **Tool: `analyze_low_score_queries`**

```
@mcp.tool()
def analyze_low_score_queries(threshold: float = 0.4, max_tools:
int = 5) -> List[str]:
```

- Scans the performance log file.
- Filters queries with a score below the threshold (default: 0.4).
- Matches patterns in those queries to suggest tool ideas, for example:
    - BMI calculator
    - Area calculator
    - Subtraction tool
    - Average calculator
    - Unit converter
- Returns a list of suggested tools (up to max_tools entries).

5. **Tool: `generate_new_tools`**

```
@mcp.tool()
def generate_new_tools(suggestions: List[str]) -> str:
```

- Takes the list of suggestions from the previous tool.
- Creates actual Python function definitions (as text/code).
- Appends the tool code to **`auto_discovered_tools.py`** file.

- Each tool function is structured to be MCP-compatible with **`@mcp.tool()`** decorator.
- Returns a message summarizing what was generated.

6. **Main Server Entry Point**

```
if __name__ == "__main__":
    mcp.run()
```

- Starts the MCP server when the script is executed.

```
self_evolving_chatbot/
│
├── chat.py
├── config.py
├── .env
├── load_and_retrieve.py
│
├── tools/
│   ├── arithmetic_tools.py
│   └── auto_discovered_tools.py        ← New tools generated via MCP
│
├── agents/
│   ├── starter_agent.py
│   ├── hybrid_agent.py
│   └── rag_model.py
│
├── discovery/
│   └── mcp_phase3_server.py           ← PLACE IT HERE
│
├── scoring/
│   └── evaluator.py
│
├── utils/
│   └── logging_utils.py
│
├── logs/
│   └── performance_log.json
│
└── state_data/
    ├── Wisconsin_embeddings.npy
    └── Wisconsin.csv
```

Figure 14.5: *An example of a production-ready folder structure*

We have developed a self-evolving or Adaptive multi-agent system (AMAS), inspired by **Genetic Algorithms (GA)**, where agents autonomously evolve through mutation, crossover, and fitness-based selection. Each agent represents an organism with traits such as tools, prompts, reasoning chains, and memory. Poor-performing agents are replaced by offspring with adapted traits, mimicking biological evolution. This architecture integrates **LLM-powered reasoning**, **FAISS-based context retrieval**, and **modular tool usage**, forming a closed learning and adaptation loop.

To scale this system, we now incorporate the **Model Context Protocol (MCP)**—a standardized protocol by **Anthropic** that allows seamless exposure of tools, prompts, and resources to LLMs. MCP decouples tool provisioning from internal agent logic, enabling agents to **introspect, discover, and use tools dynamically**, a core requirement for evolving systems. MCP acts as the **tool discovery and integration engine**, crucial for Phase 3: **autonomous tool generation based on low-scoring agent queries**. Agents now gain the ability to self-assess, evolve new tools via MCP servers, and inherit capabilities across generations. Thus, MCP not only enhances modularity but also aligns with evolutionary learning—transitioning our system from **designed intelligence to emergent intelligence**, where agents evolve their boundaries independently.

As we look toward the future of Genetic Algorithms (GAs) in the context of Generative AI and Agentic AI systems, it becomes increasingly evident that GAs hold transformative potential—not just as optimization engines, but as core enablers of adaptive, self-evolving intelligence. Integrating genetic principles into generative and agentic systems offers a pathway to dynamic adaptability, emergent behavior modeling, and autonomous decision refinement. However, to truly harness this potential, it is essential to ground innovation in well-established design patterns and disciplined execution. This brings us to the critical foundation: the best practices for implementing GA systems—starting from classical methods and extending toward deep learning-enhanced evolutionary architectures.

Best Practices for Implementing the GA System

Genetic Algorithms (GAs) have long been a cornerstone of evolutionary computation, offering powerful solutions to complex optimization problems through principles inspired by natural selection. Over time, their versatility has extended far beyond traditional use cases, evolving into hybrid systems that integrate seamlessly with advanced Deep Learning techniques. This convergence of classical evolutionary strategies with modern neural architectures has opened new frontiers in solving high-dimensional, non-differentiable, and multi-objective problems.

Implementing a GA system effectively requires careful design choices, from encoding strategies and fitness functions to adaptive operators and convergence criteria. As these algorithms scale in complexity and integrate with machine learning and deep learning pipelines, best practices become essential to ensure robust performance, computational efficiency, and meaningful results.

This section highlights key best practices across the spectrum–from foundational GA implementation to state-of-the-art deep learning-enhanced variants–providing a roadmap for building powerful, scalable, and intelligent optimization systems.

1. **Problem Definition and Encoding Strategy**
   - Clearly define the optimization problem (classification, regression, feature selection, and so on).
   - Choose an appropriate encoding: **binary, real-valued, tree-based**, or **graph-based** representations depending on the problem domain.
   - Ensure the chromosome structure aligns well with the problem constraints and objectives.
2. **Fitness Function Design**
   - Develop a **robust and scalable fitness function** to evaluate solutions effectively.
   - If multiple objectives are involved, consider **multi-objective optimization** approaches such as **NSGA-II**.
   - Normalize or scale fitness scores if the value range skews selection pressure.
3. **Selection Mechanisms**
   - Use effective selection strategies such as:
     - **Roulette Wheel**
     - **Tournament Selection**
     - **Rank Selection**
   - Balance **exploitation vs. exploration** by adjusting selection pressure appropriately.
4. **Crossover and Mutation Operators**
   - Choose crossover types wisely: **single-point, multi-point, uniform, or arithmetic.**
   - Tune **mutation rates** carefully to maintain diversity but avoid random search behavior.
   - Consider **adaptive mutation and crossover rates** that evolve over generations.
5. **Elitism and Diversity Preservation**
   - Preserve the best individuals through **elitism** to ensure progressive improvement.
   - Prevent premature convergence by maintaining **population diversity**.
     - Use techniques such as **crowding, fitness sharing, or speciation**.

6. **Termination Criteria**
    - Define clear stopping criteria:
        - Max generations
        - Convergence threshold
        - No significant improvement over several generations
7. **Parallelism and Speed Optimization**
    - Leverage **parallel processing or GPUs** for large population evaluations.
    - Use **vectorized operations and efficient data structures** to accelerate computation.

Deep Learning-Enhanced GA Practices

1. **Neuroevolution (Evolving Neural Networks)**
    a. Use GA to evolve **weights, architectures, or hyperparameters** of neural networks.
    b. Choose between:
        - **Direct encoding**: every weight is part of the chromosome.
        - **Indirect encoding**: evolve network topology using schemes such as **NEAT (NeuroEvolution of Augmenting Topologies)**.
2. **Hybrid GA + Deep Learning Approaches**
    a. Combine GA with Deep Learning for:
        - **Hyperparameter tuning**
        - **Model compression (e.g., pruning, quantization)**
        - **AutoML tasks**
    b. Use **GA as an outer-loop optimizer** and gradient based learning in the inner loop.
3. **Transfer Learning with GA**
    a. Fine-tune pretrained models using GA for non-differentiable objectives.
    b. Apply GA to **optimize final layers or loss function parameters** in downstream tasks.
4. **Fitness Prediction Models**
    a. Use **surrogate models (meta-models)** such as small neural networks to approximate fitness values and reduce computation cost.

   b. Retrain surrogates periodically to maintain reliability.

5. **Reinforcement Learning Synergy**
   a. Implement **GA-RL hybrid systems**, for example, using GA to evolve RL agent policies or reward functions.
   b. Apply **policy evolution** for discrete or non-differentiable environments.
6. **Monitoring and Evaluation**
   a. Track **diversity metrics, fitness progression curves, and convergence trends**.
   b. Log and analyze **dominant genes, mutation effects, and structural patterns** in evolved solutions.
7. **Benchmarking and Generalization**
   a. Validate GA performance on **standard benchmark datasets** before applying it to real-world problems.
   b. Test **robustness and generalization capability** under noisy or varying environments.

While adhering to best practices lays the foundation for a well-structured and efficient Genetic Algorithm system, real-world applications often demand more than just theoretical soundness. Subtle refinements, clever heuristics, and practical tweaks can significantly enhance GA performance, adaptability, and convergence speed. These hands-on insights, often learned through experience, can make the difference between a good solution and a great one.

With that in mind, let us explore some tips and tricks in GAs that can help you fine-tune the implementations and unlock even greater optimization potential.

Tips and Tricks in Genetic Algorithms

- **Start with a Diverse Initial Population:** A common mistake is initializing the population with values too close to each other. A diverse starting population increases exploration in early generations and reduces the risk of premature convergence.
- **Use Adaptive Mutation and Crossover Rates:** Instead of static rates, let mutation and crossover probabilities adapt dynamically based on population diversity or fitness stagnation. This helps maintain exploration when needed and supports exploitation when nearing convergence.
- **Apply Constraint Handling Techniques:** When dealing with constrained optimization, use methods such as penalty functions, repair functions, or feasibility rules to ensure solutions remain within acceptable bounds.

- **Elitism is Essential, But Do not Overuse It:** Preserve the best individuals across generations to avoid losing high-quality solutions, but avoid excessive elitism as it can reduce diversity and lead to stagnation.
- **Use Niching or Speciation for Multimodal Problems:** For problems with multiple good solutions, apply techniques such as fitness sharing, crowding, or niching to encourage diverse subpopulations to thrive.
- **Maintain a History of Best Solutions:** Logging or storing elite solutions across generations allows for later analysis or hybridization. It also helps if you want to restart the algorithm with informed seeding.
- **Consider Hybrid Approaches:** Combine GA with local search methods (for example, hill climbing or simulated annealing) to improve convergence speed – known as memetic algorithms.
- **Parallelize Fitness Evaluation:** If the fitness function is computationally heavy, distribute fitness evaluations across multiple cores or GPUs to reduce runtime significantly.
- **Use Problem-Specific Operators:** Design custom crossover or mutation operators that respect domain-specific structures (for example, permutation-based operators for scheduling or routing problems).
- **Monitor Genetic Diversity Metrics:** Track entropy, gene distribution, or population variance to ensure diversity does not collapse too early, which is a key indicator of potential stagnation.
- **Tune Population Size Thoughtfully:** Larger populations allow better exploration but increase computational cost. Experiment with different sizes to strike a balance between diversity and speed.
- **Visualize the Evolution Process:** Plotting fitness curves, diversity trends, and solution space distributions can offer insights into convergence behavior and help debug anomalies.
- **Use Surrogate Models When Fitness is Expensive:** If fitness evaluations are slow or costly, use approximate models (for example, decision trees, regression models, or neural networks) as fitness surrogates to accelerate early-stage search.
- **Random Restarts can Help Avoid Local Optima:** If convergence stalls, restarting the GA with a new population seeded by the best individuals from the previous run can help escape local optima.
- **Cross-validate Solutions in Noisy Environments:** In noisy or stochastic environments, average the fitness over multiple evaluations to obtain a more reliable score and prevent overfitting to noise.

Note: *The tips and tricks shared above serve as a general guide for improving Genetic Algorithm performance across a wide range of applications. However, optimization* *problems can vary greatly in structure and complexity. Depending on the specific problem statement, domain constraints, and objectives, additional problem-specific strategies may be required for best results.*

As we reach the final leg of this fascinating journey through the world of Genetic Algorithms and Evolutionary Intelligence, it is clear that the path of optimization is as much an art as it is science. From decoding nature's blueprint to engineering intelligent systems, we've explored how ideas born in biology can evolve into powerful tools across domains such as machine learning, deep learning, computer vision, natural language processing, and beyond.

Along the way, the practical insights, tips, and tricks have helped us sharpen our implementations and expand our problem-solving toolkit. But beyond code and algorithms lies a deeper understanding–of adaptability, emergence, and iterative refinement–core principles that mirror the evolutionary process itself.

Now, as we pause to reflect and synthesize, it's time to revisit what each chapter has offered–chapter by chapter–drawing connections between theory, practice, and potential. Let us step into the **chapter-wise conclusion**, not just to summarize, but to appreciate how each layer of knowledge contributes to the larger ecosystem of intelligent optimization.

Conclusion

As we reach the final chapter of this journey, it becomes clear that **Genetic Algorithms (GAs)** represent far more than a computational optimization technique–they symbolize a paradigm shift toward **adaptive, self-evolving intelligence** in the age of Generative AI.

Throughout this book, we have explored how the evolutionary principles of natural selection, crossover, and mutation can be strategically harnessed to build systems that not only learn but continuously improve. From enhancing **generative agentic AI** to enabling **self-evolving multi-agent systems**, GAs provide the necessary foundation for creating intelligent architectures capable of **adapting to change, optimizing performance, and generating innovation autonomously**.

Looking ahead, the **future of Genetic Algorithms** lies in their integration with contextual intelligence frameworks such as the **Model Context Protocol (MCP)**. Such protocols will enable agents to understand their environment, access relevant tools dynamically, and evolve their strategies accordingly–blurring the line between fixed-program AI and truly **self-directed intelligence**.

The convergence of GAs with generative systems also introduces exciting possibilities in **creative problem solving, autonomous robotics, intelligent simulations, and AI-driven decision-making**. As these domains evolve, GAs will play a pivotal role in fostering AI systems that are not just intelligent but **resilient, self-optimizing, and context-aware**.

We have also emphasized **best practices and practical tips** for implementing GA-based systems, recognizing that technical excellence and thoughtful design go hand in hand when building for scalability and adaptability.

Final Thoughts

This book concludes, but the real journey is just beginning. The vision of **AI systems that evolve like living organisms, adapt like ecosystems, and create like artists** is no longer distant. It is now within reach–driven by the principles we have explored and the architectures we've envisioned.

Genetic Algorithms will be the heartbeat of this future–fueling an era of generative intelligence that is not static, but alive.

Let this final chapter serve as both a conclusion and an invitation–to innovate, to explore, and to evolve.

Index

A

B

C

D

E

F

I

M

R

S

T

V